STRATEGIC MANAGEMENT: AN INTEGRATIVE PERSPECTIVE

STRATEGIC MANAGEMENT: AN INTEGRATIVE PERSPECTIVE

Arnoldo C. Hax
Massachusetts Institute of Technology

Nicolas S. Majluf
Universidad Catolica de Chile

PRENTICE HALL, Englewood Cliffs, New Jersey 07632

Library of Congress Cataloging in Publication Data

HAX, ARNOLDO C.
  Strategic management

  Includes index.
  1. Corporate planning. 2. Management. I. Majluf,
Nicolás S. II. Title.
HD30.28.H388 1984   658.4'012   84-6939
ISBN 0-13-851270-1

Printed in the United States of America

10

ISBN 0-13-851270-1

Prentice-Hall International (UK) Limited, *London*
Prentice-Hall of Australia Pty. Limited, *Sydney*
Prentice-Hall Canada Inc., *Toronto*
Prentice-Hall Hispanoamericana, S.A., *Mexico*
Prentice-Hall of India Private Limited, *New Delhi*
Prentice-Hall of Japan, Inc., *Tokyo*
Simon & Schuster Asia Pte. Ltd., *Singapore*
Editora Prentice-Hall do Brasil, Ltda., *Rio de Janeiro*

To our dear wives, Neva Hax and Lichy Majluf, for their constant encouragement and support. Also, to our children Andrew and Neva Hax, and Lichita, Nicolas, Javier, Cristobal and Maria Paz Majluf for their love and understanding.

Finally, to the peaceful setting of Martha's Vineyard which provided much inspiration.

CONTENTS

PREFACE

This book is intended to serve both as a text for students of strategic management as well as a valuable reference tool for managers and corporate planners. It grew out of several years of research and consulting work aimed at translating the rich concepts of corporate strategy into a disciplined methodology to assist in the development and implementation of strategic objectives and programs. We have tested earlier versions of this book, both in the classroom and in business organizations throughout the world; invariably the response that we have been getting has been quite encouraging. We would therefore like to share with you our perspective on strategic management, as well as the process that we have followed to help organizations achieve more effective strategic thinking throughout all hierarchical and functional levels.

The book is organized into four distinct parts—each one containing a unique contribution.

PART I—THE EVOLUTION OF STRATEGIC PLANNING THINKING

Planning is presented from an evolutionary perspective, progressing from simple to more comprehensive stages. In this way, each firm will be able to adjust its planning process to its actual needs, depending upon the degree of complexity of the firm's businesses as well as its internal culture. Part I recognizes five major stages in the evolution of planning: budget and financial control (Chapter 1), long-range planning (Chapter 2), business strategic planning (Chapter 3), corporate strategic planning (Chapter 4), and strategic management (Chapter 5). Strategic management represents the most advanced and coherent form of strategic thinking. Not only does it attempt to extend the strategic vision through-out all the operational and functional units of the firm, it also encompasses every administrative system and recognizes the central role to be played by the individuals and groups within the organization, and its resulting culture.

PART II—CONCEPTS AND TOOLS
FOR STRATEGIC PLANNING

This part offers a comprehensive review of the best of strategic planning tools and concepts, all of which are extensively discussed, analyzed, evaluated, and illustrated. The role of the experience curve in strategic planning is presented in Chapter 6. Subsequent chapters discuss the most widely used portfolio ma-trices: the growth-share matrix developed by the Boston Consulting Group (Chapter 7); the industry attractiveness–business strength matrix, developed jointly by General Electric and McKinsey (Chapter 8); the life-cycle portfolio matrix, developed by Arthur D. Little (Chapter 9); and the profitability matrix, developed by Marakon Associates (Chapter 10). This last chapter also addresses the economic contribution of strategy and the market-to-book value model. Chapter 11, the last chapter of Part II, reviews different approaches for industry and competitive analysis.

PART III—A METHODOLOGY FOR THE DEVELOPMENT
OF A CORPORATE STRATEGIC PLAN

One of the primary objectives of our work is based on the development of a methodology to facilitate the translation of broad strategic concepts and tools into a well-defined set of steps that can be used to implement a corporate strategic planning process. Part III discusses and illustrates this methodology in detail. Chapters 12 through 19 describe a twelve-step planning process that involves corporate, business, and functional managers. General Motors of Venezuela, Citicorp, and the Aluminum Company of Martin Marietta are used to exemplify the application of this methodology. Different alternative formats are included to provide concrete suggestions for implementing the planning process of the firm.

PART IV—THE CONGRUENCY BETWEEN
ORGANIZATIONAL STRUCTURE AND STRATEGY

One of the key concerns of strategic management is the proper linkage between strategy and the organizational structure. Chapter 20 discusses the main arche-types of organizational structure and proposes a novel and pragmatic approach to organizational design, seeking congruency between strategy and structure. Chapter 21 illustrates the application of this methodology through a fully developed case.

Throughout the book, our emphasis has been to present a clear formulation of the basic issues and concepts related to strategic management, to describe in detail the most relevant and up-to-date methodologies and tools to address those issues, and to facilitate the actual development of a strategic planning process through a pragmatic set of well-proven recommendations.

This book evolved from many years of work. Throughout this time we learned a great deal from many of our colleagues at the Sloan School of Management at M.I.T. through joint teaching and research activities. Among them we would like to acknowledge the important contributions that shaped our thinking in the area of strategy made by Mel Horwitch, John D. C. Little, Stewart Myers, William Pounds, Edward Roberts, John Rockart, Edgar Schein, Michael Scott Morton, Gordon Walker, Zenon Zannetos, Edward Bowman, and Peter Lorange. These last two are now at the Wharton School at the University of Pennsylvania.

We also benefited greatly from many of our students who wrote theses in the strategy field. We would especially like to recognize Marianne Kunschak, Lily K. Lai, Otto K. Soulavy, Luis F. Tena-Ramirez, and Antoinette M. Williams; their thesis material is cited as illustrations of the methodology developed in Part III of the book.

The important role that consulting firms have played in the advancement of strategic thinking is widely known. Certainly our work reflects the strong influence from some of the leading firms. In particular, we would like to thank William Alberts at Marakon Associates and the University of Washington, Walker Lewis at Strategic Planning Associates, Howard Schwartz at Management Analysis Center, and John White at Arthur D. Little.

Finally, we would like to express our deepest gratitude to the number of executives, both in the U.S. and abroad, whose organizations became central laboratories for testing our ideas as well as providing constant sources of inspiration. We would particularly like to thank David Bishop and James Ledwith then at Technicon, John Leng and Andrew Knowles, both at that time at Digital Equipment Corporation, Richard LeFauve at Chevrolet, Elmer Reese at Delco Remy and Packard Electric at General Motors, Donald Rosselini then at G. D. Searle, Carlos Salvatori at Citibank, Robert Scifres at National Gypsum, Gerhard Schulmeyer at Motorola, Ray Stata and Graham Sterling at Analog Devices, Fernando Buttazoni at Codelco (Chile), Ramón Corral and José Santos Gutiérrez of Mezquital del Oro (Mexico), H. Schulthess at Brown Boveri (Switzerland), and Tomas Voticky at Bufete Industrial (Mexico).

In the production of this book we owe our deep thanks to Deborah Cohen for an outstanding job of typing, editing, and proofreading the many versions of the original manuscript.

STRATEGIC MANAGEMENT: AN INTEGRATIVE PERSPECTIVE

Part One

THE EVOLUTION OF STRATEGIC PLANNING THINKING

Planning is an elusive subject. There is no such thing as "an effective unique way to plan." Planning is a complex social activity that cannot be simply structured by rules of thumb or quantitative procedures. The essence of planning is to organize, in a disciplined way, the major tasks that the firm has to address to maintain an operational efficiency in its existing businesses and to guide the organization into a new and better future.

An effective planning system has to deal with two relevant dimensions: responding to changes in the external environment and creatively deploying internal resources to improve the competitive position of the firm. The maintenance of a vigilant attitude toward external changes is a major driving force behind the capability shown by firms to survive in a hostile environment. The lack of alertness to changes in economic, competitive, social, political, technological, demographic, and legal factors can become extremely detrimental for the sustained growth and profitability of firms.

Planning is the core capacity developed by firms to adapt to environmental movements. This adaptability is not a purely passive response to external forces, but an active, creative, and most decisive search for the conditions that can secure a profitable niche for the firm's businesses.

The internal response of the firm to environmental challenges is given in terms of a clearly defined set of implementable action programs aimed at enhancing the existing and long-term position of the firm vis-a-vis its competitors. Since these action programs define the totality of the major tasks the firm has to face, planning is a most valuable device to coordinate the efforts of the entire organization.

An appropriate planning process must be reflected in adequate functional responses. Manufacturing, distribution, sales, R&D, engineering, personnel, finance, and all functions of the firm should be constantly adapted to respond to new conditions and to achieve increased excellence. But most important still, an effective planning process should be responsive to the individual talents and capabilities that reside in the organization, to the personal aspirations of its members, to the organizational style and corporate values, and to long held beliefs and traditions; in essence, to the organizational culture.

We find no better way to describe the challenges of developing an adequate planning process than to reflect upon the evolution that strategic planning thinking

*has experienced in the last three decades, and learn from the benefits and pitfalls
of each stage of development.*

In this part we recognize five major stages in the evolution of planning:

—budgeting and financial control
—long-range planning
—business strategic planning
—corporate strategic planning
—strategic management

*A firm does have an appropriate planning system in place when its degree of
planning competence matches the degree of complexity of the firm's businesses
as well as its internal culture. Each of the above planning stages represents a
response to different needs for planning capabilities. Firms do not have the same
needs, so it is not surprising to find today many organizations still firmly anchored
in the early stages of the planning evolution.*

*We stated at the beginning that there is no unique way to plan. The type of
businesses, the managerial competence, the intensity of competition, the turbulence
in the environment, and different cultural conditions call for a planning system
coherent with this reality. Moreover, there is more than one way to plan effectively.
Rather than looking for the process, business firms should tailor their systems
to fit their corporate culture, organizational structure, and administrative processes.*

1

STAGE 1: BUDGETING AND FINANCIAL CONTROL

The earliest manifestations of managerial systems are budgeting and financial
control. They emerged more than fifty years ago to maintain within managerial
reach the increasing number of activities developed by a firm. Both of them
are powerful formal procedures that constitute an integral part of the set of
administrative processes used by managers to run a firm and must be intimately
related to the formulation and development of strategies in the organization.

In this chapter we provide a brief discussion of budgeting and financial control.
We will not be concerned with the methodologies used to develop them since
there is abundant literature on this subject.

BUDGETING

Budgets represent projections of revenues and costs normally covering a one year period. The *master budget* of a firm includes all those activities whose monitoring is judged to be important for a healthy development of the firm's businesses, among them sales, manufacturing, administrative activities, investment, and cash management. Figure 1.1 provides a schematic view of the budget-

Figure 1.1 A Schematic Representation of a Master Budget

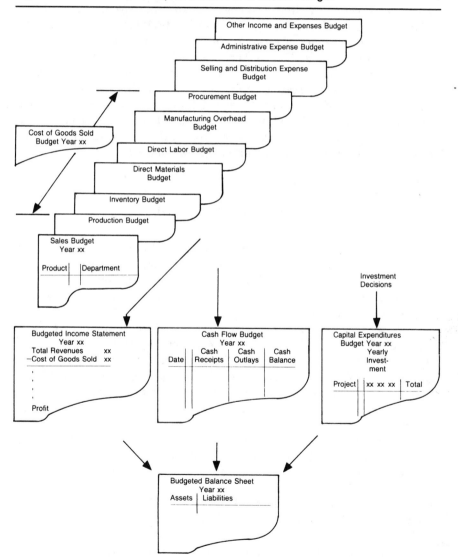

ing process, which is fully described in relevant literature (Sweeny and Rachlin 1981, Welsch 1976, and Anthony and Welsch 1981).

Efficiency standards with regard to all of the above activities are implicit in the budgetary projections. The estimated productivity figures are commonly based upon standards of performance derived from historical observations, both internal data drawn from the firm's experience and external figures obtained from financial statements of competitors are frequently used to set budgetary targets. (This issue will be addressed in Chapter 11.) A new approach to budgeting calls for the use not only of historical data, but for the establishment of commitments that emerge from a strategic plan, or from negotiations conducted within a Management by Objectives framework (MBO) (Carrol and Tosi 1973).

Thanks to many years of experience with the formulation of budgets, this process has been under continuous refinement and new mechanisms for defining the budget have appeared. For example, *flexible budgets* permit the original standards being used to measure performance to be modified with the changes in the actual level of operations (Horngren 1982). Also, *Zero-Base Budgeting* (ZBB) establishes a set of very comprehensive rules to force managers to justify their budgetary allocations from ground zero, rather than defining the new budget in an incremental way (Pyhrr 1973 and Stonich 1977).

FINANCIAL CONTROL

Originally, financial control was adopted as an administrative system to respond to pressures for better cash management, higher operational efficiency, cost reductions, and constrained financial resources. It provided also a useful mechanism for a decentralized accountability for profit and cost performance at various levels in the organization.

Today, with the increased knowledge in the field of accounting and the advent of computerized information systems, financial control has become much more sophisticated; however, it retains still the basic spirit of the original versions. Financial control is a structured process aimed at the efficient and effective use of financial resources, in consonance with corporate strategy.

Financial control measurements are used to judge the performance of the corporation as a whole and of well-defined segments within the corporation. For the latter case, the notion of *responsibility center* has been developed. This is an organizational unit with a clearly identified scope of activities that has been entrusted to a responsible manager. Depending on the nature of the managerial control, it can be defined as an expense center, revenue center, profit center, and investment center. (Anthony and Dearden 1980, Anthony and Welsch 1981, Solomons 1965, and Vancil 1973 and 1979).

The financial control system is built around a rather limited number of *key variables* whose careful monitoring allows managers to track monthly the perfor-

Figure 1.2 Key Planning and Control Parameters Used by United Technologies Corporation

Growth	Assets	Ratios
Sales	Total assets	Return on Assets
Orders	Accounts receivable	Return on Sales
Cost of Sales	Inventories	Asset Turnover
Research and Development Expense	Capital Appropriations and Expenditures	Collection Period
	Customer Payments	Inventory Turnover
Pretax Profit		

mance of the various functional activities and business units of the firm. These indicators are derived from the same information used for putting the budget together. This concept will be revisited and further explored within the framework of Strategic Management in Chapter 5.

To illustrate the essence of the financial control system in a major American corporation, Figure 1.2 identifies the key planning and control parameters used by United Technologies Corporation; and Figure 1.3 illustrates the monthly report used for the control of financial performance against plan.

The financial control system commonly includes some absolute measures of performance related to size and growth of the firm operations and a set of selected financial ratios, as in the case of United Technologies Corporation (see Figures 1.2 and 1.3). A more comprehensive list of the most frequently used financial ratios is presented in Figure 1.4 (Foster 1978) and discussed in Chapter 11.

The use of financial ratios facilitates the comparison of performance among units of different size and among different firms competing in the same industry. With the required financial disclosures imposed upon publicly owned corporations in the United States, ratios have become important standards for competitive comparison. Often, they are used also by external financial analysts as guides for investment decisions.

THE RELEVANCE AND LIMITATIONS OF BUDGETING AND FINANCIAL CONTROL AS A FORM OF PLANNING

Financial performance is at the heart of every business firm. Although profit making is not the only objective to be pursued, it cannot be ignored. Lack of profitability will affect adversely all other objectives of the firm.

Figure 1.3 Reporting Mechanism for the Monthly Control of Financial Performance in United Technologies Corporation

Selected Operating Data for Month of _____

(Amounts in thousands of dollars)

Month				Data	Month			
Actual	Budget	Variance			Actual	Budget	Variance	
		Amount	%				Amount	%
				Income Statement				
				Sales				
				Gross Margin				
				SG&A Expenses				
				R&D Expenses				
				Pretax Profit				
				Assets				
				Cash				
				Accounts Receivable				
				Finished Product Inventory				
				WIP Inventory				
				Total Assets Employed				
				Orders and Backlogs				
				Orders Booked				
				Backlog				
				Billings				
				Other Data				
				Cash Flow from Operations				
				Capital Expenditures				
				# of Non-Salaried Employees				
				# of Salaried Employees				
				Ratios				
				Return on Assets				
				Return on Sales				
				Asset Turnover				
				Inventory Turnover				
				Collection Period				
				Forward Months of Supply				

Figure 1.4 A List of Commonly used Financial Ratios

(1) *Liquidity Ratios*

$$\text{Current Ratio} = \frac{\text{Current Assets}}{\text{Current Liabilities}}$$

where: Current Assets = Cash + Short-Term Marketable Securities + Accounts Receivable + Inventories + Prepaid Expenses
Current Liabilities = Accounts Payable + Dividends + Taxes due within one year + Short-Term Bank Loans

$$\text{Quick Ratio} = \frac{\text{Total Defensive Assets}}{\text{Current Liabilities}}$$

where: Total Defensive Assets = Cash + Short-Term Marketable Securities + Accounts Receivable

$$\frac{\text{Defensive Interval}}{\text{Measure}} = \frac{\text{Total Defensive Assets}}{\text{Projected Daily Operating Expenditures}}$$

where: Projected Daily Operating Expenditures = [(Cost of Goods Sold + Excise Taxes + Marketing, Administrative, and General Expenses + Interest Expense + Other Expenses) − (Depreciation + Deferred Tax)]/365

(2) *Leverage / Capital Structure Ratios*

$$\frac{\text{Long-Term Debt to}}{\text{Equity Ratio}} = \frac{\text{Long-Term Debt}}{\text{Shareholders' Equity}}$$

$$\frac{\text{Total Debt to}}{\text{Equity Ratio}} = \frac{\text{Current Liabilities + Long-Term Debt}}{\text{Shareholders' Equity}}$$

$$\frac{\text{Times Interest}}{\text{Earned Ratio}} = \frac{\text{Operating Income}}{\text{Annual Interest Payments}}$$

where: Operating Income = Sales − (Cost of Goods Sold + Excise Tax + Marketing, Administrative, and General Expenses)

(3) *Profitability Ratios*

$$\frac{\text{Return on}}{\text{Total Assets}} = \frac{\text{Net Income After Tax + Interest Expense} - \text{Tax Benefit of Interest Expense}}{\text{Total Assets}}$$

$$\frac{\text{Return on}}{\text{Equity}} = \frac{\text{Net Income Available to Common}}{\text{Common Shareholders' Equity}}$$

$$\text{Sales Margin} = \frac{\text{Revenues} - \text{Operating Expenses}}{\text{Revenues}}$$

(4) *Turnover Ratios*

$$\text{Total Asset Turnover} = \frac{\text{Sales}}{\text{Average Total Assets}}$$

$$\frac{\text{Average Collection}}{\text{Period (days)}} = \frac{\text{Average (net) Accounts Receivable}}{\text{Daily Sales}}$$

$$\text{Inventory Turnover} = \frac{\text{Sales}}{\text{Average Inventory}}$$

Figure 1.4 *Continued*

or

$$\text{Inventory Turnover} = \frac{\text{Cost of Goods Sold}}{\text{Average Inventory}}$$

(5) *Common Stock Security Ratios*

$$\text{Earnings per Share (EPS)} = \frac{\text{Net Income Available for Common}}{\text{Number of Shares Outstanding}}$$

$$\text{Book Value per Share} = \frac{\text{Shareholders' Equity}}{\text{Number of Shares Outstanding}}$$

$$\text{Dividends per Share} = \frac{\text{Dividends Paid on Common}}{\text{Number of Shares Outstanding}}$$

$$\text{Market to Book Value} = \frac{\text{Price per Share}}{\text{Book Value per Share}}$$

Source: George Foster, *Financial Statement Analysis*, © 1978, pp. 28–37. Adapted by permission of Prentice-Hall, Inc., Englewood Cliffs, NJ.

Managers, particularly the CEO, consider profitability as one of their central concerns. Well designed and implemented budgeting and financial control systems are powerful tools for the definition, monitoring, and attainment of profit targets. The major issue, however, is to prevent excessive myopia and undue concern for short-term profitability at the expense of the long-term development of the firm. Much has been said on the pitfalls of depending too strongly on achieving good ROI performances in the short-term (see, for example, Dearden 1969). Many organizations have found themselves inadvertently weakening their asset base and discouraging necessary investments by compromising the long-term competitive standing of the firm in exchange for a hefty next-year ROI.

The conceptual answer to this dilemma is relatively straightforward, budgeted, ROI figures should stem from the strategic direction selected by the firm rather than becoming goals unto themselves. In other words, strategic commitments should condition financial performance in the short- and long-run. We should keep in mind that a good financial performance is originated by the proper management and development of all physical, technological, and human resources; consequently, rather than manipulating the ROI-index, we should act over the determinants of that index.

Firms which depend entirely on budgetary and financial control measurements for their planning system quite often are exceedingly vulnerable to fall into near-sighted ROI traps. Unless there is a clear articulation of the business competitive strategy, properly understood at all organizational levels, a pure budgeting and financial control system will prove inadequate to avoid undesirable consequences.

Thus, the proper development and communication of the business strategy and the translation of the resulting strategic commitments into meaningful financial indicators are essential requirements to prevent the misuse of budgeting and financial control. One way of assuring this quality of strategy articulation is to adopt a formal strategic planning system. This matter constitutes the core of this book. Companies which do not adopt some kind of a formal planning system have to rely on other mechanisms to develop and communicate their strategies, like implicit rather than explicit avenues for strategy formulation, entrepreneurial strategic thinking on the part of the CEO and his top team, and opportunistic decision making. But this planning approach could become increasingly dysfunctional when the complexity of businesses grows. The excessive financial bias would prevent a proper diagnosis of the underlying causes of short- and long-term profitability and would cloud the sense of priorities. Financial targets for a given year can probably be achieved. The main question is, at what price?

REFERENCES

Anthony, Robert N. and John Dearden, *Management Control Systems*, Richard D. Irwin, Homewood, IL, 1980.

Anthony, Robert N. and Glenn A. Welsch, *Fundamentals of Management Accounting*, Richard D. Irwin, Homewood, IL, 1981.

Carroll, Stephen J. and Henry L. Tosi, *Management by Objectives*, NY, 1973.

Dearden, John, "The Case Against ROI Control," *Harvard Business Review*, Vol. 49, No. 3, May–June 1969, pp. 124–135.

Foster, George, *Financial Statement Analysis*, Prentice-Hall, Englewood Cliffs, NJ, 1978.

Horngren, Charles T., *Cost Accounting: A Managerial Emphasis*, 5th edition, Prentice-Hall, Englewood Cliffs, NJ, 1982.

Pyhrr, Peter A., *Zero-Base Budgeting*, John Wiley, New York, 1973.

Solomons, David, *Divisional Performance: Measurement and Control*, Richard D. Irwin, Homewood, IL, 1965.

Stonich, Paul J., *Zero-Base Planning and Budgeting*, Richard D. Irwin, Homewood, IL, 1977.

Sweeny, H. W. Allen and Robert Rachlin (editors), *Handbook of Budgeting*, John Wiley, NY, 1981.

Vancil, Richard F., "What Kind of Management Control Do You Need?", *Harvard Business Review*, Vol. 51, No. 2, March–April 1973, pp. 75–86.

Vancil, Richard F., *Decentralization: Managerial Ambiguity by Design*, Financial Executives Research Foundation, Dow Jones-Irwin, Homewood, IL, 1979.

Welsch, Glenn A., *Budgeting: Profit, Planning and Control*, Prentice-Hall, Englewood Cliffs, NJ, 1976.

2

STAGE 2: LONG-RANGE PLANNING

THE EMERGENCE OF LONG-RANGE PLANNING

Substantive progress toward the development of a more comprehensive planning system was made with the introduction of long-range planning in the 1950s. This system called for an organizational-wide effort to define objectives, goals, programs, and budgets over a period of many years.

The underlying idea behind long-range planning is to make a thoughtful projection of the environmental trends and establish challenging objectives to guide the operation of the firm and the actions of everyone involved in its development.

Long-range planning was a response adopted by many firms to manage more effectively the extraordinary boom triggered during the post World War II period. In order for American firms to respond to this unprecedented growth, it was not enough to rely on a one-year budgetary projection. To meet the required expansions of capacity and to find the corresponding financial resources, it became necessary to extend this planning horizon.

The starting point for long-range planning is a multi-year forecast of the firm's sales. Subsequently, manufacturing, marketing, personnel, and all other functional plans are issued around these initial sales forecasts, which represent a growth commitment on the part of the firm. The final step is the aggregation of the resulting projections into a financial plan that retains the typical measurements of budgeting and financial control, but covering an extended horizon.

The forecasting effort relies heavily on historical projections, typically covering a five-year period. Long-range planning is a bottom-up functional process which generates a set of plans that are little more than budgets extended over a longer time horizon. Perhaps the only additional managerial tool that is introduced with long-range planning is the use of pay-back and discounted cash-flow techniques to evaluate capital expenditures, popularized by Joel Dean's influential book on capital budgeting (1951).

In Figure 2.1, we present the form used by a typical American corporation to report its long-range plans in 1982. The plan spans eleven years: the first five correspond to historical information, the sixth year represents partly budgetary and partly actual data, and the last five years are filled with forecasted figures, a customary procedure used in the United States. The presentation of historical results facilitates the comparison of observed and forecasted trends. For example, it is a simple matter to detect the so-called "hockey sticks," which are plans that project a sudden recovery of sales and profitability since the beginning of the first forecasted year, after a sustained period of declining performance. In fact, in the illustration given in Figure 2.1, the projected sales growth, although slightly optimistic, does not seem to generate a gross discontinuity between the past and the future. This, however, does not mean the plan does not have any hockey sticks. The RONA figures contain projected levels of performance which cannot be explained by looking at the corresponding historical data (particularly, if we disregard 1979, which was an abnormally good year). Based on those profitability expectations, the plan calls for heavy allocations of cash during 1982, 1983, and 1984, as reflected by the cash flow numbers. This is typical of the hockey stick behavior. The role of higher level management in cases like this, is to grasp the premises on which plans are based, to detect whether hockey sticks represent futile illusions or realistic changes of the business position which call for full support.

LIMITATIONS OF LONG-RANGE PLANNING

Long-range planning makes sense under the conditions that prevailed after World War II; that is, high market growth, fairly predictable trends, firms with essentially a single dominant business, and relatively low degree of rivalry among competitors.

If the above conditions are not met, long-range planning could become a very frustrating activity. Managers would find time and again that their sales projections would not match actual results and that the tools to diagnose and understand the causes of those deviations would be lacking.

Beginning the planning process with sales forecasts represents a serious flaw, one should forecast total markets, not sales. The first step in the development of sales projections calls for an analysis of the dynamics exhibited by the market for the various businesses in which the firm is engaged, trying to understand underlying economic, demographic, and attitudinal factors that might be causing its observed behavior. The linkage between total market and sales is market share, which is a decision variable critically important in the definition of the business strategic position. The adoption of a strategic posture can be expressed in terms of market share such as: increase, maintain, disinvest, look for a special niche in the market, etc.

Figure 2.1 Form Used by a Typical American Corporation to Report Its Long-Range Plans

Historical and Forecasted Performance (World Wide)

	Actual					Ob-served 1982	Fore-casted 1982	Forecasted					Compounded Growth-Rate %	
	1977	1978	1979	1980	1981	1982	1982	1983	1984	1985	1986	1987	1977–1982	1982–1987
Sales $M	48.2	56.0	71.1	77.0	75.2	86.7	76.9	88.2	108.6	131.2	143.3	140.7	9.8	12.2
Profit After Tax %	3.6	0.2	4.5	0.2	(1.8)	1.4	0.3	2.0	4.4	6.9	7.2	5.5		
Net Asset Turnover	1.6	1.9	2.4	2.4	2.5	2.6	2.4	2.3	2.4	2.7	2.8	3.0		
RONA %	5.6	0.4	10.9	0.5	(4.4)	3.7	0.7	4.6	10.7	18.5	20.5	16.5		
Cash-flow $M	0.6	0.8	0.6	1.0	(1.2)	(1.9)	(3.1)	(3.8)	(0.3)	4.2	7.9	8.4		
Fundable Growth $M	1.1	0.6	1.7	0.7	(1.7)	(1.5)	(3.1)	(3.3)	1.1	6.7	10.4	9.9		

(RONA = Return on Net Assets)

The historical projections of sales, so typical of long-range planning, assume that the future will offer a smooth continuity of the past. This is against the very nature of strategic planning, which often leads to drastic discontinuities between the past and the future. Long-range planning can make us fall into the trap of thinking that we are creating a sustained growth situation when, in fact, we are just being driven by highly favorable external forces. When these conditions cease to exist, we are confronted with the difficult task of managing a business in a stagnant economy, which calls for a much more creative form of planning.

Long-range planning does not work under changing external conditions and very intense competitive activities. Likewise, it does not work for a diversified company engaged in a variety of businesses. The functional orientation of long-range planning presupposes a monolithic business structure. When there is a multiplicity of businesses, we have to understand first their inherent differences to provide the support they need for their distinctive development. A bottom-up process will seldom work under these conditions.

Finally, resource allocations in long-range planning are normally done by project, using discounted cash-flow methods. Besides the inability to produce accurate future projections and reliable indicators of financial performance, there is a dangerous loss of strategic vision in approving capital expenditures on a project-by-project basis instead of having a broader view of the long-term implications for the business development. It is relatively easy to evaluate a project in isolation, but it is quite difficult to assess the actual value contributed by a project to a business or a set of businesses of the corporation.

MERITS OF LONG-RANGE PLANNING

Though it is unlikely that a firm will face today the conditions of environmental stability that would make long-range planning an appropriate strategic process, it constitutes an important first step in the quest for increasing managerial competence. Incidentally, this is a very difficult step to skip because it provides the organization with a valuable learning experience. As the limitations of this process become apparent to managers, it will be relatively easy to advance into the next stage of planning evolution.

For additional reading on the subject of long-range planning see Kastens 1976, Linneman 1980, O'Connors 1976, and Steiner 1969.

REFERENCES

Dean, Joel, *Capital Budgeting*, Columbia University Press, New York, NY, 1951.

Kastens, Merritt, *Long-Range Planning for Your Business*, AMACOM, New York, 1976.

Linneman, Robert E., *Shirt-Sleeve Approach to Long-Range Planning*, Prentice-Hall, Englewood Cliffs, New Jersey, 1980.

O'Connors, Rochelle, *Corporate Guides to Long-Range Planning*, The Conference Board, New York, 1976.

Steiner, George A., *Top Management Planning*, Macmillan, New York, 1969.

3

STAGE 3: BUSINESS STRATEGIC PLANNING

During the 1960s, some important environmental changes began to take place in the United States. The extraordinary growth of the previous period started gradually to temper down, driving up the degree of rivalry among competitors in some of the key American industries.

As a result of this process, the focus of managerial attention switched from production to marketing. Previously, every manufactured good could find a place in the market once it was produced; but low industry growth forced firms to pay special attention to the understanding of marketing forces and causes of profitability in order to achieve a defensible position in those areas the firm elected to compete.

Moreover, there was an increase in diversification by the most important business firms, often attained via aggressive acquisitions that led in the late 1960s to the third big wave of conglomeration in the United States (Scherer 1980).

THE EMERGENCE OF BUSINESS SEGMENTATION

Once the conditions that made possible the successful development of long-range planning ceased to exist, a major new concept emerged creating a most significant development in the practice of planning: the concept of business segmentation. This concept originated in 1970, when Fred Borch, then Chairman of General Electric, decided to break the G.E. businesses into a set of autonomous units, following a recommendation made by McKinsey and Company. G.E. had evolved from a company restricted to the electrical motors and lighting businesses into a conglomerate of activities spanning a wide variety of industries. Complexity increased as size, diversity, international scope, and a spectrum of technologies began to impose an unprecedented challenge to G.E. top managers.

Confronted with this formidable task, G.E.'s answer was to break down the businesses of the firm into independent autonomous units that could be managed as viable and isolated business concerns. Those entities were labelled Strategic Business Units, or SBU for short. The SBU concept has produced a long lasting influence in the way companies design, develop, and implement formal strategic planning processes.

Quoting from a case study prepared by the Harvard Business School (General Electric Company 1981):

> [The SBUs were initially designed] so as to assure organizational integrity, while permitting the SBU general manager to carry out the business strategy effectively and competitively (without affecting the strategies of other SBUs within the firm). The SBUs could have stood alone as viable and completely successful independent companies, each with . . . its own defined market or market segment.

Rothschild (1980, p. 14), a manager of Corporate Strategy Development and Integration at G.E., has listed the following criteria to be met before an organizational component is classified as an SBU:

—First of all, an SBU must serve an external, rather than an internal, market; that is, it must have a set of external customers and not merely serve as an internal supplier or opportunistic external supplier.

—Second, it should have a clear set of external competitors which it is trying to equal or surpass.

—Third, it should have control over its own destiny. This means that it must be able to decide by itself what products to offer, how and when to go to market, and where to obtain its supplies, components, or even products. This does not mean that it cannot use pooled resources, such as a common manufacturing plant, or a combined sales force, or even corporate R&D. The key is choice. It must be able to choose and not merely be the victim of someone else's decision. It must have options from which it may select the alternative(s) that best achieves the corporate and its business objectives.

—Fourth, its performance must be measurable in terms of profits and losses; that is, it must be a true profit center.

No organization is a pure SBU, but most SBUs should meet most of these criteria, and all must meet the third one.

A similar notion has been espoused by Arthur D. Little, Inc. (ADL), which defines an SBU as a business area with an external marketplace for goods and services, whose objectives can be established and strategies executed independently of other business areas. It is a unit that could stand alone if divested from the corporation.

ADL's segmentation criteria is based primarily on conditions determined by the external market place rather than production-cost linkages (for example, common manufacturing facilities), technical linkages (for example, common technology), or common distribution channels. They suggest that an SBU is a collection of products and markets that face the same set of competitors, are similarly affected by changes in price, are satisfying a single set of customers, are equally impacted by changes in quality and style, are composed by products which are substitutes of one another, and can be divested without affecting other businesses of the corporation. (This topic is expanded in Chapter 9.)

The segmentation process does not finish with the definition of SBUs, this process is applied at different hierarchical levels in the organization. There is a span of control issue when positioning businesses from the corporate perspective. The resulting number of SBUs should not be so large as to impair the ability of top managers to understand the broad characteristics of each business and effectively contribute to their proper management. By necessity, therefore, the corporate segmentation in a large firm is rather broad and aggregated.

Normally, the resulting SBUs are thus composed by a plurality of products and markets which have to be properly identified by a secondary segmentation taking place at the business level. This segmentation provides the necessary intelligence for the SBU manager to establish meaningful priorities for the development of each individual segment, including possible abandonment of some of them, in order to concentrate all of the business competencies in a more narrowly focused market.

THE FUNDAMENTAL ELEMENTS IN FORMAL BUSINESS STRATEGIC PLANNING

The major tasks to be conducted in a formal business strategic planning process are identified in Figure 3.1. The process is centered in the formulation of the business strategy and their supporting strategic programs. The corporation will evaluate those programs, allocate resources, and make a formal commitment through the agreed-upon budget figures. By adhering to this procedure, the business strategy becomes the end product of a thoughtful process that includes an environmental scan and an internal scrutiny, and requires a previous articulation of the business mission. Now we offer some comments on these steps.

The Mission of the Business

An expression of the business purpose, as well as the required degree of excellence to assume a position of competitive leadership, is an essential first step in the formulation of a business strategy. This overall statement of business direction is what we refer to as the mission of the business.

The primary information that should be contained in a statement of mission is a clear definition of current and future expected business scope. This is expressed as a broad description of the products, markets, and geographical coverage of the business today and within a reasonably short time frame, commonly three to five years. The statement of business scope is informative not only for what it includes; it is equally telling for what it leaves out.

The specification of current and future product, market, and geographic business scope communicates the degree of permanence that the business is expected to have. In a widely popular article, Leavitt (1960) warns against excessive

Figure 3.1   The Fundamental Elements in Formal Business Strategic Planning

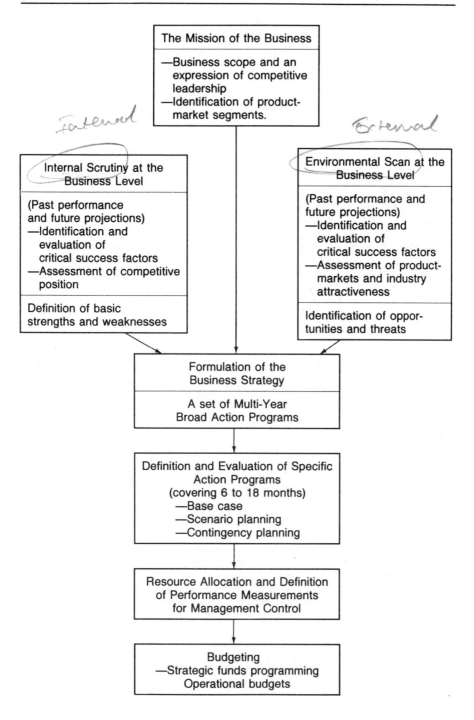

marketing myopia. The essence of his message is to allow for a broad enough definition of business scope in order to detect changes in the industry trends, the repositioning of competitors in terms of products, markets, geographical coverage, and the availability of new substitutes. The contrast between current and future scope is an effective diagnostic tool to warn against myopic positioning of the business.

An example of a mission statement which clearly communicates the three dimensions of the business scope is provided by the Automotive and Industrial Electronics Group of Motorola:

> The mission of the Automotive and Industrial Electronics Group is the development and production of electronic modules and power conversion equipment for sale to original equipment manufacturers (OEMs) and the associated replacement parts market.
> The product scope centers on volume production of electronic modules, in a variety of manufacturing technologies, for monitoring, control, information transmission, information display, and power conversion.
> The market scope is the OEM and replacement market segment for instrumentation, electronic power conversion systems, wire line communication equipment, vehicle power trains, appliances, OEM passenger car entertainment, and systems refining visual display capabilities.
> The geographic scope is primarily North America and Europe, and secondarily Japan, Latin America, and South Africa.

The other important piece of information that should be contained in the mission statement of a business is the selection of a way to pursue a position of either leadership or sustainable competitive advantage. In this respect, we find Emhart's corporate mission statement to be unambiguously clear. Although it involves a corporate rather than a business statement, we offer it for purposes of illustration:

> The businesses within the Company are expected to achieve and maintain a leadership position in attractive industries. A true leadership position means having a significant and well-defined advantage over all competitors. This can be achieved through continuous, single-minded determination to achieve one or both of the following positions within an industry:
> 1. Lowest Delivered Cost Position
>   A business with the lowest delivered cost has greater economies of scale than other competitors. Economies of scale are available in the manufacturing, distribution, and installation steps where large amounts of costs are incurred. Success at achieving the position of lowest delivered cost is dependent upon identifying and concentrating upon that step where a concentration of effort will produce the most dramatic results.
> 2. Differentiated Products
>   Differentiated products are those which offer the customer some important and unique benefit. Typically, patents, trademarks, brand names, or specialized skills prevent competitors from copying such products. If a product is truly differentiated, the customer is selectively insensitive to price. Increasing customer price sensitivity is a sign that a product is losing its advantage of differentiation.

Environmental Scan and Internal Scrutiny

Prior to the development of strategies for the individual businesses, it is necessary to perform a thorough analysis regarding the current and future business position in terms of two dimensions:

—the noncontrollable forces which are associated with the external environment and determine the industry trends and market opportunities; and

—the internal competencies residing in the firm, which will determine the unique competitive leadership potential that the firm could mobilize in order to establish a business superiority against competitors.

The business strategy constitutes a response to deal with these two dimensions. When addressing the external environment, the strategic orientation will try to take advantage of market opportunities and neutralize adverse environmental impacts; when facing the internal environment, the direction will be to reinforce internal strengths and improve upon perceived weaknesses with regard to competition.

During the late 1960s and throughout the 1970s, a planning methodology known as the *business portfolio approach* was developed to assist managers in addressing these two dimensions of strategic diagnosis. The essence of these methodologies consists in positioning a business within a matrix in accordance with its competitive strength and the attractiveness of its industry. The result of this effort, presented in a simple graphical display, allows managers to visualize the contribution of each business to the corporate portfolio. The most popular among business portfolio matrices (presented in Figure 3.2) are:

—The growth-share matrix, originally developed by the Boston Consulting Group (BCG), covered in Chapter 7.

—The industry attractiveness-business strength matrix, originally developed by General Electric jointly with McKinsey and Co., presented in Chapter 8.

—The life-cycle approach, developed by Arthur D. Little, Inc., discussed in Chapter 9.

Portfolio approaches have made important contributions to the improvement of strategic planning thinking. Some of the most significant among them are:

—They represent simple and effective ways to facilitate the decomposition of the firm's activities into a set of well-defined businesses. Moreover, while conducting the necessary analysis to position the businesses in the two-dimensional matrix, ample opportunities exist to reassess the merits of the proposed segmentation.

—By permitting a clear differentiation of the nature of each business in terms of industry attractiveness and competitive position, portfolio approaches allow top managers to set appropriate and distinct strategies for each business in accordance to its inherent potential and developmental needs. Gone are the days in which a manager would impose a global and uniform objective, such as "let's get an ROE of 15%," expecting that every business would stand on the same ground to fulfill that goal.

Figure 3.2   Portfolio Matrices Used in Strategic Planning

The Growth-Share Matrix
(Boston Consulting Group Approach)

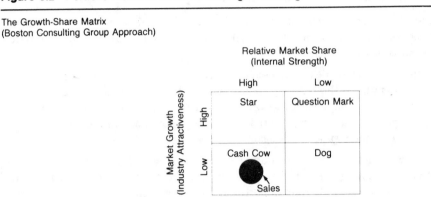

The Industry Attractiveness-Business Strength Matrix
(The General Electric-McKinsey Approach)

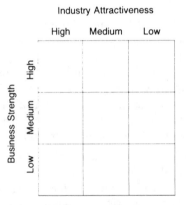

The Life-Cycle Approach
(Arthur D. Little, Inc.)

Competitive Position	Stages of the Life-Cycle			
	Embryonic	Growth	Maturity	Aging
Dominant				
Strong				
Favorable				
Tenable				
Weak				
Nonviable				

—Portfolio approaches represent a pragmatic way to capture the essence of strategic analysis. By means of a simple visual display of the portfolio of businesses, they provide a useful device to understand and communicate some important characteristics of the strategic options confronted by the firm.

—Portfolio approaches were most significant in raising the strategic alertness of most managers. To a great extent, the use of portfolio matrices was responsible for accelerating the adoption of formal competitive analyses and for increasing the competitive awareness in American firms. This was accomplished because the implementation of the portfolio approach requires the collection and processing of some minimum quantitative information regarding competitors, which constitutes a useful first step in improving competitive intelligence. Also, portfolio matrices can be easily constructed for major competitors, generating some valuable insights with regard to their overall strengths and some ability to anticipate their potential responses and moves. At the very least, this judgmental call would put in evidence the need to improve the firm's understanding of its major competitors.

—Portfolio approaches have two basic levels of applicability: corporate and business. At the corporate level, they provide the CEO with a useful tool to set up criteria for resource allocation, to reflect upon growth-profitability trade-offs, and to address the question of cash balancing. At the business level, the focus of attention changes from the entire business to product-market segments, but the same portfolio techniques can be used in the process of strategy formulation at a more detailed level.

—Portfolio approaches, by representing the complete collection of businesses of the firm, provide a useful mechanism to consider potential acquisitions and divestitures.

Recent analyses of the various portfolio management techniques have been performed by Wind and Mahajan (1981) and Haspeslagh (1982).

Formulation of Business Strategies and Definition of Strategic Programs

The strategic planning process leads to the formulation of the strategy for a business unit. A business strategy is a set of well-coordinated action programs aimed at securing a long-term sustainable competitive advantage. These programs are defined at two different levels of specificity: broad action programs covering a multi-year planning horizon and specific action programs covering a 6 to 18 month period. Therefore, the business strategy is operationally expressed in terms of a series of broad action programs and each one of these is, in turn, explicit as a set of specific action programs. All of these action programs, broad and specific, often involve functional commitments, transforming business strategy in the articulation of properly integrated multifunctional activities.

Perhaps the most significant and permanent contribution of the portfolio approach resides in the generation of a set of *natural* or *generic strategies* to be considered by each business depending on their position in the industry attractiveness and competitive strength dimensions.

The first proposal of generic strategies came from the BCG approach, which relies on desirable market share positioning as a primary input to convey the strategic objectives for a business unit. The categories of market share thrusts initially defined by BCG are:

—Increase
—Hold
—Harvest
—Withdraw or Divest

Macmillan (1982) expands the strategic roles which could be played by a business unit depending on its position in the portfolio matrix. Figure 3.3 identifies each strategic role and provides its definition.

Figure 3.3   Business Strategic Roles Emerging from the Portfolio Approach to Strategic Planning

Build aggressively.   The business is in a strong position in a highly attractive, fast-growing industry and management wants to build share as rapidly as possible. This role is usually assigned to an SBU early in the life cycle, especially when there is little doubt that this rapid growth will be sustained.

Build gradually.   The business is in a strong position in a very attractive, moderate growth industry and management wants to build share, or there is rapid growth but some doubt as to whether this rapid growth will be sustained.

Build selectively.   The business has *some* good positions in a highly attractive industry and wants to build share where it feels it has strength, or can develop strength, to do so.

Maintain aggressively.   The business is in a strong position in a currently attractive industry and management is determined to aggressively maintain that position.

Maintain selectively.   Either the business is in a strong position in an industry that is gettting less attractive, or the business is in a moderate position in a highly attractive industry. Management wishes to exploit the situation by maximizing the profitability benefits of selectively serving where it best can do so, but with the minimum additional resource deployments.

Prove viability.   The business is in a less than satisfactory position in a less attractive industry. If the business can provide resources for use elsewhere, management may decide to retain it, but without additional resource support. The onus is on the business to justify retention.

Divest-Liquidate.   Neither the business nor the industry has any redeeming features. Barring major exit barriers, the business should be divested.

Competitive harasser.   This is a business with a poor position in either an attractive or highly attractive industry and where competitors with a good position in the industry also compete with the company in other industries. The role of competitive harasser is to sporadically or continuously attack the competitor's position, not necessarily with the intention of long-run success. The object is to distract the competition from other areas, deny them from revenue business, or use the business to cross-parry when the competition attacks an important sister business of the strategic aggressor.

Source: Adapted from Ian C. Macmillan "Seizing Competitive Initiative," Spring 1982. Reprinted by permission of *The Journal of Business Strategy*, Boston, MA.

Arthur D. Little, Inc. proposes an even further structured and more comprehensive set of generic strategies which are listed in Figure 3.4, and whose use is explored in Chapter 9.

The intent behind the use of generic strategies is not to convert strategic planning in a mechanistic exercise or to reduce the development of strategies to those which naturally coincide with the positioning of the business in the portfolio matrix, but rather to give a menu of reasonable strategic alternatives to the business manager.

The generic strategies can be grouped into six major categories, which emphasize their primary purpose for strategic development.

I. *Marketing Strategies*
    Export/Same Product
    Initial market development
    Market Penetration
    New Products/New Markets
    New Products/Same Market
    Same Products/New Markets

II. *Integration Strategies*
    Backward Integration
    Forward Integration

Figure 3.4   Generic Strategies Proposed by Arthur D. Little, Inc.

Backward Integration
Development of Overseas Business
Development of Overseas Facilities
Distribution Rationalization
Excess Capacity
Export/Same Product
Forward Integration
Hesitation
Initial Market Development
Licensing Abroad
Complete Rationalization
Market Penetration
Market Rationalization
Methods and Functions Efficiency
New Products/New Markets
New Products/Same Market
Production Rationalization
Product Line Rationalization
Pure Survival
Same Products/New Markets
Same Products/Same Markets
Technological Efficiency
Traditional Cost Cutting Efficiency
Unit Abandonment

III. *Go Overseas Strategies*
    Development of an Overseas Business
    Development of Overseas Production Facilities
    Licensing Abroad

IV. *Logistics Strategies*
    Distribution Rationalization
    Excess Capacity
    Market Rationalization
    Production Rationalization
    Product Line Rationalization

V. *Efficiency Strategies*
    Methods and Functions Efficiency
    Technological Efficiency
    Traditional Cost Cutting Efficiency

VI. *Harvest Strategies*
    Hesitation
    Little Jewel
    Pure Survival
    Maintenance
    Unit Abandonment

Resource Allocation and Definition of Performance Measurements for Management Control

The ultimate sanctioning of the merits of the business strategy has to reside at the top of the organization where the key resources of the firm are allocated. Once again, the portfolio approach provides useful guidelines for top managers to address the question of business strategy evaluation and resource allocation.

1. It allows the establishment of an orderly set of priorities for investment, depending on the business potential for growth and profitability derived from its position in the portfolio matrix.
2. It provides a mechanism to check the consistency between business requests of financial and human resources and their inherent needs obtained from their position in the portfolio matrix.
3. It facilitates the proper balancing of cash-requirements and cash-supplies among businesses of the corporation.
4. It permits the establishment of management control mechanisms suitable for monitoring the performance of each business using key variables consistent with their current and future potential.

Budgeting

The result of this planning process leads toward the development of an "intelligent budget," which is not a mere extrapolation of the past into the future, but an instrument that contains both strategic and operational commitments. Strategic commitments pursue the development of new opportunities which very often introduce significant changes in the existing business conditions. Operational commitments, on the other hand, are aimed at the effective maintenance of the existing business base.

A way to break this dichotomy within the budget is to make use of strategic funds and operational funds to distinguish the role that those financial resources will have. *Strategic funds* are expense items required for the implementation of strategic action programs whose benefits are expected to be accrued in the long-term, beyond the current budget period (Vancil 1972 and Stonich 1980). *Operational funds* are those expense items required to maintain the business in its present position.

There are three major components of strategic funds:

1. Investment in tangible assets, such as new production capacity, new machinery and tools, new vehicles for distribution, new office space, new warehouse space, and new acquisitions.
2. Increases (or decreases) in working capital generated from strategic commitments, such as the impact of increases of inventories and receivables resulting from an increase in sale; the need to accumulate larger inventories to provide better services; increasing receivables resulting from a change in the policy of loans to customers, etc.
3. Developmental expenses, that are over and above the needs of existing businesses, such as advertising to introduce a new product or to reposition an existing one; R&D expenses of new products; major cost reduction programs for existing products; introductory discounts, sales promotions, and free samples to stimulate first purchases; development of management systems such as planning, control, and compensation; certain engineering studies, etc.

It is important to recognize these three forms of strategic funds. Although all of them contribute to the same purpose, namely, the improvement of future capabilities of the firm, financial accounting rules treat these three items quite differently. Investment is shown as increase in net assets in the balance sheet and as annual expenses through depreciation in the profit and loss statement. Increases in working capital also enlarge the net assets of the firm, but they have no annual cost repercussion. Developmental expenses are charged as expenses in the current year income statement and have no impact on the balance sheet. Since there are no immediate profitability results derived from these strategic funds, it is important to make a manager accountable for the proper and timely allocation of those expenditures using performance measurements related to the inherent characteristics of the action programs they are attempting to support.

If the business has developed a sound strategy, it will be easy to see how the key performance variables begin to improve with the years. What is more difficult is to measure the short-term contribution of a multitude of programs requiring strategic expenses. Often, it is necessary to resort to project-management type of control mechanisms, centered in cost and time efficiency, as the only way to measure the quality of the implementation of strategic funds.

THE BUSINESS STRATEGIC PLANNING PROCESS

A planning process is an organized and disciplined way of implementing the sequence of major tasks that are needed for the full development of the business strategy. Figure 3.5 illustrates the nature of that sequence when conducting a business strategic planning process. The six tasks represented in the figure coincide with the fundamental elements described previously. Now we are merely emphasizing the role to be played by the corporate and business levels in the planning process. The corporation limits itself to evaluate business proposals, allocate resources (mostly financial), and provide a final approval for the resulting

Figure 3.5   The Formal Business Strategic Planning Process

Hierachical Levels of Planning	Less Frequent than Annual Review Structural Conditioners	Annual Review		
		Strategy Formulation	Strategic Programming	Strategic and Operational Budgeting
Corporate				④	⑥
Business	①	②	③	⑤	

1 The Mission of the business
2 Formulation of business strategy and broad action programs
3 Formulation and evaluation of specific action programs
4 Resource allocation and definition of performance measurements for management control
5 Budgeting at the business level
6 Budgeting considerations and approval of strategic and operational funds

budget. Since each business unit is supposed to be an autonomous entity having full functional support, the functional participation is implicit at the business level.

We will enrich the description of the formal strategic process when discussing in Chapter 4 the wider role of the corporation in the next stage of the planning evolution.

AN EXAMPLE OF FORMAL BUSINESS STRATEGIC PLANNING

Figure 3.6 illustrates the format being used by a major American corporation to summarize the highlights of its business strategy. Although it does not match exactly the steps we have just discussed, it covers most of the issues we addressed in the previous section. The business strategy description contains also a numerical statement of historic and forecasted performance. We have omitted it because it follows exactly the same reporting pattern given in Figure 2.1.

THE CONTRIBUTION OF BUSINESS STRATEGIC PLANNING

Business strategic planning is characterized by the introduction of the concept of business segmentation and the rise of competitive assessment to the primary level of managerial attention. This form of planning introduces the portfolio approach to address formally the issues of attractiveness and competitive strength. Moreover, the business manager is made fully accountable for the strategic and operational performance of the business and he is given total control over the resources needed to fulfill his managerial duties. All of this constitutes significant accomplishments and represents an extraordinary progress from the long-range planning approach, its historical predecessor.

We have purposely described here the purest form of business strategic planning. By that we mean a situational setting in which there is almost complete autonomy at the business level, except for the necessary sanctioning of the business plans and the allocation of resources to be done at the corporate level. We will address the proper role of the corporation in the next stage of the planning evolution covered in Chapter 4.

The Relevance of Business Strategic Planning

This is a legitimate form of strategic planning process whenever the corporation is composed of a loosely connected set of unrelated businesses, as in the case of a conglomerate firm. In that situation, the corporation merely acts as a holding company, monitoring the divisional performance, balancing cash flows, and allocating resources to the competing business activities.

Also, this is an acceptable procedure for a divisional manager in a corporation which has not adopted a more progressive form of planning system. In those circumstances, the divisional manager can move forward creatively in his own area of concern, without waiting for the whole corporation to put its act together. At the same time, this manager could set a constructive example which might inspire other business managers and the corporate officers to improve the quality of the administrative process they have currently in place.

Finally, the evolutionary process that we are describing involves profound educational lessons. Strategic planning requires, more than any other effort,

Figure 3.6   An Example of a Business Strategic Plan

SUMMARY OF BUSINESS STRATEGY
(1982)
BUSINESS: Electronic Controls (E.C.)

MISSION STATEMENT: To design, develop, and manufacture electronic control systems for electric engines, for sale to OEMs and the associated replacement market in the U.S.

INDUSTRY PERSPECTIVE

MARKET OVERVIEW	COMPETITIVE ENVIRONMENT

• Total Available Market
    1982   1987   %Gr.
 $M   500   1856   30
	• Narrative
	   • Growing industry attracting a large number of national and international firms
	   • Total production capacity in the industry is expected to double in the next two years

• Trends
 	
   • Japanese competition is expected to increase through the 80's
 	
   • New applications in trains and subways
	• Market Share
	
	   Firm %
	   E.C. 28
	   Bosch 22
	   Delco 20
	   Hitachi 15
	   Motorola 10
	   Toshiba 5

	• Competitors profile • Bosch has ownership and technical tie-ups with Japanese firms

Figure 3.6 *Continued*

BUSINESS DESCRIPTION

MARKETS AND DISTRIBUTION	PRODUCTS-TECHNOL-OGY SCOPE	MANUFACTURING
• Major OEMs in the electric engines market • Service parts to independent distributors and repackagers	• Current products: Generator set controls and transmission controls • New Products: Pump control • New technologies: Electronic testing	• Current operations at Boston and California • New operations: Increase capacity in actual locations. No new locations being considered

BUSINESS SALES: $140 M
AFTER TAX PROFITS: 9.2%

BUSINESS KEY VARIABLES AND IDENTIFICATION OF DISTINCTIVE COMPETENCES

KEY VARIABLE	BUSINESS COMPE-TENCE	COMMENTARY
• OEM capability	Very Strong	Our disctinctive competence
• Technology	Strong	Better than average, but there are substitutes
• Quality	Medium	Comparable to competitors'
• Cost	Weak	Production inefficiencies

BUSINESS STRATEGY: DEFINITION OF BROAD ACTION PROGRAMS

- Become the technological leader
- Reduce manufacturing costs
- Develop OEM sales capability to support new products
- Look for ways to improve quality

BUSINESS PERFORMANCE OBJECTIVES

- Growth   30% per year
- After-tax profits   11%

HISTORIC AND FORECASTED PERFORMANCE

- Follows the format presented in Figure 2.1.

the development of a core management team sharing a sense of values, corporate philosophy, corporate priorities, a deep understanding of the collection of businesses of the firm, and a professional background and managerial competence which will push them to the limits of their creativity. This cannot be acquired overnight, it is the result of a slow process of joint learning through common experiences, which is partly developed by their participation in the formal process of business planning.

The Limitations of Business Strategic Planning and Further Developments

There are six important limitations that we could cite with regard to the business strategic planning process and the use of portfolio matrices:

1. By emphasizing the autonomy of business units, the corporation might fail to take advantage of what could be great potentials for sharing resources and concerns among distinct but yet related business activities.
2. By failing to start the planning process with a proper corporate vision, the totality of business plans will not be necessarily convergent toward the betterment of the corporation as a whole.
3. The use of portfolio approaches might become a subtle trap for business executives. The orderly implementation of portfolio analysis and the careful selection of generic strategies might constrain managers to a framework which represses rather than enhances creative thinking, precluding innovation within the firm.
4. In the early stages of the portfolio methodology, there was an excessive reliance in the use of market share as a primary measure of competitive strength. This was partly due to the adherence to the experience curve effect (that we present in Chapter 6), which suggests that the firm with the largest accumulated experience enjoys the highest profitability according to the following reasoning:

$$\text{High Market Share} \rightarrow \text{High Accumulated Volume} \rightarrow \text{Lower Unit Cost} \rightarrow \text{High Profitability}$$

Exclusive reliance on these arguments creates the impression that there is only one effective way to compete: go after volume and market share. Porter, in his book *Competitive Strategies* (1980), has presented a convincing argument to cast a doubt on the legitimacy of the above position. He postulates that there is not one but three potentially successful generic strategic approaches to outperform another firm in an industry: overall cost leadership, differentiation, and focus. (A brief definition is given in Figure 3.7.) The

Figure 3.7 Porter's Generic Strategies

1. *Overall cost leadership* requires aggressive construction of efficient-scale facilities, vigorous pursuit of cost reductions from experience, tight costs and overhead control, avoidance of marginal customer accounts, and cost minimization in areas like R&D, service, sales force, advertising, and so on.
2. *Differentiation* calls for creating something that is perceived *industry-wide* as being unique. Approaches to differentiating can take many forms: design or brand image, technology, features, customer service, dealer network, or other dimensions.
3. *Focus* consists on concentrating on a particular buyer group, segment of the product-line or geographic market. As with differentiation, focus may take many forms. Although the low cost and differentiation strategies are aimed at achieving those objectives industry-wide, the entire focus strategy is built around servicing a particular target very well, and each functional policy is developed with this in mind.

Source: Adapted from Michael E. Porter, *Competitive Strategy*, © 1980. Reprinted by permission of the Free Press, New York, NY.

influence of Porter's framework in the formulation of Emhart's mission statement included on page 18 is noteworthy.

5. The traditional portfolio approaches deal with competitive analysis in a fairly informal way. In the book previously referred, Porter (1980), supported by the Industrial Organization conceptual framework (Caves 1964 and Scherer 1980), proposes a comprehensive methodology for conducting industry and competitive analysis which has strong relevance to business strategic planning. He identifies five basic forces as determinants of industry profitability which are illustrated in Figure 3.8. An industry will enjoy high and stable profits whenever the firms within that industry can deal effectively with the threats of new entrants and substitutes, neutralize the bargaining power of suppliers and buyers, and establish a moderate to low rivalry among themselves. An explicit description of components affecting each one of these five forces and the way in which they impact the profitability of industry, developed by Management Analysis Center (MAC), is presented in Figure 3.9.
6. The conventional portfolio approaches do not incorporate explicitly the profitability of each individual business unit. It is assumed that a business having a high competitive strength will enjoy a high profitability. Moreover, by providing too much emphasis on cash balancing considerations, the firm could be either ignoring attractive investment opportunities or investing in unprofitable ventures. In response to these concerns, Marakon, a consulting company based in San Francisco, has proposed a different type of portfolio matrix, which they refer to as the profitability matrix, and is discussed in Chapter 10.

After pondering the merits and limitations of business strategic planning, it is an undeniable fact that this stage represents an important step forward in

Figure 3.8   Porter's Framework for Industry and Competitive Analysis

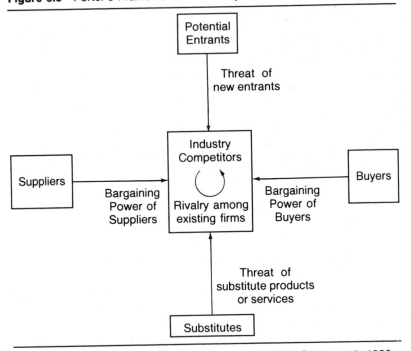

Source: Adapted from Michael E. Porter, *Competitive Strategy*, © 1980.
Reprinted by permission of the Free Press, New York, NY.

the evolution of planning methodologies. But there is, still, one important question unanswered: What is the proper role to be played by the corporate level in the formulation of business strategy? We will turn to this question in the next chapter.

Figure 3.9   Some of the Critical Components Affecting Industry Competitiveness

	Will Lower Profitability	Will Raise Profitability
	Easy to Enter	*Difficult to Enter*
Ease of entry	> Low scale threshold > Little brand franchise > Common technology > Access to distribution channels	> High scale threshhold > Brand switching difficult > Proprietary know-how > Restricted distribution channels
	Difficult to Exit	*Easy to Exit*
Ease of exit	> Specialized assets > High exit costs > Interrelated businesses	> Saleable assets > Independent business

Figure 3.9 *Continued*

	Will Lower Profitability	Will Raise Profitability
	Suppliers Powerful	*Suppliers Weak*
Power of suppliers	> Credible forward integration threat by suppliers > Suppliers concentrated > Significant cost to switch suppliers	> Many competitive suppliers > Purchase commodity products > Credible backward integration threat by purchasers > Concentrated purchasers
	Customers Powerful	*Customers Weak*
Power of customers	> Buyers concentrated > Buyers purchase a significant proportion of output > Buyers possess credible backward integration threat	> Producers threaten forward integration > Significant buyer switching costs > Buyers fragmented > Producers supply critical portions of buyers' input
	Substitution Easy	*Substitution Difficult*
Availability of substitutes	> Low user switching costs > Substitute producers profitable and aggressive	> High user switching costs > Substitute producers unprofitable and passive
	Many Competitors	*Small Number of Competitors*
Industry conditions	> Competitors equal in size > Slow demand growth > High fixed costs > Excess capacity > Commodity products > Diversity of approach and historical background	> Diversity of competitor size > Industry leader > Fast demand growth > Low fixed costs > Differentiated products > Commonality of approach and historical background

REFERENCES

Caves, Richard E., *American Industry: Structure, Conduct, Performance*, Prentice-Hall, Englewood Cliffs, NJ, 1964.

General Electric Company, "Background Note on Management Systems: 1981," Case #181-111, Harvard Business School, Boston, MA, 1981.

Haspeslagh, Philippe, "Portfolio Planning: Uses and Limits," *Harvard Business Review*, Vol. 60, No. 1, January–February 1982, pp. 58–73.

Leavitt, Theodore, "Marketing Myopia," *Harvard Business Review*, Vol. 38, No. 4, July–August, 1960, pp. 45–56.

Macmillan, Ian C., "Seizing Competitive Initiative," *The Journal of Business Strategy*, Vol. 2, No. 4, Spring 1982.

Management Analysis Center, "Strategy Formulation," Cambridge, MA, undated publication.

Porter, Michael E., *Competitive Strategy*, Free Press, New York, 1980.

Rothschild, William E., "How to Insure the Continuous Growth of Strategic Planning," *The Journal of Business Strategy*, Vol. 1, No. 1, Summer 1980, pp. 11–18.

Scherer, F. M., *Industrial Market Structure and Economic Performance*, Rand McNally, Chicago, 1980.

Stonich, Paul J., "How to Use Strategic Funds Programming," *The Journal of Business Strategy*, Vol. 1, No. 2, Fall 1980, pp. 35–40.

Vancil, Richard F., "Better Management of Corporate Development," *Harvard Business Review*, Vol. 50, No. 5, September–October 1972, pp. 53–62.

Wind, Yoram, and Vijay Mahajan, "Designing Product and Business Portfolios," *Harvard Business Review*, Vol. 59, No. 1, January–February 1981, pp. 155–165.

4

STAGE 4: CORPORATE STRATEGIC PLANNING

The 1960s marked a major change in the socio-political environment in America and the world. Then, the 1970s deepened this already profound transformation of society and brought the energy and environmental problems to prime levels of societal concerns. We are living through a period of growing technological changes, particularly as a result of what is happening in the electronic area. Business firms are facing new competitive forces among which Japanese firms appear as a most powerful adversary. There is also a projection toward international markets, which must be made in the midst of uncertainties created by inflation, foreign exchange rates, and the different economic conditions of all countries competing for the world markets.

Another major contributor to the creation of this turbulence has been the more militant attitude from different groups in the society, which calls for an enlargement of the relevant environment of a firm in what is commonly named the group of stakeholders. In this group belong not only shareholders, debtholders, clients, suppliers, managers, and other personnel but also the government, the community, and all groups that are bound to affect or be affected in some way by the direction of the firm, like environmentalists, consumers, and others.

In the early 1950s, the focus of managerial attention was production, since markets were plentiful for the goods delivered by business enterprises. The increasing competition observed during the 1960s switched the interest from production to marketing. Paradoxically, the continuous increase in competition, particularly from international firms, and the slowdown of economic growth again raised productivity, quality, and cost at the level of primary managerial concerns.

The trend toward decentralization and the development of autonomous business units had to be reconsidered. External pressures forced more careful considerations to all potential sharing of resources, such as manufacturing facilities, distribution networks, common sales forces, and centralized purchasing. Qualified attention to cost reduction and increased efficiency could give a business firm the necessary competitive edge to outperform competitors.

SEGMENTATION REVISITED

We stressed in the previous discussion of business segmentation the need to address this question by identifying business units which constituted independent viable entities. An important exception to the applicability of this definition is the business firm primarily engaged in a single or dominant business activity with a purely functional organizational structure. This is a prevalent situation in small enterprises, and it is commonly observed in medium and large size organizations in process oriented industries characterized by high levels of vertical integration.

Our inability to establish autonomous entities in those cases, however, does not preclude the firm from engaging in a plurality of external markets, each one possessing very distinct opportunities and demanding very different competitive efforts. We have to manage a situation in which there is no easy matching between the functional organizational structure and the strategic focus for different market segments.

A second important exception to the definition of independent business units is the firm which can be broken into highly distinct businesses, but if those units were to be managed in a totally autonomous way, unacceptable inefficiencies would result. Very often, a proper strategy would address two primary dimensions among distinct but related business units, shared resources and shared concerns. We can identify situations where different units, in order to be run effectively, have to share some common resources like manufacturing facilities, distribution channels, or other functional support. Ignoring these potentials would deprive the organization of significant benefits to be derived from shared experiences and economies of scale. The other form of interrelationship that can be found among distinct business units is the existence of shared concerns, like common geographical areas and key customer accounts.

The cornerstone to identify shared resources opportunities is the value-added chain, which covers all stages in the development of a product, from product development to delivery of the finished product to the final customer. We can apply the experience-curve effect (to be discussed in Chapter 6), not only to the final product, but to every stage in the value-added chain, opening new avenues for increased efficiency when businesses share various forms of functional support. A typical value-added chain covers the following steps:

PROD-UCT R&D	PROC-ESS R&D	PURCHASING OF RAW MATERIALS	TRANSPOR-TATION OF RAW MATERIALS	MANUFAC-TURING OF PARTS AND COMPONENTS	ASSEM-BLY	TESTING AND QUALITY CONTROL	MARKET-ING	SALES	WHOLE-SALE DISTRI-BUTION	RETAIL-ING

A simple procedure to diagnose the potentials for shared resources among various business units is to construct a two-dimensional matrix for the appropriate stages for value added and business units of the firm. In each of the resulting cells, a comment can be made on the nature of the potential sharing of resources, if any. (This procedure is illustrated in Chapter 12.)

Porter (1981) has identified various kinds of business interrelationships among markets, product costs, and technologies which might be of assistance to identify the form of leverage among the firm businesses (Figure 4.1).

Lewis (1984) has used this approach to produce a description of shared resources in what he refers to as the *Strategic Field Theory*, an illustration of which is presented in Figure 4.2. The figure shows quite clearly that P&G brings powerful skills in distribution, marketing, manufacturing, and R&D strengths to a wide variety of apparently unrelated businesses. It is this corporate "field" of strengths that has allowed P&G to develop an effective and tightly focused corporate strategy.

THE DIFFERENT HIERARCHICAL LEVELS OF PLANNING

The considerations which we have just expressed point out the difficulties in segmenting the businesses of the firm in a way that is consistent with its existing organizational structure. Whenever this segmentation does not result in completely autonomous units, it is likely to generate significant ambiguity regarding the strategic and operational responsibilities of the firm's managers. In other words, a considerable effort would have to be made to match strategy and structure.

Gluck, Kaufman, and Walleck (1982) characterize the problems with a definition of an SBU as a type of chicken-and-egg situation:

> You can only really know the proper definition of an SBU when you have an agreed strategy; different strategic thrusts require the inclusion of different product-market units and functional capabilities within the SBU. But one purpose of the SBU strategy is to provide a framework for planning. Which came first, strategy or structure?
>
> Second, in most companies the planning structure is force-fitted into the current organizational structure, or the other way around. Both are equally unsatisfactory. The planning structure should be shaped around tomorrow's concepts of the business. An organizational structure is responsible for implementing today's strategies well; when the two are different, conflict is inevitable.
>
> It should not be surprising, therefore, that no one has been able to prescribe an entirely acceptable definition of an SBU, or describe satisfactorily how to derive an SBU structure. SBU definition remains something of a black art. . . .

In this excerpt, Gluck and others refer to a situation in which the existing formal organization structure cannot be logically mapped with the business

Figure 4.1 Different Forms of Leverage Among Businesses

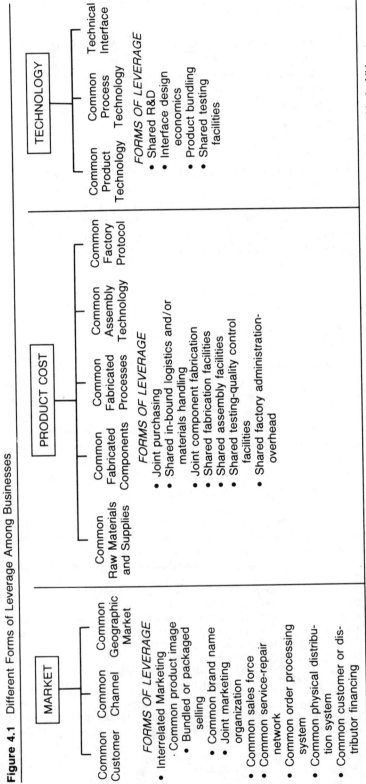

Source: Adapted from Michael E. Porter, *Competitive Strategy*, © 1981. Reprinted by permission of the Free Press, New York, NY.

Figure 4.2   Procter & Gamble Strategic Field

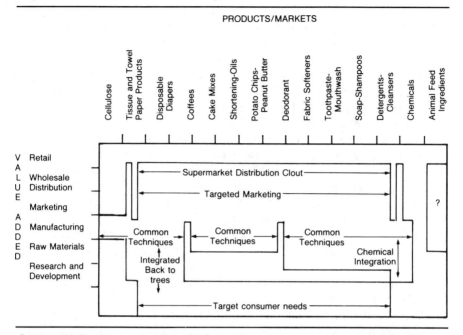

Source: Walker W. Lewis, "The CEO and Corporate Strategy in the 80's: Back to Basics," © 1984. Reprinted by permission of Interfaces, University Park, PA.

segmentation scheme, which is one of the two conditions that invalidates the definition of an SBU, as autonomous business unit to which we alluded in the previous section. Their proposal for resolving this problem is based upon a comprehensive strategic planning framework which defines a hierarchy of planning levels composed by five different layers:

> —*Corporate-level planning*. To establish the vision of the firm, state corporate objectives and strategic thrusts, define a corporate philosophy and values, identify the domains in which the firm will operate, recognize worldwide technical and market trends, and allocate resources with a sense of corporate priorities.
>
> —*Share-concern planning*. To meet unique needs of certain industrial or geographical customer groups or to plan for technologies used by a number of business units.
>
> —*Shared resource planning*. To achieve economies of scale or to avoid problems of subcritical mass for example R&D). Whenever a critical resource relies on a function centralized at the corporate level, the development of that functional strategy could be critically important to either determine or constrain a business unit strategy.
>
> —*Business-unit planning*. Business units are defined having external markets and competitors in mind. Most of the strategic planning effort is done at this level, where the business unit manager seeks control of its own market position and cost structure.
>
> —*Product-market planning*. The lowest level at which strategic planning takes place, where typically product, price, sales, and services are planned.

From the perspective of this framework, the essential task is to identify what are the issues to be faced by each hierarchical level, and what is the role that they have to play in shaping corporate, business, and functional strategy. Also, individual responsibilities for developing, implementing, and controlling the proper strategic tasks have to be assigned at all levels in the organization.

By adopting this way of resolving the dilemma between strategy and structure, we are de facto admitting that there could be two coexistent types of organization within the firm. One, the formal organizational structure, is designed to deal in an effective manner with the ongoing operational tasks, and requires a clearly spelled out hierarchy of responsibilities and authorities allowing little or no reporting ambiguity. The other, the strategy structure, has its own reporting system according to the hierarchical strategic levels we just described. Many managers assume dual roles: operational and strategic, and therefore are measured and rewarded by a dual control system. In the terminology of Texas Instruments, these individuals wear "two hats."

There is also no ambiguity in the strategic reporting structure except that it might not coincide with the operational reporting mechanism. As far as we know, General Electric was the first organization to formally adopt this dual operational and strategic approach to structuring an organization (General Electric Company 1981).

The second condition we have identified in the previous section that limits the definition of SBUs as autonomous entities applies to firms which, though clearly segmented in accordance with largely self-contained business units, do share significant resources and concerns among them.

A very popular way of resolving this issue has been to interpose a new hierarchical level in the organizational structure, normally referred to as group or sector. It represents a collection of distinct but interrelated business units which share resources or concerns or both and, therefore, cannot state strategic plans in a completely independent fashion.

The group or sector management fulfills many roles: it serves as a buffer between the corporate and business levels; it assists in the translation of corporate objectives, thrusts, and planning challenges for the participating SBUs; it assures that the adequate resources and concerns are properly dealt with and developed by business units; and it coordinates the strategic and operational activities pertaining to SBUs.

Two additional tasks conducted by group managers in some organizations are the allocation of resources among SBUs and the extension of existing businesses into new and related product-market segments. This is particularly true in firms such as General Electric, where the various sectors are differentiated by type of industry. The corporate level lacks an intimate knowledge of the wide array of businesses spanning a broad spectrum of industries, so it delegates in group executives what actually is the management of a fairly complex segment of the corporation, but it retains the responsibility for diversification opportunities into new industries not covered by existing groups.

The issue of matching strategy and structure is further discussed in Chapter 5. Part IV of this book is solely dedicated to the issue of organizational design.

THE CORPORATE STRATEGIC PLANNING PROCESS

The corporate strategic planning process is a disciplined and well-defined organizational effort aimed at the complete specification of corporate strategy. In the words of Andrews (1980):

> Corporate strategy is the pattern of decisions in a company that determines and reveals its objectives, purposes, or goals, produces the principal policies and plans for achieving those goals, and defines the range of businesses the company is to pursue, the kind of economic and human organization it is or intends to be, and the nature of the economic and noneconomic contribution it intends to make to its shareholders, employees, customers, and communities . . . [It] defines the businesses in which a company will compete, preferably in a way that focuses resources to convey distinctive competences into competitive advantages.

It is a complex matter to describe this process in general terms. We need to identify not only the major tasks that have to be addressed in setting up corporate strategy and the sequence in which they must be completed, but also the assignment of responsibilities for the execution of those tasks.

It is apparent from our previous discussion that there are many hierarchical levels that depend very heavily upon the diversity of businesses of the firm, its organizational structure, and the interrelationship between strategy and structure. It becomes clear that the precise specification of a corporate strategic planning process depends on the particular characteristics of the situational setting confronted by the firm. The planning process appropriate for a single business firm with a purely functional organizational structure is quite different from the one suitable for addressing the strategic tasks of a highly diversified multinational corporation. We believe, however, that there are some common properties whose adequate use can help in delineating the formal planning process for most business firms.

At the risk of being overly simplistic, we will go back to basics. In Figure 4.3 we have identified three conceptual hierarchical levels, which have always been recognized as the essential layers of any corporate planning process: a corporate, a business, and a functional level. One should keep in mind, however, that imbedded in what we are describing as the corporate level is a need to address the matter of shared resources and shared concerns, both enrich and constrain the formulation of business strategies. At the business level, managers have to deal with the more detailed questions pertaining to the strategic options of product-market segments. Finally, functional strategies not only consolidate the functional requirements demanded by the composite of businesses of the firm, but also impose legitimate strategic directions and developmental constraints to those businesses.

Figure 4.3 The Formal Corporate Strategic Planning Process

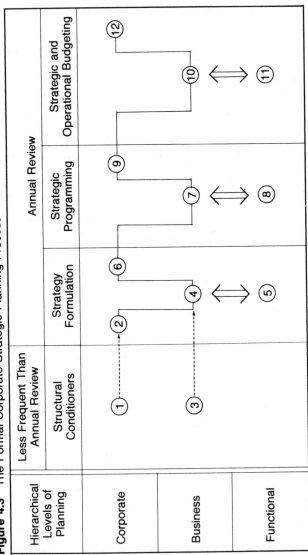

1 The vision of the firm: corporate philosophy, mission of the firm, and identification of SBUs and their interactions.

2 Strategic posture and planning guidelines: corporate strategic thrusts, corporate performance objectives, and planning challenges.

3 The mission of the business: business scope and identification of product-market segments.

4 Formulation of business strategy and broad action programs.

5 Formulation of functional strategy: participation in business planning, concurrence or nonconcurrence to business strategy proposals, and broad action programs.

6 Consolidation of business and functional strategies.

7 Definition and evaluation of specific action programs at the business level.

8 Definition and evaluation of specific action programs at the functional level.

9 Resource allocation and definition of performance measurements for management control.

10 Budgeting at the business level.

11 Budgeting at the functional level.

12 Budgeting consolidations and approval of strategic and operational funds.

Regarding the nature of the planning tasks, we believe it is important to distinguish, first, some activities which have a more permanent character. Although planning is a continuous process which is repeated year in and year out in the life of an organization, there are certain basic conditions that seem to be more permanent and are not significantly altered in each planning cycle. We have referred to them as the structural conditioners of the business firm and thus are represented in Figure 4.3 by the vision of the firm, and the mission of the business.

At the same time, there are three major tasks which need to be updated and revised at every planning cycle: strategy formulation, strategic programming, and strategic and operational budgeting. Essentially, these three tasks were discussed when we addressed the issue of strategic planning at the business level. Figures 3.5 and 4.3 provide a sharp contrast of the interactions required to undertake those tasks from a business and a corporate strategic planning perspective. In the latter case, the corporation becomes a primary actor, mainly at the early stages of the strategic planning process.

The essence of the message portrayed in Figure 4.3 is that corporate planning is neither a top-down nor a bottom-up process. It is a much more complex activity which requires a strong participation of the key managers of the firm, where objectives are being proposed from the top, and specific pragmatic alternatives are being suggested from business and functional levels. It is a process that, properly conducted, generates a wealth of individual commitments and personal participation from everybody who has a definitive say in sharpening up the direction of the firm. It is a rich communication device, where the key managers have an opportunity to voice their personal beliefs about the conduct of businesses of the firm, and offer a valuable joint experience as well as an educational opportunity to be shared by key participants.

Tom MacAvoy, the president of Corning-Glass Works, once said that the most important role of a CEO was to identify, develop, and promote "the one hundred centurions." In the old Roman empire, the Centurion was a soldier who received instructions from the Caesar, was sent to remote lands, and the Caesar knew that, regardless of the number of years he would take for his task, he would always be fighting for the Caesar's interests. If the planning process has any definitive objective and basic influence, it is to develop a strong esprit-de-corps among the one hundred centurions of the firm.

We recognize the following basic steps in the corporate strategic planning process:

1. The vision of the firm: corporate philosophy, mission of the firm, and identification of SBUs and their interactions.
2. Strategic posture and planning guidelines: corporate strategic thrusts, corporate performance objectives, and planning challenges.
3. The mission of the business: business scope and identification of product-market segments.

4. Formulation of business strategy and broad action programs.
5. Formulation of functional strategy: participation in business strategic planning, concurrence or nonconcurrence to business strategy proposals, and formulation of broad action programs for each function.
6. Consolidation of business and functional strategies.
7. Definition and evaluation of specific action programs at the business level.
8. Definition and evaluation of specific action programs at the functional level.
9. Resource allocation and definition of performance measurements for management control.
10. Budgeting at the business level.
11. Budgeting at the functional level.
12. Budget consolidation and approval of strategic and operational funds.

We provide now a brief description of the content of these corporate strategic planning steps. A detailed methodology to implement these steps is presented and illustrated in Part III of this book.

Step 1: The Vision of the Firm

The vision of the firm is a rather permanent statement articulated primarily by its Chief Executive Officer, that is issued to:

1. Communicate the very nature of existence of the organization in terms of corporate purpose, business scope, and competitive leadership.
2. Provide a framework that regulates the relationships between the firm and its primary stakeholders: employees, customers, shareholders, suppliers, and the communities in which the firm operates.
3. State the broad objectives of the firm's performance in terms of growth and profitability.

The vision of the firm has to be expressed as to provide a unifying theme and a vital challenge to all organizational units, communicate a sense of achievable ideals, serve as a source of inspiration for confronting the daily activities, and become a contagious, motivating, and guiding force congruent with the corporate ethic and values.

The vision is a statement of basic principles that set apart those firms which have been able to articulate it in a positive manner from those which lag behind in this respect. There are very few firms which can show well-defined statements of vision. Perhaps the most notorious distinction of firms which have reached the stage of corporate strategic planning is the presentation of a clearly articulated vision of the firm.

An individual working for a firm has to become an active collaborator in the pursuit of the corporate purposes; he must share the vision of the firm and feel comfortable with the way in which it is translated or expressed in traditions and values. The behavior of individuals is conditioned by this framework and they must intimately sense that by following these guidelines, they are fulfilling their most personal needs for achievement. The vision of the firm is a *personal* drive for their own lives.

Though the vision of the firm is a central thrust for a smooth development of corporate concerns, it is very hard to be precise in unambiguous and pragmatic terms, and explain what it takes to develop and communicate the proper sense of vision. The proper realization of corporate strategic planning requires, as a first step, that a statement of the vision of the firm be issued. We believe that three major components should be present in such a statement:

1. An expression of the mission of the firm in terms of product, market, and geographical scope and a statement of the way to achieve competitive leadership.
2. The identification of SBUs and their interactions in terms of shared resources and shared concerns.
3. An articulation of the corporate philosophy in terms of corporate policies and cultural values.

The expression of the mission of the firm was already alluded to when presenting the business strategic planning in Chapter 3, where we provided an example of Emhart's mission. We should emphasize that the statement of the firm's domain ought to be expressed in terms of the current as well as the future expected product, market, and geographical scope. This allows communicating a sense of the future direction selected by the corporation in order to prevent a myopic positioning of its businesses.

Likewise, we have already addressed the question of business segmentation, first at the business level where we defined an SBU as an independent autonomous unit, and at the corporate level, where the independence assumption was dropped and we discussed at certain length the issues of shared resources and shared concerns.

Therefore, it remains for us to comment on the third component of the vision of the firm, which is a statement of corporate philosophy. Needless to say, this is the most subtle of the issues involved in shaping up the corporate vision. Rather than offering an abstract discussion on this subject, we provide an actual example on how Analog Devices, Inc., a progressive firm, has decided to communicate its corporate philosophy (Figure 4.4), its corporate policies (Figure 4.5), and its value system (Figure 4.6), all of them summing up a broad statement of corporate culture. This subject is treated extensively in Chapter 5.

In Chapter 12 we present an illustration of a methodology to develop the vision of the firm.

Figure 4.4   The Statement of Corporate Philosophy of Analog Devices, Inc.

Corporate Purpose and Scope of Business

Our purpose is to search continuously for opportunities where we can make unique or valuable contributions to the application of measurement and control technology and by so doing increase the productivity of human and capital resources, improve the quality and reliability of products and more generally upgrade the quality of life and the advancement of society.

The scope of our business includes industrial automation and process control, medical electronics, navigation and guidance controls, laboratory test and measurements, environmental monitoring and energy conservation both domestically and around the world.

Our Employees

Personal motivation and interests are primarily related to ascending needs for security, safety, purpose, recognition, identity and the realization of one's full potential. Our corporate goals are best achieved in an environment that encourages and assists employees to achieve their personal goals while helping Analog Devices to achieve its own.

Our goals are to offer our employees a challenging and stable working environment, above-average compensation, and an unrestricted opportunity for personal advancement irrespective of race, creed, color, sex or national origin. Our objective is to build mutual respect, confidence and trust in our personal relationships based upon commitments to integrity, honesty, openness and competence. Our policy is to share Analog Devices' success with the people who make it possible.

Our Customers

Satisfying the needs of our customers is fundamental to our survival and our prosperity. These needs can best be understood in terms of the support we lend in helping our customers meet their objectives with the minimum use of their resources. Thus, our goals must be to provide reliable and superior products which offer innovative solutions to our customers' problems, dependable delivery, quick response to inquiries, easy-to-use products and product literature, and strong service and applications assistance. We must work hard at understanding the business of our customers so that we may anticipate *their* needs and enhance *their* effectiveness. We wish to be major suppliers to our key customers and to establish long lasting business relationships based on performance and integrity.

Our Stockholders

Our responsibility is to satisfy our stockholders' desire for a secure and liquid investment at an attractive rate of return. Our objective is to consistently earn a return on invested capital that is well above the average for all manufacturing companies and comparable to the most successful companies in our industry. To date our policy has been to retain all of our earnings to finance our growth. Our goal is to achieve return on capital at a level where we can both finance our growth and pay a dividend.

Our Suppliers

Our suppliers are partners in our efforts to develop market share by fulfilling our customers' needs. This requires that we be open and frank about our future

Figure 4.4 *Continued*

requirements and plans as they would affect our suppliers. It also requires that we seek to understand what constraints are placed upon them by their technology, cost structure and financial resources. We place strong emphasis on associating with suppliers who are financially stable, competent and honest and who are consistent in meeting their delivery and quality commitments to us.

Our Community

Our goal is to be an asset to every community in which we operate by creating stable employment, by lending our effort and support to worthy causes and by developing people with leadership skills who can be valuable in community affairs. Our people are encouraged to take an active interest in their community and to contribute their efforts to the solution of community problems.

Growth

Growth is an important means by which we satisfy the interest of our employees, our stockholders and our customers. High caliber people are looking for opportunities for personal development and advancement which can best be achieved in a growth environment. Our stockholders are looking for an above average return which can be achieved more assuredly by a growth company.

Our growth objective is to penetrate selected segments of the worldwide instrumentation market which are growing at an annual rate of 15% or more. Thus, for us, no growth means extinction and growth in excess of the market is a requirement for increased strength. Our goal is to achieve a three year average growth of 25% per year which is nearly twice the growth rate of the markets we serve. We accomplish this growth primarily by continuously broadening the range of our product line through internal developments, but also through venture investments in new companies and through selected acquisitions that fall within the scope of our business definition.

Profit generated by our business is the primary source of funds required to finance our growth and ultimately to pay a return to our stockholders. Without growth and profits we cannot achieve our corporate objectives. Our goal is to earn 12% return on assets employed and 19% return on invested capital which translates to about 6.5% profit after tax on sales for our business. With this rate of return we can finance our growth and over the long term pay a dividend to our stockholders without taking unreasonable risk.

Market Leadership

Our goal is to obtain the largest share of each market segment we serve. We believe the key to achieving market share is to enter growth markets early with superior, innovative products and to provide a high level of customer service and communications. Our markets are worldwide in scope and our objective is to develop comparable penetration in every major geographical market.

Summary

Achieving our goals for growth, profits and market share creates the environment and economic means to satisfy the interests and needs of our employees, stockholders, customers and others associated with the firm. Our success depends on people who understand the interdependence and congruence of their personal goals with those of the company and who are thus motivated to contribute toward achieving these goals.

Source: Analog Devices, Inc., "Corporate Objectives." Reprinted by permission of Analog Devices, Inc., Norwood, MA.

Figure 4.5 A Brief Summary of Corporate Policies of Analog Devices, Inc.

Analog Devices, Inc.
Policies

Centralized business strategy
Highly decentralized organization, aligned to strategies and cultural values
Depend more on champions than on committees and broad studies
Management by objectives
Consultative management style
Open, frank communications
Concern for the individual and respect for his commitment and judgement
More dependency on judgement than on rules and regulations
Respect for different points of view and tolerance of conflict in goal setting
Expectation of full commitment to agreed goals
Risk oriented, entrepreneurial climate
Tolerance and understanding of occasional failures
High value placed on innovative, creative results
Congruence between individual and corporate goals
High standards for personal and business ethics
High standards for positive, inspirational leadership
Broad sharing of the fruits of success

Figure 4.6 A Brief Summary of the Value System of Analog Devices, Inc.

Analog Devices, Inc.
Value System

Management processes and policies are based on assumptions about people and how they behave. Specifically people—
—Are honest and trustworthy
—Should be treated with respect and dignity
—Want to achieve to their full potential and will work hard to do so
—Want to understand the purpose of their work and the goals of their organization
—Want a strong hand in determining what to do and how to do it
—Want to be held accountable for results and to be recognized and rewarded for achievements.

Step 2: The Process of Arriving at the Strategic Posture of the Firm

The corporate vision is a rather permanent statement of the central purpose of the organization, its policies and corporate values. Normally, it is not updated at the beginning of each planning cycle but it is subject to a thorough review at much longer intervals, say every five years or so. The vision, however, has to be translated into more pragmatic and concrete guidelines which serve as immediate challenges for the development of strategic proposals at the businesses and major functions of the firm.

This is expressed by means of the strategic posture of the firm, which has to be distilled from the vision of the firm and the situational analysis of the external and internal environments. In Figure 4.7 we represent these interactions and indicate the primary elements in these strategic activities.

Environmental Scan at the Corporate Level

Environmental scan attempts to diagnose the general health of the industrial sectors relevant to the businesses in which the corporation is engaged. It concentrates on assessing the overall economic, political, technological, and social climates that affect the corporation as a whole. This assessment has to be conducted, first, from a historical perspective to determine how well the corporation has mobilized its resources to meet the challenges presented by the external environ-

Figure 4.7   The Vision of the Firm and Its Strategic Posture

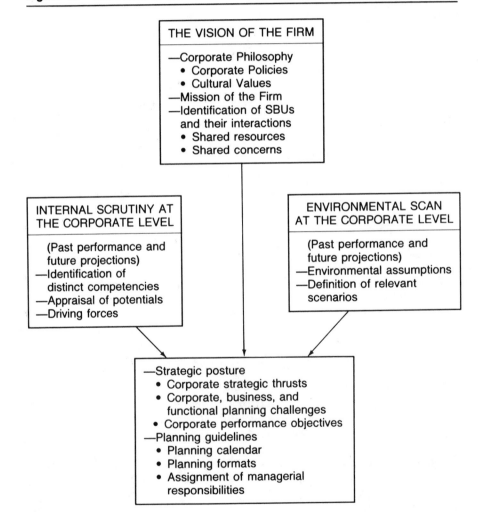

ment; and then, with a futuristic view in mind, to forecast future trends in the environment and seek a repositioning of the internal resources to adapt the organization to those environmental trends.

The output of the environmental scan normally starts with an economic scenario which exhibits the most likely trends affecting the next planning cycle and, possibly, a call for the development of contingency plans addressing either optimistic or pessimistic departures from this most likely trend. Topics to be included in this economic scenario are:

—economic growth: GNP and major influencing factors
—inflation rate
—prime interest rate
—unemployment
—overview of foreign markets and foreign exchange rates considerations
—population growth in critical geographical areas
—disposable income
—growth of critical industrial sectors, such as housing, defense, health, and so forth

A second important component of the environmental scan is the projection of global trends in the primary markets in which the firm competes. Although a more detailed industry and competitive analysis has to be conducted at the business level, it is important to provide some macro-trends mutually agreed upon by corporate officers and key business managers in order to assure a sense of overall consistency in the formulation of business strategies and action programs.

For a firm competing in a high-technology environment, an essential third ingredient of the environmental scanning process is a thorough analysis of the change of pace of emerging technologies and the threats and opportunities this situation creates for the firm.

Besides economic, market, and technological considerations, a question that deserves special attention is the availability and quality of the supply of human resources. For some firms, this is the most critical and constraining resource. Therefore, it is essential to understand the composition and trends of specially critical professional and technical skills.

Finally, the environmental scan has to address more subtle but, at times, crucial issues pertaining to the political, social, and legal environments. Concrete items which are central to most business firms are regulatory issues, questions of unionization, minority concerns, environmentalists pressures, public opinion groups, community activities, and so forth.

Internal Scrutiny at the Corporate Level

The subject of the internal scrutiny at the corporate level is concerned with a broad evaluation of the human, financial, productive, physical, and technological resources available to the corporation. As with the environmental scan, the analysis has to include the historical background as well as the forecasted trends.

As we indicated in the business strategic planning process, a detailed analysis of internal strengths and weaknesses has to be performed at the SBU level where all the pertinent information resides. What is intended to be distilled from the internal scrutiny at the corporate level is the identification of the major areas of competence existing across the organization which are going to be exploited to achieve a position of leadership.

A tool which could be useful to reflect upon the primary thrust of the firm is what Tregoe and Zimmerman (1980) designate as the *driving force*. According to their definition, a driving force is a central determinant of *changes* in the mission of the firm; that is, in its product, market, and geographical scope. They suggest that there are nine basic strategic areas, grouped in three broad categories, all of which can decisively affect and influence the nature and direction of any organization. In Figure 4.8, we present excerpts of the definition of these nine driving forces extracted from their book.

Figure 4.8 Driving Force and The Nine Basic Strategic Areas

CATEGORY	STRATEGIC AREAS
Product/Markets	*Products Offered* The products-offered driven organization will continue to produce and deliver products similar to those it has. New products will have characteristics very similar to those of current products. This organization will seek a new geographic market and market-segments where there is a need for its products. It will constantly look for ways to improve or extend these products. *Market Needs* The market-needs driven organization will be constantly looking for alternative ways to fill the needs it is currently filling; and searching for new or emerging needs in the market-segment itself. It develops or acquires new different products to meet needs in its market-segment. New geographic market and market segments will have characteristics similar to those it currently serves.
Capabilities	*Technology* The technology driven organization offers *only* products or services that emanate from or capitalize on its technological capabilities. It would seek a variety of applications for its technology and strives to be the technological innovative leader in its field. *Production Capabilities* The production-capabilities driven organization offers *only* those products that can be made or developed using its production know-how, processes, systems, and equipments. There are two different forms of production capability as a driving force: the commodity type of business, which manufactures products in long-runs and with economies of scale; and the job-shop type of business, which produces a wide range of products, sub-products, or parts.

Figure 4.8 *Continued*

CATEGORY	STRATEGIC AREAS
	Method of Sale The method-of-sale driven organization determines its product, markets, and geographical scope based on the capabilities and limitations on its method of sale; that is, the *primary* way the organization convinces current or potential customers or users to buy its products. *Method of Distribution* The method-of-distribution driven organization determines the products it sells, the customers it sells them to, and its geographic scope on the basis of those kinds of products or services and customers which can be handled through its established distribution channels. *Natural Resources* The natural-resources driven company would develop its products and markets through the use and conservation of those natural resources. It would concentrate on control of those resources as a way of increasing their value.
Results	*Size-Growth* The size-growth driven organization determines its business scope in its desire to become larger or smaller. It will set levels of size and growth significantly different from its current level of performance, and will push into new unrelated products and markets. *Return-Profits* The return-profits driven organization determines the scope of its business from its desire for specific levels of return-profits. To be return-profit driven, the return and profit targets must be used to determine the scope of future products or markets and *not* as a screen for particular products or markets to select within the existing product scope. This driving force may lead an organization to seek a variety of unrelated products over time or it may lead an organization to change from one line of related products to a different line of related products because of return-profit considerations.

Source: Adapted from B. B. Tregoe and John W. Zimmerman, *Top Management Strategy*, © 1980, by Kepner-Tregoe, Inc. Reprinted by permission of Simon & Schuster, Inc., New York, NY.

Tregoe and Zimmerman suggest that, although all nine strategic areas are critically important to every company, one and only one of the nine areas should be the driving force for the total organization. Likewise, for any business unit within the organization, there should be only one driving force, though not necessarily the same as in the total organization. Moreover, the driving force might change as the organization modifies its strategic posture through time, due to changes in the environment, in the competitive picture, in internal capabilities, or in the desire of top managment.

The strategic areas identified under the category "capabilities" represent driving forces which are supported by some special kind of functional excellence, while the others address broader issues of business concerns.

The Strategic Posture of the Firm

The strategic posture of the firm is a set of pragmatic requirements developed at the corporate level to guide the formulation of business and functional strategies. The principal inputs to accomplish this task are the vision of the firm, and the environmental scan and internal scrutiny at the corporate level.

This is accomplished through the formulation of corporate strategic thrusts, the identification of specific planning challenges for the corporation, businesses and functional areas, and the statement of corporate performance objectives.

A detailed methodology to develop the strategic posture of the firm is discussed and exemplified in Chapter 13.

Corporate Strategic Thrusts

The corporate strategic thrusts constitute a powerful mechanism we recommend to use in order to translate the broad sense of directions the organization wants to follow into a practical set of instructives to all key managers involved in the strategic process. We define strategic thrusts as the primary issues the firm has to address during the next three to five years to establish a healthy competitive position in the key markets in which it participates.

Strategic thrusts should contain specific and meaningful planning challenges for each of the business units of the firm. In addition, depending on the nature of the organizational structure, the strategic thrusts could also contain challenges addressed at the corporate level as well as some key centralized functions.

We have found that the mere process of collective reflection upon the strategic thrusts by a group of top managers, conducive to the listing of these primary issues, and assignment of priorities and identification of responsible individuals in charge of responding to those thrusts, represent a major advance in the strategic thinking of the firm. On the surface, it may sound as a relatively simple and straightforward exercise. This is far from being the case. The formulation of strategic thrusts permits raising the central questions the firm should address for a meaningful strategic development. Once the strategic thrusts are stated and agreed upon, we have established an important part of a coherent and relatively stable framework in which the strategic planning process will be conducted.

There is a significant power in the actions that are set in motion by the definition of strategic thrusts. Regardless of the individual concerns and situational issues residing at every level in the organization, we know that those managers who have been entrusted with the responsibility of responding to strategic thrusts will have to produce proper answers to those questions, mobilizing every unit in the organization in the desired overall direction. This provides an opportunity for all competencies and talents in the organization to be thoroughly applied in the pursuit of clearly established lines of action. It is a most constructive procedure to call for the maximum participation of all individuals in the firm.

For example, suppose that one issue considered critical at a given point in time is the excessive maturity of the firm's businesses. A thrust demanding the identification of new business opportunities will create a flare of energy to be channeled into this question. Although there is no guarantee that an edict of that sort will necessarily solve that particular problem, at least it assumes that every key manager will search for alternatives to be contributed to its solution, will report on its finding, and will communicate to its peers the result of his probes. In other words, it will generate a challenge and a sense of urgency to a strategic concern that, otherwise, could have continued to be neglected.

Figure 4.9 illustrates in a very succinct way the statement of strategic thrusts for a manufacturing firm, as well as the assignment of planning challenges to those organizational levels in charge of responding to those thrusts. Notice that there is a priority assigned to those planning challenges, depending on the level of intensity of the necessary participation required. We have formulated these thrusts in a very concise way. It could be beneficial, in a given situation, to expand the description of each thrust to allow for a better communication of the issues that are intended to be covered.

Corporate Performance Objectives

Normally, the expression of corporate objectives are quantitative indicators related to the overall financial performance of the firm. Typically, corporations choose to express corporate financial objectives via a very limited number of

Figure 4.9   Statement of Strategic Thrusts and Assignment of Planning Challenges

Strategic Thrusts	Corp	Businesses			Functions	
		SBU-1	SBU-2	SBU-3	Manuf	Tech
Reduce production costs	—	1	1	3	1	2
Improve product quality	—	2	1	1	1	2
Develop new products	2	3	1	1	3	1
Increase penetration in key accounts	1	1	2	2	—	—
Increase international participation	1	3	2	1	—	—
Seek diversification outside existing business base	1	—	—	—	—	2
Improve customer service	—	1	3	2	—	2

CODE: 1 Vital
2 Important
3 Secondary
— Not applicable

selected indicators related to total revenues, profit performance, and growth rate.

Examples of performance objectives formulated in two different corporations, one in the electronic products and the other in the forest products industries are given below:

	Electronic Products (%)	Forest products (%)
Growth rate (per-year)	30	10
Profit ratios		
—Gross margin	55	n.s.
—Return on equity	20	17
Reinvestment rates		
—Capital investment (% of sales)	16	n.s.
—R&D (% of sales)	8	n.s.
Debt-Equity ratio	75	50
Dividend payout	0	30

n.s. = Not specified as an objective

There is no universal set of indicators companies use to express their corporate objectives. Moreover, as can be easily seen in the example above, the financial targets could be quite different among firms, depending both on external market opportunities and the external competencies of the firm.

Various considerations serve as a base to arrive at a numerical expression of goals. First, the historical performance achieved by the corporation; second, the projected trends expected from the existing and new business lines; and third, the financial position of the firm's competitors. It is important to recognize the financial performance of the key competitors not only from the perspective of comparative analysis, but also because firms in the same industry attract the same group of investors in the capital markets.

By articulating broad financial expectations, the corporation adds to the challenges implicit in the strategic thrust but, at the same time, provides a more realistic framework to guide the desirability of proposed action programs that will emerge from the subsequent steps in the strategic planning process.

At the risk of being repetitive, we should reiterate that these corporate performance objectives should not be applied indiscriminately to every business of the firm, but should be adjusted to recognize the different contribution they make to the short- and long-run performance of the firm. The issue of setting financial performance objectives is thoroughly discussed in Chapter 11.

Step 3: The Mission of the Business

The basic concept of the mission of the business is similar to its equivalent at the corporate level, and is expressed in terms of products, market, and geographical scope, together with a statement of competitive uniqueness. When applied at the business level, however, the mission becomes sharper and more detailed, as shown in the examples we presented in Chapter 3 when discussing this subject, but, in this case, there is a strong influence emanating from the corporate vision and posture statements. Finally, it is possible that the existing or desirable competitive leadership of a given business might not coincide with that of the overall corporation.

The methodology we suggest to complete this step is indicated and discussed in Chapter 14.

Step 4: *Formulation of Business Strategy and Broad Action Programs*

As we stated in Chapter 3, a business strategy is a set of well-coordinated action programs aimed at securing a long-term sustainable advantage. In order to address properly the formulation of business strategy at the SBU level, it is necessary to perform a thorough analysis regarding the current and future business position in terms of two dimensions:

—the non-controllable forces which are associated with the external environment and determine the industry trends and market opportunities; and
—the internal competencies residing in the firm, which will determine the unique competitive leadership potential that the firm could mobilize in order to establish a business superiority against competitors.

The business strategy has to deal with these two dimensions, so as to take advantage of market opportunities and neutralize adverse environmental impacts, and at the same time reinforce internal strengths and improve upon perceived weaknesses with regard to competition. But in the context of corporate planning, the business strategy should be guided by directions provided at the corporate level, most importantly, those expressed by the strategic thrusts which generate specific planning challenges for the business under consideration (Figure 4.10).

The step is one of the most time consuming in the planning process, because it requires the detailed examination and evaluation of external and internal critical success factors. There are very many methodologies that have been proposed to complete this assignment, like the different business portfolio approaches which we discuss extensively in Part Two of this book. Moreover, in Chapter 15 we propose pragmatic procedures to perform this task.

Step 5: *Formulation of Functional Strategy and Broad Action Programs*

The intensity of the functional participation at this stage of the planning process depends strongly on the characteristics of the organizational structure of the firm. When the firm is heavily decentralized, with strong self-sufficient divisionalized businesses, the functional managers are directly involved in the development of their corresponding functional strategies to support each business at Step 4

Figure 4.10 Formulation of Business Strategy and Broad Action Programs Under a Corporate Planning Process

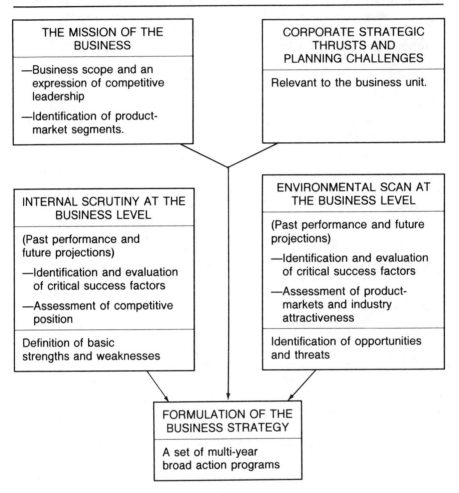

in the planning process. Therefore, at this stage, their role is relatively minimal, reduced to resolve some minor inconsistencies and fine tuning. The only important involvement might be derived from responses a functional manager has to provide to a corporate strategic thrust, which concerns directly his particular function, and is not contained in any proposed business plan. Normally, actions of this sort represent requirements for increasing existing competencies of a given function in order to create a unique competitive strength, to be transferred in the future to various businesses of the firm.

These functional responses to strategic thrusts are articulated in terms of broad action programs, containing multi-year milestones, and expressed in fairly aggregate terms. They will, in turn, be supported by a set of specific action programs later in the planning process.

In the formulation of broad action programs, it might be useful to resort to environmental scan and internal scrutiny processes, similar to those discussed at the business level, except that this time the focus of attention is the actual standing and proper development of functional capabilities in the firm.

Whenever businesses share centralized functional resources, either in a purely functional organization or in a hybrid organization having some strong centralized functional presence, the functional manager might be in the position of analyzing the business strategies and broad action programs proposed by business managers, and cast a concurrence or nonconcurrence vote.

If functional managers decide that a business plan is not acceptable because it is judged to contain inadequate or unrealistic commitments in some functional area, the corresponding functional manager will issue a nonconcurrence statement. Most of the nonconcurrences should be resolved through bilateral discussions between business and functional managers. If this is not the case, the nonconcurrence issue escalates through the organizational hierarchy until it is finally resolved. This planning mode has been adopted by IBM (IBM Corporation 1979).

Chapter 16 provides a detailed description of a methodology we propose for the development of this step.

Step 6: *Consolidation of Business and Functional Strategies at the Corporate Level*

This crucial step in the planning process calls for a critical review and sanctioning at the corporate level of the set of broad action programs proposed by business and functional managers. It requires the involvement of all key executives who share the responsibility of shaping the strategic direction of the firm, and it is conducted normally through a one or two day meeting, totally dedicated for this purpose. If properly done, it serves as a powerful communication device which allows for the emergence of a clear consensus and a personal commitment of all participating managers.

We recommend that, at a minimum, the following four issues be addressed at this step.

1. Resolution of nonconcurrence conflicts. If bilateral discussions undertaken by business and functional managers to resolve a nonconcurrence issue has not resulted in a satisfactory solution, the issue could escalate at this level, where it has to be finally resolved. Depending on the nature of the problem as well as the organizational style, we might not want to address publicly and openly this conflict at the managers meeting. In this case, efforts should be underaken to resolve the questions prior to the meeting and merely report on the final decision.
2. Balancing the business portfolio of the firm. This activity spans several dimensions of concern. The most crucial one has to do with short-term profitability versus long-term development. To some extent, that is also linked to the

trade-offs between risk and return. Finally there is a question of cash-flow balance, which does not imply that a balanced portfolio is necessarily optimum, but it serves to address the question of seeking some equilibrium between sources and uses of funds in the organization. The portfolio matrices whose merits and pitfalls we have already discussed in Chapter 3 in relation to its use at the business level, can be very helpful to guide managers in their search for a good compromise resulting in an appropriate balanced portfolio.

3. Defining the availability of strategic funds, the debt policy, and the maximum sustainable growth. Another task which is important to undertake at this step is the determination of total strategic funds available at the corporate level to support investment in fixed assets, and in increases in working capital and developmental expenses. A sound way of calculating these funds is first to forecast the sources of funds forthcoming to the firm. The primary components of the sources of funds are:

—earnings
—depreciation
—new debt issuing
—new equity issuing
—divestitures

Notice that earnings contain, as part of the cost of goods sold, the normal levels of developmental expenses which are assigned to the various functions of the organization, in particular R&D.

The second part of the computation requires the forecast of uses of funds, whose most important items are:

—dividends
—debt repayment (principal)
—strategic funds
    —new fixed assets and acquisitions
    —increases in working capital
    —increases in developmental expenses

Therefore, the total strategic funds available can be estimated as:

$$\begin{array}{l}\text{Total strategic funds}\\\text{availability}\end{array} = \begin{array}{l}\text{Total}\\\text{sources of funds}\end{array} - \begin{array}{l}\text{Dividend}\\\text{payments}\end{array} - \begin{array}{l}\text{Debt}\\\text{repayment}\end{array}$$

It is apparent from this relation that the firm's debt capacity and financial leverage policies have a significant impact on the ability of the firm to increase its growth. Establishing a sound debt policy, congruent with the company's financing requirements, is another issue to be addressed at this point. A good treatment of this topic is presented by Piper and Weinhold (1982).

Another useful guide to address the question of corporate growth is the calculation of the *maximum sustainable growth* of the firm. This represents the maximum growth the firm can support by using its internal resources as well as its debt capacity. A relation proposed by Zakon (1976) to estimate this limit to company growth is:

$$g = p\left[ROA + \frac{D}{E}(ROA - i) \right]$$

where: g = maximum sustainable growth expressed as a yearly rate of increase of the equity base. (It corresponds also to the increase
in the total assets base, because the debt-equity ratio is assumed
to remain constant.)

p = percentage of retained earnings

ROA = after-tax return on assets

D = total debt outstanding

E = total equity

i = after-tax interest on debt.

The derivation of this expression is presented in Chapter 7.

This expression represents a first cut and gross approximation of the maximum sustainable growth, that assumes a stable debt-equity ratio and dividend-
payout policy, as well as a fixed overall rate of return on assets, and cost
of debt. Although a coarse approximation, this number serves as a guidance
for corporate growth that should be taken into consideration at the corporate
level.

4. Preliminary evaluation of proposed action programs and assignment of priorities for resource allocation.

The previous considerations have allowed us to assess the affordable growth
of the corporation and the total funds available for its future development.
Having that information in mind, we should now turn our attention to the
assignment of priorities to be given to each business unit in terms of resource
allocation. This will allow realistic programs to be formulated, which not
only respond properly to the desired strategic direction of each business
unit, but also are consistent with the financial and human resources in place.

There are various ways to establish those priorities. An adequate expression
could be to use the categories of strategic growth previously identified; such
as, build aggressively, build gradually, build selectively, maintain aggressively,
maintain selectively, prove viability, divest-liquidate, and competitive-ha-
rasser. Corning Glass Works uses a slightly different categorization: super
thrust, thrust, emphasis, sustain, reposition, and harvest-divest. The original
General Electric categorization uses the following labels: invest to increase
market-share, invest to hold position, invest to gradually give-up share, and
divest to exit.

These classifications have in common an orderly ranking of priorities for
all business units of the firm, derived from their strategic positioning. What
is left to be done is to assign the total resources available to the firm among
the business units.

There are two major philosophies to accomplish that task. One allocates
directly the resources to the SBUs, based upon the previously identified priorities, leaving up to the SBU managers the assignment of those resources among
the individual projects generated at the SBU level. Those who favor this

approach argue that this guarantees a strategic fit between the allocation of resources and the strategic positioning of each SBU.

The second philosophy for resource allocation is based upon the examination of each project emanating from the business level. A project should be funded if its net present value (NPV) is positive, when the future cash flows associated with the project are discounted at the corresponding cost of capital. Those who favor this approach argue that the NPV is a meaningful representation of the addition to market value of a given project; therefore, projects with a positive NPV should have no difficulty in attracting all necessary resources to support them. Although this represents in theory a sound methodology for resource allocation, it can lead to incongruencies between the perceived priority of a business and the resources allocated to it, due to the different behavior regarding generation of projects on the part of the managers in charge of each SBU. Specifically, managers in charge of a "maintain business" could present a much larger number of profitable projects than those in charge of a "build aggressively business," simply because of differences in their eagerness to identify meaningful projects as opposed to reflecting true opportunities available in the respective businesses.

We advocate a tentative allocation of the overall strategic funds available to the firm, already identified in the previous task, among various SBUs ranked according to their strategic priorities.

It is important, at this point, to make a strong warning about resource allocation. We have been stressing throughout only the assignment of financial resources among business units. Often, those resources are the easiest to transfer and the most plentiful available; human resources being, instead, the most constrained ones. This is the case faced by many high technology firms which find themselves restricted in their growth not because of the availability of financial resources, but rather because of the unavailability of the more scarce technical talents. Therefore, resources should be interpreted here in its broadest sense.

A fairly effective way for assessing the economic performance of a set of strategic alternatives pertaining to the development of a given business unit is to use the market-to-book value model, which we have extensively treated in Chapter 10, and whose application we have presented in Chapter 16. This last chapter provides a methodology relevant for the entire development of this step in the planning process.

Steps 7 and 8: Definition and Evaluation of Specific Action Programs at the Business and Functional Levels

The essence of these steps consists in the translation of every broad action program, identified both at the business and functional levels, into concrete tasks which can be closely monitored, and whose contributions to the businesses and functions can be measured preferably in quantitative terms. If this translation fails to be done properly, business and functional strategies will be reduced to represent mere wishful thinking on the part of managers, with little, if any, implementation and follow-up qualities.

A specific action program is a structured, coherent, timed, and evaluated continuum of actions, with a clearly defined schedule for completion in a relatively short time span covering, normally, from six to eighteen months. In the military terminology, they represent the tactical plans that support the strategy.

The definition of a specific action program must include:

—a verbal description
—a statement of priority indicating the desirability of the program for the competitive position of the firm
  ("Absolute first priority"—postponement will hurt significantly the competitive position.
  "Highly desirable"—postponement will affect adversely the competitive position.
  "Desirable"—if funds were to be available, the competitive position could be enhanced.)
—the estimated cost and benefits
—the manpower requirements
—the schedule of completion
—the identification of a single individual responsible for its implementation
—the procedure for controlling its execution (normally of the project-control kind, like CPM and Gantt-schedules).

The inclusion of this normalized description of specific action programs greatly facilitates their evaluation and sanctioning at the corporate level. The final approval of these programs is partly based on a qualitative assessment of the strategic positioning of the business or function supported by them, partly on the resources available to the firm, and partly on quantitative measures of the goodness of the program obtained by using normal evaluation techniques.

Specific action programs are instruments to deploy strategic funds. As presented in Chapter 3, there are three major categories of strategic funds: capital investments, increases in working capital, and developmental expenses. There are action programs in each one of these three categories, but the great majority of them correspond to increases in working capital, and developmental expenses. The difficulty about this kind of funds allocation is that their benefits are very hard to evaluate quantitatively. Their financial merits can only be properly assessed in terms of their collective impact either for the business units or for the broad action programs they are intended to support. Therefore, when managers are confronted with the responsibility of controlling those funds, they resort to project-control approaches, assigning clearly milestones, identifying the resources required for its execution, and setting up operational variables intended to follow up the appropriate execution of those tasks.

When dealing with capital investments, normally specific action programs cover only part of their execution since investments span a period which is much longer than the duration of specific action programs. To assess the benefits of capital investments, it is necessary to resort to the more standard methodologies of project evaluation, leading toward the computation of the Net Present Value of the stream of cash-flows generated by the project. Once the project begins to be executed, it is necessary to define control procedures to assure that the agreed upon capital appropriations are being properly spent, and in accordance with the intended schedule. Finally, at the end of the project it is useful to conduct a postmortem analysis with the purpose of extracting relevant experiences to guide future capital budgeting decisions.

A distinctive characteristic of the evaluation process conducted at the corporate level is its incremental nature. In fact, a specific action program can be either added or eliminated depending on the importance and worth assigned to it.

Finally, it is a common practice to address in the cash-flow projections, different scenarios that correspond to optimistic, most likely, and pessimistic assumptions. A simple analytical procedure for evaluating specific action programs on an incremental basis is suggested by Rappaport (1981).

The methodology corresponding to this step is treated in Chapter 18.

Step 9: Resource Allocation and Definition of Performance Measurements for Management Control

At this step of the planning process, top managers are confronted with the difficult task of making a final evaluation of the proposals originated at the business and functional levels with a corporate perspective, in order to assign the necessary resources for their proper development.

The resource allocation process begins with the determination of the total funds available for supporting broad and specific action programs being presented by businesses and functions during the actual planning cycle. This is done by deducting from the total appropriated for investment, those funds which are required to fulfill legal obligations or correspond to previous commitments to ongoing projects.

The appropriation process for the remaining funds requires the completion of the following tasks:

—Collection and classification of all the information submitted by SBUs and functional units.
—Analysis of the coherence between the strategic role assigned to SBUs and functional units and the requests for funds.
—Analysis of economic indicators and value creation potentials of proposed programs.
—Final allocation of resources for the coming year.
—Development of performance measurements to facilitate the controlling and monitoring of the broad and specific action programs supporting business and functional strategies:

—In the short-run

—Over an extended planning horizon.

We have already identified in the previous step the two philosophies for resource allocation at the corporate level. When resources are allocated among SBUs, in this stage we should only be concerned about checking for final consistency between the priorities assigned to each SBU, and the final requests for funds.

When resources are allocated on a project-by-project basis, there is a much heavier concentration of responsibilities at the corporate level to evaluate the SBUs' proposal, both in terms of conventional financial performance measures, such as Net Present Value, as well as their consistency with the strategic positioning of each business unit.

The relevant methodology to judge the economic contribution of a business strategy is presented in Chapter 10. Detailed analysis and applications of resource allocation and performance measurement issues are further explored in Chapter 19.

Steps 10, 11, and 12: The Final Cycle of Strategic Planning: Strategic and Operational Budgeting

Once all strategic programs have been approved and resources allocated accordingly, business and functional managers are left with the task of translating those commitments into detailed operating budgets and precise statements of strategic funds. These steps require heavy functional involvement, and also call for a final consolidation and sanctioning from top management. The essential characteristics of this process were discussed in Chapter 3.

Budgeting was the first structured methodology to provide assistance to managers in the planning process; therefore, there is a great deal of solid knowledge residing in most organizations on how to prepare a good master budget (see references in Chapter 1). The new concept that has emerged in recent years has been the insistence in separating strategic from operational budgets, in order to sharpen and make more controllable the strategic commitments of the firm.

THE MERITS OF CORPORATE STRATEGIC PLANNING

Corporate strategic planning constitutes a powerful contribution to enhance managerial understanding and decision making. Among the most salient accomplishments we could cite the following:

1. The planning process helps to unify corporate directions.
   By starting the process with a proper articulation of the vision of the firm, subsequently extended by the mission of each business, and the recognition of functional competencies, the planning process mobilizes all of the key

managers in the pursuit of agreed upon and shared objectives. This unifying thrust could be very hard to accomplish without the formalization and discipline of a systematic process.

2. The segmentation of the firm is greatly improved.

Organizational theory has always had as a central concern the assignment and proper coordination of tasks to the members of a firm. Rather than relying on simple operational motifs, the strategic planning process contributes a significant enrichment to the firm segmentation by addressing the recognition of the various strategic hierarchical levels and its matching with the organizational structure. A key determinant of this process is not only to seek business autonomy oriented toward serving external markets, but it is also the recognition that shared resources and shared concerns must be truly accomplished to realize all the potentials for the firm.

3. The planning process introduces a discipline for long-term thinking in the firm.

The nature of the managerial tasks is so heavily dependent on taking care of an extraordinary amount of routine operational duties, that unless a careful discipline is instituted, the managerial time could entirely be devoted to operational issues. By enforcing upon the organization a logical process of thinking, with a clearly defined sequence of tasks linked to a calendar, planning raises the vision of all key managers, encouraging them to reflect creatively upon the strategic direction of the businesses.

4. The planning process as an educational device.

Perhaps the most important of the attributes of a formal strategic planning process is that it allows the development of a managerial competence of the key members of the firm, by enriching their common understanding of corporate objectives and businesses, and the way in which those objectives can be transformed into reality. In other words, the most important contribution of the planning process is the process itself. A mere by-product is the final content of the "planning book." The engaging communicational efforts, the multiple interpersonal negotiations generated, the need to understand and articulate the primary factors affecting the business, and the required personal involvement in the pursuit of constructive answers to the pressing business questions, is what truly makes the planning process a most vital experience.

THE LIMITATIONS OF CORPORATE STRATEGIC PLANNING

In spite of the many contributions of corporate strategic planning, as in any human endeavor, it has some limitations that, if not properly recognized, could destroy its effectiveness.

1. Risk of excessive bureaucratization.
One of the inherent risks in formalizing any process is to create conditions which impose a bureaucratic burden into an organization, stifling creativity, and losing the sense of the primary objectives intended by that process. Planning could become an end in itself, and pretty soon could be transformed into a meaningless game of filling in the numbers, impairing strategic alertness, which is the central concern of planning.

There is an issue about being able to maintain strong vitality and interest in a process which is time-consuming and repetitive. Often, the initial stages of introducing a well-conceived planning process in an organization is accompanied with an exhilarating challenge generating a strong personal commitment and enthusiasm. As time goes by, the threat of the planning process becoming a routine bureaucratic activity is very real.

There are several ways to prevent this undesirable situation. One is not to force a revision of all the steps of the planning process outlined in this writing; instead, one might conduct a comprehensive and extensive strategic audit, say every five years, and in the interim deal simply with minor upgrading of strategies and programs.

Another approach is to identify selectively each year the planning units that deserve more careful attention in the planning process, either because of changes in environmental conditions, or due to internal organizational issues. This discriminatory emphasis could help to avoid spending unnecessary efforts on businesses which do not require such attention.

A third organizational device to prevent bureaucratization is to select each year a planning theme which will require the attention of all key managers in their annual planning effort. Gluck and others (1980), provide examples of possible themes: international businesses, new manufacturing process technologies, the value of the firm products to customers, and alternative channels of distribution.

With regard to the objections raised about the danger of stifling innovation by institutionalizing the planning process, Haggerty (1981), the late President of Texas Instruments, argues very convincingly that institutionalization is the cost we have to pay for durability and staying power of any idea. Commenting on the Objectives-Strategies-Tactics (OST) System at TI, he expressed:

What Texas Instruments' OST system does is to provide the management with the mechanism for identifying, selecting, and pursuing the strategies and tactics which are to attain the objectives sought. What organizational learning achieves is the building into the culture of the organization of the process and the attitudes conceived by one or a few key individuals who fill a leadership role through a fraction of the overall lifetime of the institution and so extend the ideas and the processes and the attitudes of these key leaders beyond the span of either influence or time they could attain as individuals. Such an extension and span in time is essentially what organizational learning is all about.

2. Lack of an integration with other formal management systems.

Planning cannot be viewed as an isolated activity. Rather, it is part of a set of formal managerial processes and systems whose aim is to improve the understanding of managers in identifying and executing the organizational tasks.

There is an inherent danger in organizations which decide to implement its strategic planning process with a heavy planning department. Although there are legitimate activities that it could undertake, such as collecting the external information, serving as catalyst in the planning process, offering logistical support for the conduct of the planning process, and assuming an educational role to facilitate the understanding of the planning methodology, it is crucial to understand that planning is done by line executives and not by planners. Moreover, the establishment of heavy planning departments might tend to isolate the planning process from the mainstream of managerial decisions.

Strategic Management, the next stage in the evolution of planning systems, which we discuss in Chapter 5, is the response that is being offered today as a way to integrate all managerial capabilities within corporate values and corporate culture to assure effective strategic thinking at all levels in the organization.

3. Grand design versus logical incrementalism.

A question that has been raised is whether creative strategic thinking can ever emerge from a formal disciplined process. Some go even further and question whether it is desirable to commit to a rational grand scheme as a way of projecting the organization forward. A leading scholar who casts a serious doubt about the merits of formal planning is James Brian Quinn (1980, 1981). He regards formal planning as an important building block in a continuously evolving structure of analytical and political events that combine to determine overall strategy. He states that the actual process used to arrive at a total strategy, however, is usually fragmented, evolutionary, and largely intuitive. He claims that in well-run organizations managers proactively guide streams of actions and events incrementally toward a strategy embodying many of the principles of formal strategies. But top executives rarely design their overall strategy, or even major segments of them, in the formal planning cycle of the corporation. Instead they use a series of incremental processes which build strategies largely at more disaggregated levels, and then integrate these subsystem strategies step by step for the total corporation. The rationale behind this kind of incremental strategy formulation is so powerful that it, rather than the formal system planning approach, seems to provide an improved normative model for strategic decision-making.

We believe that the notion of logical incrementalism is not necessarily contradictory to a well-conceived corporate strategic planning process. By that we mean a process which is supported in the corporate values of the organization, that is participatory in character, which has a sense of vision given from the top, but shared by all key managers, which allows for meaningful negotiations to take place within an organizational framework. This process does not blindly set up long-term objectives, but rather expresses a sense of desired long-term direction and is incrementally attempting to adjust its course of action with a strategic posture in mind.

4. Formal planning versus opportunistic planning.

Formal planning systems represent an organized way of identifying and coordinating the major tasks of the organization. If all the planning capabilities were to be dependent entirely on the formal planning structure, the firm would be in a highly vulnerable position, unable to face unexpected events not properly foreseen within the assumptions underlying the strategy formulation process. Therefore, coexisting with formal planning, there is another form of planning referred to as *opportunistic planning*. In Figure 4.11 a comparison is presented on the characteristics of formal and opportunistic planning.

Since opportunistic planning is triggered by unexpected events and it is concentrated normally in a more narrow segment of the corporate activities, it seems unlikely that the triggering event affects all the businesses of the corporation. The key capability that is essential for the prompt response to the external event is the existence of *slack*. Often, organizations assign untapped financial resources to be quickly mobilized at the discretion of the corresponding manager to meet the unforeseen emergency. This is a form of financial slack. More important, it is what we might call an organizational slack. By that we mean the availability of human resources which are not

Figure 4.11 The Characteristics of Formal and Opportunistic Planning

Factors	Formal Planning	Opportunistic Planning
Timing	Systematic process that follows a prescribed calendar	Responses to unexpected emergencies of opportunities and threats
Scope	Corporate-wide	Usually concentrated on a segment of the corporation
Purpose	Attempts to develop a coordinated and proactive adaptation to the external environment, while seeking internal effectiveness and efficiency	It is based on existing capabilities that permit slack and flexibility to respond to unplanned events

overly burdened by their program commitments, so that they can absorb additional duties without experiencing a severe organizational constraint.

There is a need to balance the weight of these two coexisting planning processes. In organizations which rely exclusively on formal planning, they could trap themselves into unbearable rigidities. On the other hand, a firm whose decision making capability rests entirely on purely opportunistic schemes, will be constantly reacting to external forces, without having a clear sense of direction. The answer lies in a good compromise between these two extremes. Formal planning, providing a permanent strategic framework, without binding every action of the enterprise, while opportunistic planning allowing for creative responses to be made within that organized framework.

The development of the managerial knowledge and talent required to exercise effectively the opportunistic planning task is in itself a demanding job, which is the essence of the organizational learning issues that were addressed in the previous comments we quoted from Haggerty.

5. A calendar-driven planning process is not the only form of a formal planning system.

Implicit in the sequence of steps that we used to describe the formal corporate strategic planning process was the notion of a calendar-driven system. In fact, many American corporations have adopted variations of this type of planning approach. This, however, is not the only way of addressing a disciplined formalization of the planning activities. The most important alternative to the calendar-driven system is a program-period planning process, instituted in organizations such as IBM and Texas Instruments.

The essence of this process consists in allowing for program initiatives to be generated at any time during the year, as opposed to waiting for the prescribed timing in which broad and specific strategic action programs are supposed to be formulated. It is necessary, however, at a given point in time, to consolidate all the program proposals into a meaningful integrated document. This is what is referred to as period planning. According to an IBM executive commenting on this point: "Strategic decisions are often made in a formal process, but are made visible in an integrated way in the period process" (IBM Corporation 1979). In that way, period planning becomes a mechanism for adding up all the bottoms-up generated technical and business activities which are part of program planning to be sure they make a consistent all.

Program-period planning processes are specially suited for organizations which face a high degree of technical complexity with a rapid pace of change dealing primarily with an integrated business, such as IBM and TI. In those cases, program planning is focused on either product development or productivity improvements in a functional area; while period planning is characterized by its regular, calendar-driven sequence of events.

REFERENCES

Analog Devices, Inc., "Corporate Objectives," Norwood, Massachusetts.

Andrews, Kenneth R., *The Concept of Corporate Strategy*, Richard D. Irwin, Homewood, IL., 1980.

General Electric Company, "Background Note on Management Systems: 1981," Case #181–111, Harvard Business School, Boston, MA, 1981.

Gluck, Frederick W., Stephen P. Kaufman, and A. Steven Walleck, "The Four Phases of Strategic Management," *The Journal of Business Strategy*, Vol. 2, No. 3, Winter 1982, pp. 9–21.

Gluck, Frederick W., Stephen P. Kaufman, and A. Steven Walleck, "Strategic Management for Competitive Advantage," *Harvard Business Review*, Vol. 58, No. 4, July–August 1980, pp. 154–161.

Haggerty, Patrick E., "The Corporation and Innovation," *Strategic Management Journal*, Vol. 2, No. 2, April–June 1981, pp. 98–118.

IBM Corporation, "Background Note," Case #180–034, Harvard Business School, Boston, MA, 1979.

Lewis, Walker, W., "The CEO and Corporate Strategy in the Eighties: Back to Basics," *Interfaces*, Vol. 14, No. 1, January–February 1984.

Piper, Thomas R., and Wolf A. Weinhold, "How Much Debt is Right for Your Company?", *Harvard Business Review*, Vol. 60, No. 4, July–August 1982, pp. 106–114.

Porter, Michael E., "Strategies for Interrelated Business Units," Working Paper, Harvard Business School, Boston, MA, June 1981.

Quinn, James Brian, *Strategy for Changes—Logical Incrementalism*, Richard D. Irwin, Homewood, IL, 1980.

Quinn, James Brian, "Formulating Strategy One Step at a Time," *The Journal of Business Strategy*, Vol. 1, No. 3, Winter 1981, pp. 42–63.

Rappaport, Alfred, "Selecting Strategies that Create Shareholder Value," *Harvard Business Review*, Vol. 59, No. 3, May–June 1981, pp. 139–149.

Tregoe, Benjamin B., and John W. Zimmerman, *Top Management Strategy*, Simon & Schuster, NY, 1980.

Zakon, Alan G., "Capital-Structure Optimization," in J. F. Weston and M. B. Goudzwaard (editors), *The Treasurer's Handbook*, Dow Jones-Irwin, Homewood, IL, 1976.

5

STAGE 5: STRATEGIC MANAGEMENT

Most of what we have discussed so far centers on strategic planning as if it were the sole administrative process available for managers to reach a better understanding of the issues they are facing. This is certainly not the case. Although planning is, in our opinion, the key process to properly define critical tasks of the organization, it is also, perhaps, the simplest one to develop. It has the attractive characteristic of being a highly rational and analytical process which, as we have indicated many times, serves as a most appealing communicational device. Planning alone, however, will never produce the massive mobilization of resources and people, and will never generate the high quality of strategic thinking required in complex organizations. For that to happen, planning should be carefully integrated with other important administrative systems, like management control, communication and information, and motivation and rewards. Moreover, all of these systems are supported by the organizational structure, which provides a necessary definition of authority and responsibilities to guide and regulate relationships among members of the firm, mainly in the upper levels of management. Finally, these basic expressions of managerial infrastructure—administrative systems, and organizational structure—must be well-balanced with the culture of the firm, which adds a much broader and subtler set of dimensions to the management problem.

Strategic management has, as an ultimate objective, the development of corporate values, managerial capabilities, organizational responsibilities, and administrative systems which link strategic and operational decision-making, at all hierarchical levels, and across all businesses and functional lines of authority in a firm. Institutions which have reached this stage of management development have eliminated the conflicts between long-term development and short-term profitability. Strategies and operations are not in conflict with one another, but they are inherently coupled defining the managerial tasks at each level in the organization. This form of conducting a firm is deeply anchored in managerial style, beliefs, values, ethics, and accepted forms of behavior in the organization, which make strategic thinking congruent with the organizational culture.

These basic characteristics of strategic management are illustrated in Figure 5.1, which shows the interaction among the administrative systems, the organizational structure and its culture. All need to be *fitted* for the organization to be really effective. For example, the best planning system will take the firm to nowhere if it is not adequately complemented by the management control system. The creation of a future implied by an active planning system requires follow up and close monitoring provided by the management control system for the firm to succeed in this kind of effort. Also, this figure shows the required integration with the organizational culture, in order to generate a climate conducive to the achievement of the organizational objectives, and to the satisfaction of individual needs.

In this chapter we discuss some fundamental concepts of strategic management, concentrating our attention in those aspects that provide a broader perspective for looking at the problem of strategic planning. The presentation is organized around the following issues:

—the need for integration among administrative systems and the organizational structure,
—the need to conduct this integration in two modes: strategic and operational, and
—the need to seek congruency between the managerial infrastructure and the corporate culture.

INTEGRATION AMONG ADMINISTRATIVE SYSTEMS

Integration between Planning and Management Control

One could argue that planning and control are indivisible activities; two sides of the same coin. The process of planning—formulating objectives, programs, and budgets—cannot be terminated properly without defining appropriate procedures for monitoring, analyzing, and controlling the planning activities. Otherwise planning simply becomes an abstract expression of too general and broad commitments, with little, if any, implementation qualities. In other words, a well designed planning process should include the definition of performance measurements which are the essence of management control.

There is a clear continuity between planning and management control. The focus of attention of planning is the next fiscal year. In the planning process we look ahead in order to get the entire organization prepared to confront successfully the challenges lying in the future. Management control takes over

Figure 5.1 Strategic Management: Integration among Administrative Systems, Structure, and Culture in Strategic and Operational Modes

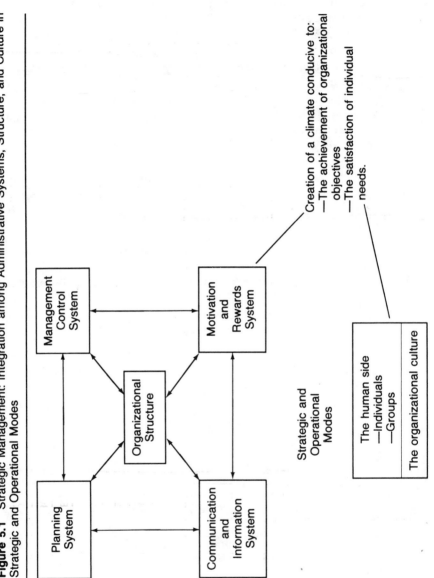

after the planning effort has been completed. Its focus of attention is the current year, and it simply monitors, diagnoses, and evaluates the actual results against the targets developed by the plan, and take corrective actions when needed. Thus, planning involves a great deal of control and control involves a great deal of planning.

Figure 5.2 represents the essence of integration between planning and control processes. This figure emphasizes the role of budgeting as a bridge between

Figure 5.2   Integration of the Planning and Management Control Process

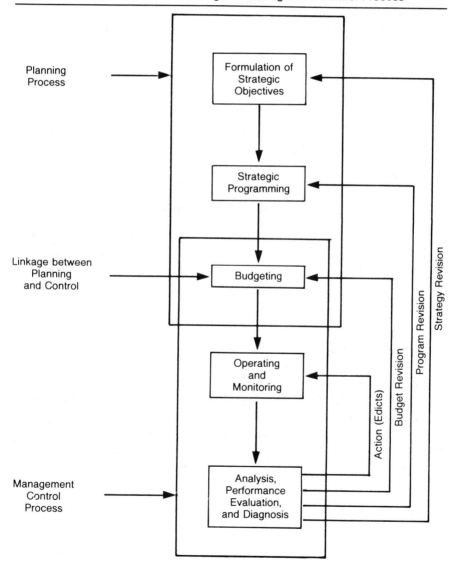

planning and control. From this perspective, budgeting can be viewed as a part of both the planning process and the management control process.

From a planning standpoint, the budget produces a set of financial statements identical to those used in financial accounting: balance sheet, income statement, and a statement of changes in the financial position. The basic difference is that budget figures are estimates of the intended future results rather than historical data of what has happened in the past.

From a management control standpoint, the budget provides all necessary support for monitoring, analyzing, and programming the development of strategic and operational programs.

The figure also illustrates that an important element of the management control process is to incorporate revisions in either budgets, strategic programs, or the strategic objectives whenever the deviations between proposed plans and actual results are so significant, so as to warrant the incorporation of those changes prior to beginning a new planning cycle.

Integration between Planning, Management Control, and the Organizational Structure

The planning and management control systems are intended to guide and support managers at all hierarchical levels, in their definition of meaningful tasks and in the specification of procedures to monitor their completion. When viewed from that perspective, it is easy to recognize the central importance of the organizational structure in the necessary integration required by strategic management. The organizational structure provides the hierarchical definition of responsibilities and authorities for the firm. _Responsibility_ has to do with the nature of the task entrusted to each manager. Obviously, the planning process is a primary vehicle to identify, in a coordinated manner, the major tasks faced by the firm. Likewise, management control deals with the issue of segmenting the organization into responsibility centers which allow for proper decentralized accountability at all levels of the firm. _Authority_ represents the means available to the manager for the effective execution of the tasks under his responsibility. Again, both the planning and control process are directly concerned with the issue of balancing responsibility and authority, as well as allocating resources and monitoring their use.

We believe that the issue of organizational structure is so central to the discussion of strategic management, that we have devoted Chapters 20 and 21 to the development of this subject.

Integration with the Communication and Information Systems

Information and communication are ubiquitous in a firm. After all, every administrative system is information based and managers are coordinated primarily via information-driven mechanisms. Most of the managerial time and energy are spent processing massive amounts of very dissimilar information and establishing significant communications with interested parties, external and internal to the firm. This makes clear that an effective information and communication system cannot be independent of planning, management control, and the organizational structure. One more time, there should be a clear balance and integration among all of them.

We attach the label information system to the more formal process of gathering, digesting, filtering, and distributing the information relevant to managers at all hierarchical levels. The term communication is reserved to mean a more sophisticated and elaborate managerial activity, implying the ability to transmit at all organizational levels, as well as the relevant external stakeholders, the messages that managers think should be given to interested parties related with the organization.

The development of an effective communication and information system is an order of magnitude more difficult, in our opinion, than the development of a planning system. First, it has to gather, process, and evaluate large volumes of data, coming both from internal and external sources. Second, it has to filter, diagnose, and discriminate relevant information to be made available to the different levels of managerial hierarchy. Rather than submitting large volumes of unprocessed data, which tend to saturate managers' ability to digest a large number of trivia, a proper information system should be intelligent enough to discriminate the essential from the secondary at each level, and to provide supporting detail only by means of exceptional reporting. And third, managers should have the ability to translate that information into meaningful messages to relevant audiences, by developing clear and well-defined communicational actions.

Integration with the Motivational and Reward Systems

To a great extent, the motivational and reward systems are responsible for shaping behavior in the organization and assuring, if properly done, congruency between individual and corporate objectives. People tend to behave according to the explicit or implicit mechanisms which regulate their rewards; therefore, if we want the commitments identified in the planning process to become vivid realities, certainly we have to assure the establishment of a well-designed management control system, consistent with the assignment of responsibilities and authorities reflected in the organizational structure, and able to provide the right clues for problem solving and managerial decision-making. But this is not enough, we have to make sure that the motivation and reward systems reinforce the implementation of those planned commitments. Otherwise, planning will become again a worthless exercise.

A Brief Comment on the Role of Planning Departments

Parenthetically, a relatively common pitfall in some organizations is to rely on a centralized planning department as the major force behind the development of a balanced system. This is normally a serious pitfall on two accounts. First, planners should not plan. Planning, as we have stressed throughout, is an inherent managerial responsibility that cannot be delegated to staff units. A legitimate role for planners is the gathering of information, primarily external to the firm, to enlighten managerial decision-making. Also, they should act as catalysts, inquirers, educators, and synthesizers to guide the planning process in an effective manner. But planners do not plan, this is done by the line executives.

It is probably better to have very lean planning departments composed by intelligent and energetic young individuals who could benefit from a brief stay there, a location with a remarkable vantage point in the organization, and be moved later to a more permanent line or staff position.

The second potential pitfall of having a centralized planning department is that it tends to isolate the planning activity from the remaining administrative systems. This is the sure way of transforming planning in a largely irrelevant activity. No wonder then that, in many instances, planning becomes a yearly ritual, conducted by staff members, which culminates in a thick book that gathers dust on the shelves of those managers who were not involved in their preparation, but whose tasks the book is intended to define. Most of the benefits of the planning process, if properly done, accrue in the realization of the process itself. Planning is a decision-making activity, and the planning books are simply sub-products for refreshing our memory and documenting the decisions made. They are certainly not the final aims of the planning process.

INTEGRATION IN STRATEGIC AND OPERATIONAL MODES

The issues that we have discussed in the previous section, regarding the requirements for integration among the administrative systems and structure are only half the story. That integration should be conducted to assure continuity, not only in an operational mode, but also in the strategic thinking across all administrative systems and across all hierarchical levels present in the organizational structure. This second message apparently is not that obvious because significant flaws are detected in many business firms with regard to the quality of integration in the strategic mode.

Let us review again each one of the elements in Figure 5.1 having now the strategic concerns in mind. Throughout this discussion, the emphasis will be placed on requirements that each administrative system has to meet in order to seek integration in the strategic mode. In particular, we will assume the reader is knowledgeable about the basis of management control and managerial accounting to support operational systems. Good references on this subject matter are Anthony and Welsch (1981), and Anthony and Dearden (1980).

Planning and Management Control in the Strategic Mode

Regarding the planning system, it is hard to find organizations even with some minor degree of complexity, which do not embark, in one way or another in some form of strategic planning. The intensity of competition, both domestic and foreign, and the turbulence of the external environment in which most firms operate, have made strategic planning almost universally adopted by American firms. The strategic interest, however, seems to stop there. What happens with management control? Very often firms resort to the budgeting and financial control mechanisms which we outlined in stage 1 of the evolution of strategic planning systems, thus falling into the trap of short-term accounting-driven control instruments. There is very little, if any, strategic control under those conditions. Therefore, the ability of the firm to implement, monitor, evaluate, and correct strategic commitments is almost entirely lost.

A strategic control system shares the same conceptual requirements as an operational control system; namely, it has to identify a unit which will be a focus of control (the so-called responsibility center), and the definition of key quantifiable variables to measure the performance of those units. The difference resides, however, in the distinct nature of these two entities. While operational control tends to look at responsibility centers as either expense, profit or investment centers, strategic control should be based on the notion of an SBU. When both, responsibility centers and SBU coincide with one another, there is no conflict for overlapping of measurements, but when this is not the case, much more careful design is required to implement sound management control practices, leading very often to double or matrix accountability.

Regarding key variables used as performance measurements, an operational control system tends to center managerial attention on fairly straightforward financial results, such as those presented in Figures 1.2, 1.3, and 1.4. This is not necessarily the case with strategic control systems. Much more creativity is required for quantifying the long-term impact of the chosen strategic plan. Now, we have to observe and closely monitor strategic programs, as well as the deployment of strategic funds (which we discussed in Chapter 3).

There are several ways of expressing in the reporting system this dichotomy between operational and strategic accountability. One of the first firms to adopt this separation of funds was Texas Instruments, whose simplified profit and Loss Statement, for a given PCC (Product-Customer Center) is presented in Figure 5.3.

Normally, a PCC manager is expected to wear "two hats," the first as an operating manager concerned with today's operating results, and the second as a strategic manager concerned with longer range results. As Figure 5.3 shows, operating results are being measured through operating profits; strategic results are measured by how effectively a manager utilizes the strategic expenses at his disposal. In TI, those strategic expenses are centrally assigned through the OST (Objectives-Strategies-Tactics) System. It is interesting to notice that the allocation of strategic expenses results from allocating resources to specific projects which finally will become the responsibility of the PCC manager.

Figure 5.4 shows a seemingly very similar reporting document for the decentralized departmental manager at GE, who is also a profit center. The three categories of expenses listed beneath the contribution margin are collectively called "base costs." Readiness-to-serve costs are the fixed expenses of the operat-

Figure 5.3 Simplified Profit and Loss Statement Used by Texas Instruments

Strategic Activities	PCC* Profit/Loss Statement		Operating Activities
Corporate Development	Net Sales Billed	xxx	Group
↑	Direct Product Costs	xxx	↑
Objective			Division
↑	Gross Product Margin	xxx	↑
Strategy			
↑	Operating Expense	xxx	PCC
Tactic	Operating Profit	xxx —	↑
↑ ⌐—————————	Strategic Expense**	xxx	
	Organization Profit	xxx	

* PCC = (Product-Customer Center).
** Also called Developmental Expense.
Source: Richard F. Vancil and Ronald Hall, Texas Instruments, Inc.: Management Systems, 1972. Boston: Harvard Business School, Case 9–172–054, p. 11. Reprinted by permission.

Figure 5.4 Simplified Profit and Loss Statement Used by General Electric Co.

Net sales billed	xxx
Less: Materials in cost of goods sold	(xxx)
Contributed value from operations	xxx
Less: Direct labor	(xxx)
Other variable costs	(xxx)
LIFO revaluation provision	(xxx)
Contribution margin	xxx
Less: Readiness-to-serve costs	(xxx)
Program expenses	(xxx)
Assessments from corporate, sector, group, and division	(xxx)
Operating profit	xxx
Less: Interest expense/income	(xxx)
Income taxes	(xxx)
Net income	xxx

Source: Richard F. Vancil and Paul Browne, General Electric Company, Background Note on Management Systems. Boston: Harvard Business School, Case 9–181–111, p. 8, Table A. Reprinted by permission.

ing component stemming from its current capacity. It includes depreciation, other manufacturing costs, and sales and administrative overhead. Program expenses are discretionary expenses intended to increase future profits through specific strategic programs (developing new products, entering new markets, or improving productivity). Assessment from corporate headquarters and allocations of corporate overhead are based on the department's cost of operations and are expressed as a proportion of such costs in all departments—roughly 1% of sales (General Electric Company, Background Note on Management Systems, 1981).

There are two basic differences between the TI and GE reporting systems. One, at GE, the department manager himself proposes what he considers to be a desirable amount for operating and strategic expenses. This amount is modified or accepted at the Sectoral level according to the position of the business within the corporate portfolio. This represents an allocation of resources in terms of overall strategic attractiveness, rather than an assignment in a project by project basis conducted at the corporate level, as is done by TI. The second difference resides on the bottom line accountability used by GE, forcing managers to absorb their share of interests and taxes prior to determining the net income generated by each department. This seems to contradict some sound basic principles of accountability that requires a manager to be made responsible only for expenses which are truly under his control. However, by making managers responsible for the true bottom line, one begins to instill the utmost sense of managerial accountability, and this provides a genuine training ground for general managers development.

A third form of splitting operational and strategic expense reporting is illustrated in Figure 5.5. The conventional statement column shows the profit and loss statement which is generated by applying the generally accepted financial

Figure 5.5 Splitting the Profit and Loss Statement of a Division in Terms of Operational and Strategic Expenses

	Conventional Statement	Operational Expenses	Strategic* Expenses
Net Sales	100	100	—
Less: Variable Manufacturing Costs	30	30	—
Depreciation	20	20	—
Other Fixed Manufacturing Costs	10	5	5
Gross Margin	40	45	—
Less: Marketing Expenses	15	5	10
Administrative Expenses	10	5	5
Research Expenses	5	0	5
Division Margin	10		
Operating Margin		35	
Total Strategic Expenses			25

* Also called Developmental Expenses.

accounting principles. The two additional columns break every expense category into operational expenses (efforts supporting the ongoing business), and strategic expenses (efforts applied to the development of a future position for the firm). Notice the remarkable difference in terms of managerial accountability when comparing the conventional statement to the revised breakdown, in terms of operational and strategic expenses. In the conventional statement, a division manager is supposed to generate 10 units of profit. When the business conditions get rough, it is entirely possible for the manager to deliver those 10 units by curtailing severely strategic expenses, and thus jeopardizing the future development of this unit. However, in the breakdown statement, the manager is entrusted with a much more difficult task, he is expected to deliver 35 units of divisional profit from its existing business base, and to wisely use 25 units in strategic expenses intended to strengthen the future development of this unit. Each entry in the strategic expense column identifies strategic action programs, whose purpose is to reinforce the competitive position of the firm in the long term, as opposed to simply delivering short-term profitability.

Organizational Structure in the Strategic Mode

Again we find that a large number of firms adopt an organizational form whose major objective is to facilitate the day-to-day operational activities. Very often, it is hard to identify who are the true strategic managers in those organizational settings. In other words, responsibility and accountability are formally expressed in terms of relatively short-sighted operational issues. Chandler (1962), in his now classic historical analysis of major American firms, was the first to draw the attention to the significance of strategy in prescribing a sound organizational structure, by enunciating the principle "structure follows strategy," meaning that an organization should be designed in such a way as to facilitate primarily the pursuit of its strategic commitment.

When addressing the question of organizational design, we are confronted with two primary issues: how to divide the tasks of the organization in an effective way (the issue of segmentation and differentiation), and how to assure that those tasks are properly coordinated (the question of coordination and integration). Simply stated, when seeking congruency between strategy and operations, we need to address those tasks not only by looking at the day-to-day operational requirements, but rather, and most significantly, by reflecting upon the strategic commitments the organization is seeking to fulfill. Pragmatically, this means that the organizational structure should:

1. Facilitate the allocation of resources among the various businesses of the firm.
2. Support the implementation of preferred strategies for each business.
3. Permit the adaptation of existing businesses to a changing environment.
4. Allow for the efficient execution of short-term operational tasks.

The segmentation issue should centrally consider the questions of how the various SBUs are going to receive the proper managerial attention. When the organizational structure is segmented according to SBUs, we find no real conflict between strategic and operational performance. A given manager simply has to wear two hats and becomes accountable in these two modes. When this is not the case, significant coordinational pressures are exercised upon the organization to maintain a degree of alertness in both strategic and operational responsibilities.

Some business firms face a fairly complex dilemma. On the one hand, they find themselves competing in a variety of markets which forces them to identify several SBUs in order to conduct an appropriate strategic process. However, because of pressures to share resources and seek economies of scale to achieve operational efficiencies, the organization cannot be structured according to independent SBUs. Rather, the SBUs become simply a planning focus, which cut across several organizational units, insofar as the development and implementation of its corresponding strategic programs is concerned.

We have found there are just a few alternatives available as coordinating mechanisms to address these issues:

Assign to the SBU Manager a Permanent Coordinating Role. This is a solution often adopted in professional organizations such as engineering and consulting firms, and universities, where the segmentation structure is done according to major disciplines, while coordinating managers are in charge of developing the firm's position in its primary programs, markets or, more broadly speaking, businesses. It is essential in those cases to maintain a high level of disciplinary excellence, which is the basic resource of those institutions. Therefore, it would be unacceptable to fragment disciplinary groups, giving away the benefits to be derived from a large professional critical mass. If a concerted effort, however, is not made to respond effectively to the requirements of the external businesses of the firm, the organization will significantly lack strategic alertness. That role is assumed by the SBU coordinating manager. It is a difficult role, because his responsibility by far exceeds his authority. As a minimum, there are two conditions that should coexist for the SBU manager to have a meaningful chance for success. First, there should be a full understanding and complete support on the part of the CEO and top operating managers, on the significance of the SBU coordinating manager's tasks. Second, the SBU manager should have full authority over the strategic component of the SBU budget, which constitutes his only meaningful weapon for exercising some leverage over operating managers.

We have found some misconceptions with regard to how these organizational solutions are perceived in practice. Many people tend to associate a matrix form with this organizational structure. This is clearly not the case. Under this scheme, the SBU manager does not have direct authority over the individuals working in various organizational units. Therefore, there is no duality of bosses, which is an essential attribute of a matrix organization. The SBU manager is strictly a *coordinating* manager.

This alternative can also be used in functional organizations, which participate in a plurality of businesses.

Assign to a Top Management Committee the Responsibilities for SBUs Management. This second coordinating mechanism consists of assigning a committee, normally composed by the CEO and the top operational managers, the task of developing and implementing the necessary SBUs' strategic programs. This organizational form is prevalent in many European nations, foremost in England. The committee meets normally once a week to discuss questions of operational and strategic significance. It is central for the success of this organizational solution, that managers distinguish very clearly their duality of roles. As heads of their corresponding operational units, they have the normal profit and loss, or expense accountability which emanates from their routine operational activities. However, as members of the SBU management committee, they are supposed to act on behalf of the ultimate corporate interests, and not as parochial defenders of their own areas of operational responsibilities. In that capacity their role is essentially strategic in character.

Adopt a Matrix Form of Organization for Dealing with Operational and Strategic Responsibilities. The most extreme form that can be adopted in seeking integration between operational and strategic responsibilities, when these responsibilities cannot be squarely assigned to a single individual (in which case he wears "two hats"), is the matrix structure. That organizational structure institutionalizes the dual responsibilities and accountabilities in both strategic and operational modes.

Normally the operational side of the matrix is represented by functional managers, who are responsible for expense centers, while the strategic dimensions correspond to SBU managers, as indicated in Figure 5.6. In Chapter 21 we provide an extensive discussion on the characteristics, advantages, and disadvantages of the matrix form of organization. For the purposes of this discussion, we would like to emphasize just a few points.

For the matrix to operate effectively, it is important that each functional unit is segmented according to SBU lines. Under those conditions, the SBU managers would have clear access to functional resources, thus avoiding some of the inherent ambiguity of the matrix form. Moreover, it is necessary to establish a coordinating committee, chaired by the SBU manager, and composed by one representative from each functional specialty linked to the SBU, thus institutionalizing the necessary coordination that has to take place among the various functional units from a business dimension. Finally, every administrative system (planning, control, information, and reward systems) should be designed so as to support the matrix structure. If all of these recommendations are properly implemented, the matrix can become an effective organizational form. One, however, has to recognize from the outset that the matrix implies an

Figure 5.6 Matrix Form of Organization to Deal with Strategic and Operational
Responsibilities

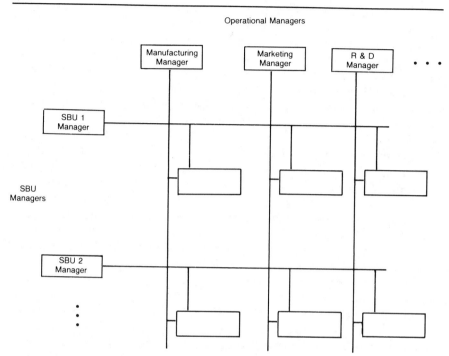

exceedingly complex form of management. It is much more than an organizational structure; it has overwhelming cultural, behavioral, and administrative implications, all of which should be properly balanced for the matrix
to be viable.

Organizational design is an art, not a science. We adhere to concepts expressed
by the contingency theory approach which suggests that there is no single way
to establish the best organizational structure of the firm. That does not mean,
however, that any organizational alternative is equally acceptable. The effectiveness of a given organizational structure depends on situational characteristics
such as the environment that the firm faces, the nature of the tasks the organization is to undertake, and the people involved in the performance of those tasks
(Lawrence and Lorsch 1967).

Information and Communication Systems in the Strategic Mode

When analyzing the information and communication system of a firm, searching
for their strategic quality, again one observes serious deficiencies. A most common one is the excessive reliance on internal sources, mainly the accounting
base, as the primary vehicle for supplying information to managers. Needless
to say, accounting-driven sources have little relevance for guiding strategic decision-making and strategic performance. From a strategic point of view, it is

not enough to know our own cost structure; rather, it is the industry cost structure and our relative position in it that is relevant. The same can be said about every other financial measure of performance that could be originated from internally-driven data.

In particular, the cost accounting system must be designed to permit the breaking down of expenses into strategic and operational concerns, to support the strategic control system we alluded to in a previous section. Some companies, like TI, have chosen to classify every expense, either as operational or strategic, and charge the corresponding account accordingly. This requires an extraordinary effort to adjust the overall cost-accounting system of a firm. To avoid that, some firms simply treat strategic programs as independent projects, and report them within the framework of the existing management control system, without necessarily changing the accounting procedures of the firm as a whole.

When going beyond the purely accounting measurements, several approaches have been designed to provide managers at all levels with relevant information, both of a strategic and operational nature. Rockart (1979) provides a good classification of those approaches. We will comment briefly on two of the leading contenders to satisfy executive information needs: the key performance indicator method, and the critical success factor method.

The key performance indicator method requires the selection of a set of key variables, meaning a stable set of indicators that allow managers to detect and monitor the competitive position of all businesses the firm is engaged in. Obviously, information has to be collected to report the performance of each indicator, and the results are made available to the pertinent managers at all levels, possibly on an exception basis. Only those indicators whose performance is significantly differently from a predefined target are reported to managers.

One of the first companies to institutionalize this process was General Electric, which more than twenty years ago began to measure performance in all its departments according to the eight key result areas listed in Figure 5.7.

The critical success factor method (CSF) was first proposed by Daniel (1961). However, it has been Rockart who has championed this idea as central for the design of top-management information systems. He defines CSFs as "the limited number of areas in which results, if they are satisfactory, will ensure successful competitive performance for the organization. They are the few key areas where 'things must go right' for the business to flourish. If results in these areas are not adequate, the organization's efforts for the period will be less than desired." (Rockart 1979) Figure 5.8 provides an example of the critical success factors identified for Microwave Associates, Inc., as reported by Rockart.

Rockart considers that there are four primary sources of CSFs:

—The structure of the particular industry.
—The company's competitive strategy, its industry position, and its geographical location.
—Environmental factors.
—Temporal factors, which refers to areas or activities that become significant for an organization for a limited period of time.

Figure 5.7 Key Result Areas and Performance Measurements Originally Defined by General Electric

Area	Performance Measurement
1. Profitability	Residual Income
2. Market Position	Market Share
3. Productivity	Output (Value Added)/Input (Payroll + Depreciation)
4. Product Leadership	—Competitive standing —R&D and innovation in Engineering, Manufacturing, and Marketing
5. Personnel Development	—Development programs —Inventory of promotable people —Effectiveness of program implementation
6. Employee Attitudes	—Statistical indicators —Periodic employee surveys
7. Public Responsibility	Surveys
8. Balance between Short- and Long-range Goals	All previous factors have short and long-term dimensions

Adapted from Robert N. Anthony and Robert H. Caplan, General Electric Company. Boston: Harvard Business School; Case 6–113–121 in Robert N. Anthony and John Dearden, *Management Control Systems*. Homewood: Richard D. Irwin, 1980, pp. 101–109. Copyright © 1964 By the President and Fellows of Harvard College. Used with permission of the Harvard Business School.

Figure 5.8 Critical Success Factors Developed to Meet Microwave Associates' Organizational Goals

Critical Success Factors	Prime Measures
1. Image in financial markets	Price/Earnings ratio
2. Technological reputation with customers	Orders/Bid ratio Customer "perception" interview review
3. Market success	Change in market share (each product) Growth rates of company markets
4. Risk recognition in bids and contracts	Company's years of experience with similar products "New" or "old" customer Prior customer relationship
5. Profit margin on jobs	Bid profit margin as ratio of profit on similar jobs in this product line
6. Company morale	Turnover, absenteeism, etc. Informal feedback
7. Performance to budget on major jobs	Job cost budgeted/actual

Reprinted by permission of the Harvard Business Review. An exhibit & excerpt from "Chief Executives Define Their Own Data Needs" by J. F. Rockart (November/December 1979). Copyright © 1979 by the President and Fellows of Harvard College; all rights reserved.

The primary differences between the key performance indicator method and the CSF-method is that the former tends to be more permanent and uniformly applied to all organizational units of the firm, as stated in the GE example; while the latter is tailor-made to fit each manager, and the characteristics of his units, and it is constantly adapted to reflect changes taking place in the organization or its environment.

More recently, Rockart and Treacy (1982) have proposed a framework for the development of an Executive Information System (EIS). This sytem is supported by a common core of data, identified as the "data cube" (Figure 5.9), which contains important business indicators (dimension one), through time (dimension two) for all businesses of the firm, competitors, customers, and industries (dimension three). These data can be used in two modes: *Status access*, which provides simple displays of the data in the cube; and *personalized analysis*,

Figure 5.9   The Data Cube

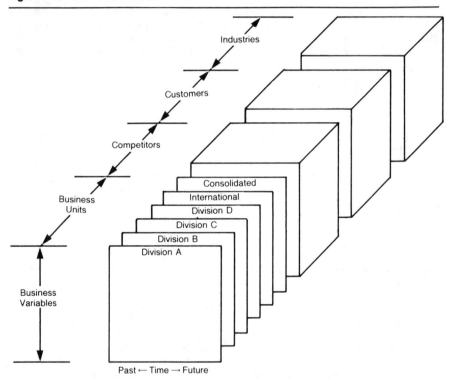

which permits a more advanced manipulation of data through special statistical programs and other kinds of models.

Let us now turn our attention to the requirements for a strategic communication system. We define as the primary thrust of the communication process, the articulation of the central objectives and programs the organization is intending to pursue in a way which is amenable to key external and internal audiences, with the purpose of increasing the level of understanding and the degree of commitments of the firm to its stakeholders.

When viewed from this perspective, the central roles of the CEO appears to be that of communicating the basic strategic goals of the organization. Every publicly owned firm needs to keep external groups informed of the main strategic direction the organization is following. Particularly, providing sound information to the financial community is a most relevant task, since the market value of the stock of the firm develops from the expectation of future cash flows derived not only from assets the firm has already in place, but also from those it intends to deploy in the future. Appropriate external communications, therefore, are essential to achieve the warranted market value of the firm. Likewise, internal communications fraught with strategic content are essential to mobilize all the individuals working in the firm in the same desired direction. Everybody, even the most modest workers, has a role to play in shaping up the future of the organization. If strategy is treated as if it were a top secret and a highly confidential matter that can be trusted only to a select few, it will never become a real driving force. It is a central role of the CEO, not only to serve as the key architect for shaping the strategy of the firm, but equally important to effectively communicate it to all levels in the organization.

This matter has been just recently receiving a full understanding and significant attention from American firms, particularly after recognizing the strengths that their Japanese counterparts have enjoyed in this area, and the significant competitive advantage resulting from that strength. For the first time, we have seen direct involvement on the part of the CEO of major corporations in the U.S. to take significant time to carefully address the strategic communication role, not only to key middle managers, but also to the entire blue-collar force.

Motivational and Rewards Systems in the Strategic Mode

As we have pointed out previously, undoubtedly the reward system is the one that has the most definitive influence in determining individual behavior in the organization. Naturally, people tend to act in a way consistent with the performance measures which are exercised upon them, and which in turn determine future career paths in the organization. Therefore, if we are seeking a strong organizational commitment in the pursuit of an agreed upon strategy, there is not a more central administrative system to seek congruency with than establishing individual rewards and motivations. Yet, it is this lack of congruency that is perhaps the most appalling when one performs an audit for American Corporations. Most U.S. firms suffer significantly from the use of short-term, accounting-driven measures of performance to establish the reward mechanisms for high-level managers, who are mainly responsible for implementing strategic actions. Particularly, the exceeding reliance on return on investment (ROI) has been singled out as a primary cause for discouraging investments in industrial firms, and as a strong determinant for the continuous erosion of the U.S. presence in world markets. There have been organizations which have used ROI as the sole performance measurement for assigning bonuses to their top managers. This is a dangerous practice. In an inflationary economy, total investment inaction could be translated into a short-term increase in ROI. Profits would tend to increase numerically, simply because of the inflationary effects. Moreover, the lack of investment commitments would reduce the investment base significantly since its replacement value would not be updated, according to the existing accounting practices in the U.S., and depreciation would further decrease it. A manager who is forced to match an ROI target, might temporarily reach it while contributing to the destruction of the long-term development of the firm.

Another common faulty design in the reward system of some American firms resides in creating internal competition by rewarding different divisions within a firm in accordance with the relevant ROI-performance. In this case, a percentage of the total profits of the organization is reported to be distributed as bonuses; the amount to be given to each divisional manager depending upon its ROI-performance vis-a-vis the other divisions of the firm. Not only does this procedure have the disadvantages of short-term responses to which we already alluded, but it creates a parochial attitude of divisiveness, aggressiveness, and conflict among units that might benefit from working together against their real competitors, which are the other firms participating in the industry.

These two limitations lead us to propose a different way of looking at the implications of a reward system, which is characterized by the simple 2 x 2 matrix depicted in Figure 5.10 modified from the compensation scheme of Corning Glass Works. The figure shows the two critical dimensions for establishing a well-balanced reward system: the observed results, as measured by individual

Figure 5.10   Determinants of Managerial Compensation

	Period of Observation	
	Short term	Long term
Observed individual performance	Salary Increases	Incentive Plan
Observed group performance	Bonus	Stock Options

and group performance, and the period of observation, defined as short or long term.

In our previous comments, we have addressed situations where almost all the weight resides on observed individual performance in the short term, defined by the ROI, which tends to create myopic and aggressively dysfunctional behavior in the organization. The great challenge is how to expand the performance measurement and reward system into the other three cells of the matrix. The basic idea behind this scheme is to align the compensation of a given manager with the overall performance of the organization, so as to make his final monetary compensation increase whenever the entire firm shows a sustained profit generating capability. Let us discuss briefly the other three cells in the matrix.

It seems obvious that an individual should benefit from the performance of the group in which he belongs. The major question is what is the relevant group that should be used as a reference point. Corning Glass Works has opted for what we consider to be a rather fascinating solution. In this case, the reference group is always one step above the hierarchical level of the manager. For example, a department manager will have as a relevant group the division in which it belongs. In turn, the divisional manager will have the group in which the division fits. Finally, the group manager will have the corporation as a whole as a reference level.

What kind of behavioral responses does such a system generate? It is an attempt to create a reasonable broad attitude; thus, when a good manager is confronted with a decision that could affect favorably on his own group, but could be dysfunctional to the overall corporation, he has the proper kind of forces acting upon him, so that he could decide more objectively on the trade-offs of that decision. In any event, it is important to identify which is the relevant group, and what percentage of the individual reward will be determined by the group performance in the short term.

Regarding the long term, it is relatively easy to measure group performance in that mode. What is normally done is to take the corporation as the relevant group, and to use mechanisms such as stock options to reward executives for the improvements of corporate performance at a future date. Stock options is a financial arrangement by which managers are offered the right to purchase corporate stock at a future date, and at a price agreed upon when the option is granted (normally the current market price or a slightly lower figure).

The most difficult task involves measuring individual performance in the long term. People normally do not stay indefinitely in a given job, inherit conditions shaped by others, and leave conditions to their successors for which they should receive full credit or blame. Keeping track of individual achievements through time requires a great deal of skill. If the manager has been responsible for developing and implementing strategic commitments for his business units, it might be feasible to keep track of his performance record. Many different schema for compensating managers for the long-run impact of his decisions have been instituted (see, for example Kaplan 1982).

Regardless of the allocation of weights to be used on individual versus group, and short versus long term performance, it is imperative to find mechanisms for obtaining a better integration of management incentives and strategic plans. Rappaport (1978) proposes three approaches addressing that issue:

—the extended performance evaluation approach
—the strategic factors approach, and
—the management accounting approach.

In the *extended performance evaluation approach*, the firm rewards managers for achieving certain performance levels over a multi-year period, by awarding him with deferred stock or stock options according to his ability to fulfill various strategic goals over the agreed upon planning horizon. This method also allows for a more appropriate use of accounting measurements. For example, ROI is used as a target, based upon expected profits and the investment deployments the manager is committed to make over an extended time horizon.

The *strategic factors approach* involves the identification of the critical success factors governing the future profitability of the business, and the assignment of proper weights depending on the inherent characteristics of the business unit, and its agreed upon strategy. This approach allows for establishing congruency in terms of the performance measurements to be used, and the position of the business within the corporate portfolio. Stonich (1981) proposes the use of four measurements of performance [Return on Assets (ROA), Cash Flow, Strategic Funds Programs, and Market Share Increase], receiving different weights depending on the expected growth of the corresponding business unit. Figure 5.11 illustrates his suggestion. In different situations, and according to the nature of the SBU, many other factors could be used, such as productivity levels, product-quality measures, product-development measures, and personnel-development measures.

The *management accounting approach* considers the motivation and implications of accounting measurements, and therefore adjusts, rather than adopts, the financial accounting model for the company's internal usage. The reasons behind these modifications of the financial accounting rules have already been discussed when we were addressing the strategic funds subject in Chapter 3. The primary mechanism to seek congruency between strategic objectives and managerial measures of performance is to resort to a break down of expenses

Figure 5.11 An Illustration of the Strategic Factors Approach for the Reward of Managers

SBU Category	Weights to be Assigned to Strategic Factors (%)			
	ROA	Cash Flow	Strategic Funds	Market Share Increase
High Growth	10	0	45	45
Medium Growth	25	25	25	25
Low Growth	50	50	0	0

Figure 5.12 Conventional versus Strategic Funds Accountability

Conventional Statement		Strategic Expenses Statement	
Sales	100	Sales	100
Cost of Goods Sold	60	Operating Cost of Goods Sold	55
Gross margin	40	Gross Operating Margin	45
Sales, General and Ad. Exp.	30	Operating SG&A	10
Division Margin	10	Operating Margin	35
		Strategic Expenses	25
		Division Margin	10

Note: Same numbers as in Figure 5.5

into operational and strategic categories (see Figure 5.5, already presented). At the risk of being redundant, we should emphasize the unusual aspects of strategic funds accountability. Developmental expenses, such as R&D, are conventionally included as overhead in the Sales, General and Administrative Expenses, as shown in the conventional statement of Figure 5.12. Under the strategic funds accountability, however, it will be taken out of SG&A, which now will include only operating expenses, transferring all other expenses into the strategic expense item.

Rappaport (1978) also recommends capitalizing certain R&D expenses, and expensing them gradually in subsequent years to encourage executives to take some reasonable business risks without affecting their operating margins too severely. Likewise, if companies were to use accelerated depreciation for tax purposes, it might be desirable in the management accounting approach to have less rather than more depreciation during the initial years of investment.

All of these comments amount to one single lesson, and that is financial accounting, which intends to provide objective information to external parties to the firm, might tend to discourage some sound managerial actions, particularly if the reward system stresses short-term operational performance. Managers could benefit from changing some of these rules if necessary, to create conditions that support the desired strategic directions of the firm.

INTEGRATION BETWEEN THE MANAGERIAL INFRASTRUCTURE AND THE CORPORATE CULTURE

So far, we have dealt entirely with administrative processes and structure. This might lead one to believe that strategic management is a rather mechanistic and abstract activity. Obviously, this is far from true. There are no quick recipes and universal rules of thumb on how to plan, control, organize, inform, and set rewards for a business firm. What makes these tasks immensely challenging is people and what is usually referred to as the culture prevailing in the organization. We have purposely left to the very end of these reflections on the requirements for strategic management, the most subtle of all integration demands.

Strategy does not need only to be congruent with the organizational structure and the key administrative processes; but, most centrally, it has to be integrated within the corporate culture. This last section will attempt to shed some light on this issue.

The Increasing Awareness of the Importance of Corporate Culture: The Seven S Model

Perhaps the most important element which triggered the interest of American managers in the issue of culture was the emergence of Japanese competition. As Japan began to take a leading role in one basic industry after another, the question of cultural differences emerged as a causal factor to explain Japanese superiority. There are those who signal the deterioration of sound cultural values as the central reason behind the slippage of America as a worldwide industrial power. They suggest that Americans have gotten too fat, demanding too much from society without imposing any equivalent internal demands on themselves, and that they seem to have lost a sense of pride and self-satisfaction derived from a job well done. When contrasted with their Japanese counterparts, the gap seems to be enormous and still growing. Somehow, there is a basic erosion of standards of excellence that seems to undermine the basic fabric of American society. This is a message of gloom, and the popular press, as well as the academic writers, when contrasting American and Japanese management styles have been repeatedly conveying that message in recent years. The most notable exception, which might be the cause of its enormous popularity, has been the book *In Search of Excellence* by Peters and Waterman (1982), where they emphasize the lessons to be derived from America's best run companies. Paradoxically, it is interesting to observe that the best compliment that can be made to an American firm is that it resembles a Japanese company. We will not attempt to summarize Peters and Waterman's findings. What is more meaningful in this discussion is to reflect upon the framework they use to evaluate the best managed companies, which has become known as the McKinsey's Seven S model (Figure 5.13).

According to that model, there are seven basic dimensions which represent the core of managerial activities. These are the "levers" which executives use to influence complex and large organizations. Obviously, there was a concerted effort on the part of the originators of the model to coin the managerial variables with words beginning with the letter S, so as to increase the communication power of the model. The Seven Ss are:

1. *Strategy.* A coherent set of actions aimed at gaining a sustainable advantage over competition, improving position vis-a-vis customers, and allocating resources.
2. *Structure.* The organization chart and accompanying baggage that show who reports to whom and how tasks are both divided up and integrated.

Figure 5.13 McKinsey Seven S's Model

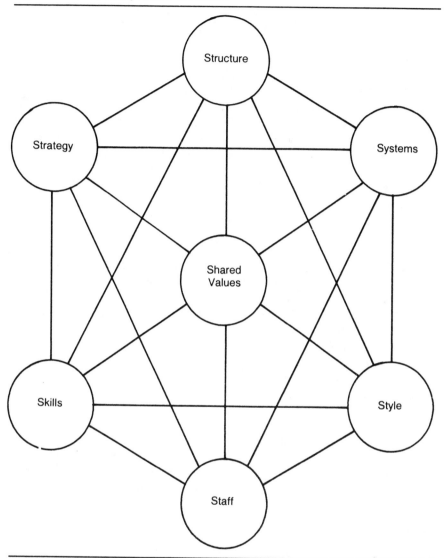

Source: McKinsey 7-S Framework (p. 10) from In Search of Excellence: Lessons from America's Best-Run Companies by Thomas J. Peters and Robert H. Waterman, Jr. Copyright © 1982 by Thomas J. Peters and Robert H. Waterman, Jr. Reprinted by permission of Harper & Row, Publishers, Inc.

3. *Systems*. The processes and flows that show how an organization gets things done from day to day. (Information systems, capital budgeting systems, manufacturing processes, quality control systems, and performance measurement systems all would be good examples.)

4. *Style*. Tangible evidence of what management considers important by the way it collectively spends time and attention and uses symbolic behavior. If it is not what management says is important, it is the way management behaves.

5. *Staff*. The people in an organization. Here it is very useful to think not about individual personalities, but about corporate demographics.

6. *Skills*. A derivative of the rest. Skills are those capabilities that are possessed by an organization as a whole as opposed to the people in it. (The concept of corporate skills as something different from the summation of the people seems difficult for many to grasp; however, some organizations that hire only the best and the brightest cannot get seemingly simple things done, while others perform extraordinary feats with ordinary people.)

7. *Shared Values*. The values that go beyond, but might well include, simple goal statements in determining corporate destiny. To fit the concept, these values must be shared by most people in an organization.

Pascale and Athos (1981), in their book *The Art of Japanese Management*, use this framework to contrast American with Japanese firms. They argue that when things go wrong, Americans tend to manipulate the so-called three hard Ss—Strategy, Structure, and Systems. These have been a major center of concern up to this point. Perhaps the most important set of variables, however, is that describing the soft Ss—Style, Staff, Skills, and Shared Values. This last one—Shared Values or Superordinate Goals—is centrally responsible for providing a core mission to the organization, used as an umbrella which embraces all the other managerial activities. We have addressed those concepts under the label "The Vision of the Firm" in Chapter 4. These four soft Ss are the primary forces which shape the culture of the organization.

One more time, we should emphasize that the quality of strategic management depends on the goodness of fit among all those key managerial dimensions. The best run companies have been able to develop Strategies, Systems, and Structures which are not only centrally congruent, but also support and enrich the organization's Superordinate Goals, Style, Skills, and Staff.

Toward a Definition of Corporate Culture

In spite of the central importance that organizational culture has in shaping corporate performance and individual satisfaction, it is still a subject highly misunderstood. To trace any scientific foundation for the definition of culture, one would have to resort to the anthropological approach. Ed Schein (1981) has made a significant contribution to the study of management culture drawing from the anthropological work. He proposes a framework for studying culture, presented in Figure 5.14, which includes three interconnected levels.

According to it, the culture of a group is made visible in the *artifacts* and *creations* produced, like language, technology, art, stratification, and status sys-

Figure 5.14 Schein's Framework for Studying Culture from an Anthropological Perspective

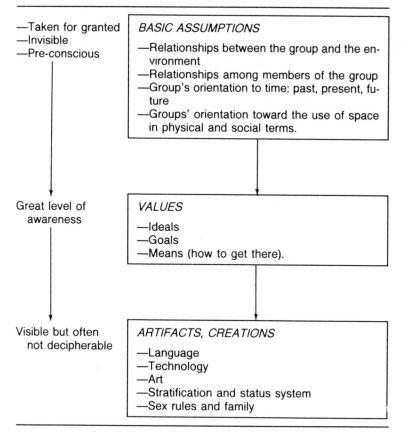

—Taken for granted
—Invisible
—Pre-conscious

BASIC ASSUMPTIONS

—Relationships between the group and the environment
—Relationships among members of the group
—Group's orientation to time: past, present, future
—Groups' orientation toward the use of space in physical and social terms.

Great level of awareness

VALUES

—Ideals
—Goals
—Means (how to get there).

Visible but often not decipherable

ARTIFACTS, CREATIONS

—Language
—Technology
—Art
—Stratification and status system
—Sex rules and family

Source: Edgar Schein, "Does Japanese Management Style Have a Message for American Managers?" © 1981, p. 64. Reprinted by permission of Edgar Schein.

tem, and rules regarding sex and family. There is a high level of awareness on these issues. They correspond to things we can see, use, or clearly perceive. But they are no more than the reflection of a more primary and underlying set of *values*, which are defined in terms of ideals, goals, and means to achieve them. The student of a culture cannot be satisfied with the description and cataloging of artifacts, but should probe into the underlying set of values which are more deeply buried in the formulations that only "old-timers" of the group can provide. They have been able to arrive at a higher level of abstraction in the preservation of cultural traditions and they know about the more profound meaning of visible artifacts. A final representation of the culture of a group goes even deeper, and is constructed on only a few *basic assumptions* regarding the rules of interaction between man and nature, among members of the group, within a time framework, and subject to the use of space in physical and social terms. This is a more demanding task because basic assumptions are not consciously held. They are invisible and taken for granted. It is only through a series of observations and abstractions that an acceptable formulation for these basic assumptions can emerge. Kluckhohn and Stodtbeck (1961) suggest that these basic assumptions can be traced back to only four types:

—Relationship between the group and the environment. Kluckhohn and Stodtbeck (1961) propose three different orientations which determine how members of a group respond to environmental forces:
One, a basic belief that the group can master the environment.
Two, a basic belief that the group is subjugated to a powerful and immutable environment.
Three, a basic belief that the group should neither master nor be subjugated by the environment, but it should harmonize with it.
—Relationships among members of the group. There are two dimensions within this assumption.
First, the number of ways in which relationships may be arranged, including: strict hierarchy, solidarity and integrity, and individual achievement.
Second, the group's assumptions about human nature, including whether man is ultimately good, evil, or neither; whether man can be perfected or is doomed to imperfection; as well as the meaning of birth and death, heroic ideas, taboos and sins in how people relate to each other.
—Group's orientation to time. Kluckhohn and Stodtbeck (1961) suggests that all societies have some conceptions of the past, present, and future, but they will be primarily oriented toward one of them at a particular point in time.
—Group's orientation toward the use of space. Here we distinguish among the various assumptions a group has about the use of physical space (design of physical facilities, closeness to others, and so forth) as well as social space (arrangements reflecting social positions, status, and power).

Schein suggests that a cultural analysis should have as an ultimate objective the unveiling of the basic assumptions of cultural values in a firm, and that we can "structure our observations around the question of how the organization relates to its environment, how it manages time, how it deals with space, and what can be observed about the relationships of people to each other."

Borrowing from this anthropological perspective, Schein has suggested the following definition of culture:

Culture is the set of basic assumptions which members of a group invent to solve the basic problems of physical survival in the external environment (adaptation) and social survival in the internal environment (internal integration). Once invented, these basic assumptions serve the function of helping members of the group to avoid or reduce anxiety by reducing anxiety and cognitive overload. Once invented, those solutions which work are passed on to successive generations as ways for them to avoid the anxiety which may have motivated the invention in the first place.

There are several elements of this definition which are worth discussing. First, culture is expressed as a way of responding to external environmental pressures through the process of adaptation, by designing rules, perspectives and ways of thinking, which are internalized as norms of behavior for the group. Not surprisingly, these are the same central dimensions of strategic planning: *adaptation* towards the external environment, and *integration* in terms of internal commitments. Next, if properly executed, these norms of conduct represent explicit or implicit ways of affecting communication within the group, which develops a sort of character or personality for an institution. Finally, there is the element of permanence of accepted solutions, which are passed from one generation to the next. This means that there is some degree of molding of values and ethics which are recognized and become acceptable patterns of conduct in a given organization.

In his concluding remarks, Schein suggests some recommendations on how to study organizational culture. First, he advises to look for units that have a reasonably long history and stable membership. For analytical purposes, he distinguishes sharply between *artifacts*, which are "the visible creations of the culture"; *values*, which are "the stated operating principles of the culture"; and *basic assumptions*, which are "the essence of the culture, a pattern which permits us to decipher the significance of values and artifacts." He also suggests that the best model for studying organizational culture is a combination of anthropology and clinical psychology. The clinical method implies that each cultural analysis is, in essence, a case study. Even if one finds common elements across cultures, one must know how to pull data from many informants into the patterns which make up the unique culture of a particular organization. For an excellent case analysis following this approach, the reader is referred to Dyer (1982).

In an independent study, Schwartz and Davis (1981) provide a definition of culture which is fairly consistent with Schein's: "a pattern of beliefs and expectations shared by members of an organization. These beliefs and expectations produce rules for behavior—norms—that powerfully shape the behavior of individuals and groups in the organization."

They proceed to distinguish between corporate culture and climate. This last is a measure of people's expectations about what it *should* be like to work in an organization, and the degree to which they are being met.

They also indicate that:

What climate really measures is the fit between the prevailing culture and the individual values of the employees. If the employees have adopted the values of the prevailing culture, the climate is "good." If they have not, the climate is "poor," and motivation and presumably performance suffer . . .

While climate is often transitory, tactical, and can be managed over the relatively short term, culture is usually long-term and strategic. It is very difficult to change. Culture is rooted in deeply held beliefs and values in which individuals hold a substantial investment as the result of some processing or analysis of data about organizational life.

No wonder then, that influencing the climate of an organization by means of changes in the administrative systems appears as much more likely than modifying the prevailing culture. To alter the culture is, undoubtedly, a tough undertaking.

Cultural Audit

We have discussed already the anthropological and clinical approach proposed by Schein on how to conduct a cultural audit. We will review now some more pragmatic frameworks for structuring a process of finding out the underlying cultural characteristics of a firm.

Likert (1967) proposes an approach to describe an organization from the perspective of its human side, and the quality of interaction affecting its members. He argues that an organization can be described through eight basic processes: (1) leadership, (2) motivation, (3) communication, (4) interpersonal interactions and influence, (5) decision-making, (6) goal-setting or ordering, (7) control, and (8) performance goals and training. The nature of each of these characteristics can be located in a continuum spanning four general types of organizational management systems:

—System one, Exploitive Authoritative, provides an environment where there is low motivation, little interpersonal support and participation, only downward communication, and authoritarian control.
—System two, Benevolent Authoritative, is similar to system one but it is more paternalistic.
—System three, Consultative, provides an environment having upward and downward communication, supporting leadership, a certain degree of self-regulation, and consultative goal-setting.
—System four, Participative, provides an environment with more emphasis on self-regulation and mutual support, openness and trust, high performance goals, and more involved participation at all levels.

We will further discuss the implications of Likert in Chapter 21. What is important to emphasize here is that he has provided a well structured process, supported with detailed questionnaires, to categorize an organization within the continuum from system one to system four. Those questionnaires, which are reproduced in Likert's book, can greatly facilitate what otherwise would be a highly judgmental and subjective process.

Figure 5.15 presents an illustration of what a profile might look like after applying Likert's methodology. There are two major benefits to be derived from assessing such a profile. One is the value of having a description of important cultural components of the organization, and second its conclusions might lead to undertaking some normative efforts intended to correct perceived inconsistencies among the managerial processes. Most organizations find themselves in system two or three.

Figure 5.15 Organizational Profile as Part of a Cultural Audit

Organizational Variables	System of Organization			
	Exploitive Authoritative	Benevolent Authoritative	Consultative	Participative Group
Leadership process used				
Character of motivational forces				
Character of communication process				
Character of interaction-influence process				
Character of decision-making process				
Character of goal setting or ordering				
Character of control process				
Performance goals and training				

Schwartz and Davis (1981) suggest an approach for cultural audits, based on an assessment of the managerial tasks and their key relationships in the organization. They define six managerial tasks, somewhat reminiscent of Likert's which they believe are central for performing a cultural assessment: innovating, decision-making, communicating, organizing, monitoring, and appraising and rewarding. Each task should be described in terms of how it is handled within the context of four types of relationships: company-wide, boss-subordinate, peer, and interdepartmental. This results in a matrix, such as the one presented in Figure 5.16, which serves both as a checklist to conduct a cultural analysis, and as a framework in interpreting the meaning of the artifacts, in which much of the data about organizational culture is reflected. For an example on how to use the matrix, the reader is referred to Schwartz and Davis's original paper.

The final framework which we consider useful when performing a cultural audit is the Rockwell International Culture Analysis described in the Appendix

Figure 5.16 Corporate Culture Matrix

Tasks	Relationships			
	Company-Wide	Boss-Subordinate	Peer	Interdepartmental
Innovating				
Decision-Making				
Communicating				
Organizing				
Monitoring				
Appraising and Rewarding				

Howard Schwartz and Stanley M. Davis, "Matching Corporate Culture and Business Strategy," © 1981, p. 36. Reprinted by permission of Organizational Dynamics, New York, NY.

of Ouchi's book *Theory Z* (1982). Rockwell uses five categories to describe the cultural profile: short- versus long-term environment, communication, information sharing, individual orientation, and job security. Each of these categories is represented in terms of past, present, and future characteristics, according to the form illustrated in Figure 5.17.

Figure 5.17 Rockwell International Culture Analysis

Culture Category	Where We Were Mid-70's	What We've Done	Where We Are 1 3 5 7 10	Future Direction
Short vs. Long Term Environment				
Organization Communication				
Information Sharing				
Individual Orientation				
Job Security				

Adapted from William G. Ouchi, *Theory Z,* © 1981. Reprinted by permission of Addison-Wesley, Reading, MA. Adapted material. Reprinted with permission.

The most significant contribution of this approach is that it forces the cultural description to span a time dimension showing the evolution of cultural changes.

Congruency between Strategy and Corporate Culture

From the perspective of strategy formulation and implementation, we cannot be satisfied by a mere description of the cultural characteristics of the firm. Having done that, the major question still remaining is whether or not the proposed strategies are congruent with the culture, and if not, what to do about it.

In order to address the first part of this question, we should decompose the overall strategy into its major tasks, which is what we have referred to as broad strategic action programs. Having those tasks as a central focus of analysis, we can address one, the importance of each task to the success of the strategy, and two, the degree of compatibility that exists between the strategy and the organizational culture. Schwarz and Davis (1982) propose a matrix to portray these two dimensions of cultural risk assessment, as illustrated in Figure 5.18. Their approach requires positioning each task in the matrix, by exercising crude managerial judgment. The result of this effort should serve as a guide to start reflecting upon what ought to be done when serious incompatibilities arise. Actions taken to make the implementation of the strategy more compatible with culture will tend to decrease the cultural risk and, consequently, enhance the chances of a successful implementation.

Schwartz and Davis offer four generic alternatives to deal with this question of strategy and cultural compatibility.

1. Ignore the culture, which is a dangerous and unacceptable alternative when significant inconsistencies still remain.
2. Manage around the culture by changing the implementation plan. This alternative is based upon recognizing the cultural barriers which represent serious obstacles for the implementation of the desirable strategy, and offering alternative approaches to bypass the cultural obstacles, but without changing the intended strategic focus. Figure 5.19 reproduces a list of examples suggested by Schwartz and Davis on how to accomplish this task.
3. Attempt to change the culture to fit the strategy. This is an extremely difficult task to accomplish, requiring a lengthy process and significant resources. There are, however, situations where this could be a central determinant for the long term success of a firm. One of the clearest illustrations of this case is represented by AT&T. Due to the dramatic change in AT&T's external and internal environment, it will be hard to conceive that a successful strategy will not call for a deep and permanent change in its culture. When a cultural change is explicitly intended, it should be coordinated with all the necessary internal changes in management systems and organizational structure to seek a mutual and positive reinforcement of overall strategic management infrastructure.

Figure 5.18 Cultural Risk Assessment

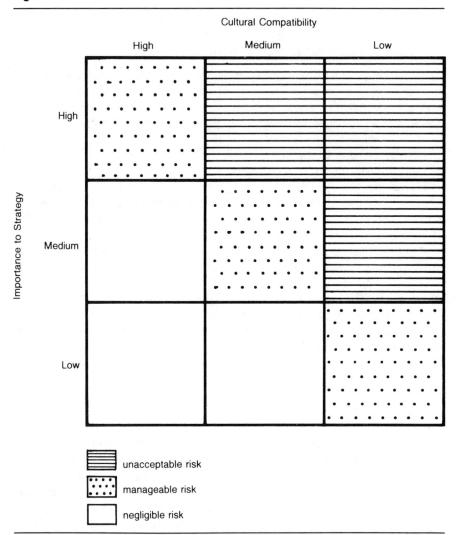

Source: Howard Schwartz and Stanley M. Davis, "Matching Corporate Culture and Business Strategy," © 1981, p. 36. Reprinted by permission of Organizational Dynamics, New York, NY.

4. Change the strategy to fit the culture, perhaps by reducing performance expectations.

The lessons to be derived from these brief comments on cultural and strategic compatibility is that every effort should be made to minimize the cultural risk

Figure 5.19 How to Manage Around the Company Culture

	Strategy	"Right" Approach	Cultural Barriers	Alternative Approaches
Company A	Product/market diversification	—Divisionalization	—Centralized power —One-man rule —Functional —Hierarchical	—Business teams —Explicit strategic planning —Business measurement
Company B	Focus marketing on most profitable segments	—Fine tune reward system —Adjust MIS	—Diffused power —Highly individualized —Relationship-oriented	—Dedicate full-time personnel to each key market
Company C	Extend technology to new markets	—Matrix organization	—Multiple power centers —Functional focus	—Program coordinators —Planning committees —Greater top management involvement

Adapted from Howard Schwartz and Stanley M. Davis, "Matching Corporate Culture and Business Strategy," © 1981, p. 44. Reprinted by permission of Organizational Dynamics, New York, NY.

inherent in a proposed strategy. When this cannot be avoided, either because of structural changes in the industry in which the firm is located, or because of critical and serious lack of performance, a combination of the last three alternatives—managing around the culture, changing the culture, and modifying the strategy—should be used to bring cultural risk to an acceptable level.

Merits and Limitations of Strategic Management

Strategic management represents the most advanced and coherent form of strategic thinking. Not only does it attempt to extend the strategic vision throughout all the operational and functional units of the firm, but it also encompasses every administrative system recognizing the central role to be played by the individual and groups within an organization, and its resulting culture.

Stated in this form, it is hard to argue against strategic management. In itself, it is a mature and overall-encompassing concept which embraces most of what we know about the practice, art, and science of management.

The first overwhelming fact that one encounters when analyzing a large number of organizations is that very few have reached the quality of excellence that would be naturally resulting from a fully implemented strategic management system. Occasionally, one wonders why such an obviously desirable managerial state, so easily describable in conceptual terms, is so hard to accomplish. The answer to this question can be argued in many different ways.

First and foremost, as we have said in the opening paragraphs of this book, management is a very complex social activity which cannot be comprehended by a simple set of rules and normative processes. We lack now, and probably will always lack, a well developed body of knowledge which will provide the scientific foundation for the development of a managerial methodology to facilitate the implementation of strategic management. We are left with broad concepts and pragmatic responses based on experiencial perceptions, rather than undisputable principles. We are forced to admit, therefore, that strategy is an ad-hoc process and that there is no single way to guide us into the realizations of this ultimate goal which is represented by the strategic management ideal.

If we admit this concept of strategic management as an ideal, it is not hard to explain that we only see it, at best, partially realized in most organizations. Therefore, we will be forced to strive constantly and endlessly toward the pursuit of this form of management. Implicit in this search is the constant development and learning which provides an enrichment and maturity for all members in an organization. That is why it is hard, if not impossible, to skip stages or greatly accelerate this process. Time is of the essence to consolidate the goal for integration, which is so basic in strategic management. Integration which brings in its more methodological dimension, the quality of congruency of all the administrative processes with the organizational structure in strategic and operational mode. But most significantly, integration which consolidates a common strategic vision among all the members of the organization, supported by rich and highly shared values and beliefs creating a top quality of cultural support.

REFERENCES

Anthony, Robert N., and John Dearden, *Management Control Systems*, Richard D. Irwin, Homewood, IL, 1980.

Anthony, Robert N., and Glenn A. Welsch, *Fundamentals of Management Accounting*, Richard D. Irwin, Homewood, IL, 1981.

Chandler, Alfred D., Jr., *Strategy and Structure: Chapters in the History of the American Industrial Enterprise*, The MIT Press, Cambridge, MA, 1962.

Corning Glass Works, "Tom MacAvoy," Case #179-074, Harvard Business School, Boston, MA, 1978.

Daniel, D. Ronald, "Management Information Crisis," *Harvard Business Review*, Vol. 39, No. 5, September–October 1961, pp. 111–121.

Dyer, Gibb, W., Jr., "Culture in Organizations: A Case Study and Analysis," Unpublished Master's Thesis, Massachusetts Institute of Technology, 1982.

General Electric Company, "Background Note on Management Systems," 1981, Case #181-111, Harvard Business School, Boston, MA, 1981.

Kaplan, Robert S., *Advanced Management Accounting*, Prentice-Hall, Englewood Cliffs, NJ, 1982.

Kluckhohn, Florence R., and Fred L. Stodtbeck, *Variations in Value Orientations*, Row, Peterson, Evanston, IL, 1961.

Lawrence, Paul R., and Jay W. Lorsch, *Organization and Environment: Managing Differentiation and Integration*, Richard D. Irwin, Homewood, IL, 1967.

Likert, Rensis, *The Human Organization: Its Management and Value*, McGraw-Hill, New York, 1967.

Ouchi, William G., Theory Z, Addison-Wesley, Reading, MA, 1981.

Pascale, Richard T., and Anthony G. Athos, *The Art of Japanese Management*, Simon & Schuster, New York, 1981.

Peters, Thomas J., and Richard H. Waterman, Jr., *In Search of Excellence*, Harper & Row, Pub., New York, 1982.

Rappaport, Alfred, "Executive Incentives vs. Corporate Growth," *Harvard Business Review*, Vol. 56, No. 4, July–August 1978, pp. 81–88.

Rockart, John F., "Chief Executives Define Their Own Data Needs," *Harvard Business Review*, Vol. 57, No. 2, March–April 1979, pp. 81–92.

Rockart, John F., and Michael E. Treacy, "The CEO Goes On-Line," *Harvard Business Review*, Vol. 60, No. 1, January–February 1982, pp. 82–88.

Schein, Edgar S., "Does Japanese Management Style Have a Message for American Managers?" *Sloan Management Review*, Vol. 23, No. 1, Fall 1981, pp. 55–67.

Schwartz, Howard, and Stanley M. Davis, "Matching Corporate Culture and Business Strategy," *Organizational Dynamics*, Vol. 10, Summer 1981, pp. 30–48.

Stonich, Paul J., "Using Rewards in Implementing Strategy," *Strategic Management Journal*, Vol. 2, No. 4, October–December 1981, pp. 345–352.

Texas Instruments Incorporated, "Management Systems," Case #172-052, Harvard Business School, Boston, MA, 1972.

Part Two

CONCEPTS AND TOOLS FOR STRATEGIC PLANNING

6

COMPETITIVE COST DYNAMICS: THE EXPERIENCE CURVE

PRESENTATION OF THE EXPERIENCE CURVE

The effective management of the total cost of manufactured products is a fundamental concern for the long-term profitability of a firm operating in competitive markets. To a great extent, the internal strength of a business rests on the firm's ability to deliver products at costs which are lower than those of the competitors. From this perspective, the cost of a product should not be viewed as the simple accumulation of direct and allocated expenses required for its manufacturing and sale, but as a central indicator of the firm's capability for managing its internal resources to attain a productivity advantage over its competitors.

In this chapter we discuss the experience curve, which is a key tool to assist managers in addressing more formally the question of the competitive cost structure. The experience curve provides an empirical relationship between changes in direct manufacturing cost and the accumulated volume of production. Although its origins go back to the beginning of this century, it was only in the late 1960s that the Boston Consulting Group began to emphasize its role for strategic decision making [Boston Consulting Group (1972)]. Our presentation follows Hax and Majluf (1982).

In Figure 6.1 we present an 85% experience curve. In the horizontal axis we have the accumulated volume of production (in units), and in the vertical axis the deflated direct cost per unit, which is the actual cost corrected by the inflation rate. The experience curve shows that the cost of doing a repetitive

Figure 6.1   An 85% Experience Curve

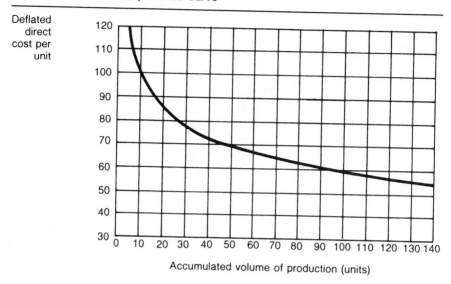

task decreases by a fixed percentage each time the total accumulated volume of production (in units) doubles. In the example given in the figure, the total cost drops from 100 when the total production was 10 units, to 85 (= 100 × 0.85) when it increased to 20 units, and to 72.25 (= 85 × 0.85) when it reached 40 units. This relationship between accumulated volume of production and deflated direct cost is expressed in a log-log graph as a straight line, which is easier to work with. In Figure 6.2, we display the 85% experience curve shown above in this kind of graph.

If nominal rather than deflated cost were to be used in plotting the experience curve, none of the previous effects could be observed. Most likely, instead of a decreasing cost curve, we would have obtained an increasing and unsystematic cost pattern.

The cost predicted by the experience curve effect can be obtained from a simple negative exponential relationship of the following type:

$$C_t = C_o \left(\frac{P_t}{P_o}\right)^{-a}$$

where:

C_o, C_t = Cost per unit (corrected by inflation) at times 0 and t, respectively;

P_o, P_t = Accumulated production at times 0 and t, respectively;

a = Constant, industry dependent.

Figure 6.2 An 85% Experience Curve on Log-Log Scales

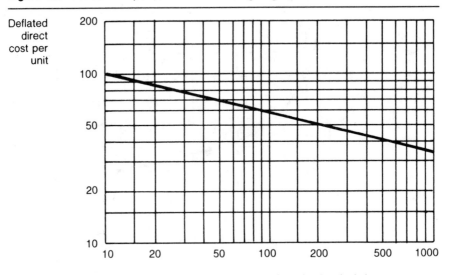

Accumulated volume of production (units)

In the 85% curve, the constant "a" can be obtained by recognizing that doubling the production reduces the cost to 85% of its initial value. This corresponds to introducing the values $C_t/C_o = 0.85$ and $P_t/P_o = 2$ in the expression:

$$\frac{C_t}{C_o} = \left(\frac{P_t}{P_o}\right)^{-a}$$

The resulting solution is $a = 0.234$. Other values of this constant for different slopes of the experience curve are presented in Figure 6.3. The reduction that may be obtained by the experience effect is dependent on the industry. For example, the manufacturing of integrated circuits approaches a 70% slope, air conditioners show an 80% slope, and primary magnesium exhibits a 90% slope (see Figure 6.4). Similar observations are obtained from other industries like cement manufacturing (70% slope), power tools (80% slope), and industrial trucks (90% slope).

The actual significance of the experience effects for a given industry depends not only on its inherent slope, but also on the speed at which experience accumulates, measured by the rate of growth in the market. Figure 6.5 provides an estimate of the potential for annual cost reductions for different combinations of experience-curve slope and annual market-growth rate.

It is apparent from the figure above that the potential for cost reduction is of the utmost importance in industries characterized by strong experience effects and highly growing markets, such as the semi-conductor and the computer industries in recent years.

Figure 6.3 Experience Curves for Different Relations Between Accumulated Production and Unit Cost

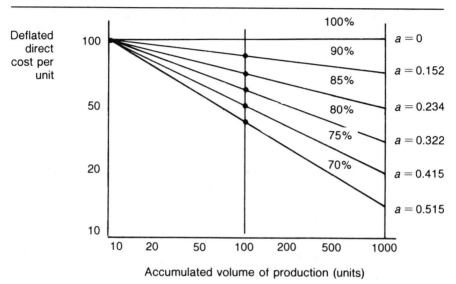

Accumulated volume of production (units)

Figure 6.4 A Sample of Experience Curves

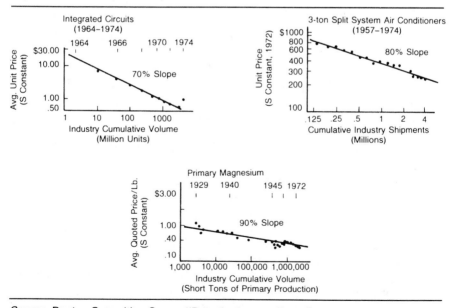

Figure 6.5 Annual Percentage of Cost Reduction Due to Experience Effects

| Experience Curve | Annual Market-Growth Rate | | | | |
Slope	2%	5%	10%	20%	30%
90%	0.3	0.7	1.4	2.7	3.9
80%	0.6	1.6	3.0	5.7	8.1
70%	1.0	2.5	4.8	9.0	12.6
60%	1.4	3.5	6.8	12.6	17.6

MANAGING THE EXPERIENCE CURVE: REASONS FOR THE REDUCTION OF COST

Although the impact of experience on lowering costs has been measured empirically in a wide spectrum of industries—ranging from broiler chickens to integrated circuits—its benefits can only be realized by careful management. The effects of the experience curve can be observed in every stage of the value added chain. Its impact affects in a distinctive way each one of the value added steps covering research and development, procurement of raw materials, fabrication, assembly, marketing, sales, and distribution. In this section we discuss the most important factors that contribute to the systematic decrease in cost with accumulated volume.

1. *Learning.* The repetitive performance of a task allows a person to develop a specialized set of skills which permits the completion of the assignment in a more efficient way. For this reason, the productivity per worker is expected to rise with the increased dexterity to handle the job's responsibilities (Hirschmann 1964).
2. *Specialization and Redesign of Labor Tasks.* The increased volume of production lends itself to a divisionalization of labor that allows for specialization and standardization to take place, thus contributing greatly to productivity improvements.
3. *Product and Process Improvements.* As volume increases, many opportunities become available for product and process improvements leading toward higher productivity and cost reductions. An important factor for the realization of these opportunities is the implementation of a broad standardization policy affecting all significant steps in the value added chain. Changes in the product characteristics that generate significant increases in productivity are design modifications, better utilization and substitution of materials, and rationalization of the product-mix; all of them dictated by the increased experience resulting from larger volumes of production. Added opportunities

for cost reduction arise from changes in the manufacturing process. Improved technologies, layout changes, better ways for handling and storing materials, parts, and products; adoption of more efficient maintenance schema, and better distribution of final products are just some of the broad alternatives open to drive costs down through the accumulation of experience. In general, the idea is to look for all those improvements of the industrial process that can profitably reduce the cost schedule.

4. *Methods and Systems Rationalization.* There is an increasing number of opportunities to improve the performance of a firm by introducing more up-to-date technology in the handling of operational activities. By introducing rationalization of procedures and extensive use of computers and automation, all hierarchical layers of firms become confronted with substantial changes in their normal administrative and managerial duties. Many of the simplest rationalization efforts can be successfully completed after some accumulation of experience, but large productivity improvements related with computerization are particularly dependent upon having reached a certain volume of production that can support the high fixed cost associated with the introduction of that technology.

5. *Economies of Scale.* The substantial cost reduction observed in an historical series of real costs can be partly explained by the impact of accumulated volume of production and partly by the changes of scale induced by the increased throughput required from a firm as time passes. The economies of scale correspond to the decline in unit costs as throughput increases. Scale economies can be present in nearly every function and many technological factors concur to explain the downward trend of the cost-curve as a result of increased volume per period. The most dominant among them are:

—The availability of improved technological processes for high-volume production;
—The indivisibility of many resources that can only be profitably used when adopted in fairly large operations;
—The backward and forward integration of manufacturing processes and business activities, which can be justified only for very large firms operating in stable environments;
—The sharing of resources, mainly the ones managed at the corporate level, which is an alternative open mainly to diversified firms with businesses in related product markets.

The typical application of a scale effect is observed in the use of the "$0.6 - 0.8$ rule" for estimating the investment required for a given plant capacity. The rule, that applies in many industrial settings, is that if capacity is doubled, the investment required increases only in 2^a with the exponent varying between 0.6 and 0.8. This corresponds to an increase between 52% and 84% of investments for a 100% increase in capacity. Similarly, scale effects can be observed in distribution, sales, R&D, general administrative activities, and in all stages of a productive operation.

It is apparent from these comments that cost reductions with scale are another clue for dedicated managers to improve their competitive cost position in the marketplace, because it signals factors that, when properly managed, can reduce the total cost of a product.

6. *Know-How.* A subtle and overall encompassing result of the benefits to be derived from experience can be collected under the label "know-how." This represents an enriched understanding of the managerial, technological, and operational factors that contribute to the efficiency of the firm. Know-how is hard to transfer because it represents the accumulated experience that has been gained through the passage of time. If know-how is properly consolidated and protected, it can give a significant competitive edge to tha' firm which is the leader in its industry.

CONVENTIONAL STRATEGIC IMPLICATIONS OF THE EXPERIENCE CURVE

The Value of Market Share

The decline in unit costs produced by an increase of accumulated production has led to the isolation of market share as a primary variable to identify the strength of the strategic position of a business within a given industry. Those who advocate this view, primarily among them the Boston Consulting Group, state the following chain of causal relationships:

$$\text{High Market Share} \rightarrow \text{High Accumulated Volume} \rightarrow \text{Low Unit Cost} \rightarrow \text{High Profitability}$$

The association between market share and profitability has received some empirical support in the work of project PIMS (Profitability Impact on Marketing Strategies; Schoeffler, Buzzel, and Heany 1974; Buzzel, Gale, and Sultan 1975).

The implications of these relationships are clearly depicted in Figure 6.6, which shows the positioning within a common experience curve of four competing firms. It can be observed that firm A, the leader of the group, has a commanding advantage over its competitors, while firm D is struggling for its survival that is determined by the strategic moves of firm A, and by its ability to sustain long-term losses. Under this approach, the only alternative for firm D to improve its situation is to move aggressively in its search for an increase in market share.

Bruce Henderson, the founder of the Boston Consulting Group, has been a leading spokesman for this approach. In his book *On Corporate Strategy* (1979) he proposes the "rule of three and four," which indicates that

Figure 6.6   The Value of Market Share

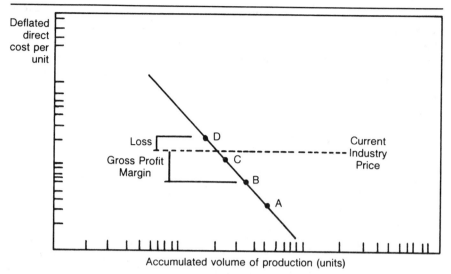

Accumulated volume of production (units)

A stable competitive market never has more than three significant competitors, the largest of which has no more than four times the market share of the smallest.

There are two primary reasons argued by Henderson to sustain this hypothesis.

A ratio of 2 to 1 in market share between any two competitors seems to be the equilibrium point in which it is neither practical nor advantageous for either competitor to increase or decrease share.
Any competitor with less than one quarter the share of the largest competitor cannot be an effective competitor.

The most important strategic implications suggested by Henderson are

If there is a large number of competitors, a shakeout is nearly inevitable in the absence of some external constraint or control on competition.
All competitors wishing to survive will have to grow faster than the market in order even to maintain their relative market shares with fewer competitors.
The eventual losers will have increasingly large negative cash flows if they try to grow at all.
All except the two largest share competitors either will be losers, and eventually be eliminated, or will be marginal cash traps reporting profits periodically and reinvesting forever.
The quicker an investment is cashed out or a market position, second only to the leader is gained, then the lower the risk and the higher the probable return on investment.
Definition of the relevant market and its boundaries becomes a major strategy evaluation.

The validity of this rule is arguable. The main reason for presenting it is to illustrate the way in which a complete set of normative implications have been derived by making a particular interpretation of the experience curve effects. What is interesting from this posture is that industry concentration should tend to be very high under stable conditions, and that failing to observe this fact may be due to a faulty definition of an appropriate market, which has very negative strategic implications for the firm, or to the presence of government regulations which prevent the natural course of strategic adjustment to take place.

The Price-Cost Relationship

Although cost has a fairly predictable trend along the experience curve, prices do not behave that way. At the early stages of a product introduction, price becomes a strategic decision variable for the innovating firm. The major question to be resolved is whether to keep a fairly high price in the initial phases, at a time which is possible for the innovator to impose a monopolistic rent and enjoy an extraordinarily high profitability level, or to lower the prices at the same rate at which costs decline to discourage the entry of competing firms into this business. The more frequent relationship observed is the one depicted in Figure 6.7. In the introduction and embryonic stages prices tend to be fairly stable, providing a real bonanza for the innovative firm. This has been the case for electronic watches, video recorders, hand electronic calculators, and similar technology-intensive consumer products. It is only at the final stages of the embryonic phase where the entry of new competitors generate a turbulent shakeout in the industry with a rate of price reductions much faster than the cost decline. Quite often, a complete restructuring of the industry takes place at this stage and even the innovator might be forced out of business. Such was the case with Bowmar in electronic hand calculators.

At the end of the shakeout phase, only a few of the most efficient producers can survive, and despite their small number, the expectation is that the profit margin is consistent with a perfect market situation throughout the maturity stage of the product.

ADDITIONAL CONSIDERATIONS FOR THE USE OF THE EXPERIENCE CURVE IN STRATEGIC PLANNING

It is undeniable that the experience curve provides important insights for strategic planning, particularly in higher-technology firms. Its use, however, requires the observance of some subtle guidelines, many having been carefully identified by a specialized consulting firm in the field, Strategic Planning Associates, Inc. The lack of recognition of these guidelines can lead to misleading uses of the experience curve implications.

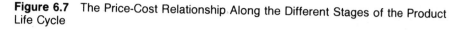

Figure 6.7 The Price-Cost Relationship Along the Different Stages of the Product Life Cycle

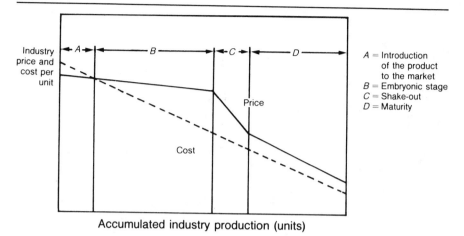

Determining the Appropriate Chronology of the Accumulated Experience

There are two basic issues regarding the chronology of the experience curve: One is the detection of the starting point for the accumulation of experience, and the other is the need to recognize that, occasionally, shifts in the experience curve tend to take place during a significantly long time span. Figure 6.8 illustrates this last point. The use of an average slope will grossly underestimate the existing experience effects due to recent technological advances, or significant capacity expansions resulting from major capital investment commitments.

Assessing the Proper Starting Position of a New Entrant

The strategic implications that we discussed in Figure 6.6 require a common experience curve applicable to every competitor in an industry. This assumption can be violated in two different situations.

First, when a new entrant is supporting its business on a technology that has a completely different experience curve behavior, as shown in the situation represented in Figure 6.9. In spite of the larger accumulated volume of firm A as compared with the new entrant, this fact is not translated into a cost advantage due to the different pattern of the respective experience curves. The dominance of the Japanese in the U.S. steel industry might be explained by the distinct technological base that supports the Japanese industry.

A second reason to explain an improved position of a new entrant, other

Figure 6.8 Illustration of Shifts in the Experience Curve: The Case of Polyvinyl Chloride

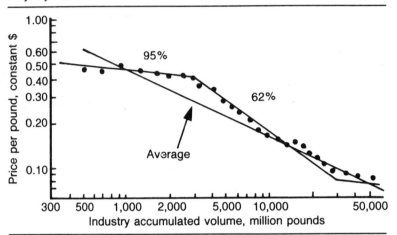

Adapted from Albert: *Handbook of Business Problem Solving* (Henderson & Zakon's "Pricing Strategy: How to Improve It (The Experience Curve)"). Figure 5–11, p. 3–57. Used by permission of McGraw-Hill Book Company, New York, NY.

than technological differences, is originated in quick transfer of technology, know-how, and smart followership. In today's industrial world, characterized by increasingly fast communications, it is often impossible to retain absolute proprietorship in process and product technology. Figure 6.10 exhibits a new entrant B with an experience curve of identical slope with leader A, but its

Figure 6.9 The Impact of a New Entrant with Improved Technology

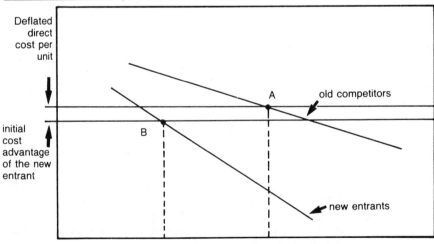

Figure 6.10   The Impact of a New Entrant with Smart Followership and Technology Transfer

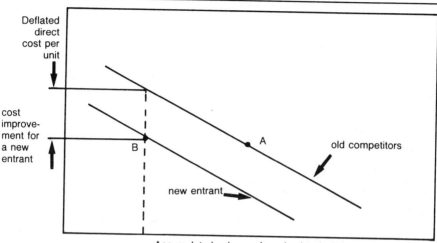

Accumulated volume of production (units)

initial position is significantly better than would have been predicted if no technological transfer had taken place.

Market Share Is Not the Only Game

There are certain industries in which experience does not seem to play a fundamental role in cost reduction. In those industries, the strategic positioning of a business does not rely exclusively in cost advantages. In this setting, it is useful to distinguish between specialty and commodity products. Commodity products are characterized by having very few, if any, opportunities for differentiation that can induce the consumer to pay a price premium. Specialty products, on the contrary, are sustained by the capability of a firm to offer very distinctive features which are highly valued by the consumer. The closer a business is to a commodity, the more significant its cost becomes as a crucial strategic decision variable.

The classical example to prove this point is the loss of Ford leadership in the automobile industry. In spite of the fact that Ford managed to reduce its costs by 15% from 1908 to 1925 (Abernathy and Wayne 1974), it was overtaken by General Motors due to a creative strategy of segmentation under the slogan "A car for every purse and every purpose." Ford was wrongly treating a car as a commodity ("I will give you any car provided it is a model T and it is black."), without realizing that the American public was ready to pay a price premium for a more distinctive type of product.

*Market Share Should Not be Measured Just at the End of the Value-
Added Chain*

A productive activity is not a monolithic process, but is composed of many
different steps and functions, that can be ordered in terms of stages of value-
added. Among these stages, one could recognize research and development,
manufacturing of parts and components, subassembly, marketing, distribution,
and retailing. Although experience will affect all these stages, seldom will its
impact be felt homogeneously across them. Figure 6.11 illustrates this point.
It shows, for example, that experience in retailing is not as important as in
the subassembly process.

Besides the different experience effect on each of the stages due to the nature
of the work, it is quite common that impact of product mixes contributes to
the accumulation of different volumes at each stage. Therefore, experience will
accrue more rapidly to those stages which are more heavily loaded by the entire
set of items produced.

Both of these two effects, the different impact of experience in cost and the
different rate of accumulation of experience in the various stages of value added,
is a message that consulting firms like Strategic Planning Associates and Braxton
are advocating quite forcefully in recent years. They argue that a trap one
could fall into is to measure market share just at the end of the productive
chain, without recognizing the two indicated effects.

One example will be used to illustrate this argument. In a business, the
leader of the market is firm A with a relative market share of four times the
one held by its competition, firm B. At first sign, it looks as if firm A has an
insurmountable advantage, but this primary impression is very much tempered
when considering that the business may be conceptualized in terms of two
stages of value added: manufacturing and distribution. In the manufacturing
stage, firm A has the 4 to 1 advantage over firm B, but in the distribution
stage, it is firm B which has an advantage of 3 to 1 in terms of market share,
because this business is just one of many others that share the same system
of distribution. Assuming that experience in both stages has the same impact
over cost, and that each stage contributes with half the final value of the product,
we could use a normalized market share to determine the relative standing of
the two firms in the business. The market share thus obtained for firm A is

$$
\begin{bmatrix} \text{Market} \\ \text{Share} \end{bmatrix} = \begin{bmatrix} \text{Manufac-} \\ \text{turing} \\ \text{Share} \end{bmatrix} \times \begin{bmatrix} \text{Manufac-} \\ \text{turing} \\ \text{Value} \\ \text{Added} \end{bmatrix} + \begin{bmatrix} \text{Distribution} \\ \text{Market} \\ \text{Share} \end{bmatrix} \times \begin{bmatrix} \text{Distribution} \\ \text{Value} \\ \text{Added} \end{bmatrix}
$$

$$
= \begin{bmatrix} 4 \text{ to } 1 \\ \text{or} \\ \tfrac{4}{5} \end{bmatrix} \times 0.5 + \begin{bmatrix} 1 \text{ to } 3 \\ \text{or} \\ \tfrac{1}{4} \end{bmatrix} \times 0.5
$$

$$
= 0.525
$$

Figure 6.11 The Effect of Accumulated Experience over the Cost Accrued in Different Stages of Value Added

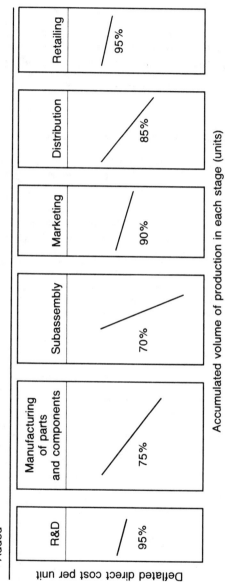

Similarly, for firm B we obtain

$$\left[\begin{array}{c} \text{Market} \\ \text{Share} \end{array}\right] = 0.475$$

The relative market share of firm A over firm B in terms of this weighted measure of experience is only $0.525/0.475 = 1.10$ times, which is far smaller than the 4 to 1 observed in the market for the final product. Figure 6.12 illustrates this point.

Rigidities Introduced by Overemphasizing Experience

Too much reliance on increasing scale and driving costs down the experience curve might have some undesirable effects. Some of these effects have already been alluded to in our previous comments. Too much emphasis on economies of scale might impair the ability of the firm to respond in a flexible way to the technological advances, environmental changes, and innovations taking place outside the firm. Likewise, it might prevent the realization of product differentiation to capture a wider range of customers.

In other words, a successful firm might find itself trapped to its existing business base preventing the needed adaptation for a long term and sustained profitability. Success could be your worst enemy!

Figure 6.12 Change in the Competitive Position of Two Firms When Using Market Share of Value-Added Stages

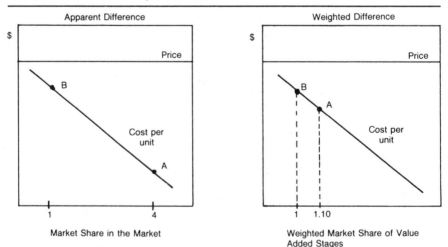

MANAGERIAL USES OF THE EXPERIENCE CURVE

So far in this chapter we have been able to understand the many insights that the experience curve provides on the dynamics of competitive cost structures. In this section we will briefly review three distinct managerial uses of this concept.

Diagnosis of the Industry Cost Structure

A critical assessment pertaining to the industry cost structure is the determination of the experience curve relevant to each one of the competitors in the industry. In the case where a single experience curve is common to everybody, the market share position of each competitor is crucial in assessing their corresponding strength. When this is not the case, the proper identification of the stages of value added and the different technologies in use could provide invaluable insights for the strategic positioning of an existing business in that industry, or for a new entrant in an established but stagnant industry.

This might explain highly successful strategies such as the entry of Phillip Morris with Miller Light into the beer industry. Normally, entry into an aging industry is regarded as a highly unnatural and unproductive strategy. The success of Phillip Morris, however, was due to a coherent integrated set of strategies which included: heavy investment in new, modern, and efficient production facilities; introduction of an innovative product with high potential market; and impressive marketing and distribution support. The final effect of this approach was to position Phillip Morris in a completely different experience curve than each one of its competitors.

The entry of Procter and Gamble into the paper towel business against Scott Paper illustrates the need to identify market share by stages of value added. If market share, and therefore accumulated experience, would only be measured by the products sold to the final consumer, one would have concluded that Procter and Gamble had nothing to do in that business. The strong dominance of Procter and Gamble at the marketing and distribution stage of value added, however, allowed them to start with a position much stronger than otherwise anticipated. It is this kind of strategic positioning that has permitted Procter and Gamble to enter late in many other consumer-product markets, without apparently having much of a disadvantage in its cost structure.

Projecting the Cost Structure

Very often high technology firms, where experience plays a fundamental role, have to bid for contracts which, if accepted, would displace them significantly to the right of the experience curve, thus affecting the cost of the units produced. In those cases, it is essential to forecast these cost projections so that the bids will incorporate the cost reduction effects.

If the bid were to be accepted, the firm would now face the imperious need to use those projections, which constituted the base for cost estimates, as a control mechanism. The actual cost being realized would then be plotted in the experience curve charts against the original estimates to detect whatever deviation might be taking place. They would call for immediate managerial attention to correct potential lack of productivity in critical areas.

Conditions similar to those described took place in the aircraft division of a major firm. This firm was successful in simultaneously gaining bids from three government agencies, which pushed its level of production by one order of magnitude. The average cost per unit that was bid was computed, assuming that cost reductions were passed along to the client. This situation required strict control of actual cost in each stage of production to make sure that the final results of those bids were to become profitable for the firm.

The Selection of a Generic Strategy

As we indicated in Chapter 3, Michael Porter (1980) has advocated three major generic strategies to be considered by a firm to identify the position of a given business. The first strategy aims at *cost leadership*, which can only be sustained if the firm is able to achieve lower costs than any of its competitors. This strategy represents the essence of exploiting the experience curve effects.

The second generic strategy seeks for *differentiation* and the basic goal is to attempt to position, in a given business, in a particular way that provides a distinctive thrust over the firm's competitors, aimed at achieving a prominence in the overall industry where the business is placed.

The third basic generic strategy consists of *targeting* a particular market segment where the firm can develop a distinctive strength.

Strategy is basically aimed at securing a long-term sustainable advantage in a competitive market. The three generic strategies discussed above attempt to pursue that goal in quite distinct ways. The justification for this positioning can be understood after recognizing the U-shape effect that is observed in the behavior of profitability of firms competing in some industrial sectors (see Figure 6.13).

The message that emerges from the observation of this curve indicates that if a firm can achieve a certain level of sales that allows the exploitation of the full benefits of the experience curve, strategies leading toward cost leadership could truly pay off. If this is not the case, two basic alternatives are still open, one leading toward unique differentiation, where the firm can enjoy a price-premium based on the special character of products offered, and the other is to resign to compete in the overall industry and find a niche by targeting the output of the firm to a particular market.

The worst alternative is to find oneself in the lower end of the U-curve with no cost advantage and no distinctive value to offer.

— Watneys Brewery (Regional)

Figure 6.13   Changes in Profitability with Market Share

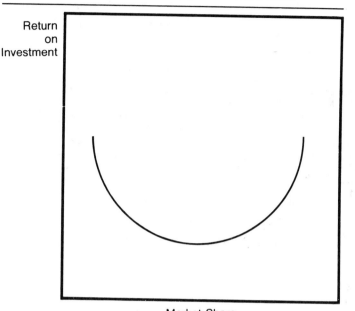

Return on Investment

Market Share

CONCLUSION

We have attempted to discuss the strategic implications of experience effects. The final message should not come as a surprise to any experienced manager. There are no simple answers to complex problems. The experience curve with its implicit message for the benefits to be attained by increased volume of production is still valid and relevant. A blind and narrow pursuit of seeking cost reductions by simply accumulating experience, however, could lead to an unexpectedly adverse position in the market place. A series of warnings has been presented to make the best of the lessons of experience.

REFERENCES

Abernathy, William J., *The Productivity Dilemma: Roadblock to Innovation in the Automobile Industry*, The John Hopkins Press, Baltimore, MD, 1978.

Abernathy, William J., and Kenneth Wayne, "Limits of the Learning Curve," *Harvard Business Review*, Vol. 52, No. 5, September–October 1974, pp. 109–119.

Boston Consulting Group, *Perspectives on Experience*, Boston Consulting Group, Inc., Boston, MA, 1982.

Buzzel, Robert D., Bradley T. Gale, and Ralph G. M. Sultan, "Market Share: A Key to Profitability," *Harvard Business Review*, Vol. 53, No. 1, January–February 1975, pp. 97–106.

Fruhan, William E., "Phyrric Victories in Fights for Market Share," *Harvard Business Review*, Vol. 50, No. 5, September–October 1982, pp. 100–107.

Hax, Arnoldo C., and Nicolas S. Majluf, "Competitive Cost Dynamics: The Experience Curve," *Interfaces*, Vol. 12, No. 5, October 1982, pp. 50–61.

Henderson, Bruce D., *Henderson on Corporate Strategy*, Abt Books, Cambridge, MA, 1979.

Henderson, Bruce D., and Alan J. Zakon, "Pricing Strategy: How to Improve It (The Experience Curve)," in Kenneth J. Albert (editor), *Handbook of Business Problem Solving*, McGraw-Hill, New York, 1980, pp. 3-51–3-68.

Hirschmann, Winfred B., "Profit from the Learning Curve," *Harvard Business Review*, Vol. 42, No. 1, January–February 1964, p. 125.

Porter, Michael E., *Competitive Strategy: Techniques for Analyzing Industries and Competitors*, Free Press, New York, 1980.

Schoeffler, Sidney R., Robert D. Buzzel, and Donald F. Heany, "Impact of Strategic Planning on Profit Performance," *Harvard Business Review*, Vol. 52, No. 2, March–April 1974, pp. 137–145.

7

THE USE OF THE GROWTH-SHARE
MATRIX IN STRATEGIC PLANNING

A decisive impulse for strategic planning activities came from the ideas promoted by the Boston Consulting Group (BCG) in the late 1960s (Henderson 1973, 1979). The essence of the BCG approach is to present the firm in terms of a portfolio of businesses, each one offering a unique contribution with regard to growth and profitability. The firm is then viewed not just as a single monolithic entity, but as composed by many largely independent units whose strategic directions are to be distinctively addressed. Our presentation follows closely Hax and Majluf (1983).

In order to visualize the particular role to be played by each business unit, BCG developed the growth-share matrix, in which each business is plotted on a four-quadrant grid, like the one shown in Figure 7.1. The horizontal axis corresponds to the relative market share enjoyed by a business, as a way of characterizing the strength of the firm in that business. The vertical axis indicates market growth, representing the attractiveness of the market in which the business is positioned. The area within each circle is proportional to the total sales generated by that particular business.

There are three basic insights a manager can gain from the growth-share matrix. First, the graphical display provides a powerful and compact visualization of the strengths of the portfolio of businesses of the firm. Second, it is a mechanism to identify the capability for cash generation as well as the requirements of cash for each business unit, and thus it contributes to assist in balancing the firm cash-flow. And third, because of the distinct characteristics of each business unit, it can suggest unique strategic directions for each business.

We will now proceed to describe the methodology to construct the matrix.

Figure 7.1 A Typical Product Portfolio Chart (Growth-Share Matrix) of a Comparatively Strong and Diversified Company

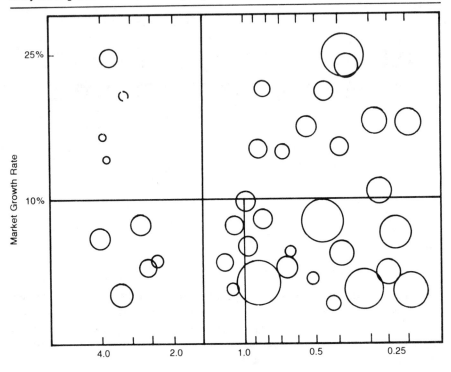

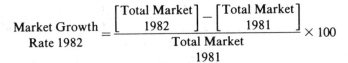

Relative Market Share

MEASURING THE EXTERNAL ATTRACTIVENESS OF THE MARKET

The market-growth rate, which is plotted in the vertical axis of the matrix, is used as a proxy to identify the external attractiveness of the market for each one of the firm's businesses. This measure is based on historical data providing a static picture of the corporation in the last year. For example, at the end of 1982 the market growth rate is measured as follows:

$$\text{Market Growth Rate 1982} = \frac{\left[\begin{array}{c}\text{Total Market} \\ 1982\end{array}\right] - \left[\begin{array}{c}\text{Total Market} \\ 1981\end{array}\right]}{\begin{array}{c}\text{Total Market} \\ 1981\end{array}} \times 100$$

This indicator provides a measure of attractiveness for the total industry irrespective of the position a given firm might have in it. The rationale for its selection stems from the business life-cycle concept, which postulates that a business follows, throughout its entire life, a process of evolution characterized by four stages identified as embryonic, growth, maturity, and aging, as shown in Figure 7.2. There are other factors besides market growth that can assist in positioning a given business in its life cycle. Nonetheless, the growth rate is a key indicator to describe the external attractiveness of that business.

This concept has enormous implications for strategic planning. When the whole industry is growing at a very high rate, it is possible for a firm to penetrate aggressively in that industry and significantly increase its market share, without necessarily eroding the total sales of its competitors. Actual sales will continue to grow for the majority of the key competitors in that industry, thus providing a comfortable feeling to them, without realizing that they may be losing participation in those markets. For a mature or aging business, however, it is no longer possible to gain market share without decreasing the dollar sales of a competitor. Managing a firm in a slow-growth economy is a difficult task.

Further implications of the life-cycle curve for strategic planning have been extensively developed by Arthur D. Little, Inc. which has proposed its own portfolio matrix based on the stages of the business life-cycle (Osell and Wright 1980). This methodology is presented in Chapter 9.

The next step required to position a business in the growth-share portfolio matrix is the selection of a cut off point to separate high growth from low growth businesses. In Figure 7.1, that cut off point is arbitrarily set up at 10%.

How is cut off point selected in practice? Whenever all the businesses of the firm belong to the same industry, the decision is straightforward. The cut off point is selected as the average growth for that industry. When businesses are above the cut off point, they are in the embryonic or growth stage, while if they are below it, they are in the maturity or aging stage. In highly diversified firms, where there is no industry commonality, one might select a measurement of the overall economy growth, such as GNP growth, if the businesses are all conducted within a given country. Otherwise, a weighted average of the growth rate of each individual business seems to be a logical selection. Occasionally, it is legitimate and convenient to set up as a cut off point a corporate growth target, which will separate those businesses which are positively contributing to the realization of the target from those which are detracting from it.

Figure 7.2 The Business Life-Cycle

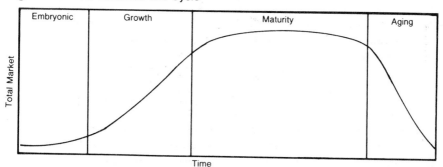

Notice that if market-growth rate is expressed in deflated dollars, the cut off point should measure the real growth of either the industry, economy, or corporate target. If nominal market-growth rates are used, the definition of the cut off point should also involve nominal values.

MEASURING THE INTERNAL STRENGTH OF THE BUSINESS

At first sight, market share seems to be a logical selection to identify the business strength in a competitive environment. What would you say, however, about a firm that in a given business conducts a 10% market share? Is the firm strong or weak? The answer to that question depends on the nature of the fragmentation of the industry in which that business is placed. If the industry were pharmaceutical, most likely the firm would have an extraordinarily strong competitive position; however, if it were the U.S. automobile industry, that firm would be about to collapse. This type of reasoning led to the adoption of relative market share as a measure for the internal strength of a given business. Going back to our 1982 example, relative market share is defined as follows:

$$\text{Relative Market Share 1982} = \frac{\left[\begin{array}{c}\text{Business Sales} \\ 1982\end{array}\right]}{\left[\begin{array}{c}\text{Leading Competitor's} \\ \text{Sales 1982}\end{array}\right]}$$

Notice that this quantity is not expressed as a percentage. It indicates the number of times the sales of a business exceed that of the most important competitor; for example, a relative market share of 2 means that business sales are two times larger than sales of the most important competitor, while a relative market share of 0.5 means that the business sales are only half as much as those of the leading competitor. Moreover, as it can be depicted from Figure 7.1, the relative market share positioning of each business is plotted in the growth-share matrix in a semi-log scale. The reason for this selection is that market share is linked to accumulated volume, and this in turn is related to the experience curve. The decline of costs resulting from the experience curve effect follows a linear relationship when plotted in a semi-log scale.

The strategic implications of the experience curve were analyzed in Chapter 6. Briefly stated:

Higher Market Share $\rightarrow$ Higher Accumulated Volume $\rightarrow$ Lower Unit Costs $\rightarrow$ Higher Profitability

The growth-share matrix requires the identification of a cut off point to separate between businesses of high and low internal strength. It should come as no surprise, after recalling Henderson's rule of three and four discussed in

Chapter 6 and presented in Henderson (1979), that in its initial proposition BCG selected a relative market share of 1.0 to perform this distinction. This implies that only being the market leader (that is, having a relative market share greater than one), can carry significant strength. Moreover, as is apparent from Figure 7.1, the basic cut off line has been drawn at a relative market share of 1.5, because only by enjoying that kind of competitive advantage, a firm can truly exercise a significant dominance in a business.

MEASURING THE CONTRIBUTION OF EACH BUSINESS UNIT TO THE FIRM

Besides positioning a business in terms of its industry attractiveness and competitive strength, there is a third parameter that is used in the growth-share matrix to characterize the portfolio of the firm. This parameter is the contribution of the business to the firm, which is measured in terms of sales, and is represented by the area within the circles in the matrix in Figure 7.1.

Sales is preferred as a measure of contribution, because it provides an easier comparison standard against the portfolio of the firm's competitors. In fact, sales is an acceptable measure to compare the fundamental strengths and weaknesses of all firms competing in an industry, given the difficulty of obtaining profitability figures for business segments by competitors. Moreover, even at the internal level, the use of profits or return on investments as measurements of the business contribution of the firm, might imply an arbitrary allocation of overhead that will tend to distort the true contribution of the business by accounting manipulations.

CASH-FLOW IMPLICATIONS OF THE GROWTH-SHARE MATRIX

A striking characteristic of the growth-share matrix is its simplicity. It attempts to capture the complex nature of a business portfolio by means of a graphical representation containing only the three indicators to which we have previously alluded.

There are several implications that emerge from this business categorization, the most important one being centered on the transfer of cash among businesses. To visualize the cash flow transactions it is useful to reexpress the same growth-share matrix, in terms of the cash-use and cash-generation dimensions being portrayed in Figure 7.3.

The separation suggested in the previous section divides the business portfolio into four quadrants. The businesses in each quadrant have distinctive characteristics with regard to cash flow, and have been labelled in what is today a very popular jargon which we will now present.

Figure 7.3 Cash-Flow Characteristics of Business Categories in the Growth-Share Matrix

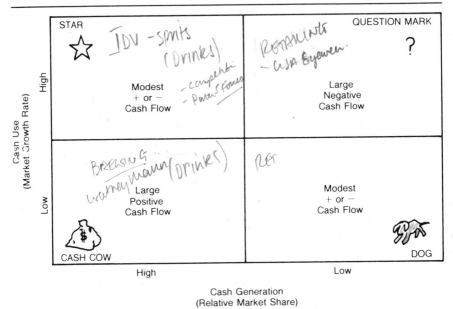

1. *The Stars.*

    These businesses are located in the upper-left corner of the matrix. They are highly attractive businesses (high market growth), in which the firm has established a strong competitive position (high relative market share). They generate large amounts of cash, because of their successful status, but at the same time, require a significant inflow of cash resources if the firm wants to sustain its competitive strength in that rapidly growing market. As a result, the final excess of cash contributed to or the deficit required from the overall organization is relatively modest.

2. *The Cash Cows.*

    These businesses are the central sources of cash for the organization. Because of their extremely high competitive strength in a declining market, they generate more cash than they can wisely reinvest into themselves. Therefore, they represent a source of large positive cash that could be available to support the development of other businesses within the firm. Incidentally, this fact clearly corroborates that, ultimately, the resource allocation process has to be centralized at a higher managerial level in the organization. Otherwise, the manager of a cash cow will tend to reinvest the proceeds of its business in its own domain, suboptimizing the uses of its resources.

3. *The Question Marks.*

    These businesses correspond to major untapped opportunities, which appear as very attractive because of the high market-growth rate they enjoy.

The firm, however, has not achieved a significant presence in the corresponding market. A decision is called for selectively identifying among them those businesses that can be successfully promoted to a leading position. This is a key strategic decision in this planning approach that carries with it the assignment of large amounts of cash to a business, because reaching a leading position in a rapidly growing market requires committing important cash resources.

At the same time, the firm might be ready to admit that its internal strengths are not appropriate for advancing a business, in spite of its high degree of attractiveness, because of the characteristics of the competitors the firm faces. This would call for the toughest of decisions: An admission that the best course of action to follow is to withdraw or liquidate.

4. *The Dogs.*

These businesses are clearly the great losers: unattractive and weak. They are normally regarded as "cash traps," because whatever little cash they generate is needed for maintaining their operations. If there is no legitimate reason to suspect a turnaround in the near future, the logical strategy to follow would be harvesting or divesting.

SUGGESTIONS FOR STRATEGIC POSITIONING

In order to discuss some of the suggestions that can be extracted out of the growth-share matrix for the strategic positioning of each one of the businesses of a firm, we are going to present first the basic philosophy underlying this approach to strategic planning.

The primary objectives of the corporation, which are implicit in the conceptualization initially done by BCG, are growth and profitability (Henderson and Zakon 1980). The argument is that the fundamental advantage that a multibusiness organization possesses is the ability to transfer cash from those businesses which are highly profitable, but have a limited potential for growth, to those which offer attractive expectations for a sustained future growth and profitability.

This philosophy leads to an integrative management of the portfolio that will make the whole larger than the sum of the parts. For this synergistic result to be obtained, a fairly centralized resource allocation process would be required which would produce a balanced portfolio in terms of the generation and uses of cash.

It is important to observe that the two dimensions used to position each business in the growth-share matrix have, as indicated in the previous section, profound implications on the issue of cash generation and cash requirements. In the association of relative market share with the experience curve, it is implicit that those businesses holding stronger shares will enjoy also higher profitability and consequently, higher cash generation. On the other dimension, those businesses pertaining to industries with higher growth rates will definitively require higher levels of cash for their future development.

Although it can be argued that a firm has access to external sources of cash, primarily through debt and equity issuing, inherent in the BCG approach is the belief that ultimately, any source of external debt will have to be sustained by a matching of internal cash flow. Therefore, the balanced assignment of internal cash resources becomes a vital concern for the proper development of the firm.

Another contribution of BCG, besides the balanced portfolio idea, resides in their selection of market share to express the basic strategic positioning desired for each business. They chose to identify four major strategic thrusts in terms of market share:

—Increase market share
—Hold market share
—Harvest
—Withdraw or divest

Although the realization of these strategic thrusts would demand spelling out the content of multifunctional programs for each business, it is unarguable that the thrusts expressed in terms of market share reveal the basic message for the desired positioning of a business in a competitive environment. This way of articulating the strategic thrust in terms of market share has been adapted by most of the alternative methodologies for portfolio analysis.

We should emphasize the different role that market share is playing as a proxy for strategic positioning as opposed to a simple description of business strength. When we use market share to designate a strategic thrust, we are attempting to summarize in a compact way what our basic intentions are in terms of the long term positioning of the business. Although normally a strategy is formed by a complex set of action programs that affect all levels of the organization, there is a forceful message implicit in just providing the market share objective to communicate the ultimate thrust of the strategy selected for a business.

Other portfolio analyses question the use of market share as an indicator of business strength, contending that there are many other factors that should be considered to establish the true competitive positioning of a business within an industry. Most of the alternative approaches to BCG, however, still retain the four categories of market share thrust as a robust way of summarizing the final direction selected for a business.

A summary of the basic suggestion for strategic positioning that emerges from the growth-share matrix, with regard to market-share thrust and cash-flow implications, is presented in Figure 7.4, which can be inferred by going back to the strategic and cash flow implications discussed in this and the previous sections. It may be observed that the cash-flow is assigned primarily from the highly positive pool of cash resources left over by cash-cow businesses, to the highly negative cash balance obtained in the selected question-market businesses whose market share to be increased.

When expanding the strategic implications of the portfolio analysis to more

Figure 7.4 Implications for Strategic Positioning Emerging from the Growth-Share Matrix

Business Category	Market Share Thrust	Business Profitability	Investment Required	Net Cash Flow
Stars	Hold/Increase	High	High	Around zero or slightly negative
Cash Cows	Hold	High	Low	Highly positive
Question Marks	Increase ╱ ﹡ ╲ Harvest/Divest	None or negative Low or negative	Very High Disinvest	Highly negative Positive
Dogs	Harvest/Divest	Low or negative	Disinvest	Positive

* There is a selective application of the strategy depending on the decision made with regard to the business: either to enter aggressively or withdraw.

than one period, we need some guidelines to judge the desirability of business movements in the growth-share matrix. In Figure 7.5 we can observe that the ideal sequence is one in which the first stage shows the transition of a question mark that gains in size and strength to become a star, and the second stage corresponds to the inevitable decline in the growth rate with the retention of the competitive strength that characterizes the final transition into a cash-cow. The figure also exhibits the undesirable sequences of evolution which might eventually lead to a catastrophic loss for the firm, due to the weak position that is finally achieved in the market, despite the sales increase shown by the areas of the circles in that figure.

FURTHER REFINEMENTS FOR THE ANALYSIS OF A PORTFOLIO OF BUSINESSES USING THE GROWTH-SHARE MATRIX

Measuring the Historical Evolution of the Growth-Share Positioning

One could argue that the graphical representation of the growth-share matrix described so far provides just a static snapshot of the business portfolio of a firm ignoring the historical trends of those businesses. We will now address this concern.

A very powerful tool that has been used to understand the implicit or explicit strategies of a firm is depicted in Figure 7.6 in the so-called "Share-Momentum Graph" (Lewis 1977).

The graph is constructed by picking a relevant time-frame, say five years, and by plotting the position of each business unit in terms of two dimensions: the total market growth for that period and the growth rate of sales for that

Figure 7.5   Conceptual Sequences of Business Evolution

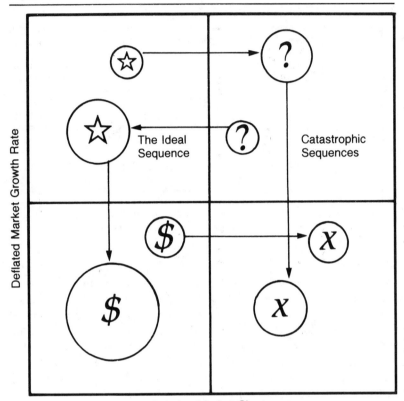

Relative Market Share

business unit for the same period. These values should be defined consistently either in nominal or real terms. As before, the area within each circle is proportional to the total sales of each business for the last year of the chosen period.

Those businesses falling in the diagonal have grown at exactly the same rate as the industry, and therefore, the firm has been able to hold market share during the period of analysis. Businesses falling below the diagonal have increased their sale at a rate higher than their respective markets. Such is the case of businesses A, B, and C in Figure 7.6. Obviously, this can only happen if those businesses have increased market share over the last five years. The opposite is true for businesses falling above the diagonal, such as businesses D and E in the same figure.

The implications of this chart are straightforward but yet quite revealing. It is entirely possible that a business in a high growth industry experiences a gain in net sales during the year while losing market share. If managers are not cognizant of this fact, they might feel quite proud of their historical performance, ignoring the grave consequences of their decline in competitive strength.

Figure 7.6   Example of a Share-Momentum Graph

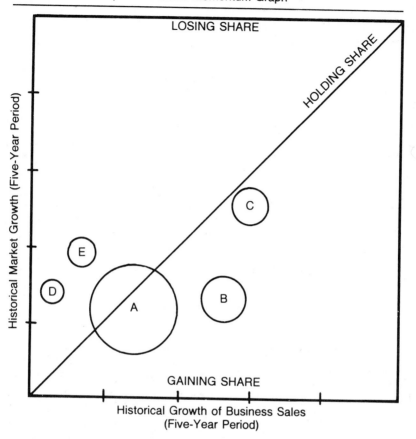

Thus, the chart provides a meaningful diagnostic tool to detect the observable trends in the growth-share positioning of their businesses, and in verifying the degree of consistency that might exist between the historical trend and the intended strategic positioning of the business.

Another use of the share-momentum chart is to apply it not only to our own firm but also to all our key competitors. The information required to develop this chart for all key competitors is basically the same information used to put together the original growth-share matrix; that is, total market figures and competitors' sales information. By properly analyzing the share-momentum chart for each competitor, we end up with a valuable intelligence with regard to their strategies. This information could reveal areas of vulnerability of key competitors that can be advantageously exploited, or areas with unsurmountable barriers for a firm to penetrate them.

Figures 7.7 and 7.8 show the growth-share matrix and the share-momentum matrix for the paper-related business of Boise-Cascade as of the end of 1979.

Figure 7.7   The Growth-Share Matrix of Boise Cascade

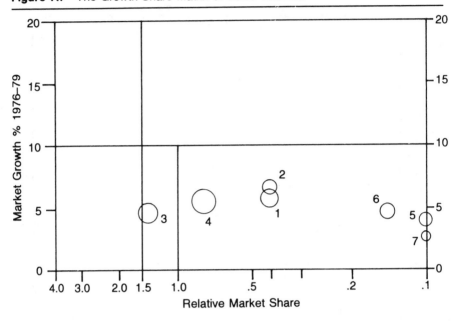

The information used in preparing this chart was extracted from publicly available records. What conclusions could be drawn by looking solely at the growth-
share matrix? Obviously, one would recognize that the whole paper industry
is plagued by slow growth, making it relatively unattractive. Moreover, Boise
Cascade seems to have a commanding strength just in business segment 3 in
that industry. Finally, it would seem clear that Boise's presence in business
segments 5 and 7 is so weak that it can be safely assumed that they might be
consciously divesting themselves out of those businesses. Now turn your attention
to the share-momentum graph in Figure 7.8. Some of the preliminary conclusions
seem to be corroborated but a major surprise is contained in the positioning
of business segment 7 in that graph. Far from abandoning that business, Boise
has experienced an extraordinary increase in market share during the last years.

A different approach to capture the dynamic nature of a portfolio is to use
the original growth-share matrix to portray the historical movements of each
business unit through a sequence of time periods (see Figure 7.9). We have
found this tool not to be as effective as a share-momentum chart, because of
the erratic variations that often are observed in a yearly analysis, and the clumsi-
ness of the resulting chart when a five-year time frame is represented in it.
Also the cut-off point to separate high from low market growth tends to change
each year. This could be remedied by simply using an average growth rate
for the five year period; however, such an average might distort the final representation of the portfolio by hiding important clues for strategic analysis which

Figure 7.8   The Share-Momentum Matrix of Boise Cascade

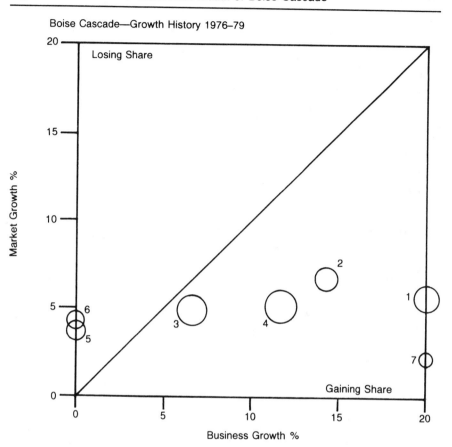

Boise Cascade—Growth History 1976–79

are only revealed by the yearly representation of data. An illustration of this approach is described in Hax and Majluf (1978).

Maximum Sustainable Growth

A concept developed by Zakon (1976), the maximum-sustainable growth, pointed to a critical dimension of the growth objective of the firm. It represents the maximum growth that the firm can support by using its internal resources as well as its debt capabilities. Expressed in very simple terms, Zakon derived the following formula for the maximum-sustainable growth:

$$g = p \cdot [ROA + \frac{D}{E}(ROA - i)]$$

Figure 7.9 Portfolio Dynamics Over a Two-Year Period Represented in a Growth-Share Matrix

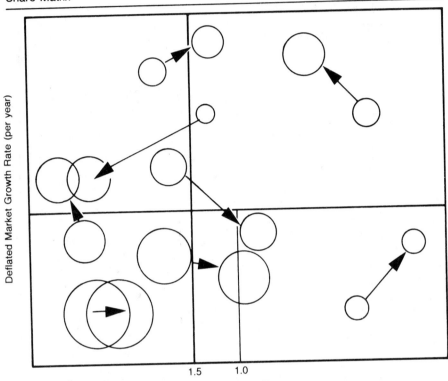

Relative Market Share

where:

g = maximum-sustainable growth, expressed as a yearly rate of increase of the equity base

p = percentage of retained earnings

ROA = after-tax return on assets

D = total debt outstanding

E = total equity

i = after-tax interest on debt

This formula is derived through the following steps. Total assets are computed as total debt plus total equity as indicated below:

$$A = D + E.$$

Therefore, after-tax profits may be computed as:

$$\Pi = (D + E) \cdot ROA - D \cdot i.$$

An equivalent expression for it is:

$$\Pi = E \cdot ROA + D(ROA - i).$$

The maximum growth of equity depends on the amount of retained earnings. Assuming that p is the retention ratio (equal to retained earnings over total earnings) and that g is the growth of equity, we can establish the following relation:

$$g = \frac{p \cdot \Pi}{E} = p \cdot [ROA + \frac{D}{E} \cdot (ROA - i)].$$

If we assume that the debt-equity ratio remains constant, and that the increment of equity will be followed by a similar increment of debt, we can conclude that the expression above corresponds to the actual growth of total assets under the stated conditions.

The expression just derived represents a first cut and gross approximation of the maximum-sustainable growth that assumes a stable debt-equity ratio and dividend-payout policy, as well as a fixed overall rate of return on assets and cost of debt. Although a coarse approximation, this number might represent a guidance for corporate growth that should be taken into consideration at a corporate level.

There are many variations of alternative expressions for the maximum-sustainable growth. Our aim has been to present the simplest of those expressions, so as to stress the underlying concept which is that a firm faces an upper bound in its objectives for future growth when the financing policy does not consider the issuing of new shares.

THE HIERARCHICAL NATURE OF THE APPLICATION OF THE GROWTH-SHARE MATRIX

The growth-share matrix is primarily intended to analyze a portfolio from a corporate perspective. It is only at that level where the fundamental message of cash balance is meaningful. However, it is perfectly legitimate to continue the segmentation of a business further in the organizational hierarchy as a diagnostic tool to understand the different positioning of individual product lines or market segments belonging to a given business.

To illustrate the application of the growth-share matrix in a hierarchical fashion, we will use the Norton Company as an example (Cushman 1979). Figure 7.10 represents the overall portfolio of Norton, a firm that was confronted with a crucial strategic decision. The base of the traditional Norton businesses resided on its leading presence in the abrasive industry, which was faced with severe cyclicalities and low growth rate. Norton understood in the middle of the 1960s the imperative need to use these profitable businesses as a way to diversify into more attractive highly growing opportunities. The company used the growth-share matrix as the primary instrument to build a successful strategy of diversification away from the abrasive industry.

Figure 7.10   Corporate Growth-Share Portfolio of the Norton Company

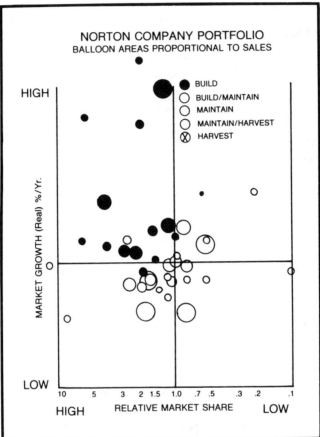

Source: Robert Cushman, "Norton's Top-Down, Bottom-Up Planning Process," © 1979, p. 6. Reprinted by permission of *Planning Review*, a bimonthly publication of the North American Society for Corporate Planning, Inc. Dayton, OH.

Figure 7.10 addresses the basic message for Norton diversification. It gives a classification of all business units in terms of the four categories whose strategic implications we have already discussed. Although it conveys a fairly meaningful message for the corporation as a whole, it is insufficient to guide the decisions of the individual managers of Norton businesses, who, legitimately, would demand a finer segmentation of the unit under their jurisdiction. Figure 7.11 provides a finer analysis of the various market segments that are part of a business unit which is characterized as a monolithic entity at the corporate level. Now we can appreciate the various contributions of those market segments to the overall business unit. A cursory look at the graph will indicate that

Figure 7.11 A Finer Analysis at the Level of One Business Unit of the Norton Company

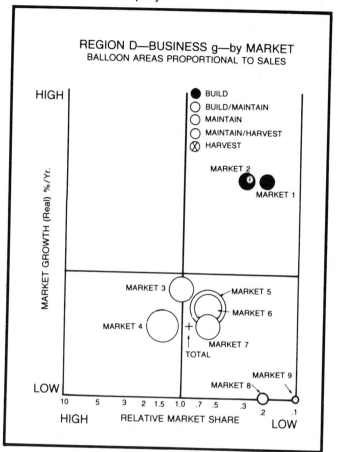

Source: Robert Cushman, "Norton's Top-Down, Bottom-Up Planning Process," © 1979, p. 6 or 7. Reprinted by permission of *Planning Review,* a bimonthly publication of the North American Society for Corporate Planning, Inc. Dayton, OH.

markets 1 and 2, the most attractive ones in terms of growth, exhibit a very weak position on the part of Norton. This might suggest that a competitor is "cherry-picking"; that is, concentrating a significant amount of effort on those market segments which appear to be most attractive. Moreover, businesses 8 and 9 are in such a dismal positioning that the only worthwhile strategy to pursue seems to be one of complete withdrawal. The ability to discriminate among components of a given business unit, being either product lines or market segments, proves to be a valuable diagnostic tool for the application of the growth-share matrix at the business unit level.

Another important segmentation which is crucial to multinational firms is to position a business unit across the various countries it serves. Normally, the most puzzling and difficult issue to be resolved by a business manager in a multinational setting is to deal with the complexities posed by contradictory positions of a given business in various countries. Using the BCG terminology, what could be a Star in the U.S. might be a Cash Cow in Colombia, a Dog in Germany, and a Question Mark in Saudi Arabia. It is a nontrivial matter to come out with a coherent international strategy under that situation. Figure 7.12 presents a segmentation of a given business unit of Norton across several countries. It is a surprising portfolio because all countries exhibit almost identical market growth rates. The only substantial difference is the strength of Norton

Figure 7.12 A Finer Analysis of a Multinational Business Unit of the Norton Company

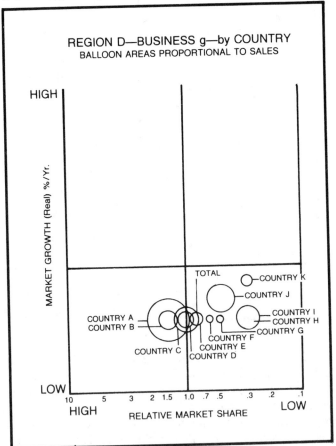

Source: Robert Cushman, "Norton's Top-Down, Bottom-Up Planning Process," © 1979, p. 6 or 7. Reprinted by permission of *Planning Review*, a bimonthly publication of the North American Society for Corporate Planning, Inc. Dayton, OH.

in each one of them. This is an atypical example, but a real one. Sometimes, reality offers amazing surprises.

A CRITIQUE OF THE BCG APPROACH

An Issue of Nomenclature

A common complaint about the approach popularized by BCG is the selection of labels that were used to classify the positioning of the various businesses of the firm. Recently, Andrews (1981) described it as a "vulgar and destructive vocabulary." In practice, the terminology has been widely accepted, in spite of its somehow derogatory connotation. For example, who wants to manage a Cash Cow or a Dog?

Mead Company, which has forcefully embraced this portfolio approach as a strategic tool, has selected what we believe is a better designation for its business units as illustrated in Figure 7.13 (Aguilar 1978).

The Reliance on Market Definition

We indicated in Chapter 6 that it could be a severe pitfall to measure the performance and, therefore, the competitive strength of the firm, on the achieved

Figure 7.13 Mead Corporation Business Strategic Matrix

		Savings Account	Sweepstake
	HIGH	*Savings Account* • Growing businesses • Self financing • Medium risk • High profit • Should maintain cost-effectiveness	*Sweepstake* • Developing businesses • Net cash user • Extremely high risk • Low profit • Not cost-effective
Market Growth %	10%		
	LOW	*Bond* • Mature business • Net cash generator • Low risk • High profit • Cost-effective	*Mortgages* • Mature business • Should be net cash generator • Medium risk • Low profit • Probably not cost-effective
		HIGH 1.5 LOW	
		Relative Market Share	

From Francis J. Aguilar, *The Mead Corporation: Strategic Planning*. Boston: Harvard Business School, Case 9-379-070. Reprinted by permission.

market-share at the end of the value added chain. The question of shared resources among various businesses at each functional level cannot be ignored.
This issue is not addressed by measuring market share at the consumer end.
For the growth-share matrix to provide a clear representation of the profitability
and competitive strength of each business, it is mandatory that each of the
business units portrayed in the matrix are totally independent and autonomous.
If this is not the case, we might face misleading representations; that is, Dogs
which are very healthy, Cash Cows which have no milk, Question Marks which
are not questionable, and Stars which are not shining.

In a rather hilarious commentary published in *Fortune* magazine (*Fortune*
1981), Kiechel described in the following way the implications of the BCG
approach.

> A balance portfolio, according to this scheme consisted a few stars shining
> away, getting ready to be cows; the bovinity throwing off cash and occasionally
> dwindling toward dogdom; and the promising question marks, in their pursuit
> of stardom, eating cash from the cows. Any money obtained from selling off the
> kennel should be employed to buy or finance question markets.*

Obviously, managing a business portfolio cannot be reduced to such a simplistic
formula. BCG never intended its tool to be applied so naively.

Another important issue has to do with the definition of the proper market
in which a business competes. Relative market share is an index that compares
a business's strength in relation to a competitor's. This introduces a subtle
issue concerning the definition of the market we use as a yardstick to measure
the business position. There are two traps that one could fall into: one is to
define the market so narrowly that we will end up invariably as the leader of
the segment; the opposite is to define it so broadly that the business is unrealisti-
cally represented as weak. A proper market definition is, as we said before, a
very subtle issue. It is unfortunate that this approach to business analysis rests
so heavily on such an imponderable matter.

Validity of the Indicators Needed to Measure Internal Strength and Market Opportunities

There are two separate issues that one could raise in terms of the indicators
used in the growth-share matrix for positioning the different business units.
The first one relates to the causality of the measurements selected to identify
profitability and growth. Is market share really a major underlying factor determining profitability? Is industry growth really the only variable that can fully
explain growth opportunities? Certainly, these are questions subject to a great
deal of debate.

The second but related objection to the indicators selected in this approach
is that a true portfolio positioning should attempt to identify the competitive

---

strengths and the industry attractiveness of each business unit. All portfolio representations offered as alternatives to the growth-share matrix depart from this approach by establishing that these two dimensions cannot be grasped by a single measurement, but are the composite result of a wider set of critical factors which need to be identified and assessed prior to producing a final positioning of the business units.

A Challenge to the Basic Premises of the BCG Approach: Marakon's Views

Marakon, a management consulting company, has presented a theoretically better grounded approach for strategic investment planning, which represents a significant challenge to the conclusions derived from the growth-share approach.

Marakon's views can be summarized in the following three statements (Marakon 1980):

—Growth and profitability are not generally tightly linked. In fact they tend to compete or tradeoff.

—Good planning should not call for passing up profitable investment opportunities.

—Ideal business portfolios are not necessarily balanced in terms of internal cash flows.

We will now briefly analyze these three statements.

The fact that growth and profitability tend to compete can be easily seen from the implications in Figure 7.14, where return on investment (ROI), a well-accepted measurement of profitability, is plotted against business growth to describe the investment options available to a given business unit. The horizontal cut-off line represents the busines-unit cost of capital. Any investment option that falls above the line implies an attractive investment opportunity. The vertical cut-off line identifies the market growth rate for that business unit. A strategy that falls on that line corresponds to a holding market-share strategy; one to the left of the line implies a decreasing market-share strategy; one to the right of the line implies an increasing market-share strategy.

As can be seen from the figure, a decreasing share strategy should be much more selective in the acceptance of its investment projects, thus leading to a higher ROI. Contrarywise, an increasing share strategy would have to accept more marginal projects, thus reducing the resulting ROI. This represents the profitability-growth tradeoff alluded to by Marakon.

Sound financial principles would suggest that a firm should accept all projects above its cost of capital. This will favor the increasing share strategy depicted in Figure 7.14, regardless of the position of the business in the growth-share matrix.

The second statement of Marakon—that a firm should not pass up profitable investment opportunities—is directly linked to the previous argument. More formally, it is supported by the so-called *additivity principle* which states that every investment opportunity should be judged on its own merits and should

Figure 7.14   The Tradeoff Between Profitability and Growth

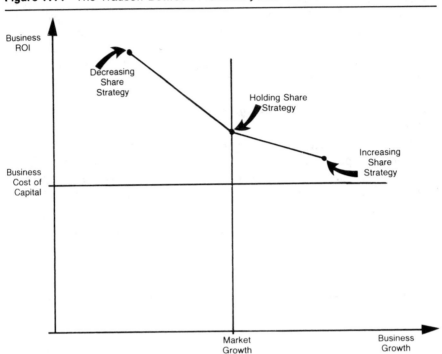

be accepted or rejected depending on whether its projected return on investment falls above or below the cost of capital associated with that investment opportunity. In other words, there are no magic financial synergisms. The value of the firm is simply equal to the sum of the values of its components.

To explain the third statement of Marakon—that ideal portfolios are not necessarily balanced—it is useful to understand first the implications of cash generation and cash use in terms of the profitability and growth dimensions. Figure 7.15 provides a valuable insight into this question. The vertical axis corresponds to the ROE earned by a given business and the horizontal axis represents the corresponding business equity growth. A business placed in the diagonal is growing at the same rate of its ROE, and neither generates cash to or requires cash from the firm: it is a cash-neutral business. Similarly, businesses above the diagonal are cash generators and those below the diagonal are cash users.

To understand this line of reasoning, consider that the total equity investment in the business is E and the earnings generated are Π. By the definition of return on equity (ROE), we can state that

$$\Pi = E \cdot ROE.$$

If we apply all earnings to the same business in order to tap new investment

Figure 7.15 Cash Generation and Cash Use Characteristics of a Business in Terms of Its Growth and Profitability

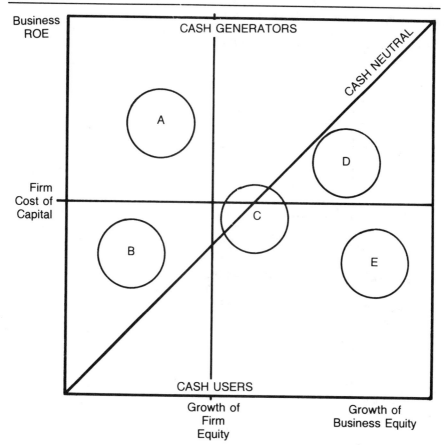

opportunities, the business growth as measured by the growth of the total investment is

$$g = \frac{\Pi}{E}.$$

This ratio is precisely the ROE of the business. Therefore, we can assert that a business growing at the same rate of its ROE is cash neutral from the corporate perspective.

We can see that there can be good businesses (that is, businesses that earn more than the cost of capital) that generate cash (for example, business A), while others require cash (for example, business D). Similarly, cases depicted as B and E are examples of poor businesses that generate and require cash, respectively.

Figure 7.16 Examples of the Relation Between the Goodness of a Portfolio and Its Cash-Balance

a) Highly Profitable Unbalanced Portfolio

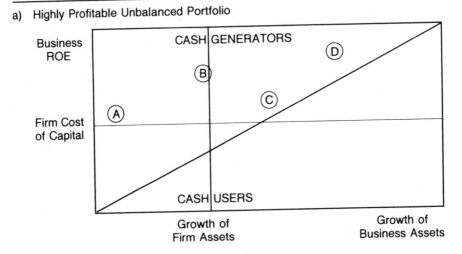

b) Balanced Portfolio with Low Profitability

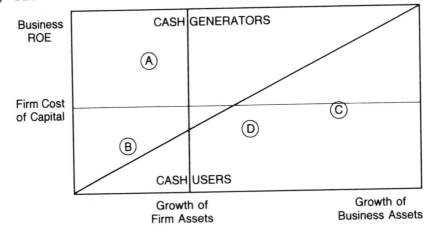

The final message became clear in Figure 7.16. We can observe that a highly profitable portfolio may well be out of cash balance, while a rather poor portfolio may be perfectly balanced. The profitability matrix and its implications for strategic planning are comprehensively discussed in Chapter 10.

THE NEW BCG APPROACH: A STRATEGY FOR THE EIGHTIES

We would like to conclude this chapter by describing briefly the new matrix advocated by BCG in response to the misleading use of the growth-share matrix, as well as to the changing nature of the competitive environment faced by business firms. Commenting on the 1981 BCG Annual Perspective, Lockridge expresses:

> In the 1970's, high inflation coupled with low growth, increased competition in the traditional fields, added regulation, and dramatic growth in international trade, again changed the rules of the game. Strategies in pursuit of market share and low-cost position alone met unexpected difficulties as segments specialists arose and multiple competitors reached economies of scale. The most successful companies achieved their success by anticipating market evolution and creating unique and defensible advantages over their competitors in the new environment.

To characterize this new environment, BCG proposes a new matrix following two different dimensions: The size of the competitive advantage, and the number of unique ways in which that advantage can be achieved. The resulting matrix and the new four-quadrant grid is shown in Figure 7.17, where four categories of businesses are recognized: Volume, Stalemate, Fragmented, and Specialization.

It is only in the Volume business where the previous strategies of market-share leadership and cost reduction are still meaningful. In this category, one would continue to observe a close association between market-share and profitability, as shown in Figure 7.18. A typical example of this industry would be the American automobile prior to the emergence of foreign competitors.

The Stalemate businesses are in industries where profitability is low for all competitors and it is not related to the size of the firm. The difference between the most profitable and the least profitable firm is relatively small (see Figure 7.18). The American steel industry provides an illustration of this category.

The profitability of businesses in the Fragmented category is uncorrelated with market share (see Figure 7.18). There are poor performers which are both

Figure 7.17 The New BCG Matrix

Number of Approaches to Achieve Advantage	Many	Fragmented	Specialization
	Few	Stalemate	Volume
		Small	Large
		Size of the Advantage	

Figure 7.18   Underlying Relationships Between ROI and Market Share in the New BCG Matrix

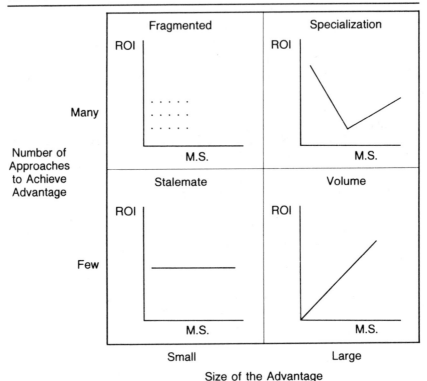

large and small firms, and there are good performers also independent of size. Their performance depends on how the firm exploits the very many ways to achieve a competitive advantage. A typical example in this category would be restaurants.

Finally, the Specialization category shows that the most attractive profitability is enjoyed by the smallest businesses which are able to distinguish themselves among their competitors by pursuing a focused strategy (see Figure 7.18). The Japanese automobile manufacturers pursue that strategy for entering the American automobile industry.

It is our interpretation of this matrix that the horizontal axis, pertaining to the size of the advantage, is definitively linked to the barriers of entry, because it is only with high barriers that a firm could sustain a long term defensible advantage over its competitors. Likewise, the number of approaches to achieve advantages seems to be strongly linked to the issue of differentiation. At the extremes of the differentiation range we encounter the commodity and specialty products.

CONCLUSION

The growth-share matrix made a major contribution to strategic thinking. It was particularly useful to support managerial decisions during the sixties and early seventies, when the U.S. economy was still exhibiting a reasonably healthy growth. These days, a naive use of the matrix could lead to inappropriate and misleading strategic recommendations.

In this chapter, we have attempted to provide a broad and critical analysis of the growth-share matrix, suggesting warnings and refinements for its applications.

REFERENCES

Aguilar, Francis J., "The Mead Corporation—Strategic Planning," Harvard Business School, Case 9-379-070, Boston, MA, 1978.

Andrews, Kenneth R., "Replaying the Board's Role in Formulating Strategy," *Harvard Business Review*, May–June 1981, pp. 18–19, 24–26.

Cushman, Robert, "Norton's Top-Down, Bottom-Up Planning Process," *Planning Review*, November 1979, pp. 3–8, 48.

Fortune, "Oh Where, Oh Where Has my Little Dog Gone? Or My Cash Cow? Or My Star?," November 2, 1981, pp. 148–154.

Hax, Arnoldo C., and Nicolas S. Majluf, "A Methodological Approach for the Development of Strategic Planning in Diversified Corporations," in Arnoldo C. Hax (editor), *Studies in Operations Management*, North-Holland, Amsterdam, 1978, pp. 41–98.

Hax, Arnoldo C., and Nicolas S. Majluf, "The Use of the Growth-Share Matrix in Strategic Planning," *Interfaces*, Vol. 13, No. 1, February 1983, pp. 46–60.

Henderson, Bruce D., "The Experience Curve Reviewed, IV. The Growth Share Matrix of the Product Portfolio," The Boston Consulting Group, Perspectives, No. 135, Boston, MA, 1973.

Henderson, Bruce D., *Henderson on Corporation Strategy*, Abt Books, Cambridge, MA, 1979.

Henderson, Bruce D., and Alan J. Zakon, "Corporate Growth Strategy: How to Develop and Implement It," in Kenneth J. Albert (editor), *Handbook of Business Problem Solving*, McGraw-Hill, New York, 1980, pp. 1.3–1.19.

Lewis, W. Walker, *Planning by Exception*, Strategic Planning Associates, Washington, D.C., 1977.

Marakon Associates, "Criteria for Determining Optimal Business Portfolio," Presentation made at The Institute of Management Sciences, November 11, 1980.

Osell, Robert R., and Robert V. L. Wright, "Allocating Resources: How to Do It in Multi-Industry Corporations," in Kenneth J. Albert (editor), *Handbook of Business Problem Solving*, McGraw-Hill, New York, 1980, pp. 1.89–1.109.

Zakon, Alan J., "Capital Structure Optimization," in J. F. Weston and M. B. Goudzwaard (editors), *The Treasurer's Handbook*, Dow Jones-Irwin, Homewood, IL, 1976.

8

THE USE OF THE INDUSTRY ATTRACTIVENESS-BUSINESS STRENGTH MATRIX IN STRATEGIC PLANNING

ESSENTIAL ELEMENTS OF THE ATTRACTIVENESS-STRENGTH MATRIX

In the early seventies, General Electric was exposed to the ideas then sponsored by the Boston Consulting Group, which are espoused in the growth-share matrix approach. GE found that approach quite appealing, particularly the ability to display in a visual representation the portfolio of the businesses of the firm in terms of two central dimensions: the industry attractiveness for each respective business, and the internal strength that the firm commands in that business. The value of such a tool for a multi-business organization was quickly detected by GE, especially for assigning priorities to each business leading toward rational investment and resource allocation decisions.

The primary objection raised by GE to the use of the growth-share matrix was the reliance upon single descriptors to characterize industry attractiveness (that is total market growth rate), and business strength (such as relative market share). It was concluded that a wide variety of critical factors, other than those enumerated in the growth-share matrix, needed to be identified and assessed in order to construct an appropriate business portfolio representation. Accordingly, GE retained the services of McKinsey and Company to develop what is now a highly popular and powerful portfolio approach: the industry attractiveness-business strength matrix. Our presentation of this subject follows Hax and Majluf (1983).

Figure 8.1 depicts the basic elements of the attractiveness-strength matrix. Prior to explaining in detail the necessary steps to implement this matrix, we will present an overview of its primary elements. They are the identification and assessment of both external and internal factors, and the suggestions for strategic action.

The identification of critical external factors, which are noncontrollable by the firm, leads to the determination of the overall attractiveness of the industry in which the business belongs. Figure 8.1 lists some external factors that have proven to be useful, in a variety of situations, to assess the attractiveness dimension.

In a similar way, we need to identify the critical internal factors, also called *critical success factors*, which are largely controllable by the firm. The position that a business achieves in these factors, vis-a-vis the key competitors, will determine the ultimate strength possessed by the firm in each business. Again, Figure 8.1 provides an illustrative list of such factors. Notice that many of them (sales, marketing, R&D, customer services, manufacturing, and distribution) represent managerial functions. This serves to emphasize the fact that, ultimately, a strategy has to be defined in terms of specific multi-functional programs for each business.

Once external and internal factors are identified, we have to assess these factors and position each business in terms of overall industry attractiveness and business strength. A nine-cell grid results, as indicated in Figure 8.1, by using three categories (high, medium, and low) to classify both attractiveness and strength.

The suggestion for strategic actions are expressed in terms of the following basic thrusts:

—Invest to grow
—Selectivity to grow
—Selectivity
—Harvest or Divest.

A METHODOLOGY FOR THE DEVELOPMENT AND USE OF THE ATTRACTIVENESS-STRENGTH MATRIX

Figure 8.2 identifies the major steps for the implementation of the attractiveness-strength matrix. A clear separation has been made between the current state and future projections in the assessment of internal and external factors. The positioning of each business unit in the current state simply involves an objective evaluation of the overall industry attractiveness and business strength performed with historical and actual data. However, the future positioning requires predict-

Figure 8.1   The Industry Attractiveness—Business Strength Matrix

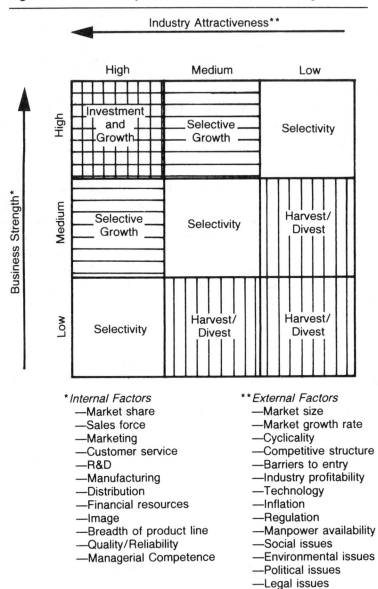

* *Internal Factors*
  —Market share
  —Sales force
  —Marketing
  —Customer service
  —R&D
  —Manufacturing
  —Distribution
  —Financial resources
  —Image
  —Breadth of product line
  —Quality/Reliability
  —Managerial Competence

** *External Factors*
  —Market size
  —Market growth rate
  —Cyclicality
  —Competitive structure
  —Barriers to entry
  —Industry profitability
  —Technology
  —Inflation
  —Regulation
  —Manpower availability
  —Social issues
  —Environmental issues
  —Political issues
  —Legal issues

ing the trends of each of the external factors in order to obtain a forecasted profile of the industry attractiveness. With this information on hand, we develop a business strategy congruent with the desired position of each business in the portfolio matrix.

Figure 8.2 Major Steps for the Implementation of the Attractiveness-Strength Matrix

Analysis of Current Situation	Analysis of Future Situation
STEP 1 Definition of critical internal and external factors *STEP 2* Assessment of external factors *STEP 3* Assessment of internal factors *STEP 4* Positioning of the business in the attractiveness-strength matrix	 *STEP 5* Forecasting of trends for each external factor *STEP 6* Developing the desired position for each internal factor *STEP 7* Desired positioning of each business in the attractiveness-strength matrix *STEP 8* Formulation of strategies for each business

We will proceed to analyze each of the proposed steps.

Step 1: Definition of Critical Internal and External Factors

A traditional way of starting a business planning effort is to conduct an *environmental scanning* process to determine the opportunities and threats that the external environment imposes upon the business unit, and an *internal scrutiny* to identify the basic internal strengths and weaknesses inherent to the business. This process is begun by recognizing the key factors which will be subjected to initial assessment.

We favor distinguishing these factors into two different groups. One is the set of critical external factors, which we define as *essentially uncontrollable* by the firm. They represent basic characteristics of the industry and competitive structure in which the business operates and a host of other concerns, such as sociopolitical, economical, legislative, regulatory, and demographic factors. The firm might, at best, attempt to mildly influence the trends of those factors by negotiating, lobbying, and bargaining with the external agents that will determine their behavior.

The other is the set of critical success factors which, to a large extent, are *controllable* by the firm. They correspond, primarily, to functional activities which have to be deployed to guarantee a successful competitive standing of the business units.

The selection of these factors is not a trivial matter. Normally, we approach this step by immersing a group of key executives of the firm, including corporate, business, and functional managers, in a collective effort oriented toward the identification and assessment of those factors. This effort represents a very subtle process that requires a great degree of intelligence, experience, and knowledge about industry and business characteristics.

It is unfortunate that the current state of knowledge in management precludes structuring this activity in a more precise way. We have to rely on a largely intuitive treatment of this subject due to the lack of a sounder and more solid scientific base. We are still far from achieving a rich and comprehensive model of the firm to facilitate the performance of this task. In the absence of this theoretical foundation, we at least can submit the managers of the firm to an orderly process aimed at extracting from them their vision of the firm and its environment.

One way to approach this descriptive task is to look at standard lists of relevant external and internal factors. Figure 8.1 already presented two broad lists of those factors. This is not an advisable procedure. An honest effort to produce meaningful lists of external and internal factors will give new and valuable insights, engaging the managers in a totally fresh exercise, probing for the identification of those issues that are truly significant to characterize the various businesses of the firm. Figures 8.3 and 8.5 identify the external and internal factors that we developed for the analysis of a business that we will use throughout this chapter to illustrate the implementation of the attractiveness-strength matrix.

Step 2: Assessment of External Factors

Once the external uncontrollable factors which are relevant to a business have been identified, we have to determine the contribution of each one of these factors to the level of attractiveness of the industry in which the business belongs. We have found that "profile charts," such as the one presented in Figure 8.3, provide a helpful visual display of the complete assessment. Each factor is graded in the following five points scale:

$\equiv$ Extremely unattractive
$-$ Mildly unattractive
E Even or Neutral
$+$ Mildly attractive
$\pm$ Extremely attractive.

The intent of this evaluation is to assess the level of attractiveness that a given industry has for the firm conducting the analysis. An industry could be highly attractive for a firm, because of the high technological standing in which the firm finds itself, but could be highly unattractive for another firm which lacks the required technological base.

To perform the industry assessment we need to classify the factors into two different groups. In one group, there are factors such as total market, market growth rate, and industry profitability, which affect in similar ways all firms competing in the industry. In this case, we favor the selection of the average

Figure 8.3 Assessment of Industry Attractiveness for the Swiss Firm Example

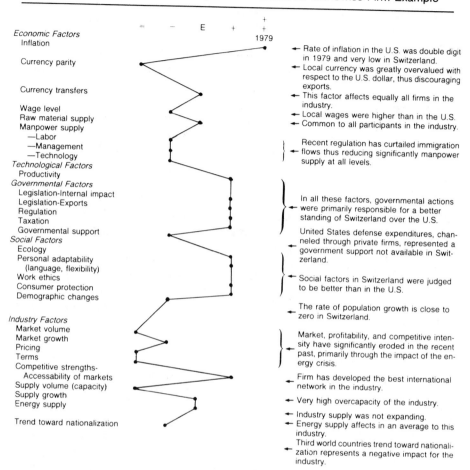

investment opportunity open to the firm as a selective basis of comparison. The reason for this selection is that the degree of attractiveness will ultimately determine the investment strategy of the firm. Thus, a business ranked in a highly attractive position will be a candidate for a larger allocation of resources than a business classified in a less favored category. When the five point scale in the profile-chart is defined in this way the "Even" or "Neutral" point identifies a degree of attractiveness for every factor which is equivalent to that enjoyed by an average investment opportunity open to the firm.

The second group is composed of factors that affect the firm and its competitors in a different way. For example, external factors tend to affect quite differently multinational corporations whose parent firms are placed in different countries, where currency parity, inflationary trends, demographic factors, and manpower supply all tend to have very different impacts. For assessing this latter group of factors, we have to resort to competitive evaluation, and the firm could select its most meaningful competitor as a basis of comparison. In this case, equal or neutral will mean that the factor affects the firm and its most important competitor in a similar way. The degree of attractiveness is then measured in terms of the relative impact to the firm with regard to the selected competitor.

The resulting assessment is going to be heavily dependent upon judgment. This is not necessarily an undesirable feature. A true understanding of a business invariably requires managerial insights. The assessment of external factors is a systematic process that allows a more orderly expression of the subjective inputs that managers have to provide when an overall diagnosis of a business is being conducted.

Obviously, there are ways to enrich the information base required to make a thorough industry analysis. Surveys, marketing research efforts, and external data sources can be valuable complements. They may be acquired either through external sources or by using the professional and research capabilities of the in-house staff. In either case, rather than launching a blind hunting expedition that might provide very little useful information at a great cost, it is better to conduct first this highly judgmental exercise, as a way of bringing in the intelligence that resides among the managers of the firm in an orderly fashion.

Figure 8.3 illustrates the industry-attractiveness assessment conducted in 1979 for a business of a Swiss firm in a highly technological industry. The order of the factors does not correspond to any particular ranking. It simply represents the sequence in which factors were identified by managers participating in the evaluation.

All of the assessments of the economic, technological, governmental and social factors, were obtained by comparing the influence of each factor in Switzerland vis-a-vis the U.S. external conditions. This is not an uncommon situation for multinational firms, which have a different set of environmental circumstances gravitating upon them. They influence adversely or positively the characteristics of their industry. However, the set of external factors grouped under the heading Industry Factors, by and large, affect in a similar way all the firms competing in that industry. The comments attached to Figure 8.3 provide a concise summary to explain the classification of each factor in the assessment of industry attractiveness.

The last step still to be resolved is the final classification of the overall attractiveness of the industry in terms of the three categories of the matrix: high, medium, and low. One school of thought, represented in the example given in Figure 8.4, advocates a quantitative approach to this issue. It requires assigning, to each factor, a weight (normalized to 100%), and a numerical grade from 1 to 5 (1 being very unattractive and 5 highly attractive). The final score of the industry attractiveness is determined as the weighted average of the numerical

Figure 8.4 An Example of the Industry Attractiveness Assessment with the Weighted Score Approach*

Attractiveness Criterion	Weight**	Rating***	Weighted Score
Size	.15	4	.60
Growth	.12	3	.36
Pricing	.05	3	.15
Market diversity	.05	2	.10
Competitive structure	.05	3	.15
Industry profitability	.20	3	.60
Technical role	.05	4	.20
Inflation vulnerability	.05	2	.10
Cyclicality	.05	2	.10
Customer Financials	.10	5	.50
Energy impact	.08	4	.32
Social	GO	4	—
Environmental	GO	4	—
Legal	GO	4	—
Human	.05	4	.20
	1.00		3.38

* Reprinted by permission from *Strategy Formulation: Analytical Concepts*, by Charles W. Hofer and Dan Schendel; Copyright © 1978 by West Publishing Company. All rights reserved.
** Some criteria may be of the GO/NO GO type.
*** 1 = very unattractive, 5 = highly attractive.

grades. This cardinal measurement will allow an exact positioning of the business unit within the matrix.

This approach is highly questionable. Within an apparent objectivity, it hides the inherent complexities of quantifying very subtle issues. Rothschild (1976, p. 151) commenting on this approach says: "I have found that weighting clouds the real issues and generates a reverence for numbers that may be unwarranted. In effect it tends to make a pseudo-science out of an art."

A better, though more judgmental way to perform the final classification of an industry, is for the managers conducting the analysis to examine in a detailed fashion the impact of each factor. Once this review is completed, they should engage in an open discussion regarding their relative importance. In this process, factors may be ranked in terms of their influence over industry attractiveness, as a way for participating managers to develop a feeling for the relative importance of each factor under consideration. The final step is to produce a collective agreement over the final classification of the industry, expressed directly in terms of the high, medium, or low categories. The reason for advocating this approach is that the nine cells defined in the attractiveness-strength matrix gives us sufficient resolution for assigning an appropriate investment strategy for each business. In our example, due to the extraordinary impact of the quite adverse industry factors, the industry attractiveness was judged to be *low* in 1979.

Step 3: *Assessment of Internal Factors*

The evaluation of the controllable success factors is normally done with regard to the leading competitor participating in the business under consideration. It is important to concentrate the evaluation on a single competitive firm. If there is more than one significant competitor against which we would like to identify competitive strategies, several evaluations should be conducted considering only one firm at a time. What should be avoided is selecting as a basis for comparison in each factor that particular firm that happens to excel in that dimension, since the resulting profile projects an unrealistic disadvantage of the firm under evaluation.

Figure 8.5 provides the business strengths profile chart for the analysis of the business whose industry attractiveness was discussed in Figure 8.3. The same five-points scale is used in the evaluation. The fact that the business strength evaluation has a clear competitor in mind makes its assessment less ambiguous than the industry attractiveness. In this case, the points of the scale identify the following competitive posture.

$=$ Severe competitive disadvantage
$-$ Mild competitive disadvantage
E Equal competitive standing
$+$ Mild competitive advantage
$+$ Great competitive advantage.

The comments in Figure 8.5 provide the reasoning for assigning the corresponding scores to each factor. Once more, we would like to emphasize that most of those factors represent a managerial function which is, by its own nature, a controllable and critical success factor. The implication is that a successful strategy for a business should coherently put together a set of well integrated R&D, production, marketing, finance, and distribution programs.

The quantitative approach favors the computation of a weighted average, which requires the assignment of weights and ratings for each factor. An example of this approach is presented in Figure 8.6.

The qualitative approach was used in the Swiss firm example presented in Figure 8.5. It was easy to conclude that the existing composite business strength was *medium*.

Step 4: *Current Positioning of the Business in the Attractiveness-Strength Matrix*

Having made the overall assessment of industry attractiveness and business strength, it is a simple matter to establish the current position of the business in the portfolio matrix, as shown in Figure 8.7. This positioning is limited to assigning the business unit in just one of the nine cells of the matrix.

Figure 8.5 Assessment of Business Strengths for the Swiss Firm Example

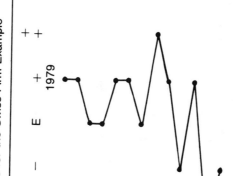

R&D concept
R&D human resources
R&D funding
Production facilities
Production human resources
Marketing work force
Distribution work force
Financing
Management competence
Management volume
Product line
Manufacturing cost
Profitability

The firm has R&D advantages in concept and human resources, in spite of an equal level of funding

Superior human resources

Extraordinary advantage in the ability of firm to offer financing terms to clients

The firm has a better quality of management, however, the total pool of managers is small

Product line is more complete

Erosion in profitability resulting primarily from higher labor rates

Figure 8.6 An Example of the Business-Strength Assessment with the Weighted Score Approach*

Critical Success Factors	Weight**	Rating***	Weighted Score
Market share	.10	5	.50
SBU growth rate	x	3	—
Breadth of product line	.05	4	.20
Sales distribution effectiveness	.20	4	.80
Proprietary and key account advantages	x	3	—
Price competitiveness	x	4	—
Advertising and promotion effectiveness	.05	4	.20
Facilities location and newness	.05	5	.25
Capacity and productivity	x	3	—
Experience curve effects	.15	4	.60
Raw materials costs	.05	4	.20
Value added	x	4	—
Relative product quality	.15	4	.60
R&D advantages/position	.05	4	.20
Cash throw-off	.10	5	.50
Caliber of personnel	x	4	—
General image	.05	5	.25
	1.00		4.30

* Reprinted by permission from *Strategy Formulation: Analytical Concepts*, by Charles W. Hofer and Dan Schendel; Copyright © 1978 by West Publishing Company. All rights reserved.
** x means that the factor does not affect the relative competitive position of the firms in that industry.
*** 1 = very weak competitive position, 5 = very strong competitive position.

A different procedure is applied when using the growth-share matrix approach popularized by the Boston Consulting Group, in which each individual business unit falls into a precise point, quantitatively determined by the value of the coordinates used in that case (growth and relative market share). Also, the relative contribution of the business is projected by the size of the area within each circle.

Those who subscribe to the weighted-score approach retain that representation in the attractiveness-strength matrix, thus providing a quantifiable set of coordinate measurements. For example, Hofer and Schendel (1978) use a graphical display similar to the one given in Figure 8.8, in which the areas of the circles are proportional to the sizes of the various industries involved, the firm's current market share in each industry is depicted by a pie-shaped wedge, and the circles are centered on the coordinates of the business units (industry attractiveness and business strength position scores).

There is one application of the attractiveness-strength matrix that deserves

Figure 8.7 Current Positioning of the Business in the Attractiveness-Strength Matrix in the Swiss Firm Example

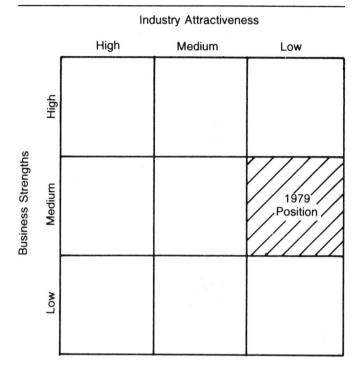

a separate comment. Rothschild (1976), a specialist in strategic planning with the General Electric Company, suggests a set of factors grouped into five major categories: market, competitive, financial and economic, technological, and sociopolitical. The detailed list of the factors in each category is presented in Figure 8.9. Rothschild, instead of prescribing the identification of a specific list of uncontrollable factors for describing the environmental characteristics and a set of controllable factors to assess the internal strengths, recommends the use of a unique generic list to be applicable to the assessment of both the industry attractiveness and the competitive strength of the firm along each factor. This procedure may also lead to an acceptable business positioning in the matrix. However, it skips the process of generation and probing of the lists of factors, which is enriching and fundamental to gain a deeper and common understanding of a business.

Step 5: Forecasting the Trends of Each External Factor

The first step in assessing the future portfolio of the firm is to forecast the trend of each of the external factors. The composite of all these trends will

Figure 8.8 An Example of the Business Positioning in the Attractiveness-Strength Matrix with the Weighted Score Approach

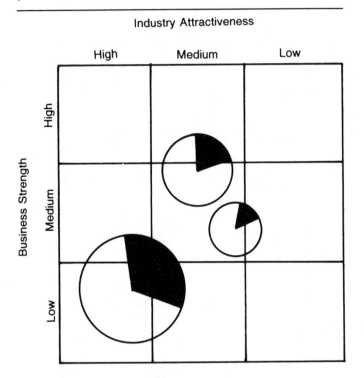

determine the future overall attractiveness of the industry. Step 5 is quite similar to step 2, except that instead of casting judgments based on objective historical information, our assessment is now relying upon our ability to understand and predict future trends. This procedure is at the core of the strategic planning effort.

The principal objective in this step is to gain an understanding of the most likely environment the firm will be facing in the foreseeable future. By determining future trends in the critical external factors, the firm will be able to anticipate explicitly what are the competitive, economic, financial, sociopolitical, technological, and legislative assumptions on which its proposed strategic actions will be based. Often, this step does not lead to the identification of a single most likely projection, but to a series of alternative meaningful scenarios. In this case, contingency plans should be readily defined to address the eventual realization of alternative scenarios that depart in a substantive manner from the most likely one.

The final aim in this effort is to determine whether the industry in which a business competes is going to maintain, increase, or decrease its current attractiveness within a planning horizon that normally covers a five year span. Ulti-

Figure 8.9 Determining Industry-Attractiveness and Business Strength

	Attractiveness of your industry	Strength of your business

Market Factors	Size (dollar, units, or both)
	Size of key segments
	Growth rate per year
	  Total
	  Segments
	Diversity of market
	Sensitivity to price, service, features, and external factors
	Cyclicality
	Seasonality
	Captive customers
		Share (in equivalent terms)
		Share of key segments
		Your annual growth rate
		  Total
		  Segments
		Your participation
		Your influence on the market
		
		Your sales lag or lead
		
		Extent to which your sales are captive

Competitive Factors	Types of competitors Degrees of concentration Changes in type and mix Entries and exits Position changes in share Functional substitution Degrees and types of integration	Where you fit, how you compare Segments you have entered or left Your relative share change Your vulnerability Your own level of integration

Financial and Economic Factors	Profitability
	  Ratios
	  Dollars
	Contribution margins
	Leverage factors such as economies of scale
	Barriers to entry or exit (both financial and nonfinancial)
	Capacity utilization
		Your profitability performance
		  Ratios
		  Dollars
		Your contributed value
		Any competitive advantage you possess
		Problems you would have in entering or exiting
		Your utilization

Technological Factors	Maturity and volatility Complexity Differentiation Patents and Copyrights Technology required Process of manufacturing	Ability to cope with change Depths of your skills Types of your skills Your position Your resources
Sociopolitical Factors	Social attitudes and trends Laws and government agency regulations Influence with pressure groups and government representatives Human factors such as unionization and community acceptance	Your company's responsiveness and flexibility Your company's ability to cope Your company's aggressiveness Your company's relationships

Adapted, by permission of the publisher, from *Putting It All Together: A Guide To Strategic Thinking*, by William E. Rothschild, pp. 144–149 & 152 © 1976 by AMACOM, a division of American Management Associations, New York. All rights reserved.

Figure 8.10 Assessment of Current and Future Trends of Industry Attractiveness for the Swiss Firm Example

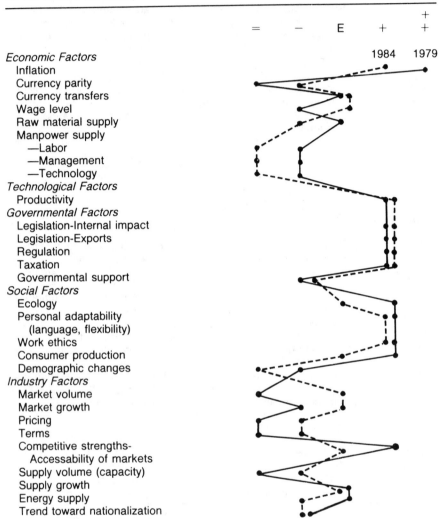

mately, the thrust of this effort is just to detect this final displacement of the attractiveness dimension, because the proper investment decision supported by the attractiveness-strength matrix will be dictated by it.

Figure 8.10 displays the assessment for 1984 of each of the critical external factors of the Swiss firm example, overimposed upon the 1979 evaluation. The most important transformations that are taking place are present in the industry factors, where a consistent improvement in the market, volume, market growth, and profitability of the industry is being predicted. These changes lead to repositioning the industry attractiveness from *low* in 1979 to *medium* in 1984.

Step 6: Developing the Desired Position for Each Internal Factor

Having resolved the future industry attractiveness corresponding to the business unit, the next step is to determine a strategic positioning for the future development of that unit. At the core of this positioning is the determination of the competitive moves to be taken in each controllable success factor to guide the business into the resulting desired competitive strength.

The essence of the formulation of a business strategy resides in establishing, in clear terms, multi-functional programs aimed at securing a long-term sustainable competitive advantage. A very useful instrument to advance in this direction is the business profile, such as in Figure 8.11, which projects each internal factor into the desired position during the planning horizon. Figure 8.11 overlaps the 1984 on the 1979 assessment conducted in Step 3.

What emerges from this figure, in our Swiss firm example, is an extraordinarily aggressive set of actions intended to reach a superior or at least equal standing with regard to the leading competitor in every one of the critical controllable dimensions of the business. The overall competitive strength of the business units, resulting from this set of decisions, relocates the business from a medium position of strength in 1979 to a *high* position in 1984.

Step 7: Desired Positioning of Each Business in the Attractiveness-Strength Matrix

After completing the forecast of the industry attractiveness and the development of the business strength, the proper positioning of a business in the attractiveness-strength matrix may appear as a simple mechanical exercise to show a graphical display. For example, Figure 8.12 shows both the business position as assessed in 1979 and its future projection for 1984.

Figure 8.11 Assessment of Business Strengths for the Swiss Firm Example

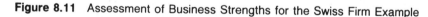

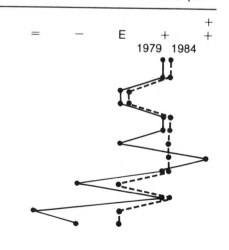

Figure 8.12 Current and Future Positioning of the Business in the Attractiveness-Strength Matrix for the Swiss Firm Example

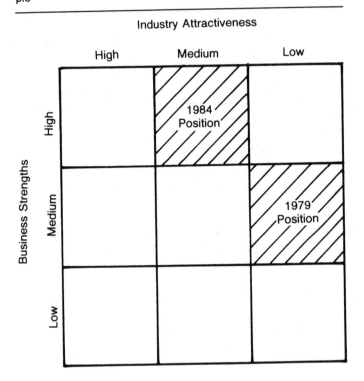

In practice, Steps 6 and 7 are carried out simultaneously. The idea is that having determined the projected attractiveness for the industry, we first decide on what the global competitive strategy should be regarding the business strength we would desire to have. Subsequently, we identify the new positioning of each one of the controllable success factors to achieve that overall business strength. The global strategy chosen has to be fitted to the actual internal capabilities of the firm.

Rothschild (1976) suggests a slightly different and provocative approach for this step. He also starts by identifying the current positioning of the business in the matrix. This position is displayed by a circle in Figure 8.13. Then, he proceeds to evaluate what the future position would be if we were to maintain our current strategy for that business, that is, if the level of resources committed to the business would remain unmodified. Figure 8.13 shows this future position by the rectangle, indicating that the industry in this case would maintain its medium level of attractiveness, but the firm's competitive position would erode from a high to a medium strength if the current strategy were to be maintained. With this information on hand, the firm should now decide what strategy should

Figure 8.13   An Alternative Display of the Current and Future Positioning of the Business in the Attractiveness-Strength Matrix

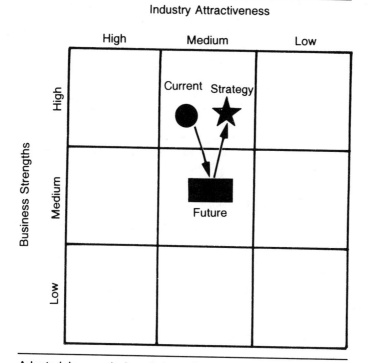

be implemented to attain the desired future position of the business, shown in Figure 8.13 by the star. In this example, the firm is committed to increase the resources currently allocated to its business, in order to maintain its strength.

Figure 8.14 is intended to summarize the basic issues being addressed in steps 5, 6, and 7. The formulation of the base case results in the identification of the most likely scenario—shaped by forecasting the trends in the external factors—and the preferred strategic action programs—determined by deciding the position that should be achieved in each of the controllable internal factors. A subsequent sensitivity analysis is intended to construct meaningful alternative scenarios and to decide the various action programs which represent the response of the firm to the eventual occurrence of those scenarios. Contingency planning is dependent on the monitoring of the critical external factors to check whether the assumptions about the environment, in which the adopted plans are based, are still valid. Leading indicators and triggering mechanisms should signal signifi-

Figure 8.14 Interplay Among External and Internal Factors in Shaping a Strategy

	Base Case	*Sensitivity Analysis*
External Factors (Uncontrollable)	Forecasting the most likely scenario	Alternative meaningful scenarios
Internal Factors (Controllable)	Deciding on the preferred strategic action programs	Contingency planning —Triggering mechanisms —Alternative action programs

cant departures of these basic assumptions and the potential selection of an alternative contingency plan.

Step 8: Formulation of Strategies for Each Business

The analysis conducted so far has provided us with all the elements necessary to enunciate the strategy to be pursued for the development of each business. At the level of a business unit the word *strategy* implies a set of broad *action programs* oriented at establishing the long-term desired competitive strengths of the business unit, and at properly managing the positive or adverse impact of external factors.

Conceived in these terms, the basic strategy is directly distilled from the assessment conducted for both internal and external factors. Thus, the strategy has two primary components:

—Broad action programs based on the controllable success factors, whose objectives are to neutralize the internal weaknesses while retaining positions of strength.

—Broad action programs based on the external factors, whose aims are to prevent the negative consequences of adverse trends over the business performance, and to take advantage of those environmental conditions which represent beneficial opportunities.

These two dimensions of strategy formulation have different degrees of creativity and complexity. It is relatively straightforward to identify action programs derived from the internal analysis, because they are directly linked to controllable functional activities. It is much more difficult to address the issues raised by uncontrollable external forces. In our opinion, it is the capturing of the essential message of the external forces and the adaptation of the firm to meet those challenges that distinguishes the creative manager.

This analysis is truly significant for the first cycle in the strategic process, where we are formulating broad statements of objectives and action programs. After these objectives have been properly sanctioned at the corporate level, the second planning cycle, dealing with strategic programming, is initiated.

At this stage, the broad strategic action programs are going to be broken down into very specific tactical plans, suitable for implementation. Also, the impact of the overall strategies will be subjected to detailed quantitative financial analyses. Those analyses will require a different kind of forecasting effort. For each of the meaningful scenarios identified in the previous steps, we will need numerical projections of parameters such as market volume, sales, prices, costs, interest rates, tax rates, and others in order to evaluate the financial attractiveness of the entire plan during a relevant planning horizon.

Figure 8.15 illustrates the broad action programs developed for the Swiss firm example. One of the most critical issues addressed in this case pertains to the question of currency parity. Although this issue appears as a devastating disadvantage for an exporting firm, it becomes obvious that it was an extraordinary weapon when considered from the point of view of purchasing strength.

Notice that there are a couple of items which recognize the need for further

Figure 8.15 Strategy Formulation for the Swiss Firm Example

I. *Broad Action Programs Based on Controllable Internal Factors*
—Maintain R&D and Technical standing above leading competitor level.
—Implement an automation program leading toward significant increases in labor productivity.
—Improve the distribution network worldwide, developing a sense of priorities according to the attractiveness of each individual market.
—Reduce manufacturing costs through proper rationalization in every stage of the production process.
—Increase number of qualified managers via proper hiring, developing, and promotional procedures.
—Maintain market positioning by the allocation of financial and human resources compatible with competitive challenges.

II. *Broad Action Programs to Deal with External Environmental Forces*
—Profit from a possibly temporarily favorable currency situation by taking advantage of a strong purchasing power, in terms of:
  —Switching from national to foreign suppliers.
  —Engaging in an active acquisition of manufacturing facilities abroad.
—Set up a task force to study the legal, financial, and sales implications of currency transfer.
—Use local manufacturing, distribution, and marketing facilities whenever possible, seeking partnerships to neutralize trends toward nationalization.
—Stockpile raw materials on critical items, and firm up long term contracts for the procurement of those raw materials, taking advantage of the temporary strong currency situation.
—Address the issue of manpower shortage by:
  —Internal development of qualified manpower at all levels.
  —Seeking an increased government support.
—Establish the base for a systematic information gathering conducive toward a better understanding of competitors and market opportunities.

---

information gathering, in order for the firm to acquire a better understanding of its competitive position. Finally, there is one issue that requires bringing in a sympathetic attitude from the government. This is a meaningful strategy for the Swiss firm, because it commands a strong presence in its own country. Probably a strategy of this nature would not make much sense for companies that do not portray such a significant influence in the economy of a country.

IMPLICATIONS FOR STRATEGIC POSITIONING

The strategic implications that are normally drawn from the attractiveness-strength matrix have, as a primary message, the assignment of investment priorities to the various businesses of the firm. In that sense, it is truly a guide for resource allocation. This matrix does not emphasize the question of cash-flow balance, a fundamental concern in the growth-share matrix.

The prescription that emerges from the matrix is to concentrate resources in those businesses that enjoy a higher degree of attractiveness and competitive strength, disengage resources when the opposite is true, and be selective in intermediate positions. The thrust of the ranking implicit for investment priorities is shown in Figure 8.16. More specific guidance in terms of supporting strategies congruent with those investment priorities have been developed by A. T. Kearney, and are shown in Figure 8.17. The Royal Shell Dutch Company adopted a slight variation of the attractiveness-strength matrix, which they name Directional-Policy Matrix. Its implications for investment priorities and corresponding supporting strategies are given in Figure 8.18.

Figure 8.16   Investment Priorities in the Attractiveness-Strength Matrix

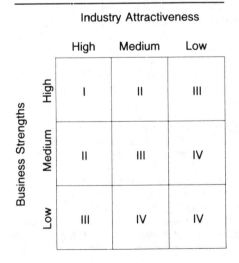

Figure 8.17 Strategic Implications from the Attractiveness-Strength Matrix Suggested by A. T. Kearney

		Industry Attractiveness	
Business Strengths	**High**	**Medium**	**Low**
High	—Grow —Seek dominance —Maximize investment	—Identify growth segments —Invest strongly —Maintain position elsewhere	—Maintain overall position —Seek cash flow —Invest at maintenance level
Medium	—Evaluate potential for leadership via segmentation —Identity weaknesses —Builds strengths	—Identify growth segments —Specialize —Invest selectively	—Prune lines —Minimize investment —Position to divest
Low	—Specialize —Seek niches —Consider acquisitions	—Specialize —Seek niches —Consider exit	—Trust leader's statesmanship —Sic on competitor's cash generators —Time exit and divest

Source: Reproduced by permission of A. T. Kearney, Inc., Chicago, Ill.

Figure 8.18 Strategic Implications from the Attractiveness-Strength Matrix Suggested by The Royal Dutch Shell Company

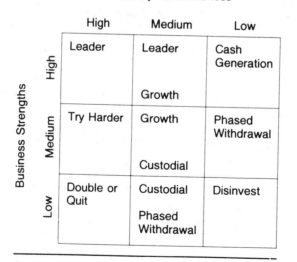

Industry Attractiveness

		High	Medium	Low
Business Strengths	**High**	Leader	Leader Growth	Cash Generation
	Medium	Try Harder	Growth Custodial	Phased Withdrawal
	Low	Double or Quit	Custodial Phased Withdrawal	Disinvest

The strategies suggested from these interpretations of the attractiveness-strength matrix are the so-called *natural strategies*, that is, logical and rational directions to be sought for the development of individual businesses consistent with the position they exhibit in the external and internal dimensions. Although they raise valid points to be considered when deciding on a business direction, natural strategies should not be followed blindly.

Another important concern is to address the dynamics of business behavior. We should avoid drawing definitive conclusions from static snapshots of the position of each business. Notice that in the example of the Swiss firm, the mere examination of the current portfolio matrix (Figure 8.12) would have indicated that the business should have been harvested or divested. However, the forecasted increase in the business attractiveness (which was based on hard facts and not on wishful thinking), led managers to pursue an investment strategy to improve the business competitive strength. Incidentally, this strategy proved to be quite effective.

PORTFOLIO VISION IN THE ATTRACTIVENESS-STRENGTH MATRIX

All portfolio matrices can be applied at several levels in the organization, with different degrees of aggregation as far as the unit that is subjected to the analysis. We have emphasized, so far, the methodology to implement the attractiveness-strength matrix at the business unit level.

Another type of powerful message can be extracted when all businesses of the firm are finally positioned in the matrix to provide us with a view of the strength of the overall corporate portfolio.

A good representation is obtained by the development of a series of matrices containing not only the position of the businesses but also their contribution measured in terms of a variety of performance indicators, such as: sales, profits, assets, and return on net assets. Figure 8.19 provides an illustration of such display. There is a powerful diagnostic message to be derived from the five matrices portrayed in this figure. For the sake of brevity, we will let the reader reflect upon it.

Although in this example the performance measurements are expressed in terms of percentages, it may be valuable to add absolute magnitudes of some selected indicators. Moreover, in this example the indicators selected are given in an aggregate form for each of the nine cells of the matrix, one might want to single out the values associated with each individual business unit.

This all-encompassing view of the firm derived by using the matrix can also be extended to produce a more detailed appreciation of a business unit. In that case, a similar in-depth analysis of each one of the product lines should be performed. This would imply a much more detailed segmentation of the matrix with the purpose of helping a diagnostic process at a business level.

Figure 8.19   Selected Set of Performance Measurements to Describe the Portfolio of Businesses in the Attractiveness-Strength Matrix

POSITIONING OF BUSINESSES*
Industry Attractiveness (IA)

		H	M	L	TOTAL
Business Strength (BS)	H	2,9,17 18,19	7,12	16	8
	M	1,3,4,14	8,10,13	11,15	9
	L	5,6	—	—	2
TOTAL		11	5	3	19

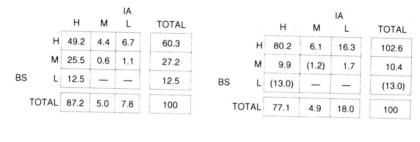

DISTRIBUTION OF CORPORATE SALES (%)

			IA		
		H	M	L	TOTAL
BS	H	49.2	4.4	6.7	60.3
	M	25.5	0.6	1.1	27.2
	L	12.5	—	—	12.5
TOTAL		87.2	5.0	7.8	100

DISTRIBUTION OF CORPORATE NET INCOMES (%)

			IA		
		H	M	L	TOTAL
BS	H	80.2	6.1	16.3	102.6
	M	9.9	(1.2)	1.7	10.4
	L	(13.0)	—	—	(13.0)
TOTAL		77.1	4.9	18.0	100

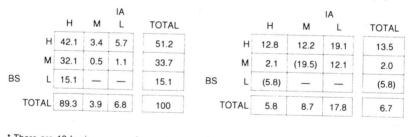

DISTRIBUTION OF CORPORATE ASSETS (%)

			IA		
		H	M	L	TOTAL
BS	H	42.1	3.4	5.7	51.2
	M	32.1	0.5	1.1	33.7
	L	15.1	—	—	15.1
TOTAL		89.3	3.9	6.8	100

RETURN ON NET ASSETS (%)

			IA		
		H	M	L	TOTAL
BS	H	12.8	12.2	19.1	13.5
	M	2.1	(19.5)	12.1	2.0
	L	(5.8)	—	—	(5.8)
TOTAL		5.8	8.7	17.8	6.7

* There are 19 businesses, each one characterized by a number from 1 through 19.

The final aim is the identification of those sub-segments that deserve either a greater or lesser degree of support.

CONSISTENCY OF INVESTMENT STRATEGIES

Rothschild (1980), proposes a procedure to check whether the resource allocation proposal for each business is consistent with the assigned investment priority for that business (see Figure 8.20). This is accomplished by measuring the historical level of expenditures during the last six years in: plant and equipment, marketing, engineering, working capital, and salaried employees. These expenditures are compared with those proposed for the next three years in terms of both real dollars and as a percent of sales. Depending on the degree of deviation of the future from the past, the plans are classified as: aggressive, moderate, maintenance, or minimum. Those proposals that fall in the diagonal of Figure 8.20 are judged to be consistent with the investment priorities. Those falling above the diagonal command a higher than expected resource allocation, and those below it, a lower one. A position of the business outside the diagonal simply signals a discrepancy from a natural strategy whose cause deserves careful investigation. There may be various reasons for a business to have more or less aggressive investment strategies than what might seem natural to adopt.

In his book on Strategic Alternatives, Rothschild (1979) devotes a great deal of attention to another consistency issue: the linking of the overall investment strategy with the natural functional strategies that might be considered to support a specific investment thrust. One message in that book is that successful management strategies tend to be driven by a concentration on a particular functional focus.

A CRITIQUE OF THE ATTRACTIVENESS-STRENGTH MATRIX APPROACH

The Ambiguity Implicit in a Multidimensional Matrix

It is an ironic paradox that one of the problems associated with the attractiveness-strength matrix arises from one of its fundamental contributions. Historically, this matrix emerges as a response to the rather simplistic approach of the growth-share matrix. The attractiveness-strength matrix requires searching for the multiplicity of factors that contribute to the strategic positioning of a business. By doing so, it rejects a rather simple-minded attempt to capture the complexity of management, and offers a richer and more mature perspective to guide the proper strategic actions for business development. In attempting to resolve that issue, it introduces the complexity of dealing with multidimensional indicators. We have criticized the weighted-score approach because of its pseudo-scientific character. However, the weighting process, when dealing with multiattributes, is unavoidable, whether you do it explicitly or implicitly.

Very often, when applying the attractiveness-strength matrix, one notices a lack of consistency in reaching a final positioning of a given business among groups of managers that have been entrusted with the same task. Also, there is a tendency to categorize a business as *medium* due to inappropriate understanding of the issues involved, and inability to reconcile diverging opinions.

Finally, it is hard to impose a uniformity of standards among businesses to ensure that the final portfolio matrix will be consistent in terms of the criteria

Figure 8.20 Consistency Check Between Investment Priorities and Resource Allocation Decisions

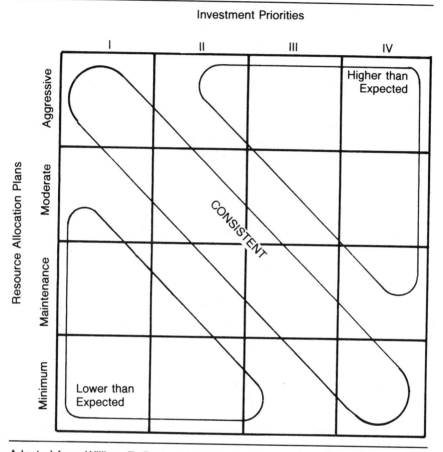

Adapted from William E. Rothschild, "How to Ensure the Continued Growth of Strategic Planning," © 1980, p. 17. Reprinted by permission of *The Journal of Business Strategy*, Boston, MA.

used in their classification. Several firms try to bypass this difficulty by developing standard lists of external and internal factors to be used by all businesses in the firm. We find that this practice prevents the recognition of the idiosyncratic characteristics of each business and presents obstacles for a rich diagnosis of its strengths and opportunities.

In contrast, the growth-share matrix becomes a much more precise and unambiguous tool. It can be easily applied to facilitate comparisons among the portfolio strength of competitive firms. Although there is conceptually nothing that would prevent applying the attractiveness-strength matrix not only for one's own firm but also for the competitor's, it is a much more difficult tool to be used objectively in that capacity. Therefore, we recommend the growth-share matrix as a useful mechanism for competitive analysis, and the attractiveness-strength matrix as a much more powerful one for diagnosis and strategic guidance tool for one's own firm.

The Difficulty of Assessing Industry Attractiveness

Although the ambiguity we have described can be applied to both dimensions in the attractiveness-strength matrix, it is clearly the industry attractiveness perspective that is most affected. In assessing business strength, at least we have a clear relative standard of comparison: the leading competitor. As we have discussed in Step 2, the evaluation of industry attractiveness is much more complex and subtle.

The Legitimacy of the Investment Priorities

A more technical point that one could raise as a critique of the attractiveness-strength matrix is the subjective nature of the priorities assigned for investment purposes among the businesses of the firm. From a strict financial theory point of view, one could argue that the only legitimate evaluation tool is the Net Present Value (NPV) of future cash-flows to be generated by a business, discounted at a proper cost of capital, which includes an adjustment for risk.

Those who support a broad categorization for an initial ranking of investment priorities, as the one resulting from the attractiveness-strength matrix, argue that the cash-flow projections required in the NPV calculations ignore the qualitative merit of an investment. If one wants to play the NPV game, it is always possible to show that an investment opportunity can meet the cost of capital hurdle. Therefore, it is better to reflect first on the overall attractiveness of the industry in which the investment will take place, and the strength that the firm will bring to bear on that business, prior to undertaking numerical computations that might not add significantly to the understanding of the decision.

We feel that both points of view are legitimate, and have important merits on their own. Rather than being alternative procedures for analyzing investment proposals, they truly complement each other.

REFERENCES

Hax, Arnoldo C., and Nicolas S. Majluf, "The Use of the Industry Attractiveness-Business Strength Matrix in Strategic Planning," *Interfaces*, Vol. 13, No. 2, April 1983, pp. 54–71.

Hofer, Charles W., and Merritt J. Davoust, *Successful Strategic Management*, A. T. Kearney, Inc., Chicago, 1977.

Hofer, Charles W., and Dan Schendel, *Strategy Formulation: Analytical Concepts*, West Publishing Co., St. Paul, MN, 1978.

Rothschild, William E., "How to Ensure the Continued Growth of Strategic Planning," *The Journal of Business Strategy*, Vol. 1, No. 1, Summer 1980, pp. 11–18.

Rothschild, William E., *Putting It All Together: A Guide to Strategic Thinking*, Amacom, NY, 1976.

Rothschild, William E., *Strategic Alternatives: Selection, Development and Implementation*, Amacom, NY, 1979.

Royal Dutch Shell Company, *The Directional Policy Matrix: A New Aid to Corporate Planning*, 1975.

Wind, Yoram, and Vijay Mahajan, "Designing Product and Business Portfolios," Harvard Business Review, Vol. 59, No. 1, January–February 1981, pp. 155–165.

9

THE LIFE-CYCLE APPROACH TO STRATEGIC PLANNING

The life-cycle concept has long been recognized as a valuable tool for analyzing the dynamic evolution of products and industries in the marketplace. It is derived from the fact that a product's and industry's sales volume follows a typical pattern that can readily be charted as a four-phase cycle known as embryonic, growth, maturity, and aging.

The managerial implications of the product life-cycle have been widely documented. See, for example, Clifford (1980), Urban and Hauser (1980), Kotler (1980). Moreover, the linkage between the industry life-cycle and strategic management has been a subject of increasing attention (Luck and Ferrell 1979; Porter 1980, Chapter 8). Also much attention has been given to the relationship between the product life-cycle and management of innovation and product technology (Abernathy and Utterback 1982, Utterback 1978, Hayes and Wheelwright 1979a and 1979b, Moore and Tushman 1982).

Although normally the stages within the industry life-cycle are characterized by their corresponding sales growth, it is important to understand how other financial characteristics impact each stage, such as profit and cash-flow. As shown in Figure 9.1, profits are negative throughout all or most of the embryonic phase, but tend to increase sharply during the growth phase, prior to leveling off and subsequent steady decline at the maturity phase, when normally competitive pressure begins to erode profit margins. At the very end of the aging phase, profits could even turn negative, if there is not a timely disinvestment of the business or product. What is even more impacting is the behavior of cash flows, which take large negative values during the embryonic and growth stages, representing an investment into the future, to be compensated during the maturity and aging phases, when positive cash flows become significant.

Obviously, the patterns just described attempt to represent the characteristics

Figure 9.1 Yearly Sales, Cash-flow, and Profits Through the Industry Life-cycle Stages

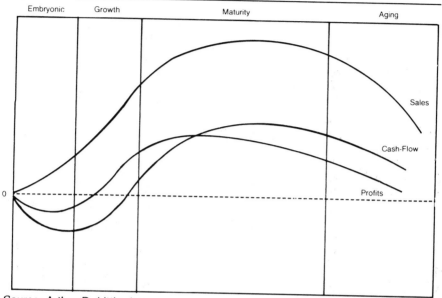

Source: Arthur D. Little, Inc.

of the "natural" behavior of a typical industry. There are numerous exceptions to this, surrounded by a high degree of controversy on the real meaning of the industry life-cycle, which we will explore at the end of this chapter.

Despite this controversy, it is understandable that very many industries, in particular high-technology ones with a rapid pace of innovation, center a great deal of attention in the challenges of managing products with short life time.

The implications of the life-cycle stages become central for the implementation and development of strategies in those industries. Accordingly, Arthur D. Little Inc. (ADL) has proposed a fairly structural methodology to guide strategic choices based on the life-cycle concept (Osell and Wright 1980, Forbes and Bate 1980, Arthur D. Little 1974, 1979, 1980).

This approach is supported by another type of portfolio matrix, whose primary dimensions are the life-cycle stages and the competitive position. Schematically, the ADL strategic planning methodology is summarized in Figure 9.2. The rest of this chapter is directed to the presentation of that methodology.

THE LIFE-CYCLE PORTFOLIO MATRIX

The business portfolio matrix suggested by ADL shares the same attributes of the previous matrices we have discussed—the growth-share matrix, and the industry attractiveness-business strength matrix—that is, it is a pictorial repre-

Figure 9.2 ADL Strategic Planning Methodology

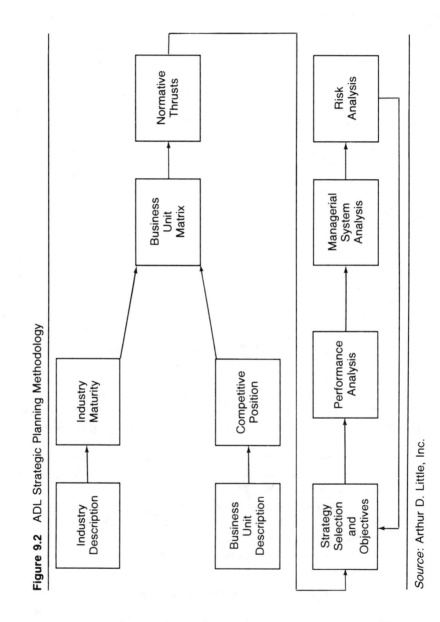

Source: Arthur D. Little, Inc.

sentation of all the businesses of the firm, in two dimensions. One represents the impact of the external forces, normally uncontrollable by the firm. ADL chose the four stages of the business life-cycle as descriptors of the industry characteristics. The second dimension represents the strengths the firm has in the industry in which each of its businesses compete. ADL selected six categories of competitive positioning (dominant, strong, favorable, tenable, weak, and nonviable).

Figure 9.3 presents the six-by-four resulting portfolio matrix. As is the case with all of the previously discussed matrices, the position of a business unit within it suggests the pursuit of some natural strategic objectives. Often, a major way of articulating those objectives is to reflect upon a desirable market share position, the need to deploy financial resources to support investment requirements, and the expectations with regard to cash flows required from or contributed to the corporation. Figures 9.4, 9 5, and 9.6 provide some suggestions for strategic positioning according to these three dimensions.

The use of this matrix is, therefore, conditioned to three primary tasks. One

Figure 9.3   The Life-cycle Portfolio Matrix

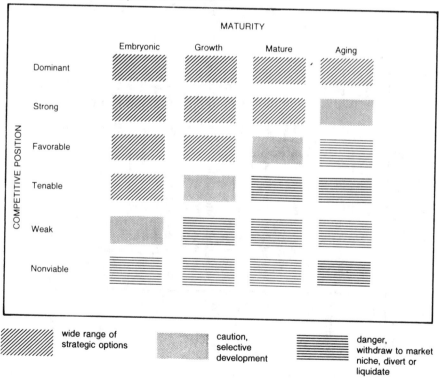

Source: Arthur D. Little, Inc.

Figure 9.4 Strategic Positioning in Terms of Market Share Suggested by the Life-cycle Portfolio Matrix

	Embryonic	Growth	Mature	Aging
Dominant	All Out Push For Share Hold Position	Hold Position Hold Share	Hold Position Grow With Industry	Hold Position
Strong	Attempt to Improve Position All Out Push For Share	Attempt to Improve Position Push For Share	Hold Position Grow With Industry	Hold Position or Harvest
Favorable	Selective or All out Push For Share Selectively Attempt to Improve Position	Attempt to Improve Position Selective Push For Share	Custodial or Maintenance Find Niche and Attempt to Protect	Harvest or Phased Withdrawal
Tenable	Selectively Push For Position	Find Niche and Protect it	Find Niche and Hang on or Phased Withdrawal	Phased Withdrawal or Abandon
Weak	Up or Out	Turnaround or Abandon	Turnaround or Phased Withdrawal	Abandon

Source: Arthur D. Little, Inc.

Figure 9.5 Strategic Positioning in Terms of the Investment Requirements Suggested by the Life-cycle Portfolio Matrix

	Embryonic	Growth	Mature	Aging
Dominant	Invest Slightly Faster Than Market Dictates	Invest to Sustain Growth Rate (and Preempt New (?) Competitors)	Reinvest as Necessary	Reinvest as Necessary
Strong	Invest as Fast as Market Dictates	Invest to Increase Growth Rate (and Improve Position)	Reinvest as Necessary	Minimum Reinvestment or Maintenance
Favorable	Invest Selectively	Selective Investment to Improve Position	Minimum and/or Selective Reinvestment	Minimum Maintenance Investment or Disinvest
Tenable	Invest (Very) Selectively	Selective Investment	Minimum Reinvestment or Disinvest	Disinvest or Divest
Weak	Invest or Divest	Invest or Divest	Invest Selectively or Disinvest	Divest

The terms invest and divest are used in the broadest sense and are not restricted to property, plant & equipment

Source: Arthur D. Little, Inc.

Figure 9.6 Strategic Positioning in Terms of Profitability and Cash-flow Suggested by the Life-cycle Portfolio Matrix

	Embryonic	Growth	Mature	Aging
Dominant	Probably Profitable, But Not Necessary Net Cash Borrower	Profitable Probably Net Cash Producer (But Not Necessary)	Profitable Net Cash Producer	Profitable Net Cash Producer
Strong	May be Unprofitable Net Cash Borrower	Probably Profitable Probably Net Cash Borrower	Profitable Net Cash Producer	Profitable Net Cash Producer
Favorable	Probably Unprofitable Net Cash Borrower	Marginally Profitable Net Cash Borrower	Moderately Profitable Net Cash Producer	Moderately Profitable Cash Flow Balance
Tenable	Unprofitable Net Cash Borrower	Unprofitable Net Cash Borrower or Cash Flow Balance	Minimally Profitable Cash Flow Balance	Minimally Profitable Cash Flow Balance
Weak	Unprofitable Net Cash Borrower	Unprofitable Net Cash Borrower or Cash Flow Balance	Unprofitable Possibly Net Cash Borrower or Net Cash Producer	Unprofitable (Write-off)

In addition, to cash throw-off or use, each grain may use or throw-off managerial resources.
Note: In some cases, the tax shield value of a unit should be taken into account in evaluating unit performance.

Source: Arthur D. Little, Inc.

is to segment the business of the firm into relatively independent SBUs, which will lend themselves to being analyzed in terms of the two dimensions of the matrix. Two, is to guide managers through a systematic process in assessing the stage of the life-cycle in which each business falls. And three, is to provide some support to identify the categories of competitive positioning of each individual business. These three subjects will be briefly reviewed now.

Criteria for Business Segmentation

ADL assigns the label "strategy center" to what we have referred to as Strategic Business Unit (SBU). A strategy center is a natural business, that is, a business area with an external marketplace for goods or services, and for which one can determine independent objectives and strategies.

In order to build business strategies, the first task of managers is to segment the firm into a set of natural businesses. To accomplish that, ADL suggests the use of a set of clues which are grounded on conditions in the marketplace rather than in internally shared resources, such as sharing of manufacturing facilities, common technology, or joint distribution channels. Once again, the emphasis on segmentation is articulated in terms of the external environment, attempting to establish the roots of business identification in the behavior of competitors, instead of being driven by internal functional arrangements. The clues which ADL offers to define a strategy center are:

1. *Competitors.*
2. *Prices.*
3. *Customers.*
4. *Quality/Style.*
5. *Substitutability.*
6. *Divestment or Liquidation.*

The first four clues indicate that a set of products belongs to a given SBU or strategy center whenever they face a single set of competitors and customers, and are similarly affected by price, quality and style changes. If this is not the case, the set of products might be split into more than one strategy center to focus more sharply its strategic actions. Moreover, all products in a strategy center should be close substitutes of one another. Finally, a strategy center could probably stand alone if divested (Arthur D. Little, 1980).

Identifying the Stage of a Business Within the Industry Life-cycle

ADL identifies eight external factors which are key descriptors of the evolutionary stage in which a business resides within its life cycle. These descriptors are: market growth rate, market growth potential, breadth of the product lines, number of competitors, distribution of market share among competitors, customer loyalty, entry barriers, and technology. (All of these correspond to the category of external uncontrollable factors, which we have addressed in the

industry attractiveness or business strength matrix.) Figure 9.7 can be used as a checklist to help positioning a business unit in the life-cycle stages according to each one of these descriptors. Obviously, it will be unlikely that a strategy center falls consistently in a single stage in every descriptor. As usual a judgmental call has to be made to finally capture the essence of the industry maturity of the strategy center.

An embryonic industry (such as laser measuring devices) is normally characterized by rapid growth, changes in technology, great pursuit of new customers, and fragmented and changing shares of market. A growth industry is one that is still growing rapidly, but customers, shares, and technology are better known

Figure 9.7 Factors Affecting the Stage of the Industry Life-Cycle for a Strategy Center

Stages of Industry Maturity: / Descriptors:	Embryonic	Growth	Mature	Aging
Growth Rate				
Industry Potential				
Product Line				
Number of Competitors				
Market Share Stability				
Purchasing Patterns				
Ease of Entry				
Technology				
OVERALL				

Source: Arthur D. Little, Inc.

and entry into the industry is more difficult (as illustrated by RCA's attempt to enter the computer business); a mature industry (like automobiles or paper in this country) is characterized by stability in known customers, technology, and in shares of market, although the industries may still be market-competitive; and aging industries (such as men's hats) are best described by falling demand, a declining number of competitors, and, in many such industries, a narrowing of the product line (Arthur D. Little, 1974).

Most industries reach the maturity phase after passing through embryonic and growth stages. Some industries stay mature for decades or even longer, while others mature quickly. However, industries can experience reversals in their maturing process. Such reversals are quite frequent. For example, as a result of the energy crisis, the aging coal mining industry has, in certain countries like the U.S., reverted to a growth phase. Other examples are the watch and bicycle industries. They tend to be caused by technological change, as in the watch industry, or changes in social values and norms (the case of bicycles), or by economic or regulatory factors (Arthur D. Little, 1980).

Figure 9.8 displays some examples of the stage of maturity for some industries, including some maturity reversals.

A more important point is that there is no "good" or "bad" maturity position. A particular stage of maturity becomes bad only if the strategies adopted by an industry participant are inappropriate for that given stage of maturity, or, indeed, if its expectations are inconsistent with that stage.

Figure 9.8 Example of Industry Maturity

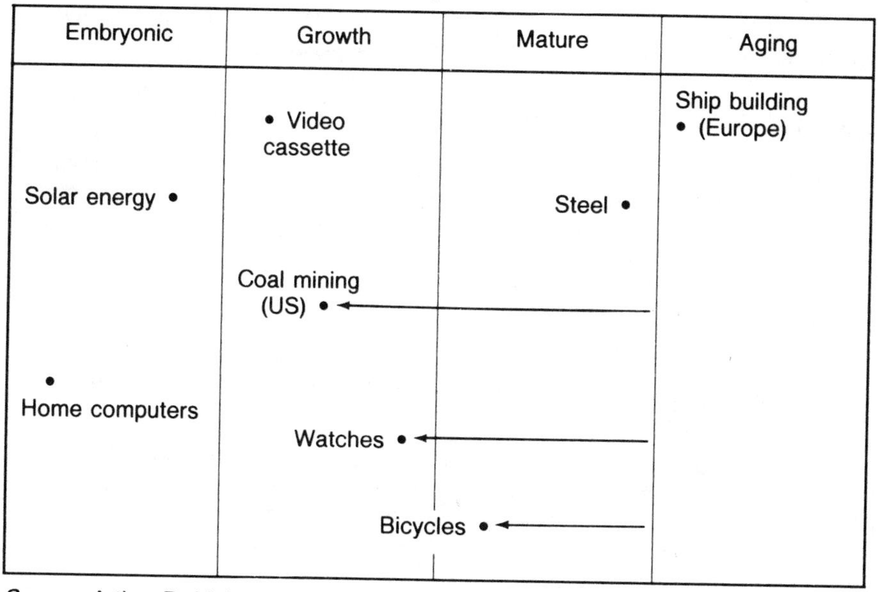

Embryonic	Growth	Mature	Aging
Solar energy • • Home computers	• Video cassette Coal mining (US) • ← Watches • ← Bicycles • ←	Steel •	Ship building • (Europe)

Source: Arthur D. Little, 1980.

Identifying the Competitive Position of a Business

ADL has decided to address the question of competitive positioning in terms of a set of subjective and qualitative categories, rather than ascribing a numerical value such as market share, to this dimension of the matrix. Figure 9.9 spells out the attributes of the first five competitive categories—dominant, strong, favorable, tenable, and weak. The sixth one, nonviable, does not need a formal description, because it represents the final recognition that the firm has really no strength whatsoever, now or in the future, in that particular business, and therefore, exiting is the only strategic response.

Although the broad descriptions provided in Figure 9.9 are meaningful enough to characterize the difference among each competitive position, it might be useful to comment briefly on the nature of their distinct role. There is only one firm in an industry, if any, that can assume a *dominant* role. If such a firm exists, it truly sets up the standards of the industry. It is Kodak in films, Boeing in commercial aircraft, and IBM in mainframe computers. A *strong* business enjoys a most definitive advantage over its competitors, with relative market share beyond 1.5, but has not reached the absolute dominance of the former category. A *favorable* position means that there is something unique about the business. It could result from a differentiating strategy or the exploitation of a particular niche where the firm happens to excell. But we are talking now about attributes in some facets of the industry, as opposed to dominant or strong positions industry-wide. A *tenable* business is beginning to have some symptoms of erosion and misperformance; however, there is little question that the business deserves full attention and has a good probability for effective recovery. Finally, a business in a *weak* position is in a transitory situation which cannot be sustained in the long run. It is either up or out.

Figure 9.9 Criteria for Classification of Competitive Position

1. "Dominant": Dominant competitors are very rare. Dominance often results from a quasi monopoly or from a strongly protected technological leadership.
2. "Strong": Not all industries have dominant or strong competitors. Strong competitors can usually follow strategies of their choice, irrespective of their competitors' moves.
3. "Favorable": When industries are fragmented, with no competitor clearly standing out, the leaders tend to be in a favorable position.
4. "Tenable": A tenable position can usually be maintained profitable through specialization in a narrow or protected market niche. This can be a geographic specialization or a product specialization.
5. "Weak": Weak competitors can be intrinsically too small to survive independently and profitable in the long term, given the competitive economics of their industry, or they can be larger and potentially stronger competitors, but suffering from costly past mistakes or from a critical weakness.

Source: Arthur D. Little, Inc. (1980)

PORTFOLIO VISION IN THE LIFE-CYCLE MATRIX

As we have indicated in the previous chapter, it is useful not only to present the position of all the business units of a firm in a portfolio matrix, but also to provide the contribution of each business unit by means of a set of financial indicators, such as sales, profits, assets, and return or net assets. Figure 9.10 represents the overall portfolio of the business of a firm in the life-cycle matrix, and Figure 9.11 further documents the financial contribution of each of these businesses. This information is helpful to confirm the role that an individual business should play according to its classification in the matrix. Obviously, a firm will be better off by having a large fraction of its business in a dominant or strong position and those businesses are expected to have handsome financial performances. However, when looking at the industry maturity dimension, a firm would benefit from having a reasonably well-balanced portfolio. If all businesses are projected toward the aging dimension, the firm might enjoy an excellent current profitability, but very little in terms of future expectations. On the contrary, if the portfolio is biased toward the embryonic side, the firm could have great future potential, but might be unable to achieve it, because of the lack of a current base to support the large commitment of resources required.

THE CONCEPT OF NATURAL STRATEGIC THRUST AND GENERIC STRATEGY

Once the portfolio of businesses has been properly positioned in the life-cycle matrix, ADL introduces three conceptual aids to assist managers in the process of identifying an appropriate strategy for each strategy center.

The first of these concepts is the so called *families of thrusts*. ADL postulates that there are four families which cover the entire spectrum of business positioning within the portfolio matrix: natural development, selective development, prove viability, and withdrawal. Figure 9.12 shows broadly where each of these four families fit. A "natural development" family corresponds to a business which, because of its industry maturity and its competitive strength, deserves a strong support to assure an industry-wide growth. A "selective development" family, as its name implies, requires concentration of resources in industries which are either particularly attractive or where the firm has a singular competitive skills to exploit. "Prove viability" is inherently a transitory situation which cannot be sustained, calling for immediate actions to change the state of affairs. "Withdrawal" calls for concerted actions to withdraw from the business.

Having selected the family of strategic thrust most appropriate for a given business, the manager should select now one *specific thrust* belonging to that

Figure 9.10 An Illustration of the Life-cycle Portfolio Matrix

Competitive position \ Maturity	Embryonic	Growth	Mature	Aging	Total
Dominant		Unit 2 (VHF and SSB radios) Unit 12 (Hi-Power tubes)		Unit 10 (Mechanical navigational systems)	3
Strong	Unit 13 (Dyna)	Unit 7 (Heat sensing devices) Unit 11 (Electron microscopes)	Unit 5 (Radar products) Unit 8 (Switching devices)		5
Favorable		Unit 1 (Electronic navigational systems) Unit 9 (Elec. temp control systems)	Unit 6 (Low pressure devices)		3
Tenable					
Weak	Unit 4 (Electronic recording systems)	Unit 3 (Mini-computers)			2
Total	2	7	3	1	13

Source: From Kenneth J. Albert (editor), *Handbook of Business Problem Solving,* Roger R. Osell and Robert V. L. Wright, "Allocating Resources: How to do it in Multi-Industry Corporations," © 1980, p. 1–98. Reprinted by permission of McGraw-Hill Book Company, New York, NY.

family. For example, the following thrusts can be applied to the natural development family:

—*Start up*, which could be applied in an embryonic stage, when the business unit has strong competitive potential to acquire rapidly a significant strength in that market.
—*Growth with industry*, which is applicable when the firm is satisfied with the current position of the business, and wants to maintain its existing market share. These conditions exist when the competitive position is either dominant or strong, and the industry has reached a certain stage of maturity.
—*Gain position gradually* useful when modest increase in market share are required for the business to have a more solid position, perhaps applicable when the firm enjoys a favorable status in a growth industry.
—*Gain position aggressively*, a clear thrust when the firm has a tenable or weak position in the early stages of maturity and wants to improve dramatically its current standing to avoid being left out of an attractive industry.
—*Defend* position, which could apply when the firm enjoys an either dominant or strong position in earlier stages of maturity.
—*Harvest*, clearly relevant for the aging stages.

The third concept is that of *generic strategy*. Having selected a specific thrust within the family, ADL proposes a set of 24 generic strategies to choose from, in order to support the development of the preferred thrust. Although these strategies were already described in Chapter 3, for the convenience of the reader they are repeated here in Figure 9.13.

ADL does not presume that this list of generic strategies exhaust the full spectrum of alternatives for strategy creation. In fact, they are persistently encouraging managers to add, expand, innovate, and offer new strategic alternatives. However, they feel the 24 generic strategies suggested constitute a reasonable broad set, so as to cover some of the more significant options related to the task of strategy formulation.

ADL has found it useful to group those strategies into subcategories which communicate the main area of concern addressed by the strategy. The resulting categories are given in Figure 9.14.

In order to link these three concepts of families, strategic thrusts, and generic strategies, ADL has provided a mapping which is given in Figure 9.15.

Strategy formulation can never be reduced to simplistic rules of thumb. However, a framework such as this one might be useful, first, to reinforce the concept of natural strategies—namely, to uncover courses of action which might be consistent with the industry and competitive portion of a business—and second, to facilitate a diagnostic process. In this capacity, the ADL framework can assist managers simply by providing a checklist against which to contrast both the strategies which are already in place, as well as those which are being proposed for the development of a business.

Figure 9.11 Distribution of Corporate Sales, Net Income, Assets and Return on Net Assets by Life-cycle Stages and Competition Positioning

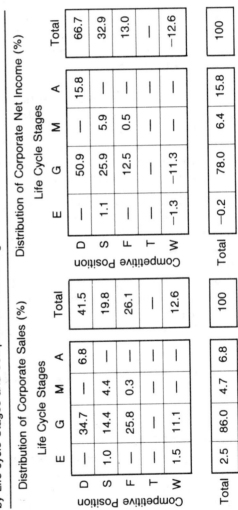

Distribution of Corporate Sales (%)

Competitive Position	Life Cycle Stages E	G	M	A	Total
D	—	34.7	—	6.8	41.5
S	1.0	14.4	4.4	—	19.8
F	—	25.8	0.3	—	26.1
T	—	—	—	—	—
W	1.5	11.1	—	—	12.6
Total	2.5	86.0	4.7	6.8	100

Distribution of Corporate Net Income (%)

Competitive Position	Life Cycle Stages E	G	M	A	Total
D	—	50.9	—	15.8	66.7
S	1.1	25.9	5.9	—	32.9
F	—	12.5	0.5	—	13.0
T	—	—	—	—	—
W	-1.3	-11.3	—	—	-12.6
Total	-0.2	78.0	6.4	15.8	100

196

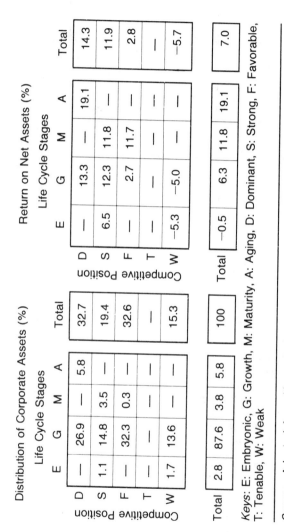

Distribution of Corporate Assets (%)

Competitive Position	Life Cycle Stages				Total
	E	G	M	A	
D	—	26.9	—	5.8	32.7
S	1.1	14.8	3.5	—	19.4
F	—	32.3	0.3	—	32.6
T	—	—	—	—	—
W	1.7	13.6	—	—	15.3
Total	2.8	87.6	3.8	5.8	100

Return on Net Assets (%)

Competitive Position	Life Cycle Stages				Total
	E	G	M	A	
D	—	13.3	—	19.1	14.3
S	6.5	12.3	11.8	—	11.9
F	—	2.7	11.7	—	2.8
T	—	—	—	—	—
W	-5.3	-5.0	—	—	-5.7
Total	-0.5	6.3	11.8	19.1	7.0

Keys: E: Embryonic, G: Growth, M: Maturity, A: Aging, D: Dominant, S: Strong, F: Favorable, T: Tenable, W: Weak

Source: Adapted from Kenneth J. Albert (editor), Handbook of Business Problem Solving. Roger R. Osell and Robert V. L. Wright, "Allocating Resources: How to do it in Multi-Industry Corporations," © 1980, p. 1–99. Reprinted by permission of McGraw-Hill Book Company, New York, NY.

Figure 9.12 Natural Strategic Thrusts

Stages of Industry Maturity: Competitive Position	Embryonic	Growth	Mature	Aging
Dominant				
Strong		Natural Development		
Favorable			Selective Development	
Tenable			Prove Viability	
Weak				Out

Source: Arthur D. Little, Inc.

Figure 9.13 Generic Strategies Proposed by Arthur D. Little, Inc.

Survey Code

A	*Backward Integration*
B	*Development of Overseas Business*
C	*Development of Overseas Facilities*
D	*Distribution Rationalization*
E	*Excess Capacity*
F	*Export/Same Product*
G	*Forward Integration*
H	*Hesitation*
I	*Initial Market Development*
J	*Licensing Abroad*
K	*Complete Rationalization*
L	*Market Penetration*
M	*Market Rationalization*
N	*Methods and Functions Efficiency*
O	*New Products/New Markets*
P	*New Products/Same Market*
Q	*Production Rationalization*
R	*Product Line Rationalization*
S	*Pure Survival*
T	*Same Products/New Markets*
U	*Same Product/Same Markets*
V	*Technological Efficiency*
W	*Traditional Cost Cutting Efficiency*
X	*Unit Abandonment*

Source: Arthur D. Little, Inc.

Figure 9.14   Grouping of Generic Strategies by Main Areas
of Concern

I. *Marketing Strategies*
   F. Export/Same Product
   I. Initial Market Development
   L. Market Penetration
   O. New Products/New Markets
   P. New Products/Same Market
   T. Same Products/New Markets
II. *Integration Strategies*
   A. Backward Integration
   G. Forward Integration
III. *Go Overseas Strategies*
   B. Development of an Overseas Business
   C. Development of Overseas Production Facilities
   J. Licensing Abroad
IV. *Logistics Strategies*
   D. Distribution Rationalization
   E. Excess Capacity
   M. Market Rationalization
   Q. Production Rationalization
   R. Product Line Rationalization
V. *Efficiency Strategies*
   N. Methods and Functions Efficiency
   V. Technological Efficiency
   W. Traditional Cost Cutting Efficiency
VI. *Harvest Strategies*
   H. Hesitation
   K. Little Jewel
   S. Pure Survival
   U. Maintenance
   X. Unit Abandonment

Source: Arthur D. Little, Inc.

PERFORMANCE ANALYSIS

In the ADL methodology, the position of a business in the life cycle affects directly the performance measurements used to monitor the quality of strategy implementation.

One tool, used for this purpose is what ADL refers to as the Ronagraph, which shows on the vertical axis the return on net assets (RONA) generated by each of the businesses of the firms portfolio, and on the horizontal axis the internal deployment of cash flows. When that number is 100%, all cash flows are redeployed and the business is cash neutral. Above 100%, the business becomes a cash user, and below 100%, a cash generator. Moreover, a negative number means that a disinvestment strategy is being applied, because more than 100% of cash flows are being taken out of the business. In the Ronagraph,

Figure 9.15   Families, Strategic Thrusts, and Related Generic Strategies

Thrusts \ Strategies	A	B	C	D	E	F	G	H	I	J	K	L	M	N	O	P	Q	R	S	T	U	V	W	X
NATURAL DEVELOPMENT																								
Startup					E				I			L												
Growth with industry	A	B	C			F	G			J				N		P				T	U			
Gain position gradually							G					L								T				
Gain position aggressively		B	C		E		G					L		N	O	P				T		V		
Defend position	A		C											N							U	V	W	
Harvest				D				H			K		M				Q	R			U		W	
SELECTIVE DEVELOPMENT																								
Find niche	A						G		I			L	M					R		T				
Exploit niche		B	C		E							L		N		P					U	V		
Hold niche			C	D										N			Q				U			
PROVE VIABILITY																								
Catchup				D	E							L	M			P	Q	R						
Renew				D									M		O	P	Q	R			U			
Turn around				D								L	M	N			Q	R				V	W	
Prolong existence	A			D		F				J	K		M	N			Q	R	S	T			W	
WITHDRAWAL																								
Withdraw				D									M				Q	R					W	
Divest				D							K						Q	R	S					
Abandon																								X

Source: Arthur D. Little, Inc.

each business unit is represented by a circle, whose area is proportional to the investment attached to that business unit.

Figure 9.16 illustrates a typical Ronagraph, which is used not only to show some key financial characteristics of the business units, but also to compare them with the performance of leading competitors. The zones in the graph indicate the performance to be expected from a strong competitor, which is

Figure 9.16 A Typical Ronagraph

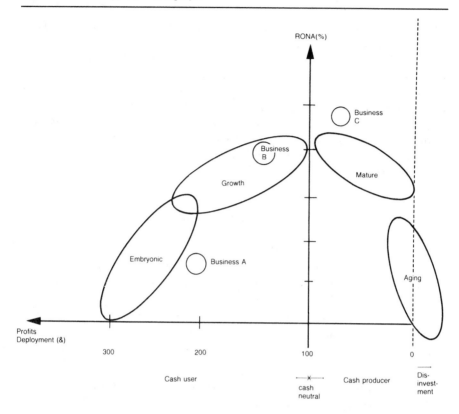

maintaining its position. Business B is performing exactly according to those expectations, while businesses C and A are above and below this benchmark, respectively.

This consistency between financial performance and stages of the life-cycle is not limited exclusively to RONA. A host of other indicators are also expected to perform in accordance with the industry maturity. Some of those indicators are: profits after taxes, net assets, net working capital/sales, costs of goods sold/sales, fixed costs/sales, variable costs/sales, profit after taxes/sales, operating cash flows/sales and net cash flow to corporation/sales. We have briefly commented on Figure 9.1 the expected behavior of sales, profits, and net cash flows, as the business travels through the life cycle. Moreover, Figures 9.5 and 9.6, establish the expected investment requirements, profitability, and cash flow requirements, respectively, according to the position of the business in the life-cycle matrix.

For an excellent illustration of the approach for allocating resources derived from the life-cycle matrix, and the financial implications for strategic performance, see Osell and Wright (1980).

MANAGERIAL SYSTEMS ANALYSIS

We indicated in Chapter 5 that the primary characteristics of strategic management is to seek congruency among all administrative systems, with corporate culture. The ADL strategic planning approach subscribes strongly to this philosophy, providing once more a consistency check among managerial systems within the stages of the life-cycle. The central idea is that the management tasks significantly change as a business goes from embryonic to aging, and therefore, administrative systems, structure, and organizational climate should change accordingly. Figure 9.17 provides a remarkably compact description of the primary characteristics of the managerial systems and organizational climate, within each stage of the life-cycle.

RISK ANALYSIS

The last step in the ADL methodology consists of mixing the degree of risk implicit in the strategy pursuit by an individual business unit. Risk is being assessed in terms of the predictability of profit performance, the more unpredictable it becomes, the greater the risk.

The risk assessment involves an exercise of high subjectivity. ADL identifies several factors which contribute to risk to be assessed independently. These factors are:

—Maturity and competitive position, which is given by the position of the business within the life-cycle matrix. The highest risk exists on an embryonic business, which is in a weak competitive position. The lower risk is the dominant business in an aging industry. The risk decreases when moving in the life-cycle matrix horizontally from left to right and vertically from the bottom to the top.

—Industry; some industries are inherently less predictable than others at the same stage of maturity.

—Strategy; some strategies are more aggressive than others, and consequently imply a larger risk.

—Assumptions; the hypotheses regarding the future, in which the strategies are based, could contain different degrees of risk.

—Past performance; units with a good track record are less risky than those with erratic records.

—Management; the demonstrated ability of the managers in charge of the unit is a central determinant to the predictability of earnings.

—Performance improvement; the magnitude of the gap between existing and expected performance is the last important conditioner of risk.

Figure 9.18 exhibits the format proposed by ADL for the assessment of the risk analysis.

Figure 9.17 Consistency of Management Systems with Industry Maturity

DESCRIPTORS / CHARACTERISTICS	Embryonic	Growth	Mature	Aging
GENERAL THRUST	Entrepreneurship • Start-up • Flexibility • Survival	Sophisticated management of markets • Growth • Develop advantageous competitive position	Critical administration • Maximize efficiency • Optimize profits	Opportunistic milking • Prolongation • Maximize profits • Survival
PLANNING SYSTEM				
• Time Frame	Long enough to encompass life cycle (10 yrs.)	Long term investment payout (7 yrs.)	Intermediate (3 yrs.)	Short term (1 yr.)
• Content	By product/customer	By product and program	By product/market/function	By plant
• Approach	Flexible	Less flexible	Formalized	Formalized
ORGANIZATION				
• Size	Small; rapidly growing	Moderate; moderate growth	Large	Large; moderate shrinkage
• Stability	Fluctuating	Less fluctuating	Stable	Less stable
• Structure	Loose/informal; authorities/responsibilities not clearly defined, with some overlapping	Becoming more formal	Tight/formal; authorities/responsibilities clearly defined and described	Formal/pared down
• Complexity	Simple; few functions and hierarchical levels	Becoming complex; increasing number and variety of functions, divisions and hierarchical levels	Complex; multifunctional, multidivisional and multi-level	Simplified functions, divisions, levels

Figure 9.17 Continued

DESCRIPTORS / CHARACTERISTICS	Embryonic	Growth	Mature	Aging
• Flexibility	High flexibility	Becoming more rigid	Rigid	Less rigid
MANAGERIAL MODE				
• Orientation	Task/growth/financing	Task/performance/people	People/performance	Performance/survival
• Style	Open; ad hoc; consultative, fire-fighting	Participative; becoming more formal; delegation	Formal; leadership; delegation; control	Autocratic; tight control; expedient
• Skills	Generalist	More specialized	Specialist	More generalist
• Risk	High	Moderately high	Moderate	Low
• Time Span/Concern	Short	Long	Intermediate	Short
• Key Activity	Innovation	Planning	Systems	Control
REWARD SYSTEM				
• Main Purpose	Incentive	Incentive/equity	Equity	Equity/incentive
• Structure of Pay Package	High variable/low fixed	Balanced variable and fixed	Low variable/high fixed	Fixed only
• Character	Loose/informal	Becoming formal	Formal/rigid	Formal/rigid
• Basis	Functional worth and individual performance	Functional worth and individual and group performance	Functional worth and group performance	Functional worth and individual and group performance
• Timing	Quarterly	Semi-annually—annually	Annually; some deferred for succeeding 2–3 years.	Annually

	Shares	Time off from work	Time off/retirement	Retirement
• Fringe Emphasis				
COMMUNICATIONS & INFORMATIVE SYSTEM				
• Main Purpose	Rapid responsiveness	Planning	Coordination/control	Control
• Character	Informal/tailored	Formal/tailored	Formal/uniform	Little or none by direction
• Content of Reporting	Qualitative; market-oriented; unsystematic	Qualitative and quantitative; early warning system, all functions	Quantitative; production-oriented; systematic	Quantitative; oriented to balance sheet; systematic
• Policies	Few	More	Many	Many
• Procedures	None	Few	Many	Many
CONTROLS AND MEASURING SYSTEM				
• Main Purpose	Identify significant need for rapid response	Early warning	Improve quality of management decisions	Control
• Principal Focus	Market/marketing/product development	Marketing/manufacturing	Manufacturing/financial performance	Financial performance
• Measures Used	Few fixed	Multiple/adjustable	Multiple/adjustable	Few/fixed
• Frequency of Measurement	Often	Relative often	Traditionally periodic	Less often
• Detail of measurement	Less	More	Great	Less
SUMMARY CHARACTERIZATION				

Source: Arthur D. Little, Inc.

Figure 9.18 Risk Analysis

Element of Risk:	Risk Level		
	Low	Medium	High
Industry			
Maturity			
Competitive Position			
Strategy			
Assumptions			
Past Performance of Unit			
Past Performance of Management			
Level of Future Performance			
Overall Risk			

Source: Arthur D. Little, Inc.

A CRITIQUE OF THE LIFE-CYCLE APPROACH

There are some major contributions that ADL has made in the area of strategic planning by proposing a comprehensive and structured process to assist managers in the identification of strategic choices. By selecting the life cycle as the central conceptual framework behind that process, ADL has recognized a relevant and widely accepted concept which has deep implications for strategic development, particularly in high technology.

Implicitly, the life cycle has been part of the previously described portfolio matrices. However, it has been ADL's contribution to raise that concept to a prominent position within strategic planning, thoroughly exploiting the strategic implications of the life-cycle.

The resulting methodological approach is, certainly, highly creative, searching for consistency of industry maturity, not only with strategic planning, but with all the other key administrative processes, organizational climate, and structure. From this perspective, the ADL methodology not only is relevant to strategic planning; it addresses also some of the key concerns of strategic management.

Finally, the articulation of strategic thrusts and generic strategies consistent with industry maturity and competitive position of the business might either offer constructive suggestions for managers who are not well seasoned in the practice of strategic planning, or, at least, might constitute a useful diagnostic base against which to contrast the existing strategies of an ongoing business.

We turn our attention now to limitations that can be raised on the ADL methodology. First, is the overall controversy surrounding the usefulness of the life-cycle concept. Dhalla and Yuspeh (1976) claim that the life-cycle has little validity and the marketing strategies typically recommended for succeeding stages of the cycle are likely to cause trouble: "In some respects, the concept has done more harm than good, by persuading top executives to neglect existing brands, and place undue emphasis on new products." Dhalla and Yuspeh particularly deplore the branch managers tendency to assume that some slump in sales is evidence of having reached its aging stage, prompting the abandonment of the brand. However, their view is drawn from nondurable goods, like cereals and cosmetics, stressing the behavior of brand sales as opposed to business units sales.

Porter (1980) also raises some criticisms regarding the life cycle:

—The duration of the life-cycle stages varies widely from industry to industry, and it is hard to specify what stage prevails in an industry at a given point in time.
—The industry maturity does not always evolve into a well behaved S-shaped pattern. Sometimes, industries rejuvenate after a period of decline. Occasionally, industries skip stages, particularly when they are affected by passing fads. Also, economic conditions, such as depression, might obscure the true developmental stage corresponding to a given industry.
—Firms can affect the shape of the life-cycle curve, primarily through product innovation and repositioning.
—The nature of competition is quite variable from industry to industry, depending on the life-cycle stage. For example, some industries evolve from a very fragmentary structure to a highly concentrated one (for example, automobiles). Others go just the other way around. They begin as concentrated industries and, as time passes, they become more and more fragmented (that is bank cash dispensers). A legitimate question to be raised is if there is any broadly applicable strategic implication to be derived from the position of a business in the life-cycle, when such important structural changes are occurring simultaneously in the industry.

All of these comments serve to stress the point that, although the life-cycle approach is a useful frame of reference, it has to be applied in a highly judicious way.

There is a final warning that we would like to address pertaining to the use and applicability of the ADL strategic planning process. There are clearly some advantages in having a well organized, disciplined methodology to facilitate the formulation and development of strategies. Its counterpart, however, is that excessive rigidity could lead to a mechanistic type of thinking which would stifle rather than enhance creativity. Although ADL would never intend to apply its methodology that way, in uninitiated hands that tool could hinder a truly innovative way of thinking.

REFERENCES

Abernathy, William J., and James M. Utterback, "Patterns of Industrial Innovation," in Michael L. Tuchman and William L. Moore, *Readings in the Management of Innovation*, Pitman, Boston, 1982.

Arthur D. Little, Inc. *A System for Managing Diversity*, Cambridge, MA, December 1974.

Arthur D. Little, Inc., *Discovering the Fountain of Youth: An Approach to Corporate Growth and Development*, San Francisco, CA, 1979.

Arthur D. Little, Inc., *A Management System for the 1980's*, San Francisco, CA, 1980.

Clifford, Donald K., Jr., "Managing the Product Life Cycle" in Philip Kotler and Keith Cox, Eds., *Marketing Management and Strategy. A Reader*, Prentice-Hall, Englewood Cliff, NJ, 1980.

Dhalla, Nariman K., and Sonia Yuspeh, "Forget the Product Life Cycle Concept!," *Harvard Business Review*, Vol. 54, No. 1, January–February 1976, pp. 102–109.

Forbes, Edward H., and Thomas J. Bate II, "The Life Cycle Approach to Strategic Planning," unpublished master thesis, Sloan School of Management, Cambridge, MA, 1980.

Hayes, Robert H., and Steven C. Wheelwright, "Link Manufacturing Process and Product Life-Cycle." *Harvard Business Review*, Vol. 57, No. 1, January–February 1979a, pp. 133–140.

Hayes, Robert H., and Steven C. Wheelwright, "The Dynamics of Process Products Life Cycles," Harvard Business Review, Vol. 57, No. 2, March–April 1979b, pp. 127–135.

Kotler, Philip, *Marketing Management*, 4th Ed., Prentice-Hall, Inc., Englewood Cliffs, NJ, 1980.

Luck, David J., and O. C. Ferrell, *Marketing Strategy and Plans*, Prentice-Hall, Englewood Cliffs, NJ, 1979.

Moore, William L., and Michael L. Tushman, "Managing Innovation over the Product Life-Cycle," in Michael L. Tushman and William L. Moore, *Readings in the Management of Innovation*, Pitman, Boston, 1982.

Osell, Roger R., and Robert V. L. Wright, "Allocating Resources: How to do it in Multi-Industry Corporations," in Kenneth J. Albert (editor), *Handbook of Business Problem Solving*, McGraw-Hill, New York, 1980, Chapter 8, pp. 1.89–1.109.

Porter, Michael E., *Competitive Strategy*, The Free Press, New York, 1980.

Urban, Glen L., and John R. Hauser, *Design and Marketing of New Products*, Prentice-Hall, Englewood Cliffs, NJ, 1980.

Utterback, James M. "Management of Technology," in Arnoldo C. Hax (Ed.), *Studies in Operations Management*, North-Holland, Amsterdam, 1978, pp. 137–160.

10

ASSESSMENT OF THE ECONOMIC CONTRIBUTION OF A STRATEGY: THE CONCEPT OF VALUE CREATION

The initial steps in the corporate strategic planning process we presented in Chapter 4 have, as a major objective, the formulation of business strategies which respond to the vision of the firm, and to the competitive pressures faced by each business unit. We are now left with the question of addressing the merits attached to each alternative strategy. In a profit making organization, it is a widely accepted economic criteria that the goodness of a strategy should be measured in terms of total value created for the firm's shareholders. In other words, the economic objective of the firm is the maximization of the shareholders' wealth.

We will pursue two different issues in this chapter. First, is the presentation of a simple rule—the market to book value (M/B) model—to guide managers in addressing the question of value creation both, at the firm and at the SBU levels. Second, we want to discuss another kind of portfolio matrix—the so-called profitability matrix—which again might cast some light on the question of the value added by each of the various businesses of a firm.

Prior to addressing these subjects, we will make a few comments on some broad conceptual issues:

1. There is no question that the best methodology available to assess the economic value of the firm, or a business unit belonging to the firm, or a project within an individual business unit, is to compute the Net Present Value

(NPV) of the future cash flows generated by that economic entity, discounted at an appropriate rate, adjusted for inflation and risk. We will assume throughout this chapter that the reader is conversant with the mechanics of cash-flow discounting, as well as the underlying principles leading toward the selection of NPV as a preferred method for economic evaluation. For a justification of this statement, see, for example, Brealey and Myers (1981, Chapter 5).

2. A meaningful proxy for the value of the equity of the firm in a country with an efficient capital market, such as the one prevailing in the United States, is given by the market value of the common stock. The assumption is that the market price of common shares represents a consensus of the present value assigned by investors to the expected cash flow streaming from the assets the firm has already in place, as well as from investments the firm will have the opportunity to make at some time in the future, once the interest payments to debtholders have been subtracted.

   Therefore, within an efficient capital market setting, the objective of the firm equates to maximizing the market value of equity, provided that the capital structure of the firm has already been defined. A broader objective would be the maximization of shareholders' wealth, considering the capital structure as one of the decision variables.

3. The market value of a firm's common shares is an indicator that can assist managers both in assessing the shareholders' wealth, as well as in measuring its economic and financial performance vis-a-vis other firms in its industry. It is not surprising, therefore, that managers carefully observe long-term trends in the capital market as an ultimate guidance for the managerial success of business firms. On the other hand, excessive concern in day-to-day movements of stock market indicators has been repeatedly stated as one of the most negative forces pressuring American managers to inappropriate short-term orientation. Therefore, there seems to be a paradox in the capital-market messages to the manager. But this is not so. There is plenty of evidence that the market does reward long-term performance, and penalizes erratic behavior intended to hide unfavorable developments in the short-run.

4. The above considerations make highly desirable the use of evaluation methodologies in which the market price of the common shares plays an essential role, while retaining the legitimacy of the NPV approach. The M/B model represents such a tool. The most attractive feature about this model is that it lends itself to a fairly simple interpretation in two basic dimensions:
   —the economic and financial performances of the firm (whether the firm is earning a return higher than its cost of capital, or equivalent, whether its economic value exceeds its accounting value), and
   —its competitive performance, measured by the resulting (M/B)s among the leading firms competing in the same industry.

THE MARKET-TO-BOOK VALUE (M/B) MODEL

The M/B model is a blend of two different perspectives of the firm. In the denominator, the book value of the firm's shares provides the accountant's perspective, which corresponds to the historical measurements of resources contributed by shareholders. In the numerator, the market value of the firm's shares gives the investor's perspective, which corresponds to an assessment of future payments generated from the assets the firm has already in place and from the investments the firm would have the opportunity to make at some time in the future. Therefore, the M/B ratio can be equated to:

$$\frac{\text{Expected future payments}}{\text{Past resources committed}}$$

The basic message of the M/B model can be summarized as follows:

—If M/B = 1, the future payments are expected to yield a fair return on the resources committed. The firm is neither creating nor destroying value.
—If M/B > 1, there is an excess return. The firm is creating value for the shareholders.
—If M/B < 1, the return is under the benchmark provided by the market. The firm is destroying value for its shareholders.

When we refer to book value, we assume that all distortions induced by accounting rules have been corrected, mainly the ones produced by inflation and the charges of certain investments as expenditures in one period (most notably R&D and advertising).

Prior to discussing the utilization of this model at both the firm and business levels, we should get a sense of the basic relationships that exist among market and book values, and some key economic and financial indicators characterizing the performance of the firm.

The essence of this model is to capture the market reaction to managerial decisions in a way consistent with NPV calculations. As with all models, a number of simplifying assumptions need to be made to make the problem more tractable from an analytical point of view. The M/B model, in its basic form, assumes a firm is in a situation of stationary growth, characterized by:

1. An initial book value of equity equal to B.
2. An initial total debt equal to D.
3. A constant yearly rate of growth of equity equal to g.
4. A constant debt-to-equity ratio, which implies that D is also growing at a constant yearly rate g. Consequently, total assets, which are equal to debt plus equity, also increase at the same rate g.
5. A constant return on assets (ROA).
6. A constant return on equity (ROE).

7. A constant cost of debt (k_D).
8. A constant cost of equity (k_E).
9. A constant payout ratio (dividends over earnings) equal to $(1 - p)$, p being the profit retention rate.
10. The reinvestment of all depreciation charges as well as retained earnings.
11. A flow of new debt that replaces the maturing debt outstanding every year, in addition to the fresh resources required to increase the total debt outstanding at the rate g.
12. New equity is never issued. All current and future dividends belong exclusively to actual stockholders. (If new equity were to be issued, and the perfect market assumption is made, the wealth of actual stockholders would be unchanged.)

In Figure 10.1 we present a diagram of the cash flows in a firm growing steadily at a rate g, which illustrates the set of assumptions introduced.

Figure 10.1 Cash-flows in a Firm Growing Steadily at Rate g

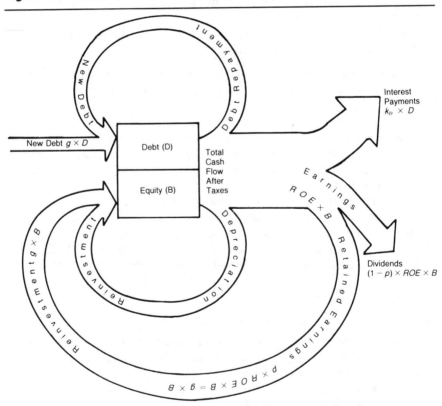

Basically, these assumptions ensure that a company's rate of growth has reached a point of stability. Experience with the use of this model, however, indicates that even if a firm does not strictly fulfill these assumptions, the model results are still useful in two dimensions: one, in providing strategic insights for increasing shareholders value; and two, in suggesting some rules of thumb for evaluating competing strategic alternatives.

Under the model assumptions, the book value of equity grows at a constant rate which may be derived by considering the total return on equity (ROE) and the reinvestment rate (p). If at the beginning of any year the book value of the firm is B, then total earnings amount to $ROE \cdot B$ and the amount reinvested is $p \cdot ROE \cdot B$. Therefore, the book value at the end of the year becomes:

$$B + p \cdot ROE \cdot B = (1 + p \cdot ROE) \cdot B$$

The yearly rate of growth is then $g = p \cdot ROE$. And the dividend paid in that same year is $(1 - p) \cdot ROE \cdot B$, which can also be computed as $(ROE - g) \cdot B$.

Under this steady situation, with a constant growth of the firm, the cash-flow stream transferred to shareholders in the form of dividend payments is derived below:

	Year 1	Year 2	• • •	Year t
Book value (beginning of year)	B	$(1 + g)B$	• • •	$(1 + g)^{t-1}B$
Earnings	$ROE \cdot B$	$ROE(1 + g)B$	• • •	$ROE(1 + g)^{t-1}B$
Retained Earnings	$g \cdot B$	$g(1 + g)B$	• • •	$g(1 + g)^{t-1}B$
Dividend Payments	$(ROE - g)B$	$(ROE - g)(1 + g)B$	• • •	$(ROE - g)(1 + g)^{t-1}B$
Book value (end of year)	$(1 + g)B$	$(1 + g)^2B$	• • •	$(1 + g)^tB$

Notice that retained earnings is computed as $p \cdot$ Earnings. Thus, for the first year, for example, the corresponding value is $p \cdot ROE \cdot B$, which is equal to $g \cdot B$.

To determine the market value of the firm shares, denoted by M, we should obtain the NPV of the dividend stream discounted at the cost of equity capital, k_E (for an explanation of this statement, see, for example, Brealey and Myers, Chapter 4). Thus:

The net present value of the dividend stream is an unbiased assessment of the market value of the firm. For a cost of capital k_E, we obtain the following value for the market value:

$$M = \sum_{t=1}^{\infty} \frac{(ROE - g)(1 + g)^{t-1} B}{(1 + k_E)^t} \tag{1}$$

The M/B ratio can be directly derived from this expression by simple algebraic manipulations. The value thus obtained for a firm growing steadily at rate g is:*

$$\frac{M}{B} = \frac{ROE - g}{k_E - g} \tag{2}$$

There is a wealth of fundamental economic and strategic implications that can be derived from this simple model:

1. The relationship between (M/B) and spread.

    As immediately apparent from the expression of the M/B model [relation (2)], the firm creates value, that is, it is economically profitable, if and only if ROE is greater than k_E. This implies the following relationship between market to book value (M/B) and spread, $(ROE - k_E)$; spread being defined as the difference between the return on equity and the cost of equity.

$$(M/B) > 1 \quad \rightleftarrows \quad ROE - k_E > 0$$
$$(M/B) = 1 \quad \rightleftarrows \quad ROE - k_E = 0$$
$$(M/B) < 1 \quad \rightleftarrows \quad ROE - k_E < 0$$

2. A key distinction between accounting and economic profitability.

    From an accounting perspective, a business is profitable if earnings are positive (the books are in the black), and, therefore, the resulting ROE is also positive.

    However, from an economic perspective, a business is profitable if the return on equity exceeds the cost of equity, which implies that the spread is positive, and consequently its (M/B) ratio is greater than 1.

    It is economic, and not accounting profitability, that determines the capability for wealth creation on the part of the firm. It is perfectly possible that a company is in the black, and yet its market value is way below its book value, which means that, from an economic point of view, its resources would be more profitable if deployed in an alternative investment of similar risk.

    Figure 10.2 contrasts the difference between accounting and economic profitability.

3. The impact of growth.

    Very often, growth is stated as one of the foremost strategic objectives, and growth goals are established without any reference to its implications for the profitability of a business or a firm. However, as can be inferred from the (M/B) model, growth cannot be separated from the profitability status. In fact, if a firm or a business is profitable, that is, its return on

---

* This relation assumes that the cost of capital is larger than the rate of growth, because otherwise we would obtain an unlimited growth in market value, which is an impossible situation to be sustained in the long run.

Figure 10.2 Economic versus Accounting Profitability

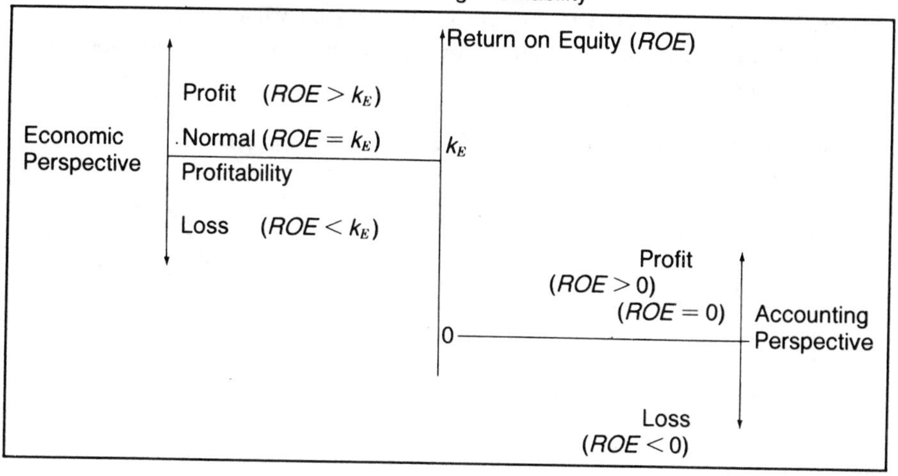

equity exceeds its cost of capital ($ROE > k_E$), growth significantly helps in increasing its market value. It is also immediately apparent from relationship (2), that when the condition of the firm or business is such that $ROE = k_E$, growth has an indifferent impact, neither damages nor hurts, the value-creating capabilities of the firm. However, if a firm or a business is economically unprofitable ($ROE < k_E$), then growth adversely affects its market value.

The statements expressed so far can be summarized in Figure 10.3.

Figure 10.3 The Essential Features of the M/B Model for a Firm under Stationary Growth

The profitable firm or business	The breakeven firm or business	The unprofitable firm or business
$ROE > k_E$	$ROE = k_E$	$ROE < k_E$
$M/B > 1$	$M/B = 1$	$M/B < 1$
Growth will increase M/B	Growth will not affect M/B	Growth will reduce M/B
$NPV > 0$	$NPV = 0$	$NPV > 0$

4. The liquidation value of the firm.

What is the lowest value that the M/B ratio can take? If M represents the value of the common shares of a firm, obviously, M/B can never be negative, since this would imply that you are being paid to acquire the stock. The value of the firm, regardless of how poorly managed it can be, has a lower bound that is represented by the liquidation value, L, which typically does not go any lower than 40 percent of the book value.

With this observation in mind, we now represent the (M/B) model in Figure 10.4.

Figure 10.4 The (M/B) Model for a Firm Under Stationary Growth

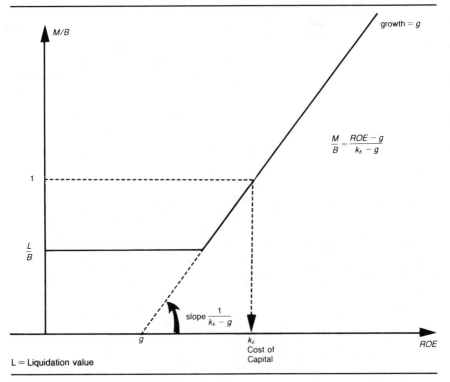

The optimal strategy for ongoing businesses that are generating an ROE below the cost of capital is to minimize growth, or even better, to disinvest and have a negative growth. In that way, market value is maximized. Eventually, the best strategy could be liquidation, particularly if the permissible disinvestment rates are very small. In Figure 10.5, for disinvestment rates larger than g^*, liquidation is not a sensible strategy to pursue (for example at rate g_2). But for smaller rates liquidation is a reasonable strategy; for example, if disinvestment is done at rate g_1, liquidation is the best course of action for ROE values below the limit ROE_1.

---

* Disinvestment rates $g_1 < g^* < g_2$.

Figure 10.5 Disinvestment versus Liquidation Strategies for Businesses with an ROE Smaller than the Cost of Capital (We Are Assuming Disinvestment Rates $g_1 < g^* < g_2$)

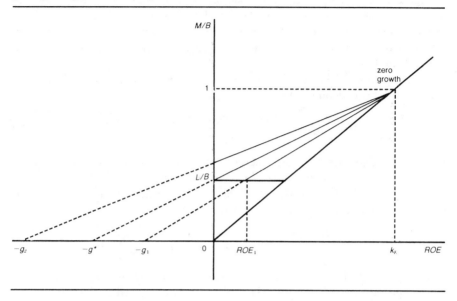

THE MARKET-TO-BOOK VALUE MODEL WITH STATIONARY GROWTH OVER A FINITE HORIZON

A slightly more realistic M/B model than the one we described in the previous section has been proposed by Fruhan (1979) in his book *Financial Strategy*. He claims that there are three factors which are essential to describe the market-to-book value ratio of the firm:

—The size of the spread = $ROE - k_E$.
—The rate of reinvestment of the firm's earnings = p.
—The number of years during which a firm will enjoy the spread identified in the first condition = n.

The model retains all of the hypotheses that we indicated in the previous section; but, rather than assuming a permanent spread, the firm will have a limited number of years where that spread applies. Subsequently, the profitability is assumed to be equal to the cost of capital (which implies that the market value of the remaining cash flow is equal to its book value).

These assumptions are grounded on the observation that many firms achieve a temporary position of economic superiority, which allows them, for a limited number of years, to enjoy significant profitability levels. But after a certain period of time, competitors catch up, and the profitability regresses to the cost of capital.

Figure 10.6 represents the three factors considered by Fruhan as well as second order determinants of those factors. For planning and management control purposes, it is important to understand the degree of influence one can exercise over those factors, in order to achieve a desired goal for the market value of the firm.

When expressing equation (1) in terms of a limited horizon n, the market value of the firm becomes:

$$M = \sum_{t=1}^{n} \frac{(ROE - g)(1 + g)^{t-1}B}{(1 + k_E)^t} + \frac{(1 + g)^n B}{(1 + k_E)^n} \tag{3}$$

The second term corresponds to the market value at the end of year n, (which is equal to the book value at that point in time) discounted to the present.

It can be derived from here the following expression for the M/B model under these conditions:

$$\frac{M}{B} = \left(\frac{ROE - g}{k_E - g}\right)\left[1 - \left(\frac{1+g}{1+k_E}\right)^n\right] + \left(\frac{1+g}{1+k_E}\right)^n \tag{4}$$

Fruhan describes the sensitivity of the (M/B) value by means of a series of tables reproduced in Figure 10.7. The information contained in this figure reinforces the findings of the M/B model which we have already discussed. Looking at the upper left side of the chart, one sees that lack of profitability destroys market value; and the longer this situation subsists, the more devastating its effect. Going down through the chart, one can see that under unprofitable conditions, growth is quite undesirable.

The opposite comments can be made if we start looking at the figure from the upper right corner, where high levels of profitability, extensions of the number of years during which that profitability is enjoyed, and higher growth rates, tends to contribute greater to value creation, translating themselves in increasingly larger M/B ratios.

THE COST OF EQUITY CAPITAL

Throughout the presentation of the model, we have carried out the constant k_E which represents the cost of equity capital. This constant is a fundamental parameter that is characteristic for each business unit. It depends on the general conditions of the economy, the situation of the industry in which this business operates, and the particular policies used by the firm in managing the business.

A sound procedure that can be used to estimate the cost of equity capital is based on the so-called Capital-Asset Pricing Model (CAPM), which is an equilibrium model for pricing securities in the capital markets that has been

Figure 10.6 Factors Affecting the *M/B* Ratio under Stationary Growth for a Finite Time Period

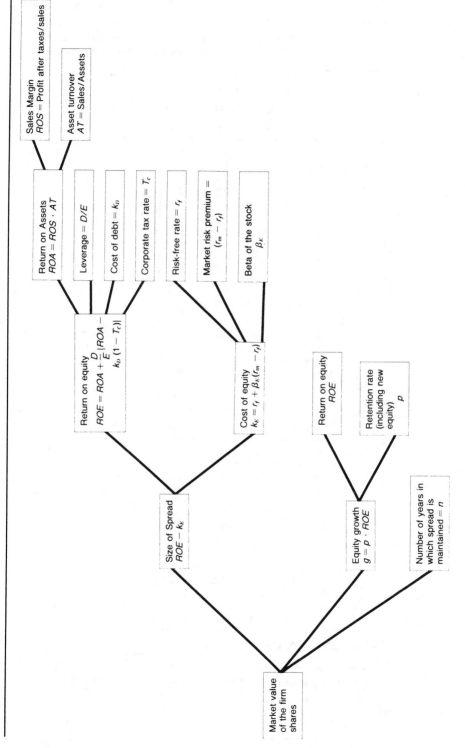

Figure 10.7 Sensitivity of the M/B Model for Different Combinations of Parameters (Model with Stationary Growth over a Finite Horizon)

$$k_E = 10\%$$

Percentage point spread: $(ROE-k_E)$ %

Number of years during which the spread holds, n	−5	0	+5	+10	+20	Reinvestment rate p (%)
5	0.8	1.0	1.2	1.4	1.9	
10	0.7	1.0	1.3	1.8	2.7	0.3
15	0.6	1.0	1.5	2.1	3.6	
30	0.5	1.0	1.7	2.7	5.8	
	−5	0	+5	+10	+20	
5	0.8	1.0	1.2	1.5	2.0	
10	0.7	1.0	1.4	1.9	3.2	0.5
15	0.6	1.0	1.6	2.4	4.8	
30	0.4	1.0	2.0	3.7	12.2	
	−5	0	+5	+10	+20	
5	0.8	1.0	1.2	1.5	2.1	
10	0.6	1.0	1.5	2.1	3.9	0.7
15	0.5	1.0	1.7	2.8	6.8	
30	0.4	1.0	2.5	5.8	30.8	
	−5	0	+5	+10	+20	
5	0.8	1.0	1.2	1.5	2.3	
10	0.6	1.0	1.6	2.4	5.3	1.0
15	0.5	1.0	1.9	3.7	12.2	
30	0.2	1.0	3.8	13.5	149.3	
	−5	0	+5	+10	+20	
5	0.8	1.0	1.3	1.8	3.2	
10	0.5	1.0	2.1	4.4	22.3	2.0*
15	0.3	1.0	3.8	13.0	161.6	

* It is assumed that the firm issues new stock.

Source: William E. Fruhan, *Financial Strategy*, © 1079, p. 12. Reprinted by permission of Richard D. Irwin, Inc., Homewood, IL.

developed by financial economists Sharpe (1964) and Lintner (1965) based on an earlier work by Markowitz (1952).

The general relation to estimate the cost of equity capital is

$$k_E = \text{Risk-free rate} + \text{Risk premium}$$

The risk-free rate corresponds to the return on an investment that offers a sure return. Normally, it is estimated as the return on government-backed treasury bills, whose nominal return may be approximated by the expected inflation rate (see Ibbotson and Sinquefield 1977).

The risk premium is dependent on two parameters: the total extra return added in the market for bearing the risk of an average risky security and the volatility coefficient (β). The corresponding relation is

$$\text{Risk-premium} = \beta \cdot (\text{Average risk premium})$$

It is apparent from this definition that when $\beta = 1$, the risk premium is equal to the average for the entire market. This average is computed as the extra return obtained by the market portfolio, which is the portfolio formed by all securities in the market. Consequently, the average risk premium is a market parameter that can be estimated as:

$$\text{Average risk premium} = \left(\begin{array}{c} \text{Expected return} \\ \text{of the market} \\ \text{portfolio} \end{array} \right) - \text{Risk-free rate}$$

Ibbotson and Sinquefield calculated the average risk premium for the Standard and Poor's portfolio of common stocks of 500 American firms to be 8.8 percent over the period 1926 to 1977.

To determine the risk-premium of an arbitrary business, an estimate of the β constant is required. This parameter represents an estimate of the riskiness of a business. It is defined as:

$$\beta(\text{business}) = \frac{\text{cov(business return, market return)}}{\text{var(market return)}}$$

The interesting result that the CAPM proposes with regard to the compensation of risk in the market is that only a fraction of the total risk is actually compensated. This fraction is called the *systematic risk* and it is related with the volatility of the security. For better understanding of the definition of the volatility coefficient (β), we now offer a brief presentation of the rationale behind the compensation of risk in the market.

The market returns of risky securities cannot be known in advance. They can be large or small, positive or negative, above or below the risk-free rate. Their riskiness stems precisely from this inability to predict their returns. The best we can do is to present an entire distribution of these uncertain returns. Some outcomes will be more likely than others, and we can single out certain intervals in which the security return can be found with high probability. Under the CAPM assumptions, the *total* risk of the security corresponds to the variance of the security returns. But, as mentioned before, this is not the risk that the market compensates, because any investor can eliminate part of that risk by *diversification*. By having more than one security in the portfolio (provided that they are not positively correlated), the total risk goes down for a given return. This is precisely the diversification effect. To understand better the impact of diversification on total risk, consider a number of securities (say n), all with the same expected return (call it μ), and the same variance of return (call it σ^2). For simplicity, suppose that these securities are uncorrelated. Let us form a portfolio with all securities participating equally, that is to say, each security has a weight $1/n$. The expected return of this portfolio stays at the level μ, but its variance goes down to σ^2/n. Figure 10.8 shows the way in which this value, which corresponds to the total risk of the portfolio, goes down with an increasing number of securities in the portfolio.

Under these assumptions, the total risk of the portfolio approaches zero. But this situation is not realistic, because, in general, securities do have a positive correlation among them. Let us consider this case. Assume again that we have n securities, with the same mean and variance of returns (μ and σ^2 respectively), but suppose also that any two securities have a positive covariance (call it cov). In this case, the total risk of an equally weighted portfolio would be

Figure 10.8 The Effect of Diversification on the Total Risk of a Portfolio Formed with Uncorrelated Securities

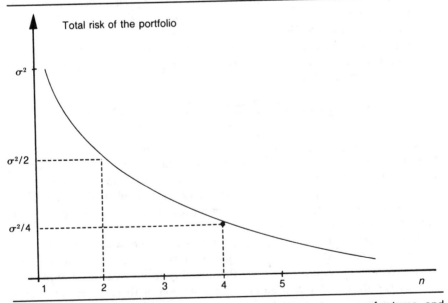

Assumptions: All securities are uncorrelated, have the same mean of returns, and variance of returns (σ^2), and all of them participate equally in the portfolio.

$\frac{\sigma^2}{n} + \frac{(n-1)}{n}$ cov. Figure 10.9 depicts the total risk under these new conditions. Again, diversification reduces the total risk but now there is no way to get to zero. The minimum risk that could be achieved through a perfectly diversified portfolio would be the covariance between any two securities (cov).

These are interesting results. In the first case, the return of securities moved without any relation among them, and diversification could wash away the total risk of the portfolio. In the second case, all the returns of the securities included in the portfolio are partially linked through their correlation. In general, there is a tendency for all of them to move partly together. It is as if the return of a particular security were the result of two independent draws, one which is common and systematic for all securities and the other that is particular for each security. As a consequence of this, the risk of a security can be decomposed into the common part which is called *systematic (or market) risk* and

Figure 10.9 The Effect of Diversification in the Total Risk of a Portfolio Formed with Positively Correlated Securities

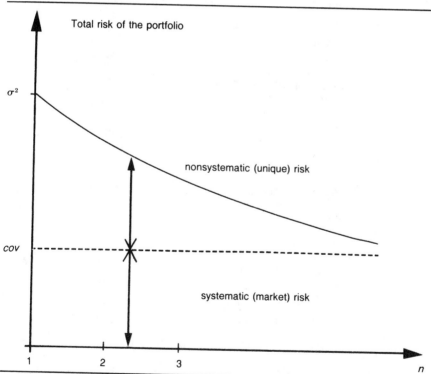

Assumptions: All securities have the same mean of returns and variance of returns (σ^2), the covariance between any two of them is cov; and all of them participate equally in the portfolio.

the particular part which is called *nonsystematic (or unique) risk*. Diversification can only eliminate this last fraction of the risk. For this reason, the systematic risk is also called *nondiversifiable*, and the nonsystematic one is known as *diversifiable*.

From these developments we can see that the market compensates only the systematic or nondiversifiable risk, because the other part of total variance can be eliminated by holding an adequately diversified portfolio. The volatility coefficient is an estimate of the contribution that a security makes to the systematic risk of the portfolio. For that reason, the market risk-premium is estimated as β times the average risk.

The β-coefficient for a given business can be estimated from historical market returns for the firm or for other firms that are present in the same industry. Beta estimates for specific companies are regularly published by Value Line and brokerage firms such as Merrill Lynch, E. F. Hutton, and others. In Figure 10.10 we present a summary table of the relative riskiness of different industries as measured through its β-coefficients.

Figure 10.10   The β Coefficient of Different Industries*

Industry	Beta
Electronic components	1.49
Crude petroleum and natural gas	1.07
Retail department stores	0.95
Petroleum refining	0.95
Motor vehicle parts	0.89
Chemicals	0.88
Metal mining	0.87
Food	0.84
Trucking	0.83
Textile mills products	0.82
Paper and allied products	0.82
Retail grocery stores	0.76
Airlines	0.75
Steel	0.66
Railroads	0.61
Natural gas transmission	0.52
Telephone companies	0.50
Electric utilities	0.46

* These are assets betas. The effect of financial leverage has been removed.

Source: Brealey and Myers, 1981, page 167.

Summarizing, the cost of equity capital for a given business can be estimated as:

$$k_E = \text{Risk-free rate} + \text{Risk Premium}$$

This relation has been shown to be equivalent to:

$$k_E = r_f + \beta_E \ (r_m - r_f) \tag{5}$$

where:

r_f = nominal risk-free rate

$r_m - r_f$ = average risk premium; that is, the expected return of the total market (r_m) minus the risk-free rate (r_f)

β_E = volatility coefficient of the equity cash flow

A last comment that is important to bear in mind has to do with the numerical value of the β_E coefficient, depending on the information used to compute it. When employing β tables which provide direct estimates of the value of β for a given firm, we could simply plug in that numerical value as β_E, because they include the existing characteristics of the firm's capital structure.

However, when using unlevered betas, such as those exhibited in Figure 10.10, a correction has to be made to take into account the specific debt-equity structure of the firm under consideration. When leverage is not too high, this correction is given by the formula:

$$\beta_E = \left\{1 + \frac{D}{E}(1 - T_c)\right\}\beta_u \tag{6}$$

where:

$$D/E = \text{debt-to-equity ratio}$$
$$T_c = \text{corporate-tax rate}$$
$$\beta_u = \text{unlevered beta}$$

A comprehensive discussion on the various forms of cost of capital and their corresponding beta, is given in the appendix to this chapter.

THE USE OF THE M/B MODEL AT THE LEVEL OF THE FIRM

One of the important uses of the M/B model has strictly a diagnostic purpose intending to position the firm against its competitors in terms of their economic and financial performance. This task is greatly facilitated due to the considerable amount of public information regarding the variables included in the M/B model. The Compustat files, Value Line reports, annual reports and financial analysts' studies, all can be used to produce estimates for the firm's current market value, book value, ROE, equity growth rate, and cost of equity capital. The broadest example of this sort is described in Figure 10.11 where the thirty Dow Jones Industrials are plotted in an M/B versus spread graph.

A first glance at that figure tends to confirm that there is a positive association between (M/B) and spread. In the upper right quadrant, perhaps the most

Figure 10.11   An M/B versus Spread Graph for the Thirty Dow Jones Industrials

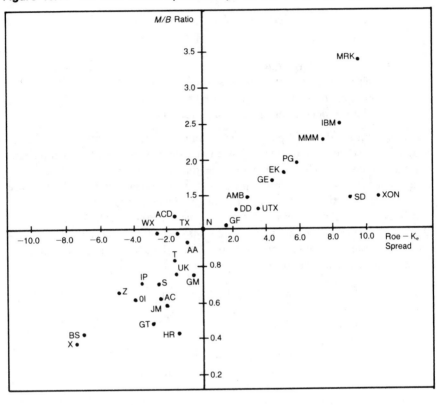

Key for the Figure

AA:	Alcoa	MMM:	Minnesota Mining
AC:	American Can	MRK:	Merck Company
ACD:	Allied Chemical	N:	Inco Limited
AMB:	American Brands	OI:	Owens Illinois
BS:	Bethlehem Steel	PG:	Procter & Gamble
DD:	du Pont	S:	Sears Roebuck
EK:	Eastman Kodak	SD:	Standard Oil of California
GE:	General Electric	T:	AT&T
GF:	General Foods	TX:	Texaco
GM:	General Motors	UK:	Union Carbide
GT:	Goodyear Tires	UTX:	United Technology
HR:	International Harvester	WX:	Westinghouse
IBM:	IBM	X:	U.S. Steel
IP:	International Paper	XON:	Exxon
JM:	Johns Manville	Z:	Woolworth

Source: Marakon Associates, "Criteria for Determining an Optimum Business Portfolio," © 1980. Reprinted by permission of Marakon Associates, San Francisco, CA.

striking deviation from that perceived association is the position of both Standard Oil of California (SD) and Exxon (XON). Those were companies that in the late 1970s were making extraordinary high profits, reflected in a large spread. However, the future expectations regarding the ability of the firm to maintain those profit levels were not as high, as reflected by an (M/B) ratio which, although greater than one, did not correspond to the historical values of the spread. These last comments serve to emphasize one of the characteristics of the model. The measurement of spread is anchored on past performance, while the (M/B) ratio contains the future expectations regarding the profitability of the firm, on the part of the shareholders.

In order to contrast the discrepancy between the market value and the historical performance of the firm, McKinsey and Co. uses a different way of examining the economic performance of a group of firms competing in a given industry (Bennett 1982). They plot the (M/B) ratio against an indicator they call Economic-to-book value ratio. The economic value calculation is based on historical performance projected out into the future. That is, a company that has earned a positive spread of 3 percentage points, has sustained a 5 percent dividend payout to investors, and has grown its equity base at 10 percent annually, in the recent past, is assumed to do so for the next ten years in the economic value calculation. (If those data are replaced in relation (4), the corresponding E/B is equal to 1.3.)

The computational methodology of McKinsey simply tends to confront the two sides of the equation (4) corresponding to the model used by Fruhan. The left-hand side can be calculated directly from publically available information. The right-hand side is calculated from projected values based on historical performance. Any significant discrepancy between these two values raises a diagnostic flag which would have to be examined carefully.

Figure 10.12 depicts (M/B) versus (E/B) plots for a group of companies in the publishing industry and in the oil industry. Those companies which are below the diagonal, are assessed by the market as expecting to have a poorer performance in the future than they have accomplished in the past. The opposite is true for a firm above the diagonal. Those firms having (M/B) and (E/B) ratios below 1, are in a more difficult position.

A slightly different approach is being used by Strategic Planning Associates (1981) in order to portray the economic performance of the various firms competing in an industry. They construct what they call the Value Curve, which is a plot of the values of M/B against (ROE/k_E), which they refer to as the Value-leverage index. (See Figure 10.13 for an example of the forest products industry.) Moreover, in the graph they also plot the average M/B curve for the industry, which they construct from the theoretical relationship $(M/B) = (ROE - g)/(k_E - g)$ for values of (ROE/k_E) greater than one, and from their own empirical observations for values of (ROE/k_E) less than one. The implications to be derived from the Value Curve Analysis are similar to those already discussed in Marakon's (M/B) versus spread graphs.

Figure 10.12 McKinsey's (M/B) versus (E/B) Graph

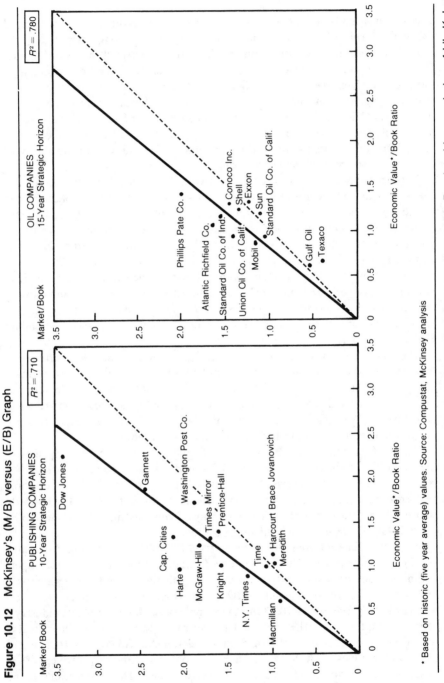

* Based on historic (five year average) values. Source: Compustat, McKinsey analysis

Source: Lily K. Lai, "Corporate Strategic Planning for a Diversified Company," © 1983. Reprinted by permission of Lily K. Lai.

Figure 10.13 The Value Curve for the Forest Products Industry

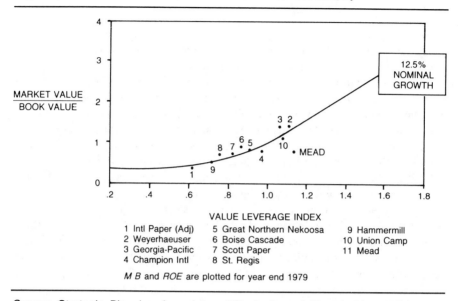

1 Intl Paper (Adj)   5 Great Northern Nekoosa   9 Hammermill
2 Weyerhaeuser   6 Boise Cascade   10 Union Camp
3 Georgia-Pacific   7 Scott Paper   11 Mead
4 Champion Intl   8 St. Regis

M B and *ROE* are plotted for year end 1979

Source: Strategic Planning Associates, "Strategic and Shareholders Value: The Value Curve," © 1981, page 12. Reprinted by permission of Strategic Planning Associates, Washington, D.C.

THE USE OF THE M/B MODEL AT THE BUSINESS LEVEL

At the level of the firm, the market value can be assessed directly through the price of common shares. However, we do not know through external information how that value is being allocated to the various businesses of the firm. Therefore, although all the concepts we have developed explaining economic performance at the level of the firm can also be applied at the level of the business, the use of the (M/B) model has to be modified. We will address now some of the central issues to accomplish that objective.

The Additivity Principle

The segmentation of the firm into a set of independent entities has been a primary concern in strategic planning. When attempting to evaluate the contribution of each of the segments, which we have referred to as SBUs, to the total market value of the firm, it is important to specify the degree of interaction among each other. If the SBUs are totally independent activities, the value of the firm is simply equal to the sum of the values of each of its businesses. In particular, if the capital market assigns a value $M(A)$ for asset A and $M(B)$

for asset B, then the market value of the firm which holds these two assets is:

$$M(A + B) = M(A) + M(B)$$

This relationship is referred to as the principle of *value additivity*, which allows a firm to evaluate new assets as independent entities.

There are situations where the profitability of a firm might be different from the simple sum of the market value of the independent businesses. A very important one is when the joint assets imply a cash flow which cannot be obtained as the simple sum of the two independent cash flows, due to a change in profitability resulting from potential synergism when the assets are integrated in a single unit. It is also worthwhile noticing that, if by any circumstance the systematic risks of the businesses are reduced by putting them together, the market value of the joint venture will be larger than just the sum of the parts.

In any event, the central task is to address what is the unique economic contribution emerging from each independent business activity, separating them from that emerging from other business entities. If this can be accomplished, we can always find the value of the firm as the sum of the contributions from each business, which is what we will be assuming in the remaining part of this section.

Assessing the Market Value of a Business

We want to comment on three distinct ways of evaluating the contribution of business units to the market value of the firm.

The simplest one is to treat the business unit as if it were a totally independent business firm, and then apply either one of the two forms of the M/B model represented by expressions (2) or (4), depending on how appropriate the assumptions of those models are with regard to the prevailing conditions of the business unit under analysis.

The second approach still requires treating each SBU as if it were a micro firm. In order to calculate its market value contribution, it will be necessary to allocate both a portion of the firm equity as well as the firm debt to each SBU, and then proceed to identify the equity cash flow emanating from the SBU according to the following computations:

> Business profits after tax
> —After tax interest payments corresponding to the SBU
> —Retained earnings for further investments in the SBU
> _____
> Equity cash flow contributed by the SBU

Normally the cash flows are projected through a limited time horizon, say five years, at the end of which a terminal value has to be attached. The actual number for the terminal value depends on the assumptions being made with regard to the nature of the cash flows after the planning horizon. If the business unit is going to have an ROE equal to its cost of capital, the terminal value should be the equity book value at the end of the planning horizon. If this results in a fairly conservative assumption, we could suppose that the business is going to enjoy for a very long period of time a positive spread, and a steady growth. We are back to the assumptions we made for the stationary model, in which case the terminal value at the end of the planning horizon could be computed as [see relation (2)]:

$$M(\text{end planning horizon}) = B(\text{end planning horizon}) \frac{ROE - g}{k_E - g}$$

These streams of cash flows have to be discounted at the cost of equity capital. Since we cannot directly observe betas for each individual business, we have to rely on betas for the industry in which the business competes. The correction for the equity beta takes into account the capital structure of the business and it is given by expression (6).

The third approach for assessing the market value contribution of an SBU is equivalent to the cash flows projections we have just described, except that more closely follows the prevailing management control practices. The idea is that a firm should be measured in terms of its profits after tax and after interests relative to its equity base, while a business should rather be accountable for its after tax profits relative to its assets, independent of the debt structure. In other words, from an accounting perspective a firm is measured in terms of its ROE, and a business unit in terms of its ROA.

When applying this concept to compute the business market value, we should now consider the stream of cash flows generated by the assets in place and discount them at a cost of capital which is determined by the beta of the unlevered firm. The correction for the debt financing (the tax shield) is only made at the corporate level for the entire firm.

The technicalities of the relationships among cash flows, cost of capital, and their corresponding betas require, at times, very subtle and deep understanding of these issues. They are the subject of an extensive appendix to this chapter.

The Profitability Matrix

Marakon (1981) developed a very useful scheme to portray the economic contribution of each business unit of a firm in terms of what they refer to as "The Profitability Matrix."

There are several ways of constructing such a matrix. The initial form proposed by Marakon is exhibited in Figure 10.14, in which the business ROE is plotted against its corresponding growth. There are two cutoff points which are of great significance to separate the status of each business. The ROE axis is divided by the cost of equity capital (k_E) into businesses which are profitable ($ROE > k_E$) versus unprofitable ($ROE < k_E$). The cutoff line for the growth axis corresponds to the total market growth (G) for the industry in which a business is competing. Thus, businesses where growth is greater than G are building market share, and those with a growth lower than G are losing market

Figure 10.14   The Profitability Matrix

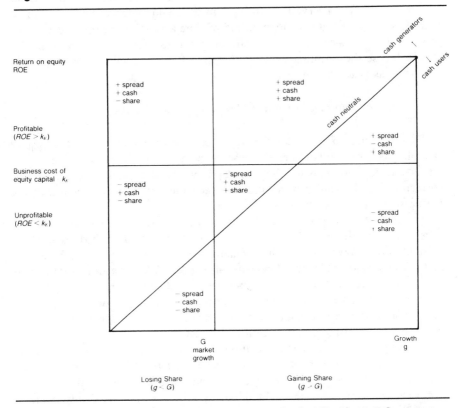

Adapted from Marakon Associates. "The Marakon Profitability Matrix," Commentary No. 7, © 1981. Reprinted by permission of Marakon Associates, San Francisco, CA.

share, perhaps for being positioned in a harvest strategic mode. Finally, the diagonal separates those businesses which are generating cash from those which are absorbing cash. This can easily be seen by realizing that a business which falls exactly in the diagonal has a profitability equal to its growth rate. Since the business growth is given by:

$$g = p \cdot ROE$$

businesses in the diagonal have p equal to one, which means that they reinvest all their profits; that is, they are cash neutral; they neither require cash from nor deliver cash to the corporation. Businesses which are above the diagonal have a profitability greater than their growth. Therefore, p is less than one, and they are cash generators. For opposite reasons, businesses below the diagonal are cash users. Therefore, the Marakon profitability matrix allows the positioning of businesses in seven different categories regarding their characteristics in terms of spread, cash flow, and changes in market share. These categories are depicted in Figure 10.14.

There is an extraordinary impacting message that is derived from this matrix, because the dimensions in which each business is positioned—profitability and growth—are the most central dimensions of strategic concern. Obviously, we would like all businesses to be profitable and we could only tolerate unprofitable ones if that is a temporary situation which will be corrected in the long run. We have already commented on how growth is desirable under profitable conditions and detrimental otherwise. Finally, the matrix states quite clearly that cash generation per se is not an attractive attribute, and thus, a balanced portfolio is not necessarily optimum, and an optimum portfolio does not have to be balanced in terms of cash flow. This last issue was discussed at more length in Chapter 7, where we contrasted the profitability matrix with the growth share matrix.

Constructing the matrix in the way just described requires measuring each business unit in terms of ROE, which needs the allocation of total corporate debt and equity among businesses. Often this is a practice left exclusively for the firm as a whole, while business units are measured in terms of ROA. These two indicators differ both in their numerators and denominators, and they are given by the following expressions:

$$ROE = \frac{\text{Profit after interests and after taxes}}{\text{equity}}$$

$$ROA = \frac{\text{Profit before interests and after taxes}}{\text{total assets}}$$

It seems logical to make a business unit manager responsible for the profitability of all the assets in place, regardless of how the corporation finances them. That is why no interest is charged to the profit earned by the business unit, and profits are measured against total assets instead of total equity. When we look at the overall firm, we are now interested in the net contribution of the firm to its shareholders, and thus we use bottom line profits (after interests and after taxes) against equity.

Therefore, an alternative way of constructing the profitability matrix is using ROA rather than ROE to position all businesses. The corresponding cutoff point should be changed to k_A, the cost of capital of the business assets, as opposed to k_E.

The parameter k_A can be obtained from tables such as that presented in Figure 10.10, which provides unlevered cost of capital for the industry in which the business competes.

The inherent limitations of the matrix as presented so far, either using ROE or ROA as measures of economic performance, reside in the representation of the two cutoff points. Since different businesses have normally different costs of capital as well as total market growth rates, it is not possible to identify single cutoff points applicable to all businesses of a corporation. Therefore, a

Figure 10.15 An Alternative Profitability Matrix

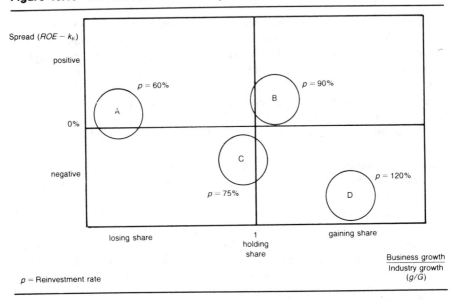

Adapted from Marakon Associates. "The Marakon Profitability Matrix," Commentary No. 7, © 1981. Reprinted by permission of Marakon Associates, San Francisco, CA.

slight modification is needed, which is illustrated in Figure 10.15, where spread $(ROE - k_E$ or $ROA - k_A)$ is used in the vertical axis, and relative growth (business growth/industry growth $= g/G$) in the horizontal axis. Unfortunately, we lose in this characterization the ability to identify what is the cash position of a business; that is, whether it is a cash generator, cash neutral, or cash user. In order to overcome this deficiency, each business unit has attached its corresponding value of the reinvestment rate (p). Obviously, if $p < 100\%$, the business is a cash generator, while if $p > 100\%$, it is a cash user. Finally, the area of each circle is proportional to total sales.

The Divestiture Decision

We have seen that the market value of a firm is always positive, even under fairly low profitability conditions. This is so because the liquidation value of the firm represents a lower bound on its market value as depicted by the horizontal line at the level L/B in Figure 10.4. However, individual businesses within a firm can, in fact, subtract value if their profitability is low and they are sustained by resources allocated from the corporate level. Businesses of this sort are referred to as "cash traps" involving a permanent negative cash flow which is diminishing the contribution of other businesses having positive cash flows. Under such conditions, divestiture might be the most logical decision for a firm to consider.

The central question pertaining to that issue is whether or not the liquidation alternative is better than holding onto that unprofitable business. A market-to-book value model can be of assistance in addressing that question.

A graphic illustration of the M/B model for a business unit within a corporation is presented in Figure 10.16. Notice that now the M/B versus ROE relation is truly a straight line, allowing M/B to assume values below L/B and even negative. In the example presented in that figure, a business with profitability ROE_1 is definitively subtracting value from the firm, and it should be liquidated,

Figure 10.16 The Representation of the M/B Model for a Business Unit which Is Part of a Diversified Corporation

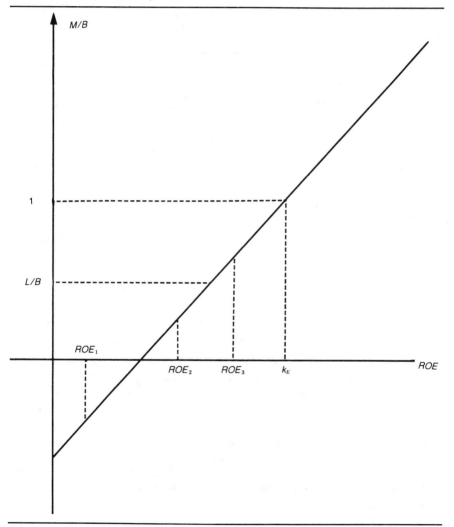

Figure 10.17 Example Showing the Contribution to Market Value of Each Business of an Hypothetical Firm

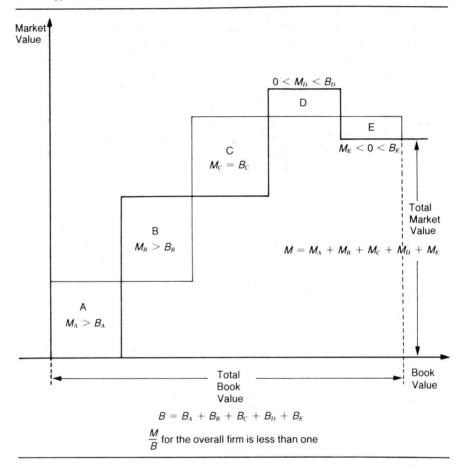

$B = B_A + B_B + B_C + B_D + B_E$

$\dfrac{M}{B}$ for the overall firm is less than one

even at a cost. If the business were to be performing at a level ROE_2, it is still adding value to the firm, but that is below the liquidation value L, and therefore should be divested. If the business performance were given by ROE_3, we have a situation where the business is unprofitable, since it is not making its cost of equity capital k_E. However, it is adding value above its liquidation value L; and, therefore, the business should not be divested.

Strategic Planning Associates (1981) have documented several situations involving Huffy, GAP Corporation, and Borden, where divestment of businesses with negative contributions to the firm have been translated into increases of the stock prices of the firm. This means that the capital markets are "intelligent" enough to understand sound decisions involving units' redeployments.

A compact way of summarizing the market value contribution of each individual business of the corporation is presented in Figure 10.17, where market value is plotted against book value. As can be seen from that graph, the company as a whole has a market value lower than its book value, which might suggest that it is an organization in trouble. However, a more careful look indicates its basic businesses A and B are pretty healthy, and business C is earning its cost of capital. Business D is adding value, but its profitability is below its cost of capital. It should be a candidate for divestment if its liquidation value L exceeds the value contributed by the business. Finally, business E should be divested as soon as possible, since it is subtracting value to the firm. With those rearrangements of the firm's portfolio, the company situation should improve markedly.

Evaluation of Broad Action Programs Supporting a Business Strategy

There are three levels of economic evaluation which are important for strategy development. One, is the assessment of the value of the firm, which we have addressed rather exhaustively in previous sections. Two, is the assessment of the value contributed by business units and particularly the understanding of how that value changes with different strategic alternatives to help support the development of this business. Three, the evaluation of projects, which is conventionally done by discounting the cash flows attributed to the project at an appropriate cost of capital.

It is the second of these evaluation issues, perhaps the most important and difficult within of the evaluation problems, which constitute the concern of this section. Within the steps of our proposed corporate strategic planning process (described in Chapter 4), this discussion is relevant to step 6, where the firm undertakes an initial assessment of the broad action programs stemming from its business units.

A primary concern which is often raised, in the strategic planning process is that there is very little of true evaluation being done at the corporate level. Frequently, strategic alternatives are generated and discarded at intermediate levels, and when the proposals finally reach the top, there is nothing left to be decided upon, and the corporation becomes a rubber stamper of economic decisions already made by business unit managers.

Marakon (1980) proposes an intelligent way of forcing true strategic options to be evaluated and reported at the corporate level. The proposed process is illustrated in Figure 10.18. It starts by requiring four options to be assessed, which summarize the competitive strategies of a business unit: build, hold, harvest, and divest. In passing, it is worthwhile to notice that these strategic options are not essentially different from the priorities for resource allocation in step 6 of our corporate planning process. For each option, the corresponding market-to-book value should have to be evaluated. We already have discussed in detail the alternatives available for evaluating market value at the business level in a preceding section of this chapter. The strategy which shows the highest M/B is the one selected for that particular business.

Figure 10.18 Selecting Business Unit Strategies

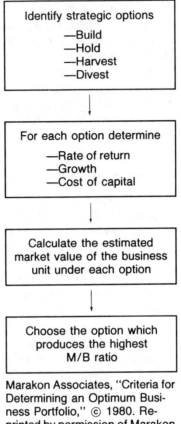

Marakon Associates, "Criteria for Determining an Optimum Business Portfolio," © 1980. Reprinted by permission of Marakon Associates, San Francisco, CA.

An illustration of the M/B values for each strategic option and for all the business units of an hypothetical firm is presented in Figure 10.19.

GENERIC STRATEGIES FOR VALUE CREATION, AND ALTERNATIVES FOR GROWTH AND DIVERSIFICATION

Before we conclude this chapter, we would like to make some final and brief comments on two important subjects relevant in guiding managerial thinking for the generation of strategic alternatives.

Generic Strategies for Value Creation

In order to review the basic options available to create value for the firm, it is useful to represent its market value in terms of the contribution stemming

Figure 10.19 Summary of M/B Values Under Different Strategic Options, for the Various Business Units of a Hypothetical Firm

Business Unit	Build	Hold	Harvest	Divest
1	1.0	1.6	1.4	1.2
2	2.1	1.5	0.9	1.8
3	0.8	1.2	1.4	1.1
4	0.3	0.5	0.7	0.8
5	2.2	2.5	1.8	1.9
6	0.5	0.7	0.6	0.5

Shaded values represent the *M/B* ratios under the optimum strategy for each business unit.

from operations (the unlevered market value) and that originated in the financial policies, mainly the debt policy:

$$\begin{matrix} \text{Market value} \\ \text{of the firm} \end{matrix} = \begin{matrix} \text{Unlevered market} \\ \text{value of the firm} \\ \text{(contribution from} \\ \text{operations)} \end{matrix} + \begin{matrix} \text{Contribution from} \\ \text{financial policies} \\ \text{(mainly debt policy)} \end{matrix}$$

We can express the unlevered value fo the firm in terms of revenues, costs and the discount rate for the business, obtaining thus an expression showing more clearly the variables that managers can influence:

$$\begin{matrix} \text{Unlevered market} \\ \text{value of the firm} \end{matrix} = \sum_{t=1}^{\infty} \frac{(\text{Revenues} - \text{Cost})_t}{(1 + k_u)^t}$$

where k_u = Cost of equity capital for the unlevered firm

Similarly the contribution from the debt policy is the value attached to the tax shield, which depends on the capital structure, and the discount rate for debt capital:

$$\begin{matrix} \text{Contribution from} \\ \text{financial policies} \end{matrix} = \sum_{t=1}^{\infty} \frac{(\text{Tax shield from debt})_t}{(1 + k_d)^t}$$

where k_d = cost of debt capital

Adding the two terms, we get:

$$\begin{matrix} \text{Market value} \\ \text{of the firm} \end{matrix} = \sum_{t=1}^{\infty} \frac{(\text{Revenues} - \text{Cost})_t}{(1 + k_u)^t} + \sum_{t=1}^{\infty} \frac{(\text{Tax shield from debt})_t}{(1 + k_d)^t}$$

Fruhan (1979) proposes the following basic options to create value suggested by the various components of the market value of the firm:

1. Increase revenues, for example by "pricing the product higher than what had been possible without the existence of some entry barrier. The barrier could be the existence of patents or some form of successful product differentiation. The barrier might also result from the simple exercise of market forces such as that enjoyed by a monopolist."

2. Reduce costs below that of competitors, "again perhaps as a result of the existence of some barrier that prevents all competitors from achieving equal costs. The barrier in this instance could be, for example, scale economies achievable by only the largest firm in a market, or the ownership of captive sources of low-cost raw materials."

3. Reduce the cost of equity capital, for example, through the "design of an equity security that appeals to a special niche in the capital markets and thereby attracts funds at a cost lower than the free-market rate for equivalent risk investments," or simply by reducing the business risk below the level enjoyed by competitors.

4. Maximize the financial contribution to the market value of the firm by increasing the tax shield from debt and reducing the cost of debt capital. This can be done by designing a debt security that is suited for a special group of investors in the market.

Alternatives for Growth and Diversification

The patterns of growth in the American industry has been well-documented by Chandler (1962). The major generic alternatives are depicted in Figure 10.20. After the introduction of a successful product, the first logical strategy to follow is that of horizontal growth; that is, keep on expanding the existing business within its current product-market structure. This can be accomplished by further penetration leading toward increased sales volumes and geographical expansion, including perhaps international coverage. Moreover, extensions of the existing market and product breadths are basic strategies for horizontal growth.

Once horizontal saturation has been reached, the second major strategy available to firms is vertical integration, which is an attempt at increasing value added within a given business base. There are two forms of vertical integration; forward integration, which leads the firm closer to its customers, and backward integration, which moves it closer to its suppliers.

Having reached a saturation of the vertical integration opportunities, a logical next step is to seek entry into new businesses via diversification. The nature of the diversification could be either related or unrelated, this last type conducive to what is referred to as conglomeration. The most logical form of related diversification is anchored in the value added chain, thus the firm could attempt to enter into new businesses, where the key for success can be traced back to

Figure 10.20   Generic Strategies for Growth and Diversification

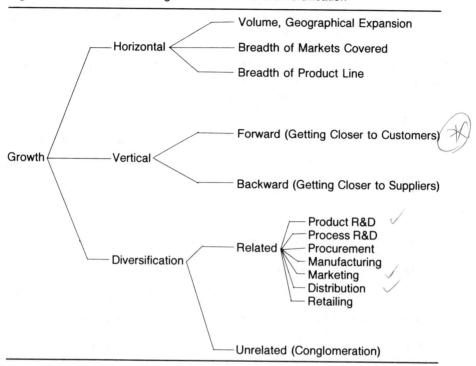

one or more of the stages of value added in which the firm currently excels, that is, product and process R&D, procurement, manufacturing, marketing, distribution, and retailing.

All of these alternatives for growth can be achieved either via internal development or acquisition. The pursuit of internal development has the advantage of establishing a strong base with deep cultural consistency. The obvious advantage of acquisition is its speedy and expedient accessibility to skill and competency not available internally to the firm. Acquisition prevails in the execution of unrelated diversification. For a good coverage of these topics, the reader is referred to Salter and Weinhold (1979), and Bradley and Korn (1981).

The selection of the strategies for growth as well as the intensity in which to carry out each one of them requires the exercise of a high level of judgment. There are clear dangers in not pursuing a strategy of extending the product line, for example, when competitors are including various features to differentiate their products. However, there are also serious problems in going too far in product line extensions, when product differences only contribute to increased inventory and lower productivity without adding significant value to the business.

Even more difficult is designing a proper strategy of vertical integration. If one is too aggressive in implementing a forward integration strategy, one could antagonize its own customers and pay dearly for it. Likewise, a backward integration strategy might result in severe negative responses on the part of one's own suppliers. And yet if one's own competitors seek a strategy of value added maximization, it would be hard to compete if vertical integration is not properly undertaken. And then, there is always the risk that your own customers integrate backwards or the suppliers integrate forward. Where would you be left if you do not know exactly what to do under those conditions?

We have found that a discipline which is enforced by carefully analyzing each one of these generic strategies contributes to the quality of the overall assessment of the opportunities available to a firm. This framework could generate alternatives to be subjected to a careful economic analysis, ultimately leading towards a preferred strategic direction for a firm.

REFERENCES

Bennett, Jim, *Strategic Management*; *Current Perspective on Frameworks and Tools*, talk at the Planning Executive Institute, March 16, 1982.

Bradley, James W., and Donald H. Korn, *Acquisition and Corporate Development*, Lexington Books, Lexington, MA, 1981.

Brealey, Richard, and Stewart Myers, *Principles of Corporate Finance*, McGraw-Hill, New York, 1981.

Chandler, Alfred D., Jr., *Strategy and Structure*, The M.I.T. Press, Cambridge, MA, 1962.

Fruhan, William E., *Financial Strategy*, Richard D. Irwin, Inc., Homewood, IL, 1979.

Ibbotson, Roger G., and Rex A. Sinquefield, *Stocks, Bonds, Bills and Inflation: The Past (1926–1976) and the Future (1977–2000)*, Financial Analysts Research Foundation, Charlottesville, VA, 1977.

Lai, Lily K., "Corporate Strategic Planning for a Diversified Company," unpublished Master Thesis, Sloan School of Management, Massachusetts Institute of Technology, 1983.

Lintner, John, "The Valuation of Risk Assets and the Selection of Risky Investments in Stock Portfolios and Capital Budgets," *Review of Economics and Statistics*, Vol. 47, February 1965, pp. 13–37.

Marakon Associates, *Criteria for Determining an Optimum Business Portfolio*, presented at the Institute of Management Science Meeting, Nov. 11, 1980.

Marakon Associates, "The Marakon profitability Matrix," *Commentary*, No. 7, San Francisco, CA, April 1981.

Markowitz, Harry M., "Portfolio Selection," *Journal of Finance*, Vol. 7, March 1952, pp. 77–91.

Salter, Malcolm S., and Wolf A. Weinhold, *Diversification Through Acquisition*, The Free Press, New York, 1979.

Sharpe, William F. "Capital Asset Prices: A Theory of Market Equilibrium Under Conditions of Risk," *Journal of Finance*, Vol. 19, September 1964, pp. 425–442.

Strategic Planning Associates, Inc., *Strategy and Shareholder Value: The Value Curve*, Washington, D.C., 1981.

APPENDIX

THE DEFINITION OF CASH FLOWS AND THE SELECTION OF PROPER DISCOUNT RATES

All the special advantages in technology, production, marketing, logistics, or any other area, that constitute the value creation capabilities of a firm should be reflected in its market value. The basic notion is that capital markets provide an economic yardstick for measuring the total contribution of a firm to the wealth of its shareholders. Every decision will impact, in some way or another, the total market value of the firm, and consequently, into the shareholders' wealth. For this reason, we need to rely on a well-defined rationale for estimating the changes in market value produced by different decisions taken by managers. For example, what is the expected increase or reduction in this indicator if a certain project is undertaken, a business of the firm is divested, a new business is acquired, or some changes in an SBU will substantially improve its total productivity?

From the perspective of capital markets, the value creation capability of a firm or any of its units, like a business or a project, is reflected in a stream of cash that this activity can generate through time. The economic evaluation of those cash flows is done through the computation of its Net Present Value (NPV) discounted at the corresponding cost of capital. A widely accepted belief is that efficient capital markets, like those operating in the United States, reflect the changes in economic value fairly closely. The questions that concern us in this section are:

—Which are the different alternatives for defining a cash flow?, and
—how to select an appropriate discount rate?

Corporate finance theory has offered many different answers to these questions, but they are valid under certain very specific assumptions which are not always clearly understood. We want to make a brief review of these ideas, and warn the reader from the very beginning that there are not definitive answers for a general case. All financial propositions have been inferred under extreme simplifying assumptions, so they should be used as rules of thumb in more realistic settings.

THE BASIC SIMPLIFYING ASSUMPTIONS

There are two forms of discounting that have received considerable attention in the financial literature:

—the multiperiod discounting under conditions of certainty, which leads to the use of NPV as a rule for assessing the market value
—the one period discounting under conditions of uncertainty, which requires the use of the CAPM (Capital Asset Pricing Model).

The great majority of situations in a business environment require the discounting of a multiperiod stream under uncertainty. The recommendation is to use the NPV rule but making an adjustment of the discount rate according to the CAPM, in order to account for the risk involved in the operation.

We limit ourselves to the discussion of NPV relationships, but the reader should bear in mind that all discount rates should be properly adjusted according to the risk implicit in the cash stream.

Another important assumption, that considerably reduces the algebraic manipulation, is to suppose that all cash flows are perpetual and stationary, so they do not change through time.

With these assumptions, we can represent the firm in very simple terms. We just need to provide, for example, the operational cash-flow, which is the profit before interest and before taxes. Moreover, given that this cash flow is perpetual and stationary, we only require the definition of one number. As an illustration, we could ask, what is the market value of a firm that has a profit before interest and taxes of X_0?

Certainly, we need to deduct taxes, therefore, an equivalent question might be: provided that corporate taxes are T_c, what is the market value of the above firm? It is not hard to realize that the profit before interest and *after* taxes is related with the value of X_0. But we will delay the presentation of that expression for later on, and we will limit ourselves to name the after tax profit by X_V.

If this is the perpetual cash flow, the present value of the stream is simply

$$V = \frac{X_V}{k_V} \tag{1}$$

where k_V is an appropriate discount rate, called the cost of capital of the firm. Unfortunately, k_V is not directly observable in the market. It is some sort of weighted average of other observable rates.

To be able to estimate this parameter, we need to recognize that there are different groups of people who have rights over the after tax profits of the firm. In the theory of corporate finance, they are reduced to just two groups: the shareholders and the debtholders. Their claims over the firm's profits are also represented in terms of perpetual cash flows. We will assume that a part of the total profit X_V goes to debtholders (which we call X_D) and the rest is received by shareholders who own the firm's equity (which we call X_E).

By definition, the shareholders receive the residual profits remaining after paying off the interests of the debt:

$$X_E = X_V - X_D.$$

Alternatively, we can say that the annual after tax profit X_V is paid out partly as interest and partly as dividends:

$$X_V = X_D + X_E \tag{2}$$

where

$X_V =$ After-tax and before interest annual profit
$X_D =$ annual interest payments
$X_E =$ annual dividend payments

Notice that there is no reinvestment, because we are assuming that the firm is stationary. Only depreciation is reinvested to maintain the level of the firm's activities. Also, debt is assumed to be perpetual, that is to say, new debt should replace old maturing debt. That is why only interests are being considered.

The importance of distinguishing the flow of interests and dividends separately is that their corresponding discount rates can be observed more easily in the market. Thus, we can obtain the total values of debt and shares outstanding by discounting those cash streams at their corresponding rates. The resulting relationship would be:

—Value of debt outstanding

$$D = \frac{X_D}{k_D} \tag{3}$$

where　　$k_D =$ cost of debt capital, or interest rate on debt.

—Value of shares outstanding

$$E = \frac{X_E}{k_E} \tag{4}$$

where k_E = cost of equity capital

The total value of the firm* is simply the sum of these two values; therefore:

$$V = D + E \qquad (5)$$

It is not hard to see, if we divide both sides of expression (2) by V, that:

$$\frac{X_V}{V} = \frac{D}{V}\frac{X_D}{D} + \frac{E}{V}\frac{X_E}{E}$$

If we now use relationships (3), (4), and (5), we find the following expression:

$$k_V = \frac{D}{V} k_D + \frac{E}{V} k_E \qquad (6)$$

This is a primary definition of the cost of capital of the firm (represented by k_V) that illustrates that it is a weighted average between the cost of debt (represented by k_D) and the cost of equity (represented by k_E). The weighting factors are related to the capital structure of the firm. Let us define θ as the fraction of debt:

$$\theta = \frac{D}{V} = \frac{D}{D + E} \qquad (7)$$

We can rewrite the expression for the weighted average cost of capital as:

$$k_V = \theta\, k_D + (1 - \theta)\, k_E \qquad (8)$$

THE UNLEVERED FIRM

Though defining the cost of capital of a firm in this way is very appealing, because the expression above has a simple structure, this definition has the undesirable property that the value of k_V changes with the capital structure selected for the firm, and the value of the firm itself moves accordingly. We would like to have a more standardized value for a given business, independent of its capital structure. For that we define the value of the unlevered firm, which corresponds to a unit which is totally financed by equity capital. The entire after tax profit goes to shareholders in this case. If we call X_U to this amount, we could establish that

$$X_U = X_0 (1 - T_c) \qquad (9)$$

where X_0 is the profit before interest and taxes. Simply stated, this expression indicates that after tax profit for the unlevered firm is the profit before interest and taxes, less taxes applied to this amount. For example, if a firm has annual

---

* We should warn the reader that what we describe as M in the (M/B) model is the market value of the shares of the firm, which in this Appendix is denoted by E. This is a widely used nomenclature, so we did not want to change it, though it might produce certain confusion.

profits before interests and taxes of 100, and the corporate tax rate is 45 percent, the annual profit for a firm wholly financed by equity capital is $100 \cdot (1 - 0.45) = 55$.

The market value of the unlevered firm can be obtained by discounting this cash flow at the *cost of capital of the unlevered firm*, as follows:

$$V_U = \frac{X_U}{k_U} = \frac{X_0(1 - T_c)}{k_U} \tag{10}$$

THE LEVERED FIRM

The value V_U is lower than the market value of a levered firm, because of the tax shield. In fact, if we assume that there are no costs induced by debts (for example bankruptcy costs), we can provide an estimate for the increase in market value generated by the tax shield through the following procedure:

—The after-tax profits for shareholders of a levered firm are obtained by deducting interest and taxes to the operational profit:

$$X_E = (X_0 - X_D)(1 - T_c). \tag{11}$$

—This relation can also be expressed in terms of the after-tax cash flow to shareholders of the unlevered firm as [see expression (9)]:

$$X_E = X_U - X_D(1 - T_c) \tag{12}$$

—The total cash flow generated by the firm that is distributed among shareholders and debtholders [see relation (2)], can then be written as:

$$X_V = X_D + (X_U - X_D(1 - T_c))$$

Rearranging terms, we get:

$$X_V = X_U + T_c X_D \tag{13}$$

—The value of the firm can then be obtained by discounting each one of the components of this cash flow at their corresponding cost of capital. For the cash flow of the unlevered firm we use k_U, and for the cash flow to bondholders we use k_D. Then:

$$V = \frac{X_U}{k_U} + T_c \frac{X_D}{k_D}.$$

It is not hard to see [by using relations (10) and (3)] that the market value of the levered firm is equal to:

$$V = V_U + T_c \cdot D \tag{14}$$

Therefore, the value of the levered firm exceeds the value of the unlevered firm by an amount $T_c \cdot D$ that corresponds to an estimate of the tax shield.

—A different but equivalent relationship between the values of the levered and unlevered firm can be obtained by expressing the debt in terms of the capital structure of the firm. We defined the parameter θ as D/V [see relation (7)]. Therefore, the total debt is $\theta \cdot V$. If we introduce this value in expression (14) and solve for the market value of the levered firm, we obtain:

$$V = \frac{V_U}{1 - T_c \cdot \theta} \tag{15}$$

This is a very interesting relationship that gives us a first opportunity for being more explicit with regard to the two questions that we posed at the beginning of this section: the definition of a cash flow and the selection of an appropriate discount rate. If we recall that the market value of the unlevered firm is simply its cash flow divided by the corresponding cost of capital [see relation (10)], then we can rewrite the expression above as:

$$V = \frac{X_U}{k_U (1 - T_c \theta)} \tag{16}$$

This expression means that we could take the after tax profit of the unlevered firm and discount it at a *"corrected" cost of capital for the firm*, defined as:

$$k^* = k_U (1 - T_c \theta) \tag{17}$$

This procedure guarantees that the value of the tax shield induced by a capital structure θ is properly being considered, not by changing the estimated profits, but by introducing a correction in the discount rate.

RELATIONSHIPS AMONG THE VARIOUS COSTS OF CAPITAL

But we still have a need to provide an estimate for k_U, the cost of capital of the unlevered firm. We said already that the most readily observable parameters are the cost of equity capital (k_E), and the cost of debt capital (k_D), and that they are closely related with the cost of capital for the entire firm (k_V) [see, for example, relation (8)].

Our aim, now, is to relate all of these parameters, so we can estimate any one of them if we happen to know the others.

1. *Relationship among k_V, k_U and k_D*

   If we want to estimate the cost of capital of the levered firm when we know the cost of capital of the unlevered firm, the cost of debt, and also the capital structure θ, we can go back to expression (13) which we reproduce below, and that relates the annual cash-flows which are relevant to this case:

   $$X_V = X_U + T_c X_D$$

Dividing both sides by V and performing some simple manipulations, we obtain:

$$\frac{X_V}{V} = \frac{V_U}{V}\frac{X_U}{V_U} + T_c\frac{D}{V}\cdot\frac{X_D}{D}$$

But we know that:

$$
\begin{array}{lll}
X_V/V = k_V & \text{relation (1)} \\
X_U/V_U = k_U & \text{relation (10)} \\
X_D/D = k_D & \text{relation (3)} \\
D/V = \theta & \text{relation (7)} \\
\text{and,} \quad V_U/V = 1 - T_c\theta & \text{relation (15)}
\end{array}
$$

Therefore, the cost of capital for the levered firm can be expressed as:

$$k_V = (1 - T_c\theta)\,k_U + T_c\theta\,k_D \tag{18}$$

If the unlevered cost of capital of the firm could be estimated—for example, through tables presenting that information for the industry in which the firm is engaged in—and if the remaining parameters of this expression—namely, k_D, T_c, and θ—are also known, the above relation could be used to estimate the value of the levered firm by discounting the total cash flow going to debtholders and shareholders with the value of k_V.

2. *Relationship among k_U, k_D, and k_E*

We have indicated that k_E and k_D are the most readily observable costs. Therefore, it is of primary interest to obtain a standardized value for the cost of capital of the unlevered firm from these parameters. Once we get this value, we can estimate, for example, the cost of capital for a firm in the same activity, but with a different capital structure. The relevant relation among cash flows is given, this time, by expression (12), which is reproduced below when solving for X_U:

$$X_U = (1 - T_c)\,X_D + X_E$$

If we divide both sides by V, we can easily obtain:

$$\frac{V_U}{V}\frac{X_U}{V_U} = (1 - T_c)\frac{D}{V}\frac{X_D}{D} + \frac{E}{V}\frac{X_E}{E}$$

All the terms in this algebraic form are parameters we have already defined:

$$
\begin{array}{lll}
V_U/V = 1 - T_c\theta & \text{relation (15)} \\
X_U/V_U = k_U & \text{relation (10)} \\
D/V = \theta & \text{relation (7)} \\
X_D/D = k_D & \text{relation (3)} \\
E/V = 1 - \theta & \text{relation (7)} \\
X_E/E = k_E & \text{relation (4)}
\end{array}
$$

This time, the expression we obtain when the replacements of these parameters are completed, is:

$$(1 - T_c\theta) k_U = (1 - T_c) \theta k_D + (1 - \theta) k_E \qquad (19)$$

3. *Relationship among k^*, k_D, and k_E*

We know from relation (17) that the corrected cost of capital k^* is equal to $k_U (1 - T_c\theta)$. Therefore, the recently derived expression can also be presented as:

$$k^* = (1 - T_c) \theta k_D + (1 - \theta) k_E \qquad (20)$$

This is a widely used relation in finance that is known as the cost of capital textbook formula, and that should be applied to discount an after-tax cash flow of the unlevered firm to derive the market value of the levered firm.

PROCEDURES FOR ESTIMATING THE MARKET VALUE OF A FIRM

There are different procedures we can use for estimating the market value of a firm. All of them can be derived from the relationships we have presented in the previous section. The most appropriate approach should be dictated by the information available to the firm. We are going to present four different alternatives to evaluate cash flows, and we will illustrate their application by means of a simple example. Consider a firm that produces an annual profit before interest and taxes of 100, that is subjected to a 45 percent corporate tax rate, and its costs of debt and equity are 12 percent and 20 percent respectively. In terms of the nomenclature we have previously defined, these data are: $X_0 = 100$, $T_c = 0.45$, $k_D = 0.12$ and $k_E = 0.20$. The question we need to answer is, what is the market value of the firm?

Procedure 1

Suppose also that the firm has defined a capital structure that requires a debt-to-equity ratio of one-half; that is to say:

$$\frac{D}{E} = \frac{1}{2} \quad \text{or} \quad \theta = \frac{D}{D + E} = \frac{1}{3}$$

We could estimate the value of the firm by discounting the cash flow of the unlevered firm with a discount rate properly adjusted by the impact of leverage.

The cash flow of the unlevered firm is [relation (9)]:

$$X_U = X_0 (1 - T_c)$$
$$= 100 (1 - 0.45) = 55$$

The corrected discount rate is [relation (20)]:

$$k^* = (1 - T_c)\,\theta\,k_D + (1 - \theta)\,k_E$$
$$= (1 - 0.45)\frac{1}{3}0.12 + \left(1 - \frac{1}{3}\right)0.20$$
$$= 0.1553$$

The market value of the firm is, then:

$$V = \frac{X_U}{k^*} = \frac{55}{0.1553} = 354$$

The contributions of debt and equity to this value are [relation (7)]:

$$D = \theta \cdot V \qquad\qquad E = (1 - \theta)\,V$$
$$= \frac{1}{3} \cdot 354 \qquad\qquad = \frac{2}{3} \cdot 354$$
$$= 118 \qquad\qquad\quad = 236$$

We could also obtain the cost of capital of the unlevered firm very easily as [relation (17)]:

$$k_u = \frac{k^*}{1 - T_c\theta}$$
$$= \frac{0.1553}{1 - 0.45 \cdot 1/3}$$
$$= 0.1827$$

Procedure 2

Suppose now that we knew the total debt outstanding and the cost of debt, but we did not have a clear estimate of the debt-to-equity ratio. This situation may arise when we are dealing with a project or a business unit with a clearly defined source of funds, but still unsure value for the resulting capital structure.

So, we have $D = 118$, $k_D = 0.12$, and we require an estimate of the value of the firm. In this case we have to get the market value of all outstanding shares, which corresponds to E. Then we simply add D and E for obtaining the total market value of the firm.

The cash flow that goes to debtholders is [relation (3)]:

$$X_D = k_D \cdot D$$
$$= 0.12 \times 118$$
$$= 14.16$$

On the other hand, the profit after interest and taxes that goes to shareholders is (relation 11)):

$$X_E = (X_0 - X_D)(1 - T_c)$$
$$= (100 - 14.16)(1 - .45)$$
$$= 47.212$$

The market value of this cash flow can be obtained as (relation (4)):

$$E = \frac{X_E}{k_E}$$
$$= \frac{47.212}{0.20}$$
$$= 236$$

Once again we obtain the market value of the firm:

$$V = D + E$$
$$= 118 + 236$$
$$= 354$$

Procedure 3

In this case we assume that we know the total cash flows generated by the firm to both shareholders and debtholders. If we could find an appropriate average for the cost of capital of the firm, we could discount this entire stream without making our explicit recognition of what goes to the different stockholders.

The annual cash flow to both groups is [relation (2)]:

$$X_V = X_D + X_E$$

The values for X_D and X_E recently obtained are:

$$X_D = 14.16$$
$$X_E = 47.212$$

Therefore,

$$X_V = 61.372$$

Before determining the market value of the firm, let us take another look at this number. We can obtain it as [replace X_E given by relation (11)]:

$$X_V = X_D + (X_0 - X_D((1 - T_c)$$
$$= X_0(1 - T_c) + X_D T_c$$

This is the after-tax cash flow of the unlevered firm plus the annual tax shield. We check our calculation by obtaining these two numbers:

$$X_U = X_0(1 - T_c) = 100(1 - .45) = 55$$
$$X_D \cdot T_c = 14.16 \times .45 = 6.372$$

Again, we obtain:

$$X_V = 55 + 6.372$$
$$= 61.372$$

The cost of capital that should be applied to discount this cash flow is a weighted average that can be computed in two ways [relations (8) and (18)]: The first way is:

$$k_V = \theta k_D + (1 - \theta) k_E$$
$$= \frac{1}{3} 0.12 + \left(1 - \frac{1}{3}\right) 0.20$$
$$= 0.1733$$

The second way is:

$$k_V = (1 - T_c \theta) k_U + T_c \theta k_D$$
$$= \left(1 - 0.45 \cdot \frac{1}{3}\right) \times 0.1827 + 0.45 \times \frac{1}{3} \times 0.12$$
$$= 0.1733$$

The market value of the firm is then [relation (11)]:

$$V = \frac{X_V}{k_V}$$
$$= \frac{61.372}{0.1733}$$
$$= 354$$

Procedure 4—The Adjusted Present Value Method APV)

The APV methodology suggests that when we have to evaluate a new project, it is much simpler to separate the financing problem altogether. So, we could estimate the market value of the project by simply using values for the unlevered case and then adjusting to account for the value of the tax shield.

In this case we could say:

$$\begin{array}{ccc} \text{Adjusted} & \text{Value of} & \text{Value of} \\ \text{Present} = & \text{the unlevered} + & \text{the tax} \\ \text{Value} & \text{firm} & \text{shield} \end{array}$$

The corresponding relation is [expression (14)]:

$$V = V_U + T_c D$$

The market value of the unlevered firm is [relation (10)]:

$$V_U = \frac{55}{0.1827} = 301$$

Also, we can easily obtain the market value of the tax shield as:

$$T_c \cdot D = 0.45 \cdot 118 = 53$$

The market value of the firm is, then:

$$V = 301 + 53$$
$$= 354$$

The advantage of this procedure is that it separates very clearly the value contributed by the firm businesses or operation, represented by the value of the unlevered firm, from the value contributed from the financing scheme selected. Up to now, we have considered that leverage has only one impact, namely, to increase the market value of the firm due to the tax shield generated. But we could also argue that high leverages induce additional burdens, like bankruptcy costs. In that case, the contribution of leverage would be smaller than the present value of the stream of tax shields. In fact, according to most recent accounts, when we take into consideration personal taxes, the value of the tax shield could be near zero (Miller 1977).

Though the contribution of leverage is still an unsettled subject, we can still use the APV method, being careful to give to the tax shield a value that best fits with previous experiences of the firm: probably not zero, but neither as high as $T_c D$.

Moreover, the APV method can handle other influences of leverage by properly considering all side effects of the financing scheme. A general relation for that is:

$$APV = V_U + \text{Present value of all side effects}$$
$$\text{induced by the financing scheme,}$$
$$\text{including bankruptcy costs.}$$

SUMMARY OF RESULTS OF THE NUMERICAL EXAMPLE

In Figure 10.21 we summarize the results obtained by applying the different relationships presented in this section to the simple numerical case developed as illustration.

We should emphasize once more that the market value of the firm can be derived from the market value of basic cash flow streams that can be generated from the original value of profit before interest and taxes. These are:

1. Market value = Market value + Market value
   of the firm   of debt   of equity

       354   =   118   +   236

2. Market value = Market value + Market value
   of the firm   of the un-   of the tax
                  levered firm   shield

       354   =   301   +   53

3. Market value = Market value + Adjustment to
   of the firm   of the un-   market value in-
                     levered firm   duced by leverage

In this example, this relation is equivalent to the previous one, because we have assumed that the adjustment to market value induced by leverage is equal to the tax shield.

Figure 10.21 Summary of Results Obtained for the Numerical Example

Cost of capital	Cash flow to which it is applied	Market value obtained
k^* = Corrected discount rate = 0.1553	X_U = After-tax cash flow of the unlevered firm = 55	V = Market value of the firm = 354
k_U = Cost of capital of the unlevered firm = 0.1827	X_U = After-tax cash flow of the unlevered firm = 55	V_U = Market value of the unlevered firm = 301
k_D = Cost of debt capital = 0.12	X_D = Interest payments = 14.16	D = Market value of debt = 118
	$X_D \cdot T_c$ = Annual tax shield = 6.372	$D\,T_c$ = Market value of the tax shield = 53
k_E = Cost of equity capital = 0.20	X_E = Profit after interest and taxes (paid out as dividends) = 47.212	E = Market value of equity = 236
k_V = Cost of capital of the firm = 0.1733	X_V = Interest payments plus profits after interest and taxes = 14.16 + 47.212 = 61.372 *Alternatively* X_V = After-tax cash flow of the unlevered firm plus annual tax shield = 55 + 6.372 = 61.372	V = Market value of the firm = 354

SUMMARY OF RESULTS IN A GENERAL CASE

Figure 10.22, which is similar to the one recently presented, shows the general relationships derived for perpetual and stationary cash flows.

The market value of the firm can be obtained directly from the table, by using the methodologies that produce that number; or, alternatively, we can obtain the components of the market value of the firm and add those partial results. As before, the three procedures suggested for obtaining the market value of the firm are:

1. Market value $=$ Market value $+$ Market value
   of the firm   of debt   of equity

   $$V \quad = \quad D \quad + \quad E$$

2. Market value $=$ Market value $+$ Market value of
   of the firm   of the un-   the tax shield
                      levered firm

   $$V \quad = \quad V_U \quad + \quad D\,T_c$$

3. Market value $=$ Market value $+$ Adjustment to
   of the firm   of the un-   market value
                      levered firm   induced by
                                        leverage

We have assumed that these adjustments are equal to the market value of the tax shield, but a more general relation can be used to estimate this adjustment, if the necessary information is available.

THE USE OF THE CAPM IN THE ESTIMATION OF THE COST OF CAPITAL

The cost of capital under uncertainty, for a one period situation, can be estimated by the use of the CAPM. The basic relation discussed in chapter 10 is:

$$\begin{pmatrix} \text{Cost of} \\ \text{capital} \end{pmatrix} = \begin{pmatrix} \text{Risk-free} \\ \text{rate} \end{pmatrix} + \beta \left\{ \begin{pmatrix} \text{Return on the} \\ \text{market portfolio} \end{pmatrix} - \begin{pmatrix} \text{Risk-free} \\ \text{rate} \end{pmatrix} \right\}$$

or

$$k = r_f + \beta \left\{ r_m - r_f \right\}$$

The values of r_f and $(r_m - r_f)$ are assumed to be known. The estimation of the cost of capital requires an assessment of the appropriate β-coefficient, or volatility, which is a measure of the risk of the cash flow.

If we were to know the volatility coefficient of the cash streams previously

Figure 10.22 Summary of Results Obtained for Perpetual and Stationary Cash Flows

Cost of capital and its derivation	Cash flow to which it is applied	Market value obtained
$k_U =$ Cost of capital of the unlevered firm obtained from a table with standard values for the industry, or derived as [relation (19)] $$k_U = \frac{(1 - T_c)\,\theta\,k_D + (1 - \theta)\,k_E}{1 - T_c\theta}$$	$X_U =$ After-tax cash flow of the unlevered firm	$V_U =$ Market value of the unlevered firm
$k_D =$ Cost of debt capital; usually an externally given date	$X_D =$ Interest payments	$D =$ Market value of debt
	$X_D T_c =$ Annual tax shield	$D \cdot T_c =$ Market value of the tax shield
$k_E =$ Cost of equity capital. Obtained from the β-book, or derived from tables of k_U and decisions regarding the capital structure, as [relation (19)]: $$k_E = \frac{(1 - T_c\theta)\,k_U - (1 - T_c)\,\theta\,k_D}{1 - \theta}$$	$X_E =$ Profit after interest and taxes (paid out as dividends)	$E =$ Market value of equity
$k_V =$ Cost of capital of the firm. Obtained as a weighted average of previous costs of capital. There are two alternative forms: · Relation (8) $k_V = \theta\,k_D + (1 - \theta)\,k_E$ · or relation (18) $k_V = (1 - T_c\theta)\,k_U + T_c\theta k_D$	$X_V =$ Interest payments and profits after interest and taxes *Alternatively* $X_V =$ After-tax cash flow of the unlevered firm and annual tax shield	$V =$ Market value of the firm
$k^* =$ Corrected discount rate obtained as a weighted average of previous costs of capital. There are two alternative forms: · Relation (17) $k^* = k_U\,(1 - T_c)$ · Relation (20) $k^* = (1 - T_c)\theta k_D + (1 - \theta)k_E$	$X_U =$ After-tax cash flow of the unlevered firm	$V =$ Market value of the firm

defined, the determination of the cost of capital would be a simple matter. In particular, we could define the following coefficients of volatility:

Corresponding Cost of Capital	Volatility Coefficient	Estimate of the Cost of Capital
k_U	β_U	$k_U = r_f + \beta_U (r_m - r_f)$
k_D	β_D	$k_D = r_f + \beta_D (r_m - r_f)$
k_E	β_E	$k_E = r_f + \beta_E (r_m - r_f)$
k_V	β_V	$k_V = r_f + \beta_V (r_m - r_f)$

The values that are observable are β_D and β_E. Normally, β_D is close to zero, because the cash flows associated to debt have a very small component of risk, so it is usual to assume that $\beta_D = 0$. But we will carry that term in the relations to have more general expressions.

1. *Derivation of β_U if we know β_D and β_E*

   As previously indicated, β_U is a standard value that is independent of the leverage of the firm. Therefore, it is very convenient to store all available information with regard to betas in terms of β_U. If we know β_D and β_E, this last one from a beta book, for example, we can easily obtain [relation (19)]:

$$(1 - T_c\theta) \beta_U = (1 - T_c)\theta \beta_D + (1\theta) \beta_E \tag{21}$$

   In the special case of a risk-free debt ($\beta_D = 0$), we get:

$$(1 - T_c\theta) \beta_U = (1 - \theta) \beta_E \tag{22}$$

   Certainly, these relationships can also be used to derive the value of β_E if we happen to know the standardized value β_U. For example, if the firm is going into a new business, it should retrieve β_U from the average for the industry, and calculate β_E, according to relation (21) or (22) above to account for the impact of leverage on the riskiness of the cash flow.

2. *Derivation of β_V*

   The value of beta for the firm can be estimated in two different ways. If we have information of β_D and β_E, we can apply [from relation (8)]:

$$\beta_V = \theta \beta_D + (1 - \theta) \beta_E \tag{23}$$

   On the other hand, if we have the standardized value β_U instead of β_E, the derivation of β_v is [from relation (18)]:

$$\beta_V = (1 - T_c\theta) \beta_U + T_c\theta \beta_D \tag{24}$$

   Assuming a risk-free debt ($\beta_D = 0$) the preceding expressions are further simplified to:

$$\beta_V = (1 - \theta) \beta_E \tag{25}$$

and

$$\beta_V = (1 - T_c\theta)\,\beta_U \qquad (26)$$

RECOMMENDED PROCEDURES TO ESTIMATE THE MARKET VALUE OF THE FIRM

As we have indicated throughout this section, there are many different procedures to determine the market value of a firm, depending on the cash flows in which those computations are based. Under the simplifying assumptions used in the derivation of those procedures, it is indifferent which one to select. It depends on the available information, and on personal preferences. But under more general conditions, we should be much more careful. None of the expressions derived to discount a cash flow can be directly applied without making certain additional qualifications. For this reason, we want to suggest a few practical rules on the preferred procedures to estimate the market value of the firm.

1. We strongly recommend to either separate the cash flows for debtholders and shareholders and discount them with their corresponding cost of capital; or else, obtain the market value of the firm by first discounting the unlevered cash flows at their corresponding cost of capital and then adding the leverage impact by discounting the stream of interests at the cost of debt. This leads to use either one of the following two relationships:

   - Market value = Market value + Market value
     of the firm   of debt   of equity

     $$V \quad = \quad D \quad + \quad E$$

   - Market value = Market value + Adjustments to
     of the firm   of the un-   market value
                        levered firm   induced by
                                         leverage

     $$V \quad = \quad V_U \quad + \text{Adjustment}$$

   We do not recommend to base the computation of the market value of the firm, either by discounting the levered cash flows plus the interest payments at the cost of capital of the firm, or by discounting the unlevered cash flow at the corrected cost of capital. Both of these computations will require the use of weighted averages for discount rates. The assumptions which led to the correctness of the weighted average formulas proposed in this section strongly deviate under more complex situations, casting some doubts on the validity of those methods.

2. To estimate the market value of debt, we have to discount the stream of payments to debtholders with the interest paid on the market value of debt, or simply with the risk-free rate if we have no other information.

3. To estimate the market value of equity, we have to discount the stream of payments to shareholders with the appropriate rate, which can be estimated as:

$$k_E = r_f + \beta_E \,(r_m - r_f)$$

The value of β_E is either obtained directly from a β-book, or it has to be derived from the standardized value of β_U as [relation (22)]:

$$\beta_E = \frac{1 - T_c\theta}{1 - \theta}\,\beta_U = \left\{1 + \frac{D}{E}(1 - T_c)\right\}\beta_U$$

When we are dealing with the value of the firm, the stream of equity cash flows is represented by the dividend payments to shareholders. However, when analyzing a business unit within a firm, the equity cash flows are given by:

> Profits after tax
> $-$ Interest payments
> $-$ Retained earnings (for further investment)
> _____
> Equity cash-flows

This is what some people refer to as free cash flow. At the level of the firm, this corresponds to the dividends stream.

4. The market value of the unlevered firm is derived from the profit before interest and taxes of the firm. For that, we have to assume that taxes are applied over all this profit, and then discount the resulting cash flow with the corresponding cost of capital:

$$k_U = r_f + \beta_U \,(r_m - r_f)$$

The value of β_U is obtained either from standard tables (if available) or estimated from the average value of β_E as [relation (22)]:

$$\beta_U = \frac{1 - \theta}{1 - T_c\theta}\,\beta_E$$

5. Finally, the adjustment of the market value induced by leverage can be estimated as the present value of the annual tax shield, or as a fraction of that number if we have some better information on the contribution of leverage to the market value. The discount rate that should be applied to obtain the present value of the tax shield is the interest paid on the market value of debt, or the risk-free rate if we lack that information.

There is no guarantee that these procedures will generate precise estimates of the market value of a firm or of the contribution that businesses or projects make to this market value, but the practice has shown that they are more than fair estimates. Henceforth, they provide an important benchmark for measuring the goodness of a strategy by its contribution to market value, assessed through a properly discounted cash flow.

REFERENCES

Miller, M. H., "Debt and Taxes," *Journal of Finance,* May 1977, pp. 261–276.

11

INDUSTRY AND COMPETITIVE ANALYSIS—A FINANCIAL STATEMENT APPROACH

INTRODUCTION

One of the trademarks of modern planning approaches is its external orientation. Not many years ago, planning used to be a purely internally driven activity. This is no longer so. Today we have to address ourselves to the careful understanding of environmental trends and surprises. We should be alert to all developments in our industry, especially to the behavior of competitors. Only a deep knowledge of the structural characteristics of the industry in which we operate and a sound awareness of competitors' actions can generate the high-quality strategic thinking which is required for a healthy long-term development of a firm.

Definition of Industry

An industry can be defined as a group of firms offering products or services which are close substitutes of each other. Thus the boundaries of the industry are determined from a users' point of view. The relevant question is, which are the products that an individual trying to satisfy a certain need is willing to consider in his buying decision? The answer is: all products which, in the eyes of the individual, perform approximately the same function. Speaking more technically, we could answer: "close substitutes are products with high cross-elasticities of demand." This can be understood more easily if we think of two products, and only one of them suffers a price increase; close substitutability implies a transfer of the demand from the more highly priced product to the other one.

Definition of Industry and Competitive Analysis

The industry and competitive analysis is an orderly process to define the relevant environment of an industry, as well as to identify and characterize the behavior of the most significant competitors in a given market.

There are three basic procedures to perform this analysis:

1. Financial statements analysis.
2. Short-cut methods for competitive analysis.
3. The industrial economic framework, which has been incorporated by Porter (1980) into an operational approach for competitive analysis.

In this chapter, we are going to discuss and illustrate at certain length the financial statements analysis, covering only briefly the other two approaches.

SHORTCUT METHODS FOR COMPETITIVE ANALYSIS

There are many different shortcut methods to perform an industry and competitive analysis. We have commented upon some of them already when discussing the different portfolio matrix approaches. In this section, we want to point out just a few basic ideas.

Perhaps the most rudimentary form of analysis of competitors was suggested when presenting the growth-share matrix in Chapter 7. We indicated that such a tool would not produce too many surprises when applied to the business of the same firm, because their basic strategic characteristics should be relatively well known to active managers. But if applied to competitors, the growth-share matrix and the share-momentum graph would be quite revealing of their strengths and weaknesses, and of the selected strategic positioning of the business in their portfolios.

A more elaborate methodology, that forces one to take a wider view of competitors' actions, was discussed in the presentation of the industry attractiveness-business strength matrix in Chapter 8. The basic idea was to select the most relevant competitors, and then define the factors that are determinant in the analysis of relative business strengths. In Chapter 15 we suggest some formats to conduct this analysis.

The third portfolio matrix approach, based on the life cycle concept, can also be used to position the various competitors in an industry, and to contrast their resulting portfolio strengths. This methodology is presented in Chapter 9.

There are many other shortcut methods to perform competitive analysis, like the one presented in Figure 11.1. All of them are based on the identification of some significant competitors, and the subsequent comparison of the firm

Figure 11.1 An Example of a Shortcut Method for Competitive Analysis

	COMPETITORS				
KEY INTERNAL FACTORS					
—Manufacturing —Marketing —R&D and Engineering —Management — — — —					
OVERALL RANKING OF EACH COMPETITOR					

ANALYSIS OF EACH COMPETITOR
1.
2.
3.
4.
5.

CONCERNS FOR THE BUSINESS REGARDING EACH COMPETITOR
1.
2.
3.
4.
5.

OVERALL ASSESSMENT OF COMPETITIVE STRENGTH

	LOW	MEDIUM	HIGH
CURRENT			
FUTURE			

standing against each one of the competitors, in a few selected dimensions considered to be critical for success.

THE INDUSTRIAL ECONOMIC FRAMEWORK AND PORTER'S APPROACH TO COMPETITIVE ANALYSIS

In Chapter 3 we discussed Porter's framework for competitive analysis, which is grounded in the field of Industrial Economics. Porter's basic assumption is that profitability in an industry is determined by structural characteristics, so the competitive analysis should be centered on the description of all of the industry components and their interaction. The main forces driving industry profitability are rivalry among competitors (mainly affected by barriers of entry and exit), bargaining power of suppliers, bargaining power of buyers, threat of new entrants, and threat of substitute products or services (see Figures 3.8 and 3.9 in Chapter 3). A form to complete the kind of analysis suggested by Porter is presented in Chapter 15.

Rather than discussing further the characteristics and use of Porter's framework, it is worthwhile to turn our attention briefly to the more basic model underlying Porter's: the model of industrial organizational analysis, which is presented in Figure 11.2. The idea behind it is that the *basic conditions* that regulate supply and demand are the primary determinants of *market structure*, which guides the actions of all participating firms. Therefore, the observed *conduct* of firms in the market could be anticipated from the structure prevailing in the industry. Finally, the *performance* is just the final result produced by the adopted conduct. Let us comment further on the components of the industrial economic model. The performance of an industry is considered good when the industry is satisfying the societal expectations with regard to the production of goods and services. In macroeconomic terms, it might embody at least the following goals, not listed necessarily in order of social importance or priority (Scherer 1980):

1. Decisions as to what, how much, and how to produce should be efficient in two respects: scarce resources should not wasted outright, and production decisions should be responsive qualitatively and quantitatively to consumer demands.
2. The operations of producers should be progressive, taking advantage of opportunities opened up by science and technology to increase output per unit of input and to provide consumers with superior new products, in both ways contributing to the long-run growth of real income per capita.
3. The operations of producers should facilitate stable full employment of resources, especially human resources. Or at a minimum, they should not make maintenance of full employment through the use of macroeconomic policy instruments excessively difficult.
4. The distribution of income should be equitable. Equity is a notoriously slippery concept, but it implies at least that producers do not secure rewards far in excess of what is needed to call forth the amount of services supplied. A subfacet of this goal is the desire to achieve reasonable price stability, for rampant inflation distorts the distribution of income in ways widely disapproved.

In addition to the measure of performance, the industrial economic framework calls for the identification of market structure and conduct of participants. Porter's framework provides a good illustration of these two basic dimensions, because it is mainly centered on the structure-conduct link. Using the factors already defined in Figure 11.2, we could say that:

- price behavior,
- product strategy and advertising,

Figure 11.2 A Model of Industrial Organization Analysis

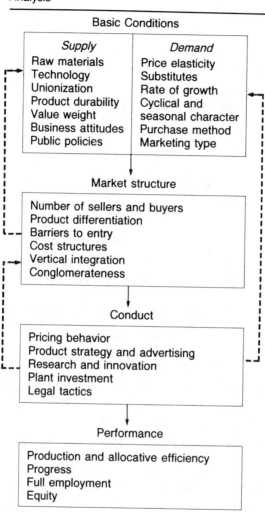

Basic Conditions

Supply	Demand
Raw materials	Price elasticity
Technology	Substitutes
Unionization	Rate of growth
Product durability	Cyclical and
Value weight	seasonal character
Business attitudes	Purchase method
Public policies	Marketing type

Market structure

Number of sellers and buyers
Product differentiation
Barriers to entry
Cost structures
Vertical integration
Conglomerateness

Conduct

Pricing behavior
Product strategy and advertising
Research and innovation
Plant investment
Legal tactics

Performance

Production and allocative efficiency
Progress
Full employment
Equity

Source: F. M. Scherer, *Industrial Market Structure and Economic Performance,* Second Edition, Copyright © 1980, Houghton Mifflin Company. Reprinted by permission.

- research and innovation,
- plant investment, and
- legal tactics,

are dependent upon (are functions of) the prevailing market structure, characterized by:

- number of sellers and buyers,
- product differentiation,
- barriers to entry,
- cost structures,
- vertical integration, and
- conglomerateness.

The structure in Porter's framework is defined by recognizing the main actors in the industry—competitors, suppliers, buyers, and potential entrants—and the substitute products. The conduct is broadly assessed in terms of the already mentioned forces driving the industry competition—rivalry among competitors, bargaining power of suppliers, bargaining power of buyers, threat of new entrants, and threat of substitution.

The seller's market structure types presented in Figure 11.3 offer another opportunity to understand the rationale behind Porter's framework. The three generic strategies proposed by Porter are:

1. Volume, which corresponds to the maximization of growth and market share, and that is a sensible strategy to pursue when the product is homogeneous, because the experience curve effects would generate competitive advantages for the market leader. The underlying industry structure is an homogeneous oligopoly.
2. Differentiation, which calls for recognizing different segments in the markets and offers a wide variety of products to satisfy more closely the consumer's needs in each one of these segments. In this case, the industry structure is a differentiated oligopoly.
3. Focus, which also emerges from the definition of different market segments, but now the firm concentrates its products in one or a few of them becoming a specialist in a facet of the market. In this case, the market structure is the monopolistic competition, which assumes the existence of many similar products which are partial substitutes among them.

Figure 11.3 Principal Seller's Market Structure Types

	one	a few	many
Homogeneous Product	Pure Monopoly	Homogeneous Oligopoly	Pure Competition
Differentiated Product	Pure Monopoly	Differentiated Oligopoly	Monopolistic Competition

Source: F. M. Scherer, *Industrial Market Structure and Economic Performance,* Second Edition, Copyright © 1980, Houghton Mifflin Company. Used by permission.

A Final Comment on the Measure of Performance

A very fundamental issue should be raised at this point. The theory of economics advances the conclusion that pure competition is the most socially desirable form of market structure, with all excess benefits of production accruing to the consumer, while providing a normal compensation to labor and capital. But this is so only under long-run equilibrium conditions. In practice we observe many different structures in the seller's market, like monopoly, oligopoly and monopolistic competition (Figure 11.3). A manager, maximizing the benefit of shareholders, should look for some sort of unique opportunity or advantage that generates, though temporarily, an extra profit beyond the pure competitive level. Viewed from this perspective, a successful strategy is one which positions the firm in its industry in such a way that the business enjoys at least temporary monopoly rents. The point is that these profits, defined as monopolistic in economic terms, are the result of some unique contribution of the firm, which separates it from its competitors. The view of society is taken care of by all the community groups and government agencies that oversee the behavior of firms, which are concerned not only with the high quality and cost effectiveness of products, but also with the broader impact on employment and income distribution.

AN INTRODUCTION TO FINANCIAL STATEMENT ANALYSIS

One of the most widely distributed sources of information of all firms in any industry are the set of three financial statements—balance sheet, income statement, and statement of changes in the financial position—and the 10K reports, which must be made public periodically by all major corporations. It is only natural, then, to make use of that information for gaining certain understanding of the competitive position of different firms in an industry. The appropriate technique to perform this task has been known for many years, and it is called *financial statement analysis* (FSA).

The raw data for FSA are the three financial statements, which are illustrated in Figures 11.4, 11.5 and 11.6, for Squibb Corporation in 1982. There are two basic procedures to make these figures more easily comparable among different competitors:

• Define common size financial statements.
• Perform a financial ratio analysis..

Let us review these procedures now.

DEFINITION OF COMMON-SIZE FINANCIAL STATEMENTS

Corporations in an industry are normally of quite different size. Therefore, to say that accounts receivable in firm A are larger than in firm B does not carry too much information. One simple transformation to make financial statements comparable across all firms in an industry is to standardize all of them to a common size, usually 100. In Figure 11.7 we present the 1981 common-size

Figure 11.4   Consolidated Balance Sheet for 1981

Consolidated Balance Sheet

Squibb Corporation and Subsidiaries
December 31, 1982, 1981 and 1980
(Dollar amounts in thousands)

	1982	1981	1980
Assets			
Current Assets:			
Cash	$ 26,813	$ 41,728	$ 9,700
Time deposits	106,669	116,570	28,525
Marketable investments, at cost	2,039	169	447
Receivables (net)	408,295	394,018	344,561
Notes receivable from sale of businesses	25,638	25,429	75,225
Inventories	371,413	390,917	388,968
Prepaid expenses	28,124	23,081	22,053
Deferred taxes on income	56,468	67,574	31,473
Total current assets	1,025,459	1,059,486	900,952
Net Assets of Businesses Sold	—	—	155,303
Investments and Long-Term Receivables	316,012	344,295	216,729
Property, Plant and Equipment (net)	511,821	479,720	479,591
Other Assets	76,420	66,859	64,476
	$1,929,712	$1,950,360	$1,817,051
Liabilities and Shareholders' Equity			
Current Liabilities:			
Current installments of long-term debt	$ 11,586	$ 3,364	$ 3,573
Notes payable	50,831	39,770	72,903
Accounts payable and accrued expenses	317,416	299,028	217,464
Taxes on income	61,839	119,435	62,280
Total current liabilities	441,672	461,597	356,220
Long-Term Debt	336,314	398,771	392,419
Deferred Taxes on Income	16,768	19,416	22,216
Other Liabilities	39,139	40,951	43,726
Shareholders' Equity:			
Common stock, par value $1.00 per share:			
Authorized 100,000,000 shares; issued 51,472,063 shares (49,993,592 in 1981 and 48,551,705 in 1980)	51,472	49,994	48,552
Additional paid-in capital	171,151	158,129	144,340
Retained earnings	955,396	857,259	809,702
Cumulative foreign currency adjustments	(82,126)	(35,717)	—
	1,095,893	1,029,665	1,002,594
Less cost of 12,071 shares of stock held in treasury (10,972 in 1981 and 24,246 in 1980)	74	40	124
Total shareholders' equity	1,095,819	1,029,625	1,002,470
	$1,929,712	$1,950,360	$1,817,051

Source: Reproduced by permission of Squibb Corporation, Princeton, NJ.

Figure 11.5 Statement of Consolidated Income

Statement of Consolidated Income

Squibb Corporation and Subsidiaries
Years ended December 31, 1982, 1981 and 1980
(Amounts in thousands except per share figures)

	1982	1981	1980
Net Sales	$1,660,766	$1,523,911	$1,334,184
Costs and Expenses:			
Cost of sales	678,472	676,444	584,892
Marketing and administrative	647,908	597,001	514,023
Research and development	122,962	95,302	73,787
Other (net)	1,890	3,818	5,825
	1,451,232	1,372,565	1,178,527
Profit from Operations	209,534	151,346	155,657
General Corporate Income (Expenses):			
Interest income	60,832	31,980	34,383
Interest expense	(40,257)	(43,453)	(49,380)
Administrative expenses and other (net)	(10,624)	(15,174)	(12,367)
	9,951	(26,647)	(27,364)
Income before Costs of Restructuring	219,485	124,699	128,293
Costs of restructuring	—	62,859	—
Income before Taxes on Income	219,485	61,840	128,293
Provision for taxes on income	65,849	20,742	24,920
Income from Continuing Businesses	153,636	41,098	103,373
Income from businesses sold (net of taxes)	—	12,181	24,371
Gain (loss) on sale of businesses (net of taxes)	—	58,068	(318)
Income before Extraordinary Charge	153,636	111,347	127,426
Extraordinary charge	—	6,532	—
Net Income	$ 153,636	$ 104,815	$ 127,426
Per Share:			
Income from continuing businesses	$3.01	$ .83	$2.15
Income from businesses sold	—	.24	.51
Gain (loss) on sale of businesses	—	1.16	(.01)
Income before extraordinary charge	3.01	2.23	2.65
Extraordinary charge	—	.13	—
Net income	$3.01	$2.10	$2.65

See accompanying notes to financial statements.

Statement of Consolidated Retained Earnings

Squibb Corporation and Subsidiaries
Years ended December 31, 1982, 1981 and 1980
(Amounts in thousands)

	1982	1981	1980
Balance at beginning of year	$ 857,259	$809,702	$734,981
Companies acquired	9,700	3,134	2,852
Net income	153,636	104,815	127,426
	1,020,595	917,651	865,259
Cash dividends–$1.28 per share ($1.21½ in 1981 and $1.15½ in 1980)	(65,199)	(60,392)	(55,557)
Balance at end of year	$ 955,396	$857,259	$809,702

Source: Reproduced by permission of Squibb Corporation, Princeton, NJ.

Figure 11.6   Statement of Changes in Consolidated Financial Position

Statement of Changes in Consolidated Financial Position

Squibb Corporation and Subsidiaries
Years ended December 31, 1982, 1981 and 1980
(Amounts in thousands)

	1982	1981	1980
Sources of Working Capital			
Income from continuing businesses	$153,636	$ 41,098	$103,373
Items not requiring (providing) working capital:			
Depreciation and amortization of fixed assets	31,270	28,175	24,003
Costs of restructuring	—	22,353	—
Other (net)	(2,402)	550	(1,871)
Working capital provided from continuing businesses	182,504	92,176	125,505
Decrease in long-term receivables from sale of businesses	27,542	12,163	8,080
Disposals of property, plant and equipment (net)	16,295	15,464	3,244
Issuance of treasury shares and shares under stock option and compensation plans (net)	14,389	1,523	869
Decrease in property, plant and equipment from foreign currency translation	13,120	13,230	—
Companies acquired	9,777	16,926	11,719
Decrease in investments by trustees under note agreements	1,599	8,286	7,338
Income from businesses sold	—	12,181	24,371
Extraordinary charge	—	(6,532)	—
Proceeds from sale of businesses (net of noncurrent notes in the principal amounts of $155,000 in 1981 and $24,900 in 1980)	—	64,871	91,622
Decrease in net assets of businesses sold	—	—	36,891
	265,226	230,288	309,639
Uses of Working Capital			
Cash dividends paid	65,199	60,392	55,557
Additions to property, plant and equipment:			
Capital expenditures	87,280	69,851	79,996
Fixed assets of businesses acquired (net)	5,506	4,441	3,443
Payment of 9.40% notes	50,000	—	—
Decrease in equity from foreign currency adjustments	46,409	35,717	—
Decrease (increase) in other long-term debt (net)	12,457	(6,352)	5,020
Increase in other assets (net)	10,665	8,527	13,218
Decrease in other liabilities (net)	1,812	4,555	5,799
	279,328	177,131	163,033
(Decrease) Increase in Working Capital	$(14,102)	$ 53,157	$146,606
Changes in Components of Working Capital–(Decrease) Increase			
Cash	$(14,915)	$ 32,028	$(19,622)
Time deposits	(9,901)	88,045	12,087
Marketable investments	1,870	(278)	(866)
Receivables (net)	14,277	49,457	32,532
Notes receivable from sale of businesses	209	(49,796)	75,225
Inventories	(19,504)	1,949	65,598
Prepaid expenses	5,043	1,028	210
Deferred taxes on income	(11,106)	36,101	10,654
Current installments of long-term debt	(8,222)	209	(2,021)
Notes payable	(11,061)	33,133	13,219
Accounts payable and accrued expenses	(18,388)	(81,564)	(25,316)
Taxes on income	57,596	(57,155)	(15,094)
(Decrease) Increase in Working Capital	$(14,102)	$ 53,157	$146,606

Source: Reproduced by permission of Squibb Corporation, Princeton, NJ.

Figure 11.7 Common Size Statements for a Group of Companies in the Pharmaceutical Industry in 1981

A. Common-Size Balance Sheet (%)

ASSETS	Abbott Labs.	Bristol Myers Co.	Syntex Corp.	Smith-Kline Corp.	Eli Lilly & Co.	Merck Co.	Searle Co.	Squibb Corp.	Group Mean
Cash and Marketable Securities	5	17	20	21	9	10	20	8	14
Accounts Receivable	16	26	15	21	22	19	19	21	20
Inventories	18	23	19	16	23	22	12	20	19
Other Current Assets	6	5	2	1	3	0	3	5	3
Net Plant and Equipment	31	23	35	31	35	41	26	25	31
Investments and Other Assets	24	6	9	10	8	8	20	21	13
	100	100	100	100	100	100	100	100	100
LIABILITIES and EQUITY									
Accounts payable	5	7	8	8	4	13	15	17	8
Other Current Liabilities	31	23	17	17	24	10	18	6	18
Long Term Debt	9	4	12	10	2	7	8	20	10
Deferred Tax & Other Liabil.	6	3	0	0	5	4	6	4	4
Stockholders' Equity	49	63	63	65	65	66	53	53	60
	100	100	100	100	100	100	100	100	100

B. Common-Size Income State (%)

	Abbott Labs.	Bristol Myers Co.	Syntex Corp.	Smith-Kline Corp.	Eli Lilly & Co.	Merck Co.	Searle Co.	Squibb Corp.	Group Mean
REVENUES	100	100	100	100	100	100	100	100	100
EXPENSES									
Cost of Goods Sold	55	38	35	31	39	39	33	41	39
Research & Development	5	4	9	8	8	8	9	6	7
Marketing, G&A Expenses	22	42	38	32	30	27	38	36	33
Interest Expense	0	0	0	1	1	1	0	3	1
Other Expense	1	0	0	2	1	1	4	5	2
Tax	6	7	4	8	7	9	6	2	6
Income After Tax	11	9	14	18	14	15	10	7	12
	100	100	100	100	100	100	100	100	100

Adapted from Marianne Kunschak and Luis F. Tena-Ramirez, "Strategic Management for a Pharmaceutical Company: A Case Study," © 1983. Reprinted by permission of Marianne Kunschak and Luis F. Tena-Ramirez.

balance sheet and income statement for a group of companies in the pharmaceutical industry. We can see, for example, that for Squibb Corp., cash and marketable securities are comparatively low, while long-term debt is comparatively high. Also, its income after taxes is the lowest in the industry.

FINANCIAL RATIO ANALYSIS

This is the most extensively used form of financial statement analysis. The ratio analysis is aimed at characterizing the firm in a few basic dimensions which are considered fundamental to assess the financial health of a company. They are usually categorized in five types (Foster 1978):

- Liquidity ratios
- Leverage/capital structure ratios
- Profitability ratios
- Turnover ratios
- Common stock security ratios.

Liquidity Ratios

A liquid firm is one that can meet short-term financial obligations without much of a problem when they fall due. This ability is normally measured in terms of three different ratios:

$$\bullet \text{ Current ratio} = \frac{\text{Current assets}}{\text{Current liabilities}}$$

This is just a ratio between short-term assets and short-term liabilities.

$$\bullet \text{ Quick ratio} = \frac{\text{Cash} + \text{Short term marketable securities} + \text{Accounts receivable}}{\text{Current liabilities}}$$

This is a more stringent definition of liquidity which is commonly called the acid test. Among the short-term assets only the most liquid ones are included, leaving aside inventories and prepaid expenses.

$$\bullet \frac{\text{Defensive}}{\text{interval (days)}} = \frac{\text{Cash} + \text{Short term marketable securities} + \text{Accounts receivable}}{\text{Projected daily operating expenses}}$$

This ratio is an estimate of the total number of days of operation that can be financed with the most liquid of short-term assets (also called defensive assets).

The values of these three ratios for a group of companies in the pharmaceutical industry in 1981 are presented in Figure 11.8. It can be observed that, in all three measures, Abbott Labs. presents the most critical condition, while Squibb

Figure 11.8 Liquidity Ratios for a Group of Companies in the Pharmaceutical Industry in 1981

	Abbott Labs.	Bristol Meyers Co.	Syntex Corp.	Smith-Kline Corp.	Eli Lilly & Co.	Merck Co.	Searle Co.	Squibb Corp.	Group Mean
Current ratio	1.22	2.38	2.23	2.28	2.40	2.04	2.40	2.29	2.20
Quick ratio	0.59	1.35	1.35	1.49	1.69	1.09	1.73	1.32	1.33
Defensive Interval (days)	97	135	135	206	220	179	222	126	165

Adapted from Marianne Kunschak and Luis F. Tena-Ramirez, "Strategic Management for a Pharmaceutical Company: A Case Study," © 1983. Reprinted by permission of Marianne Kunschak and Luis F. Tena-Ramirez.

appears well protected for fulfilling its short-term obligations, at least as reflected by the current and quick ratios.

Leverage-Capital Structure Ratios

These ratios measure the use of leverage in the firm (debt versus equity capital), and the ability it has to fulfill its long term commitments with debtholders. These are the most commonly used ratios:

$$\bullet \ \text{Leverage of long term debt} = \frac{\text{Long term debt}}{\text{Shareholders's equity}}$$

$$\bullet \ \text{Leverage of total debt} = \frac{\text{Current liabilities} + \text{Long term debt}}{\text{Shareholder's equity}}$$

These two leverage ratios measure the number of debt dollars (either long term, or total debt) per equity dollar.

$$\bullet \ \text{Times interest earned} = \frac{\text{Operating income}}{\text{Annual interest payments}}$$

This ratio measures the number of times that interest payments could be covered by operating income (profit before interest and taxes). The larger the ratio, the more security on the ability of the firm to make its interest payments, and consequently, the lower the risk borne by debtholders.

In Figure 11.9 we present the Leverage-Capital Structure ratios for a group of companies in the pharmaceutical industry in 1981. Abott Labs. appears again as the most levered company with a 0.93 ratio of total debt to equity and it is closely followed by Squibb with a 0.84 ratio. Curiously enough, Squibb shows to be very liquid in the short run, but rather illiquid in the long run, with earnings only four times interest payments.

Profitability Ratios

Profitability ratios measure the ability of the firm to generate profits. There are different measures of profitability, three being the most widely used:

$$\bullet \ \begin{array}{c} \text{Return on} \\ \text{total assets} \end{array} = \frac{\begin{array}{c} \text{Net income} \\ \text{after tax} \end{array} + \begin{array}{c} \text{Interest} \\ \text{Expenses} \end{array} - \begin{array}{c} \text{Tax benefits of} \\ \text{interest expenses} \end{array}}{\text{Total assets}}$$

This is a measure of the profitability of the business, independent of the source of financing.

$$\bullet \ \begin{array}{c} \text{Return on} \\ \text{Equity} \end{array} = \frac{\text{Net income available to common}}{\text{Common shareholder's equity}}$$

Figure 11.9 Leverage-Capital Structure Ratios for a Group of Companies in the Pharmaceutical Industry in 1981

	Abbott Labs.	Bristol Myers Co.	Syntex Corp.	Smith-Kline Corp.	Eli Lilly & Co.	Merck Co.	Searle Co.	Squibb Corp.	Group Mean
Long term debt Shareholder's Equity	0.18	0.07	0.16	0.11	0.03	0.11	0.33	0.39	0.17
Total debt Shareholder's Equity	0.93	0.59	0.54	0.50	0.46	0.46	0.76	0.84	0.64
Times interest earned	3.2	9.4	4.4	15.8	13.1	11.2	5.3	4.0	8.3

Adapted from Marianne Kunschak and Luis F. Tena-Ramirez, "Strategic Management for a Pharmaceutical Company: A Case Study," © 1983. Reprinted by permission of Marianne Kunschak and Luis F. Tena-Ramirez.

This ratio measures the profitability of the firm to common shareholders; that is to say, to equity owners. Interest payments are deducted this time from the measure of profit in the numerator.

$$\bullet \text{ Sales Margin} = \frac{\text{Revenues} - \text{Operating Expenses}}{\text{Revenues}}$$

This is a measure of the operating profit in relation to revenues from sales.

In Figure 11.10 we present the profitability ratios for a group of companies in the pharmaceutical industry in 1981. What is most noticeable in this table is the low sales margin of Squibb Corp. Over total assets the return is quite comparable with most corporations, except for Smith-Kline Corp. which shows very high profitability in all three indices. But the return on equity is only half the level of other corporations, and the sales margin is still lower. This points again to the capital structure problem, and most likely to an inadequate production-cost structure.

Turnover Ratios

Turnover are also called efficiency ratios, because they measure performance in the utilization of assets. The most popular ratios are:

$$\bullet \frac{\text{Total Assets}}{\text{Turnover}} = \frac{\text{Period sales}}{\text{Average total assets}}$$

This ratio indicates the number of times that "assets are sold" in a stated period.

$$\bullet \frac{\text{Average Collection}}{\text{Period (days)}} = \frac{\text{Average (net)accounts receivable}}{\text{Daily sales}}$$

This is the average number of days required for the collection of payments on credit sales.

$$\bullet \text{ Inventory Turnover} = \frac{\text{Period sales}}{\text{Average inventory}}$$

In this case the ratio refers to the number of times that "inventories are sold."

In Figure 11.11 we present the turnover ratios for a group of companies in the pharmaceutical industry in 1981. This time Squibb shows the lowest efficiency indicators, with only 0.81 for asset turnover (low sales compared to assets) and 3.9 for inventory turnover (too much inventory for the prevailing level of sales). Also a collection period of over 100 days speaks of credit terms more generous than other firms in the industry. Is this an intended policy or is it just the result of poor collection practices?

Common-Stock Security Ratios

Financial analysts often express some of the information contained in the financial statements on a per-share basis. This is done in order to capture information

Figure 11.10 Profitability Ratios for a Group of Companies in the Pharmaceutical Industry in 1981

	Abbott Labs.	Bristol Myers Co.	Syntex Corp.	Smith-Kline Corp.	Eli Lilly & Co.	Merck Co.	Searle Co.	Squibb Corp.	Group Mean
Return on Total Assets	0.12	0.13	0.14	0.20	0.14	0.15	0.11	0.12	0.14
Return on Shareholders' Equity	0.21	0.20	0.20	0.30	0.20	0.22	0.17	0.10	0.20
Sales (%) Margin (5-year average)	0.44	0.62	0.63	0.66	0.61	0.62	0.67	0.53	0.60

Adapted from Marianne Kunschak and Luis F. Tena-Ramirez, "Strategic Management for a Pharmaceutical Company: A Case Study," © 1983. Reprinted by permission of Marianne Kunschak and Luis F. Tena-Ramirez.

Figure 11.11 Turnover Ratios for a Group of Companies in the Pharmaceutical Industry in 1981

	Abbott Labs.	Bristol Myers Co.	Syntex Corp.	Smith-Kline Corp.	Eli Lilly & Co.	Merck Co.	Searle Co.	Squibb Corp.	Group Mean
Total Asset Turnover	1.06	1.49	0.96	1.15	0.96	1.00	0.86	0.81	1.04
Average Collection Period (days)	56	57	56	67	83	68	79	101	68
Inventory Turnover	5.8	6.3	5.3	6.3	4.1	4.6	7.3	3.9	5.5

Adapted from Marianne Kunschak and Luis F. Tena-Ramirez, "Strategic Management for a Pharmaceutical Company: A Case Study," © 1983. Reprinted by permission of Marianne Kunschak and Luis F. Tena-Ramirez.

which is central for the equity-holders to judge the firm's performance. The most commonly used of these ratios are:

- Earnings per Share (EPS) $= \dfrac{\text{Net income available for common}}{\text{Number of shares outstanding}}$

- Book value per share $= \dfrac{\text{Shareholders' equity}}{\text{Number of shares outstanding}}$

- Dividends per share $= \dfrac{\text{Dividends paid on common}}{\text{Number of shares outstanding}}$

- Market-to-Book value (M/B) $= \dfrac{\text{Price per share}}{\text{Book value per share}}$

The most relevant of these measurements for assessing the economic performance of a firm in terms of value creation is the market-to-book value ratio, which is discussed extensively in Chapter 10. In Figure 11.12, we provide the trend of M/B values from 1977 to 1981 for Squibb Corporation, Smith-Kline (an outstanding performer within its industry), and the drug industry average. The differences observed in these ratios constitute an evidence on the actual investment opportunities of the firms, as suggested by:

1. Squibb's M/B ratio experiences an important increase in 1981, when new and quite profitable products were introduced by the company.
2. Smith-Kline's M/B is very high, though it shows a persistent downward trend that could be explained by the prompt expiration of a valuable patent (Tagamet).
3. The average M/B ratio for pharmaceutical companies is relatively high, which indicates a favorable comparison with alternative investment opportunities.

Figure 11.12 The M/B Ratio for Squibb Corporation, Smith-Kline Corporation, and the Pharmaceutical Industry (1977–1981)

	1977	1978	1979	1980	1981
Squibb Corporation	1.88	1.85	1.32	1.38	1.99
Smith-Kline	6.32	5.71	5.34	4.61	3.73
Drug Industry (Worldwide)	2.00	1.88	1.76	1.89	2.19

Adapted from Marianne Kunschak and Luis F. Tena-Ramirez, "Strategic Management for a Pharmaceutical Company: A Case Study," © 1983. Reprinted by permission of Marianne Kunschak and Luis F. Tena-Ramirez.

Other Measures of Performance

Besides the five categories of financial ratios we have described, often it is useful to include other performance measurements which are particularly critical in a given industry. For instance, for high-technology firms, comparative measures pertaining to R&D expenses could be quite significant. Likewise, for firms with high capital intensity, it could be interesting to observe the ratio of capital investment over sales. In most industries, the firm's growth compared to the industry growth is an important indicator on the changes of relative market share for each of the competitors. Figure 11.13 shows some additional measures of performance which were considered significant for a group of companies in the pharmaceutical industry. The data associated with sales growth and relative market share positioning (company growth versus industry growth) present Smith-Kline and Syntex Corporations as those gaining competitive positioning more aggressively. All other companies seem more or less to maintain their existing shares. It is clear from the figures that the pharmaceutical industry is exceedingly high in the intensity of R&D expenditures. Abbott Laboratories stands alone as the lowest spender in R&D, among the group of companies being considered. This should be a matter of concern for them.

DEFINING THE STANDARD OF COMPARISON: CROSS-SECTIONAL VERSUS TIME SERIES ANALYSIS

Though a ratio is a pure number, with no dollar dimension, to fully interpret its meaning we need some standards of comparison. For example, it is a commonly held belief to think that a corporation with a liquidity ratio of 2 or more and a quick ratio of 1 or more could be considered liquid. But these absolute standards are very hard to justify. For that reason, the preferred two methodologies to define standards for the interpretation of common-size statements and financial ratio analysis use relative indicators. These methodologies are:

— *The cross-sectional analysis*, which takes all firms in an industry at a given point in time (for example, at the end of 1981), and allows the comparison of their relative standing. The usual reference selected in this case is the mean or the median for the group of industries. All Figures 11.7 through 11.11 and 11.13, which correspond to illustrations of cross-sectional analysis of both common size statements and financial ratios, include the group mean in the final column.

— *The time series analysis*. In this case the interest is centered on the evolution of an indicator through a period of many years, so the criteria for analysis are not only the behavior of some selected indicators for the competitors in the industry, but also the pattern shown by all indicators through time, including the average or median for the group of firms. For example, in Figure 11.14 we present the return on equity and return on total assets for Squibb Corporation and for the industry average between 1977 and 1981. In this period, Squibb shows a persistent deterioration of these two indicators, being more pronounced in the return on equity ratio. The interesting thing to notice

Figure 11.13 Other Measures of Performance for a Group of Companies in the Pharmaceutical Industry (Average for 1977–1981)

	Abbott Labs.	Bristol Myers Co.	Syntex Corp.	Smith-Kline Corp.	Eli Lilly & Co.	Merck Co.	Searle Co.	Squibb Corp.	Group Mean
V. GROWTH PERFORMANCE MEASURES Five-year average (77, 78, 79, 81)									
Average Sales Growth %*	16	9.4	19	23	13	9	5.3	14	14
1981 Sales Growth %*	18	14	26	17	12	12	17	18	17
R&D Expenses as % of Sales	5	9.1	9.1	7.4	8.1	8.2	8	6.1	8
Capital Investment-Sales	6.5	4.1	8	9.7	7.3	8.7	8.4	6.1	7
Company Growth-Industry Growth*	1.04	0.99	1.1	1.12	1.03	1.03	0.97	0.96	1.03

* Real Dollars.

Source: Marianne Kunschak and Luis F. Tena-Ramirez, "Strategic Management for a Pharmaceutical Company: A Case Study," © 1983, p (41) (43) (44) (45). Reprinted by permission of Marianne Kunschak and Luis F. Tena-Ramirez.

Figure 11.14 Profitability Ratios for Squibb and a Group of Companies in the Pharmaceutical Industry (1977–1981)

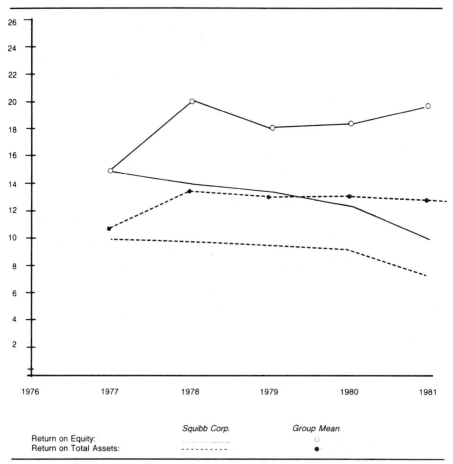

	Squibb Corp.	Group Mean
Return on Equity:	———	○
Return on Total Assets:	– – – – –	●

Source: Marianne Kunschak and Luis F. Tena-Ramirez, "Strategic Management for a Pharmaceutical Company: A Case Study," © 1983, p (41) (43) (44) (45). Reprinted by permission of Marianne Kunschak and Luis F. Tena-Ramirez.

is that back in 1977, Squibb presented an average profitability as measured by those two indicators, but in all other years it is markedly below the average.

Figures 11.15 and 11.16 compare the performance of Squibb against the mean performance of the group of companies in the pharmaceutical industry we have used in all previous analyses, by using a selected group of ratios. We leave the reader to conduct the diagnosis that this information could suggest, which could identify some of the causes of Squibb's profitability performance.

The trend analysis originated in the time series of financial indicators can

Figure 11.15 Turnover Ratios for Squibb and a Group of Companies in the Pharmaceutical Industry (1977–1981)

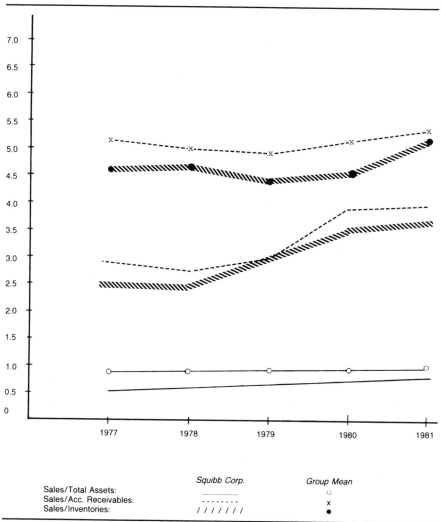

	Squibb Corp.	Group Mean
Sales/Total Assets:	————	○
Sales/Acc. Receivables:	- - - - - -	x
Sales/Inventories:	/ / / / / /	●

Source: Marianne Kunschak and Luis F. Tena-Ramirez, "Strategic Management for a Pharmaceutical Company: A Case Study," © 1983, p (41) (43) (44) (45). Reprinted by permission of Marianne Kunschak and Luis F. Tena-Ramirez.

be supported by either fairly simple tools—such as the ones that we have presented—or by making use of more advanced techniques like econometric models, Box-Jenkins analysis, and others. For a more comprehensive discussion of this subject, the reader is referred to Foster (1978).

Figure 11.16   Sales Related Financial Indicators for Squibb and a Group of Companies in the Pharmaceutical Industry (1977–1981)

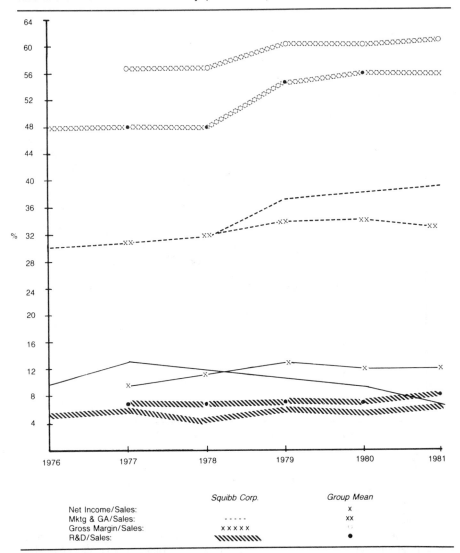

	Squibb Corp.	Group Mean
Net Income/Sales:		x
Mktg & GA/Sales:	- - - - -	xx
Gross Margin/Sales:	x x x x x	⊙
R&D/Sales:	\\\\\\\\\\\\	●

Source: Marianne Kunschak and Luis F. Tena-Ramirez, "Strategic Management for a Pharmaceutical Company, A Case Study," © 1983, p (41) (43) (44) (45). Reprinted by permission of Marianne Kunschak and Luis F. Tena-Ramirez.

FINANCIAL MODELS AND PERFORMANCE STANDARDS FOR ANALOG DEVICES

Another important use of competitive financial statement analysis is the development of meaningful and realistic financial targets for a firm. This task has received considerably attention in the recent past, and it has been greatly facilitated thanks to the availability of personal computers and software packages such as Visicalc and One, Two, Three. We have chosen Analog Devices, Inc. (ADI), a progressive high-technology company headquartered in Massachusetts that manufactures instruments and semiconductors, as an example to illustrate the use of financial models in the formulation of performance standards. Our comments are based on an annual meeting address given by Ray Stata, ADI president in March 1980.

The first step in the definition of financial standards is the identification of those companies in the industry in which the firm is competing, which will provide the base for comparison. ADI chose for this purpose a selected group of leading companies in computers, instruments, and semiconductors, whose sales growth is given in Figure 11.17. Although strictly speaking ADI is only in the instrument and semiconductor business, they perceive, properly, that they compete with this set of firms in the electronics industry for human and capital resources. The industry data given in Figures 11.17 through 11.23 are three-year averages covering 1977–1979.

Figure 11.17 Sales Growth for a Selected Group of Companies in the Electronics Industry

		SALES GROWTH	
Rank	Company	3 Yr Avg Growth	1979 Sales Growth
1	Intel (S&C)	44.1%	66.5%
2	Advanced Micro Devices (S)	63.3	60.6
3	Analog Devices (S&I)	36.6	51.6
4	National Semiconductor (S)	30.7	45.4
5	Intersil (S)	24.7	37.3
6	Hewlett-Packard (I&C)	28.7	36.6
7	Teradyne (I)	32.5	36.1
8	Data General (C)	41.7	33.6
9	Gen Rad (I)	22.1	33.2
10	Perkin-Elmer (I)	27.5	32.3
11	Tektronix (I)	29.0	31.3
12	Fluke (I)	28.5	31.1
13	Texas Instruments (S)	23.1	26.4
14	Digital Equipment Corp. (C)	35.0	25.6

(S) Semiconductors   (I) Instruments   (C) Computers

Source: Ray Stata, "Financial Models and Performance Standard for Analog Devices," © 1980. Reprinted by permission of Analog Devices, Inc., Norwood, MA.

Figure 11.17 is eloquent in communicating the extraordinary growth rate that these companies have enjoyed in the recent past. Analog Devices is standing third in 1979, with an outstanding 51.6%.

A matter of great concern for these high technology companies is the intensity of R&D investments, and how they stand regarding their competitors. Figure 11.18 shows that ADI lags the high-technology leaders when R&D expenses are measured as percentage of sales, with a relatively modest 5.7 percent. However, if R&D investments are evaluated as a ratio of sales growth rates to R&D as a percentage of sales, Analog comes out favorably. This ratio can be interpreted as a measurement of engineering productivity, and in this respect ADI gets a significant return on its engineering investment.

Figure 11.18 Ratio Average Growth to R&D Expenses (% of Sales)

Rank	Company	3 Yr Avg Growth	3 Yr Avg R&D	Ratio
1	Advanced Micro Devices (S)	63.3%	7.9%	8.0
2	Analog Devices (S&I)	36.6	5.7	6.4
3	Teradyne (I)	34.4	5.8	5.9
4	Texas Instruments (S)	23.1	4.5	5.1
5	Intel (S&C)	44.1	10.1	4.4
6	Data General (C)	41.7	10.1	4.1
7	Perkin-Elmer (I)	27.5	7.0	3.9
8	Digital Equipment Corp. (C)	35.0	9.4	3.7
9	National Semiconductor (S)	30.7	8.6	3.6
10	Tektronix (I)	29.0	8.2	3.5
11	Fluke (I)	28.5	9.0	3.2
12	Hewlett-Packard (I&C)	28.7	8.9	3.2
13	Intersil (S)	24.7	7.9	3.1
14	Gen Rad (I)	22.1	7.9	2.8

(S) Semiconductor   (I) Instruments   (C) Computers

Source: Ray Stata, "Financial Models and Performance Standard for Analog Devices," © 1980. Reprinted by permission of Analog Devices, Inc., Norwood, MA.

Figure 11.19 examines the operating expenses of the relevant group of companies as a percentage of sales. Although there does not seem to be any correlation between R&D expenses and the type of company, it is apparent that marketing and administrative expenses for instrument and computer companies are in general higher than for semiconductor companies. This is due to the traditional dependency of semiconductor component manufacturers on distributors to handle small quantity orders. ADI policy, on the contrary, handles directly a much larger percentage of small orders, thus building up its own sales and distribution capabilities. This is translated into higher growth margins than most of the semiconductor companies, because they are keeping the distribution profits for

Figure 11.19 Expense Analysis (% of Sales)

Rank	Company	R&D	Mkt/G&A	Total R&D Mkt/G&A	Int
1	Fluke (I)	9.0%	34.8%	43.8%	0.4%
2	Tektronix (I)	8.2	31.3	39.5	0.8
3	Gen Rad (I)	7.9	30.7	38.6	1.4
4	Hewlett-Packard (I&C)	8.9	27.6	36.5	0.3
5	Analog Devices (S&I)	5.8	29.3	35.1	2.7
6	Data General (C)	10.1	22.3	32.4	0.0
7	Perkin-Elmer (I)	7.0	24.3	31.3	0.6
8	Intel (S&C)	10.1	18.5	28.6	0.2
9	Digital Equipment Corp. (C)	9.4	18.3	27.7	0.0
10	Advanced Micro Devices (S)	7.9	19.0	26.9	0.4
11	Teradyne (I)	5.8	18.1	23.9	0.8
12	Intersil (S)	7.9	13.9	21.8	0.0
13	National Semiconductor (S)	8.8	13.0	21.8	0.5
14	Texas Instruments (S)	4.5	14.1	18.6	0.0

(S) Semiconductors   (I) Instruments   (C) Computers

Source: Ray Stata, "Financial Models and Performance Standard for Analog Devices," © 1980. Reprinted by permission of Analog Devices, Inc., Norwood, MA.

Figure 11.20 Margin Analysis (% of Sales)

Rank	Company	Gross Margin	Operating Profit before Taxes	Profit before Taxes	Tax Rate	Net Income
1	Fluke (I)	59.5%	15.7%	15.3%	45.9%	8.3%
2	Tektronix (I)	55.5	16.0	16.3	40.6	9.7
3	Hewlett-Packard (I&C)	53.7	17.2	16.9	48.2	8.8
4	Data General (C)	52.1	19.7	20.1	47.5	10.6
5	Gen Rad (I)	51.4	12.8	11.3	44.5	6.3
6	Intel (S&C)	50.9	22.3	22.1	48.7	11.3
7	Analog Devices (S&I)	48.5	13.4	11.2	39.8	6.4
8	Digital Equipment Corp. (C)	44.0	16.3	16.3	38.5	10.0
9	Perkin-Elmer (I)	43.6	12.3	11.6	46.3	6.2
10	Advanced Micro Devices (S)	39.4	12.5	12.1	43.9	6.8
11	Teradyne (I)	39.1	15.2	14.4	49.4	7.3
12	Intersil (S)	34.5	12.7	14.3	49.7	7.2
13	National Semiconductor (S)	28.7	7.7	7.2	44.5	4.0
14	Texas Instruments (S)	28.6	10.0	10.0	44.7	5.5

(S) Semiconductors   (I) Instruments   (C) Computers

Source: Ray Stata, "Financial Models and Performance Standard for Analog Devices," © 1980. Reprinted by permission of Analog Devices, Inc., Norwood, MA.

themselves. However, this is also translated into higher R&D, marketing, and general and administrative expenses.

The final column of Figure 11.19 shows interest expenses as a percentage of sales. The high interest expense ratio of Analog is the result of maintaining a higher debt-equity structure than most of the relevant companies.

The margin analysis shown in Figure 11.20 indicates that instruments and computer companies tend to have higher gross margins to offset the higher cost of sales and administration already mentioned. The difference between operating profits before taxes and profits before taxes is small because it is primarily due to interest expense or income, which is not very significant. Analog represents an exception to the group of companies considered, because of its high debt levels. ADI also has a substantial difference in its tax rate expressed as a percentage of profit before taxes. This is the result of such factors as tax havens, like Ireland, investment tax credits, and depreciation policies. Because of the distortions introduced by different tax rates and debt structures, Analog uses operating profits before taxes as á base of comparison.

Assets intensity (assets as percentage of sales) is analyzed in Figure 11.21, where Analog stands up in the top of the list, a matter of some concern since it is better to have low asset intensity. These figures can be understood by realizing that instruments and computer companies tend to have higher assets turnover than semiconductor firms, since they maintain higher inventories and receivables than the semiconductor companies. Moreover, ADI's policy of having their own distribution channels, and directly controlling customer service, pushes

Figure 11.21   Asset Intensity (% of Sales)

Rank	Company	Inven-tory	Receiv-ables	Net Fixed Assets	Operating Assets
1	Digital Equipment Corp. (C)	27.3%	24.7%	21.3%	73.3%
2	Analog Devices (S&I)	20.4	20.4	25.3	66.1
3	Hewlett-Packard (I&C)	18.3	18.4	25.8	62.5
4	Data General (C)	27.0	21.9	13.4	62.3
5	Tektronix (I)	23.1	17.3	21.2	61.6
6	Gen Rad (I)	29.1	22.6	9.3	61.0
7	Perkin-Elmer (I)	25.2	21.7	12.8	59.7
8	Fluke (I)	21.0	20.7	17.7	59.4
9	Teradyne (I)	18.8	19.3	21.3	59.4
10	Intel (S&C)	10.4	18.3	27.2	55.9
11	Advanced Micro Devices (S)	9.7	16.5	20.2	46.4
12	National Semiconductor (S)	15.6	13.9	16.8	46.3
13	Texas Instruments (S)	10.0	15.3	20.6	45.9
14	Intersil (S)	11.3	14.4	10.7	36.4

(S) Semiconductors   (I) Instruments   (C) Computers

Source: Ray Stata, "Financial Models and Performance Standard for Analog Devices," © 1980. Reprinted by permission of Analog Devices, Inc., Norwood, MA.

up the assets requirements. Thus, Analog decided to use 67 percent of the operating assets intensity for its financial model.

Due to the significant differences in depreciation practice, reported net fixed assets can differ substantially among companies. Figure 11.22 looks at fixed asset intensities in another way, namely, as average capital expenditures as a percentage of sales. The last column of that figure also computes the ratio of average sales growth to capital expenditures as a percentage of sales. This ratio seems to indicate that a faster growing company tends to invest a greater percentage of current sales dollars than a slower growing company. Since Analog expects to grow at a faster rate, it has selected a capital expenditure in the range from 13 to 15 percent of sales for its financial model.

All of these observations, together with strategic and competitive considerations, lead towards the formulation of Analog's financial model, whose primary targets are expressed in Figure 11.23. There, Analog's performance for 1979 is contrasted with the intended goals for 1982, as well as those of the few firms whose financial characteristics seem to be particularly relevant for ADI.

The commitments expressed in the financial model are extremely helpful to evaluate the economic merits of alternative strategies, and to establish standards for financial control. Moreover, they constitute the heart of the quantification of the financial parameters needed to generate proforma financial statements to assess the overall expected profitability of the firm.

Figure 11.22 Capital Expenditures

Rank	Company	3 Yr Avg Growth	3 Yr Capital Expenditures (% of Sales)	Ratio
1	Gen Rad (I)	22.1%	3.7%	6.0
2	Intersil (S)	24.7	4.3	5.7
3	Perkin-Elmer (I)	27.5	5.0	5.5
4	Data General (C)	41.7	7.9	5.3
5	Advanced Micro Devices (S)	63.3	13.0	4.9
6	Teradyne (I)	34.4	7.1	4.8
7	Fluke (I)	28.5	6.7	4.3
8	Digital Equipment Corp. (C)	35.0	10.1	3.5
9	Tektronix (I)	29.0	8.2	3.5
10	Hewlett-Packard (I&C)	28.7	8.6	3.3
11	National Semiconductor (S)	30.7	9.9	3.0
12	Analog Devices (S&I)	36.6	13.6	2.7
13	Intel (S&C)	44.1	18.8	2.3
14	Texas Instruments (S)	23.1	10.0	2.3

(S) Semiconductors   (I) Instruments   (C) Computers

Source: Ray Stata, "Financial Models and Performance Standard for Analog Devices," © 1980. Reprinted by permission of Analog Devices, Inc., Norwood, MA.

Figure 11.23   Profitability Model for ADI

	Analog Devices (79)	Analog Devices Model (%)	Hewlett-Packard (%)	Tektronix (%)	Data General (%)
Gross Margin	50.1	54.0	53.2	54.3	50.5
R&D	5.9	8.5	8.6	7.7	10.0
Mkt/G&A	28.9	28.0	27.7	31.2	22.6
OPBT	15.3	17.5	16.9	15.4	17.9
ROC	15.5	19.0	16.3	18.5	18.6

Source: Ray Stata, "Financial Models and Performance Standard for Analog Devices," © 1980. Reprinted by permission of Analog Devices, Inc., Norwood, MA.

REFERENCES

Kunschak, Marianne, and Luis F. Tena-Ramirez, "Strategic Management for a Pharmaceutical Company: A Case Study," unpublished Master Thesis, Sloan School of Management, Massachusetts Institute of Technology, 1983.

Foster, George, *Financial Statement Analysis*, Prentice-Hall, Englewood Cliffs, NJ, 1978.

Porter, Michael E., *Competitive Strategy*, The Free Press, NY, 1980.

Scherer, F. M., *Industrial Market Structure and Economic Performance*, Second Edition, Copyright © 1980, Houghton Mifflin Company.

Stata, Ray, "Financial Models and Performance Standard for Analog Devices," Analog Devices, Inc., Norwood, MA, March, 1980.

Part Three

A METHODOLOGY FOR THE DEVELOPMENT OF A CORPORATE STRATEGIC PLAN

In Part One we discussed the basic concepts associated with business and corporate strategy. This part is intended to illustrate how those concepts could be translated into a comprehensive corporate strategic plan. To attain that objective, we will propose a methodology which, we feel, is general enough so as to fit reasonably well a wide variety of business conditions. We have tried this methodology in a number of different settings with very encouraging results. However, as we have indicated in different contexts many times already, planning is a managerial activity that should be deeply rooted in the unique characteristics of a firm, regarding its culture, people, organizational structure, administrative systems, and the nature of its businesses and their environment. Therefore, we offer this methodology as a broad general framework, which follows the twelve steps outlined in Chapter 4. We would urge those who might consider using this approach for the development of their own corporate strategy to view it as a simple guideline, and to modify and adapt it in order to better capture the specific idiosyncrasies of their own firms.

The methodology that we cover in this part represents an attempt to structure as much as possible the corporate strategic planning process. We have done that purposely, so as to guide in a very pragmatic way the implementation of concepts and ideas pertaining to corporate strategy. When we tested this implementation in a variety of academic and consulting activities, this high degree of pragmatism was helpful and warmly received by its users. This methodology does not end with abstract concepts about the quality of strategic thinking, but it serves to guide a group of key managers into an orderly sequence of logical steps, intended to address all the key strategic issues of the organization.

Having said that about the intended objective of the methodology, we have to raise one one more time a second word of caution. Planning is not a mechanistic activity. It cannot be interpreted simply as filling in forms. The planning documents are just subproducts of the process. When they begin to get in the way of effective strategic thinking, it is time to put all forms away and provide a complete freedom in the way of documenting the basic strategic issues. A firm which is in a very embryonic stage in the development of strategy formulation might benefit from a more structured process which will assure some degree of uniformity across organizational units in the quality of strategic planning. However, firms which already have acquired a high degree of sophistication in this area could become

Figure III.1   General Electric: Topics to be Covered in Strategic Plans (1973)

1. The identification and formulation of environmental assumptions of strategic importance.
2. The identification and in-depth analysis of competitors, including assumptions about their probable strategies.
3. The analysis of the SBU's own resources.
4. The development and evaluation of Strategic Alternatives.
5. The preparation of the SBU Strategic Plan, including estimate of capital spending for the next five years.
6. The preparation of the SBU Operating Plan, which details the next year of the SBU Strategic Plan.

Source: From Francis J. Aguilar and Richard G. Hamermesh, General Electric: Strategic Position—1981. Boston: Harvard Business School, Case 9-381-174, p. 5. Reprinted by permission.

much less dependent on a rigid format. For example, General Electric simply listed a set of topics to be covered by each SBU manager (see Figure III.1).

The ensuing chapters will cover the content of the twelve steps we have identified to structure the corporate strategic planning process. Although they represent a sequence in which every outcome of a given step conditions and enlightens the subsequent ones, it should not be interpreted as a rigid linear process. More often than not, in the middle of the process, one discovers that a given issue did not receive the proper attention, and one is forced to go back and resolve that question prior to continuing with the planning process.

We have chosen a few simple cases to illustrate the implementation of this methodology. They have been extracted from master theses conducted by Sloan Fellows at MIT. These are experienced business managers who spent twelve months in a general management program leading to a master's degree at the Sloan School. The primary cases we will be presenting are General Motors of Venezuela (Soulavy 1983); Citicorp (Williams 1983); and Martin Marietta (Lai 1983).

The strategic analysis reported for each of these firms should not be interpreted as the official strategic commitments of those organizations. They represent an academic effort to apply our strategic planning framework by some MIT students under the supervision of Arnoldo Hax.

To avoid unnecessary repetitions, we are not going to cover the description material presented for each step in Chapter 4. The reader should have fresh in his mind the content of that chapter for a more fruitful reading of the material in this part.

For the sake of brevity, we are going to be extremely succinct in the descriptive material covering the content of each step and the discussion of illustrations. Most of the material presented will rely on forms, whose analysis will be largely the responsibility of the reader.

Figure III.2 reproduces, again, the sequence of twelve steps which we have adopted for the corporate strategic planning process.

Figure III.2 The Formal Corporate Strategic Planning Process

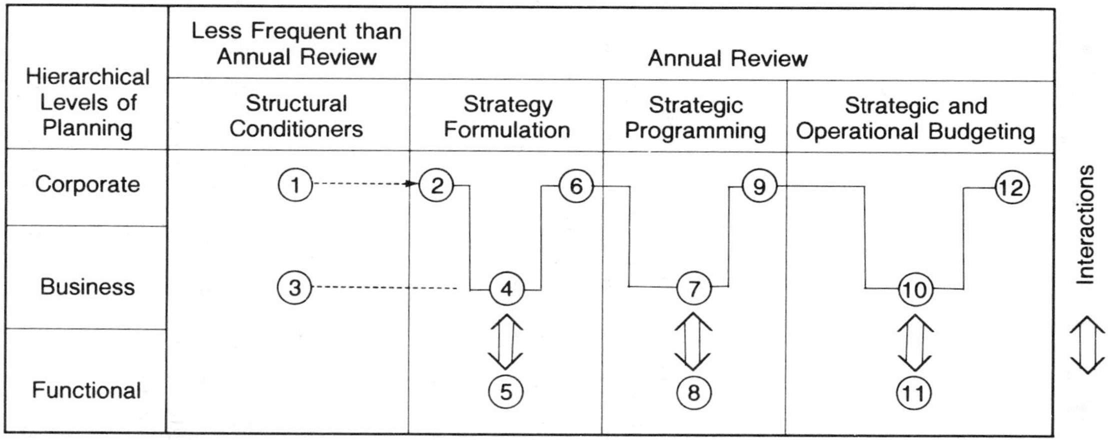

1 The vision of the firm: corporate philosophy, mission of the firm, and identification of SBUs and their interactions.
2 Strategic posture and planning guidelines: corporate strategic thrusts, corporate performance objectives, and planning challenges.
3 The mission of the business: business scope, and identification of product-market segments.
4 Formulation of business strategy and broad action programs.
5 Formulation of functional strategy: Participation in business strategic planning, concurrence or non-concurrence to business strategy proposals, broad action programs.
6 Consolidation of business and functional strategies.
7 Definition and evaluation of specific action programs at the business level.
8 Definition and evaluation of specific action programs at the functional level.
9 Resource allocation and definition of performance measurements for management control.
10 Budgeting at the business level.
11 Budgeting at the functional level.
12 Budgeting consolidations, and approval of strategic and operational funds.

12

STEP 1: THE VISION OF THE FIRM

The vision of the firm is a rather permanent statement to communicate the nature of the existence of the organization in terms of corporate purposes, business scope, and competitive leadership; to provide the framework that regulates the relationships among the firm and its primary stakeholders; and to state the broad objectives of the firm's performance.

The primary components of the vision of the firm are:

—The mission of the firm
—Identification of SBUs and their interaction
—The corporate philosophy

THE MISSION OF THE FIRM

This is a statement of the current and future expected product, market, and geographical scope, as well as a way to attain competitive leadership. The mission statement of Citicorp is being presented in Figure 12.1, and that of General Motors of Venezuela is exhibited in Figure 12.2.

IDENTIFICATION OF SBUs AND THEIR INTERACTION

The cornerstone of the strategic planning process is the segmentation of the firm's activities in terms of business units (SBUs). An SBU can be defined as an operating unit or a planning focus that sells a distinct set of products or services to an identifiable group of customers in competition with a well-defined

Figure 12.1   The Mission Statement of Citicorp

Summary Statement

The premise of Citicorp's mission is to offer an array of products and services to all of its market segments primarily where a customer need has been established. Its entry into the lucrative consumer market has begun to show signs of positive returns, while the corporate market continues to remain a highly profitable segment with strong demands for many of the products and services Citicorp offers. Its technological capability is and will continue to be a significant driving force behind many new products and improving upon its global communications network. Citicorp will also continue its active participation in legislative reform since many of the laws in existence today preclude its activities in various product-market and geographical segments within the United States.

	CURRENT	*FUTURE*
PRODUCT SCOPE:	• To provide consumer and institutional financial services which include credit extension, electronic cash management, foreign trade services, foreign exchange, savings and checking vehicles, credit cards, equipment leasing, fund-raising and investment advisory services, securities underwriting, distribution and trading, and venture capital. • Build products and services generating fee based revenue. • Package the right mix of financial services.	• Expand product scope by delivering a broader range of integrated financial services. • Continue fee based emphasis • Differentiate basic product delivery through innovation, product expertise and global communications. • Capitalize on lead position in foreign exchange, multinational finance packaging, international payments and electronic banking.
MARKET SCOPE:	• Market scope involves offering products and services to consumers, governments, private corporations, and financial institutions, through a global, communications network. • Identified consumer market as a major strategic thrust in the mid 1970s. • Consolidated business approach towards funds flow intermediation within the world capital markets.	• Capitalize on investment made in the consumer market through expansion with market share growth; to provide for attractively priced funds and new opportunities. • Leverage the communications network in order to identify and participate in new markets. • Maximize participation in the world's capital market—identification of product and market combinations.

Figure 12.1 *Continued*

	CURRENT	FUTURE
GEOGRAPHICAL SCOPE:	• Geographical scope extends to 96 countries in Asia, Australia, Middle East, Africa, Caribbean, Central and South America, Europe and North America.	• Maximum growth potential: Western Hemisphere and Asia. • Continuing expansion of the geographic boundaries of banking within the United States.
WAYS TO ACHIEVE COMPETITIVE LEADERSHIP:	• Established a global communications network connecting domestic and international branches and offices as well as major financial centers. • Reorganized the institutional business into one entity bringing together a unified business approach. • Made substantial investments in the consumer market to increase market share, capitalize on profitable opportunities, and lower funding costs. • Consolidated business segments involved in off-balance sheet financial intermediation; will provide for increased share of a $15 trillion world credit pool. • Invested heavily in technology involving computer and telecommunications research. • Established a legal focus to seek regulatory changes which will improve ability to compete in all market segments.	• Exploit advantage of global communications network. • Increase market share, efficiency, and product and service expertise. • Foster technological innovations to promote lower costs, fee revenue business, and profitability. • Develop the ability to understand the cost dynamics of the business and become a low cost supplier of financial services. • Continue major emphasis on legislative process to remove restrictive regulatory barriers.

Source: Antoinette M. Williams, "A Strategic Planning Process: The Case of Citicorp and Its Commercial Finance Subsidiary," © 1983. Reprinted by permission of Antoinette M. Williams.

set of competitors. The SBU represents the level of analysis where most of the strategic planning effort is centered.

We require the following tasks to be performed in the execution of this assignment:

1. Identify the SBUs within the firm and discuss the rationale for this segmentation.

Figure 12.2 The Mission Statement of General Motors Venezuela

Summary Statement		

The mission of GMV is the assembly and wholesale marketing of automotive vehicles, and wholesale marketing of the associated replacement parts.

	CURRENT	*FUTURE*
PRODUCT SCOPE:	• Passenger cars • Light-duty commercial vehicles • Medium-duty trucks	Expand current product scope by introducing: • Four-wheel drive vehicles (4WD) • Heavy-duty trucks • Buses
MARKET SCOPE:	• Vehicle users • Replacement parts users	Same as current
GEOGRAPHIC SCOPE:	• Only Venezuela	Same as current
WAYS TO ACHIEVE COMPETITIVE LEADERSHIP:	• Lowest cost position through greater volume and economies of scale • Maintain product differentiation through quality, technology innovation, and marketing intelligence	• Extend market coverage to all segments • Modernization of manufacturing facilities • Improvement of professional and clerical personnel • Development of component manufacturing vendors.

Adapted from Otto K. Soulavy, "Implementation of a Formal Strategic Planning Process," © 1983. Reprinted by permission of Otto K. Soulavy.

2. Identify the need to *share resources* among SBUs to achieve economies of scale or to avoid problems of subcritical mass.
3. Identify the *shared concerns* among SBUs to meet unique needs of certain industry, geography, or major customers.
4. Analyze the linkage between the proposed segmentation and the existing organizational structure.

The intent of tasks 2 and 3 is to diagnose the degree of interaction that might exist among SBUs, so as to exploit their potential synergisms. Task 4 is intended to detect possible conflicts between the proposed SBU segmentation and the existing organizational structure, which could lead to the adoption of some of the coordinating mechanisms we discussed in Chapter 5.

For purposes of this presentation, the businesses of Citicorp have been segmented into three major units: Individual Banks, Institutional Banks, and Capital Markets. These represent the three core businesses of Citicorp organized around generic customer groups on a global basis. It also matches the top segmentation of its organizational structure. Figures 12.3 and 12.4 show, respectively, the shared resources and shared concerns among the three SBUs. The intensity of these interactions suggest a critical need for cooperation among each of the businesses, especially where market-customer needs intersect, and where the effective placement of human resources becomes important. It is not surprising

Figure 12.3 The Identification of Shared Resources at Citicorp

Resource	SBU NAME		
	Individual Bank	Institutional Bank	Capital Markets
• Potential Sharing of the Same Markets Generates Overall Interdependence.	X	X	X
• Capital Base Resources.	X	X	X
• Transferable Human Resources.	X	X	X
• Account Relationship Officers.		X	X
• Global Communications Network.	X	X	X
• Treasury Funding Activities.	X	X	

Source: Antoinette M. Williams, "A Strategic Planning Process: The Case of Citicorp and Its Commercial Finance Subsidiary," © 1983. Reprinted by permission of Antoinette M. Williams.

Figure 12.4 The Identification of Shared Concerns at Citicorp

Concern	SBU NAME		
	Individual Bank	Institutional Bank	Capital Markets
Servicing major clients' needs	X	X	X
Domestic Markets	X	X	X
Major International Markets	X	X	X
Industries		X	
Regulatory Barriers	X	X	X
Foreign Bank and Nonbank Entry	X	X	X
Market Segmentation	X	X	X
Product-Service Packaging and Delivery	X	X	X
Marketing	X	X	X
Funding Costs	X	X	
Interest-Credit-Liquidity Risk Assessment	X	X	X

Source: Antoinette M. Williams, "A Strategic Planning Process: The Case of Citicorp and Its Commercial Finance Subsidiary," © 1983. Reprinted by permission of Antoinette M. Williams.

that Citicorp has adopted a fairly complex matrix organization to fulfill these integration requirements.

Figure 12.5 provides a definition of the SBUs adopted by GMV, with a brief statement indicating a rationale for segmentation Figure 12.6 shows the requirement for shared resources among those six SBUs. Note that the resources are listed in terms of the value added chain.

THE CORPORATE PHILOSOPHY

This is an articulation of:

1. The relationship between the firm and its primary stakeholders—employees, customers, shareholders, suppliers, communities—;

Figure 12.5   SBU Segmentation for General Motors Venezuela

SBU Name	SBU Code	Rationale for Segmentation	Responsible Manager
Passenger vehicles	PAM	Main business in the transportation of persons. GMV holds a leading position.	ACH
Light duty commercials and medium duty trucks	COMM	Three related segments in the transport of cargo: —Light-duty commercials (less than 600 lbs.) GMV holds a leading position. —Light-utility four wheel drive. GMV just entered this business. —Medium-duty trucks (from 19,000 to 33,000 lbs.) Strong market position.	CAH
Parts and Accessories	PARTS	Independent supporting business.	AHC
Retail and wholesale financing	FIN	Independent supporting business offering wholesale and retail financing to GM dealers.	CHA
Engines and Industrial Products	ENG	Venture market consisting in the purchasing and distribution of engines and industrial products.	
Component Manufacturing	COMP	New business in a stage of development. By law requirements, it should be independent of GMV.	HAC

Source: Otto K. Soulavy, "Implementation of a Formal Strategic Planning Process," © 1983. Reprinted by permission of Otto K. Soulavy.

Figure 12.6 THe Identification of Shared Resources at General Motors
Venezuela

	SBU NAME					
RESOURCE	PASS	COMM	PARTS	FIN	ENG	COMP.
PRODUCT R&D (Prod. Eng.)	XX	XX	XX			XX
PROCESS R&D (Ind. Eng.)	XX	XX				
PURCHASING TRANSPORT. (of Parts)	XX XX	XX XX	XX XX		XX	XX XX
ASSEMBLY	XX*					
TESTING	XX	XX	XX			XX
MARKETING	XX	XX	XX			
SALES	XX	XX	XX			
DISTRIBUTION	XX	XX				

* It refers to the potential for sharing resources among the different plants
assemblying passenger cars.
Source: Otto K. Soulavy, "Implementation of a Formal Strategic Planning
Process," © 1983. Reprinted by permission of Otto K. Soulavy.

2. a statement of broad objectives of the firm's expected performance—primarily
   in terms of growth and profitability;
3. a definition of basic corporate policies—referred to management style, organizational policies, human resource management (selection, promotion, compensation, rotation), financial policies (dividends, debt), marketing, technological—; and
4. a statement of corporate values—ethics, beliefs, and rules of personal and
   corporate behavior.

A statement of corporate philosophy for Citicorp is presented in Figure 12.7
as an example.

Figure 12.7   An Annotated Statement of Corporate Philosophy for Citicorp

---

I. Relationship with Stakeholders

Citicorp maintains that its relationship with its customers is its primary focus, for without customers the corporation recognizes that it would not be able to meet the needs of its employees, stockholders, or its communities at large.

Its relationship with its employees can be described as tough but fair, where one's intelligence, wit, and energy, without regard to race, sex, or creed can become the driving force in predicting how far one can move within the corporation.

Citicorp's commitments to its many publics can be recognized in its Public Issues Committee's underlying principle that its business franchise is grounded in the support of its corporate constituencies, and in the belief that its social responsibility is to provide to its customers the highest quality of services.

The mandate of the Public Issues Committee is to ensure that the public interest is maintained both in the performance of Citicorp's business roles and in the achievement of a more competitive business environment.

Its role during 1981 provided for the continued review of bank policies of public interest and appropriate policy guidance. More specifically, it reviewed the bank's Equal Employment Opportunity and Affirmative Action goals and accomplishments, and reviewed the goals and strategies of external affairs. In summary, the Committee confirmed the concept that public confidence in the corporation's performance, commitment to good corporate citizenship and achievement of legal and regulatory relief for the industry are all critically linked.

II. Broad Corporate Objectives

As Citicorp looks ahead towards the future by moving through the decade of the 1980s its efforts will be guided by its broad framework of corporate goals:
* Citicorp is not interested in being the largest financial institution, only one of the most profitable.
* It will endeavor to provide all financial services which the customer requires.
* The branch network is considered a major asset because of the expertise and knowledge it gives the institution, and Citicorp is committed to its enlargement domestically and worldwide.
* The customer of today wants a package of services as has been shown by the success of Merrill Lynch's Cash Management Account. Citicorp needs to develop additional thrusts for the business to meet this kind of customer demand.
* Finally, Citicorp will keep standing by its stock of human capital upon which in the last analysis its success depends and in this spirit will continue to promote its employees purely on the basis of performance and opportunity.

III. Corporate Policies

At this point, the discussion will now involve the components of Citicorp's policies. Particularly for purposes of this study; management style, human resources, and technological policies will be highlighted.

Management Style
Citicorp's management style cannot be summarized into one all embracing description, but can be traced back to various approaches which complement each

Figure 12.7 *Continued*

other in contributing to the growth of the company. There are managers who prefer to be more hands-on while others are more conceptual and yet others who are more administrative. Many managers, however, can be described as sporting an aggressive style which allows for a willingness to take chances and bring new ideas into fruition.

Managerial resources are vital to Citicorp's attainment of financial leadership and therefore it is committed to a system where talented and able people are identified, tracked, and given opportunities to develop their skills and take on greater responsibility.

This system involves consistent line management reviews of performances and career development plans of each officer from every organizational level.

Human Resources

Citicorp views the ability to hire and train highly qualified people as one of its major challenges for the future. In the words of the Chairman of the Board, "This institution owes its realization to the capabilities of its people. I've said repeatedly that people are the only game in town. We have assembled the largest body of talent that has ever existed in the financial services industry."

Its personnel policies can be defined by way of five basic principles which are exemplified as the Citicorp approach.

- To provide the climate and resources that will enable all staff to advance on merit as far as their talents and skills will take them, without regard to age, color, handicap, marital status, national origin, race, religion, sex, or veteran status.
- To offer pay and benefits that are fair and competitive.
- To make certain that ideas, concerns and problems are identified and that two-way communication is effectively maintained.
- To provide an environment that identifies, encourages, and rewards excellence, innovation, and quality customer service.
- To remember always that respect for human dignity is fundamental to our success.

In addition, the Personnel Planning Committee which was recently formed has as its task, the responsibility of ensuring that Citicorp's personnel policies and programs keep in step with changes in the internal and external environments. Even though the committee will focus on compensation, personnel policy, and staff relations, its review will encompass the full range of personnel activities.

Technological Resources

Citicorp's commitment to pursuing advancements in technology has been in existence for a long time. Even though the corporation does not consider itself a high technology company as in the case of IBM, it maintains that high technology will pervade the financial services industry.

Inherent in this commitment is the establishment of the corporate Technology Committee which is chartered with identifying and taking advantage of opportunities in telecommunications and data processing markets while maintaining a decentralized, line driven management philosophy.

Furthermore, Citicorp recognizes that its customers will be looking for information based services on a global scale and in order to respond technology will become a major force.

Figure 12.7 *Continued*

IV. Corporate Values

Citicorp's success can be attributed to a strong set of central values which are shared experiences of Citibankers across the globe. First, its innovative character rests in a strong tradition of creativity, uniqueness and a dauntless approach to solving problems. Second, Citibankers share a passion to excel with an energetic commitment to be first in whatever needs to be done. Third, integrity is a cherished quality where honesty and respect for individuals both internally and externally are exemplified through its people relationships.

The Corporation's global expansion developed an appreciation for decentralization in decisionmaking. Citibankers are expected to make decisions and solve problems wherever they are assigned without a central decisionmaking authority. It is through this decentralization that Citicorp is assured diversification in risk taking.

To an unusual extent, the Corporation has taken a great deal of chances on its people by giving them opportunities to lead, an opportunity to make mistakes, grow, develop and test new ideas.

Finally, Citicorp can be characterized for its uniquely open style and informality in its communications.

Source: Antoinette M. Williams, "A Strategic Planning Process: The Case of Citicorp and Its Commercial Finance Subsidiary," © 1983. Reprinted by permission of Antoinette M. Williams.

REFERENCES

Harvard Business School, "General Electric, Strategic Position: 1981," Case #9-381-174, Revised March 1982.

Lai, Lily K., "Corporate Strategic Planning for a Diversified Company," unpublished master thesis, Sloan School of Management, Massachusetts Institute of Technology, May 1983.

Soulavy, Otto K., "Implementation of a Formal Strategic Planning Process," unpublished master thesis, Sloan School of Management, Massachusetts Institute of Technology, May 1983.

Williams, Antoinette, M., "A Strategic Planning Process: The Case of Citicorp and its Commercial Finance Subsidiary," unpublished master thesis, Sloan School of Management, Massachusetts Institute of Technology, May 1983.

13

STEP 2: THE DEVELOPMENT OF THE STRATEGIC POSTURE OF THE FIRM

The strategic posture is a pragmatic and concrete set of guidelines which serves as immediate challenges for the development of strategic proposals at the business and major functional levels of the firm. It is expressed primarily by:

—Corporate strategic thrusts.
—Corporate, business, and functional planning challenges.
—Corporate performance objectives.

As shown in Figure 13.1, for its derivation, it is important to have completed the vision of the firm, because it provides the broad framework for strategy formulation; but two additional steps are also required:

—Environmental scan at the corporate level.
—Internal scrutiny at the corporate level.

ENVIRONMENTAL SCAN AT THE CORPORATE LEVEL

The environmental scan attempts to diagnose the general health of the industrial sectors relevant to the corporation's businesses. It concentrates on assessing the overall economic, political, technological, social, and legal climates that affect the corporation as a whole. This assessment should be conducted first, from a historical perspective; and second, from the perspective of future trends in the environment.

The output of the environmental scan normally starts with an economic scenario which exhibits the most likely trends affecting the next planning cycle

Figure 13.1   The Vision of the Firm and Its Strategic Posture

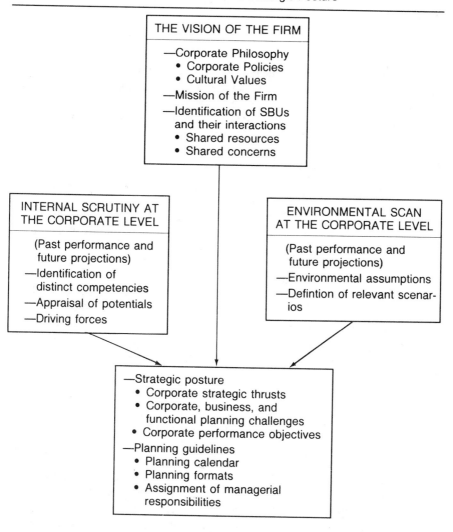

and, possibly, a call for the development of contingency plans addressing either optimistic or pessimistic departures from this most likely trend. Topics to be included in this economic scenario are:

—Economic growth: GNP and major influencing factors,

—inflation rate,

—prime interest rate,

—unemployment,

—overview of foreign markets, and foreign exchange rate considerations,

—population growth in critical geographical areas,
—disposable income,
—growth of critical industrial sectors, such as housing, defense, health, and
so forth.

A second important component of the environmental scan is the projection
of global trends in the primary markets in which the firm competes.

To provide a description of the environment, three main charts should be
filled out, containing quantitative data as well as a description of key external
factors. These are:

—The Economic Outlook
—Growth in Primary Markets
—Broad Assessment of Basic External Factors

Figures 13.2, 13.3, and 13.4 provide an example of these charts for General
Motors Venezuela and Figures 13.5 and 13.6 correspond to Citicorp.

The environmental scanning is completed with the definition of pessimistic
and optimistic planning scenarios, which give some insights into the kinds of
contingencies that can be met in the future, and that should find the organization
prepared to deal with. In Figures 13.7 and 13.8 we carry on the examples of
General Motors Venezuela and Citicorp, respectively.

It is interesting to contrast the information provided by the environmental
analysis of these two cases, one leading with a major financial institution covering
a worldwide market, and the other concentrating in the car industry a developing
country.

INTERNAL SCRUTINY AT THE CORPORATE LEVEL

The internal scrutiny is concerned with a broad evaluation of the human, financial, productive, physical, and technological resources of the corporation, with
the purpose of identifying the firm's distinct competitive strengths.

The basic purpose of this task is to assist in the identification of the distinct
competencies of the firm as a whole (strengths), as well as the required competencies which are not yet present, but need to be developed (weaknesses). Figures
13.9 and 13.10 summarize that information for General Motors Venezuela and
Citicorp respectively.

An additional tool that we have tried many times, with mixed results, to
focus the internal scrutiny in the search of distinctive competencies is the concept
of driving forces developed by Tregoe and Zimmerman, and discussed in Chapter
4. The primary idea behind that concept is to identify the main determinant
which will generate a change of the mission, both for the firm as a whole and
for each one of the SBUs. Surprisingly, we have detected a great degree of

Figure 13.2 Environmental Scan at the Corporate Level of General Motors Venezuela

ECONOMIC OUTLOOK	PAST YEARS				CURRENT	FUTURE			
	78	79	80	81	82	83	84	85	86
GNP Growth %	3.2	0.8	-1.5	-0.6	-8.0	0.6	2.0	3.0	4.3
Inflation %	7.2	12.3	21.6	16.2	8.3	8.9	8.5	8.4	8.0
Unemployment %	5.0	5.2	6.2	6.8	11.0	8.0	6.0	5.0	5.0
Per capita income*	1.2	1.1	1.1	1.1	1.0	1.0	1.0	0.9	0.9
Prime rate %	11	13	20	17	14	15	—	—	—
Population growth %	3.3	3.3	3.3	3.2	3.2	3.1	3.1	3.1	3.1
GROWTH IN CRITICAL INDUSTRIAL SECTORS (%)									
Petroleum	-2.2	7.7	-6.2	-3.6	-13.2	1.5	1.5	1.5	6.0
Construction	11.0	-9.7	-16.5	-2.6	-7.7	6.3	3.5	4.1	4.4
Agriculture	6.3	2.3	0.9	-1.5	4.5	2.6	3.0	3.0	3.0
Manufacturing	4.9	4.9	3.3	0.2	1.0	3.1	3.9	5.0	6.0
Automotive	13.9	-1.5	-2.8	19.6	4.0	4.0	4.0	4.0	4.0
GROWTH IN PRIMARY MARKETS (%)									
Passenger	4.5	-8.9	4.3	-3.9	2.5	0	1.5	1.0	1.0
Commercial & Trucks	31.9	-12.8	-10.2	+1.7	-3.8	1.2	1.2	3.7	2.3
4 Wheel Drive	20.0	-19.0	-4.0	+1.6	-7.1	0	2.4	3.5	2.5

* US $000
Source: Otto K. Soulavy, "Implementation of a Formal Strategic Planning Process," © 1983. Reprinted by permission of Otto K. Soulavy.

Figure 13.3 Environmental Scan at the Corporate Level of General Motors Venezuela (GMV)

BROAD ASSESSMENT OF BASIC EXTERNAL FACTORS

	Past	Future	Major Opportunities	Major Threats
Economic Overview	• 1974–1978: High growth rate (4–6%), economic boom, high inflation, low unemployment. • 1979–1982: Negative growth rate, recession, inflation decreased, high unemployment.	• 1983 Will be a difficult year, devaluation, high inflation in the last 3 quarters. • 1984–1986 Economy will recuperate slowly, inflation will be lower and stable (8.5%).	If economy recovers, GMV has the installed capacity to take over a considerable share of the market growth; it has new products and should make sure to bring the ones that are planned.	That recession deepens, foreign exchange control maintained and uncontrolled inflation.
Primary Market Overview	High market growth until 1978, a big drop in 1978, market stable from 1979 to 1982. It looks like a mature market, but it is not.	1983 seems bad, a decline is expected. 1984–1986 a moderate market growth 1.5 to 2.0% is expected.	GMV has new products and new capacity in place, if the market responds can obtain a bigger market share.	If market stays flat, or there is a further decline, GMV will be at a cost disadvantage, since it has higher amortization than competition. New models and new plant.
Technological Trends	Market followed mainly U.S. technologies, European models are less than 20% of total market. Japanese are only present in the 4 wheel market and through a license agreement.	GMV and Ford changing to new front wheel drive technology (GM US, Ford Brazil), but on different car lines. GMV is first changing the top of the line, the Caprice was changed this January for the Celebrity, Ford is changing the medium lower end of their product line, changed Fairmont for the Brazilian Del Rey (size of a Ford Escort).	Expansion in the manufacture of components, and sell to competition. Components will have to be manufactured by joint ventures.	New front wheel drive technology not accepted in the market for the top of the line models.

Supply of Human Resources	Has been scarce, needed much training, high turnover.	Low turnover, plenty available.	Replace imported personnel with nationals.	None.
Political	Stable, left of center nationalism.	Stable, same trend.	None.	If economic situation continues to deteriorate, the leftist parties, which today represent 10% of the voters, can gain terrain, and could create social unrest. Between 1960 and 1970 considerable guerrilla movement existed in Venezuela.
Social	Uneven distribution of wealth in the country. A small rich class, a large poor class and a strong and growing middle class.	Tendency toward middle class growth will continue, but high inflation creates extra pressure on middle class and especially on the marginal poor class.	None	Social unrest if economic stagnation and inflation continue.
Legal	Highly regulated environment, rules changed frequently but always in the same nationalistic direction.	Trend to continue, high intervention by Government in private industry.	To shape through influence and negotiations the new government regulations.	A very nationalistic Government. Force GMV to divest 51% of ownership to nationals.

Source: Otto K. Soulavy, "Implementation of a Formal Strategic Planning Process," © 1983. Reprinted by permission of Otto K. Soulavy.

Figure 13.4 Summary of the Broad Assessment of Basic External Factors at General Motors Venezuela

Primary Opportunities —Installed capacity —New technology prior to competition —Additional local content requirements, potential for expansion of component manufacture —Good local management for key management positions
Primary Threats —Recession deepens —Uncontrolled inflation —New front wheel drive technology not accepted —Social unrest —A very nationalistic government —Mandatory divestiture of 51% ownership to nationals

Source: Otto K. Soulavy, "Implementation of a Formal Stragegic Planning Process," © 1983. Reprinted by permission of Otto K. Soulavy.

ambiguity and conflict in the selection of a single driving force for each of those business entities. Nonetheless, the discussion leading toward the acceptance of a single driving force might help in focussing on the key competencies that the firm has to concentrate upon, as a first priority, in order to acquire a competitive edge.

Figure 13.11 summarizes the perception of existing as well as desired (future) driving forces for GMV and its six SBUs.

CORPORATE STRATEGIC THRUSTS AND PLANNING CHALLENGES

Corporate strategic thrusts are the primary issues the firm has to address in the next three to five years to establish a healthy competitive position. The strategic thrusts should contain specific and meaningful planning challenges addressed at:

—The corporate level,
—each business unit of the firm, and
—some key centralized functions.

The strategic thrusts are the recipients of all the analysis conducted so far, and they should be articulated in such a way as to convey a sense of the critical tasks that every unit in the organization has to deal with, in order to develop an effective strategic position. Figures 13.12 and 13.13 provide the strategic thrusts and planning challenges for GMV and Citicorp respectively.

Figure 13.5 Environmental Scan of the Corporate Level of Citicorp; Economic Outlook (Annual Growth Rates—%)

	Past Years					Current		Future Projections				
	77	78	79	80	81	82	83	84	85	86	87
Gross National Product Growth (1972 Dollars)	5.5	5.0	2.8	−0.4	1.9	−1.6	3.4	4.6	3.7	3.5	3.3
Inflation Rate (Consumer prices)	6.5	7.7	11.3	13.5	10.3	6.2	5.2	5.5	5.5	5.3	5.3
Unemployment	7.1	6.1	5.9	7.2	7.6	9.7	9.9	8.6	7.9	7.5	7.1
Disposable Personal Income Growth	4.0	4.9	2.7	0.2	2.5	1.4	3.8	3.3	2.7	2.6	2.9
Profits After Taxes Growth	19.1	19.5	13.2	−4.4	−4.4	−21.4	14.4	13.6	17.9	8.2	7.0
Rates 3 Month Certificate of Deposit	5.64	8.21	11.22	13.05	15.92	12.39	9.69	9.75	9.50	8.56	7.88
Long term Aa Utility Bond	8.33	9.09	10.24	13.11	16.25	15.12	12.00	11.09	11.13	10.25	9.31
Population (millions of persons)	220.3	222.6	225.1	227.7	229.9	232.0	234.4	236.7	239.1	241.4	243.8

Source: Antoinette M. Williams, "A Strategic Planning Process: The Case of Citicorp and Its Commercial Finance Subsidiary," © 1983. Reprinted by permission of Antoinette M. Williams.

Figure 13.6 Environmental Scan at the Corporate Level of Citicorp Broad Assessment of Basic External Factors

Factors	Past	Future	Major Opportunities and Threats
Economic Overview	—High inflation, moderate unemployment, and high interest rates. —World recession. —Monetary growth expansion in several industrial countries. —U.S. policy of temporary suspension of monetary targets has important implications for world recovery.	—Downward projection for 1983 economic growth. —Moderate U.S. recovery anticipated. —Real GNP growth of 3.8% projected for major industrial countries. —Actions by industrial economies will continue to shape the outlook for developing countries. —Unemployment levels expected to remain high. —Inflation to remain at low levels and interest rates should show modest increases (U.S.).	—Depressed credit demand and increased risk in portfolio quality resulting from economic downturn. —Loan Loss provision increases. —Sustained economic recovery will improve credit demands.
Primary Market Segments —International governments and official institutions, International Commercial banks, and International private sector markets (such as, Oil exporters, manufacturers, and so forth.)	—Liquidity problems of foreign countries resulting from political and economic conditions. —Debt repayment subject to restructuring and refinancing.	—Continued presence in this market. —Foreign policies design to facilitate international debt servicing.	—International Monetary Fund support of foreign countries. —Losses historically lower than on private sector debt. —Limited opportunity for product and service delivery (Government).

—Domestic International Corporate, and Financial Institutions.	—Growth opportunities narrowed due to adverse economic conditions. —Earnings base well diversified geographically and by source—reduced dependence on earnings from interest revenue. —Loan Loss provision increased due to worldwide economic climate.	—U.S. recovery should help stimulate foreign economic growth. —Product growth—foreign exchange, multi-national finance, international trade services, electronic banking, and asset based finance. —Specific growth markets: multi-national companies, resource industries, importers-exporters, and global financial institutions. —Competitive pricing will intensify. —Credit quality to remain within acceptable levels.	—Larger fee related revenues from provision of noncredit services. —The breadth of the corporate market's needs stimulates provision of new products and services. —Industry and geographic diversity alleviate risk due to economic cyclicalities.
Consumer Market	—Market size estimated at about $15 trillion. —Market share increased domestically and internationally. —Slow down of inflation and interest rate decline encouraged consumers reentry into housing market.	—Highly attractive market profitability potential remains high. —Attraction of funds will become more competitive as interest rate ceilings disappear. —Increased competition with nonbank institutions.	—Take over of California Savings & Loan—provides entry into California financial services market. —Market sensitive to interest rates and competition.

Figure 13.6 Continued

Factors	Past	Future	Major Opportunities and Threats
Consumer Market (continued)	—Quality of consumer loan portfolio improved.	—Economic recovery will increase demand for financial services. —Credit losses to remain within specified limits.	—Regulatory relief will provide increased opportunities for growth in innovative product offerings and geographic expansion. —The public's positive response to financial technological innovations forebodes market share growth.
Technological Trends	—Computer technology increased efficiency in repetitive back office functions. —Capital investments of $500 million since 1977. —Advancement of computer and telecommunications have allowed for global communications and technology related products.	—Financial services delivery and communications have become inseparable. —Computerized distribution systems will dominate the industry—customer needs will be for worldwide information. —Technological focus will be on data processing and communication linkages. —Divestiture of AT&T increases uncertainty of cost and delivery of communication networks.	—Satellite technology allows for control of communication channels and operational cost. —Design and development of new systems enhancing: innovative services, low cost and high reliability. —Reduced costs for branch network. —Provide better service with a competitive edge.

Political / Social	—Recent political movements towards deregulation. —Trend towards easier acquisitions and diversification. —Increased customer demand for a broader array of financial services offering higher returns and flexibility.	—Continued attention regarding legislative reform will continue. —Senate-House banking political focus on Glass Steagall form (Legal separation of banking and securities industries). —Political concern over lending practices to LDCs. —Possible changes to international financial system.	—Lobbying efforts will play an important role. —Opportunity for improved competitive position. —Likely delays in congressional action.
Legal	—Present laws restrict product and market diversification and geographic expansion. —Constraints on providing comprehensive financial services to all market segments.	—Framework established for future legislative reform—major developments foreseen five to six years hence. —Complete regulatory freedom unexpected.	—Time allowed for strategic positioning in preparation for deregulation. —Meeting competitive forces with limited freedom remains as a significant challenge.
Supply of Human Resources	—Growth, aggressiveness of style coupled with a developed corporate image allow for attraction of extremely competent people.	—Pool of talented resources should continue to exist in the immediate future, but competition will intensify. —Specific emphasis will continue to be on training and development of employees.	—Citicorp's image and established worldwide geographic scope presents a need for a well diversified level of skill.

Source: Antoinette M. Williams, "A Strategic Planning Process: The Case of Citicorp and Its Commercial Finance Subsidiary," © 1983. Reprinted by permission of Antoinette M. Williams.

Figure 13.7 Definition of Alternative Planning Scenarios for General Motors Venezuela

	Optimistic	Pessimistic
1. GENERAL DESCRIPTION	After elections, the Government will lift exchange controls and will declare an official currency devaluation of approximately 50% to 75%. Will maintain certain control over economy but allow the auto industry to operate without price controls. Economy will recuperate slowly in 1984.	Government will maintain strict foreign exchange control, enforce greater control over the total economy, impose price controls and volume controls.
2. ECONOMIC OUTLOOK • GNP—growth	GNP will decline in 1983 by 1%, and will start to recuperate slowly in 1984.	GNP will decline drastically due to further fall in oil prices, Venezuela will have a negative economic growth for the next two or three years before recuperation can be expected.
• Inflation rate	Inflation rate will be high in the second half of 1983, 20% to 30%, due to the devaluation and exchange control. It will stabilize and return to less than 10% by 1984.	
3. GROWTH IN PRIMARY MARKETS • Passenger car market	For 1983 the market will remain equal to 1982 or will even decline slightly, from 1984 onwards a small growth of 1% to 2%.	1983 will have a sharp decline, and recuperation will take at least two to three years.
• Commercial and light trucks	If economy starts to recuperate in 1984, truck sales are expected to grow at least between 2% and 3%.	Market will stay flat, even a slight downturn in 1983.
• Four wheel drives	Similar to the commercial sector, small growth 2% to 3%.	Market will stay flat.

4. RELEVANT CRITICAL FACTORS		
• Technology	New front wheel drive technology is well accepted and GMV will be able to maintain and even gain some market share. New local content requirement can be met growing vertically with joint ventures of GM component divisions.	Luxury front wheel drive cars are not accepted in the market, Government and local supplier oppose GM component divisions to create joint ventures for new local content items.
• Human Resources	Plenty of resources available, can replace foreign imported personnel with local nationals.	None.
• Political	Government will maintain stability, continue moderate nationalistic trend.	Government becomes very nationalistic, enforces regulation 24, which calls for reducing foreign capital participation in the automotive industry to 49%.
• Social	The country will be successful in its goal of redistributing national income more equitably among citizens. The middle class keeps growing strongly.	Economic situation continues to deteriorate, producing social unrest, growth of leftist political parties, and insurrection.
• Legal	Maintain status quo, no major changes. Venezuelan withdrawal from Andean pact.	Major nationalistic trend followed by new and stricter regulations against foreign capital. GMV has to divest 51% of its ownership to local national investors.

Source: Otto K. Soulavy, "Implementation of a Formal Strategic Planning Process," © 1983. Reprinted by permission of Otto K. Soulavy.

Figure 13.8 Definition of Alternative Planning Scenarios for Citicorp

	Optimistic	Pessimistic
Economic Outlook	—Reduced unemployment to acceptable levels within this decade. —Growth of 4.3% per year through 1990 (industrial countries). —Further decline in inflation and interest rates. —World export trade revitalized—will improve a country's ability to service debt as borrowings increase.	—Unemployment levels remain at higher than historical averages. —Growth of 3.3% per year through 1990 (industrial countries). —High interest rates—limit debt capacity of foreign nations. —Limited growth in developing countries.
Growth in Primary Markets	—Growth attributed to many factors primarily linked to economic considerations worldwide. —Strong recovery. —Stimulative monetary policy. —Stability in oil prices. —Improved credit demand.	—Weak recovery. —Tight monetary policy. —Erratic changes in oil prices. —Low credit demand. —International government lending restricted.
Relevant Critical Factors —Technology —Human resources —Political —Legal	—Continued advancement of computer-communications technologies. —Available pool of talent. —Congressional attention to removing competitive barriers. —Favorable legislation towards deregulation.	—No significant growth. —Inability to attract young professionals. —Political shift away from regulatory reform. —No change in existing laws and increased foreign lending regulation.

Source: Antoinette M. Williams, "A Strategic Planning Process: The Case of Citicorp and Its Commercial Finance Subsidiary," © 1983. Reprinted by permission of Antoinette M. Williams.

Figure 13.9 Identification of Distinct Competencies at the Corporate Level for General Motors Venezuela

PRESENT DISTINCT COMPETENCIES (Strengths) 1. Capacity readily available. 2. Recognized product quality and reputation. 3. Market leader, market share. 4. Well established in the market. 5. Largest dealer network in the country. 6. High customer loyalty. 7. Excellent government relations.
REQUIRED DISTINCT COMPETENCIES (Weaknesses) 1. Local company has very little freedom. It is tightly controlled by the parent company. 2. Decision process very lengthy due to required approvals from home office. 3. Company is not run by local management. It is run from headquarters in the United States. 4. Slow reaction time to market changes. Pipeline for imported and local material is very long, 5 months commitment.

Source: Otto K. Soulavy, "Implementation of a Formal Strategic Planning Process," © 1983. Reprinted by permission of Otto K. Soulavy.

Figure 13.10 Identification of Distinct Competencies at the Corporate Level for Citicorp

PRESENT DISTINCT COMPETENCIES (Strengths)

1. Well-diversified, competent staff functioning throughout the world.
2. Global communications network, connecting major operations within 96 countries.
3. Substantial ability to raise capital easily.
4. Technological commitment.
5. Risk-taking ability and willingness.
6. Innovativeness in the delivery of financial services and corporate image provides for customer attraction.
7. Higher return potential from human resources as freedom to innovate in an unregulated environment encourages higher rewards.
8. Exceptional legal support, allowing expansion of geographical boundaries within the United States.

REQUIRED DISTINCT COMPETENCIES (Weaknesses)

1. Complete understanding of the cost dynamics of the business.
2. Ability to conduct branch banking activities outside New York State.
3. Nonrestricted entry to major markets.
4. Ability to compete in the delivery of a broad spectrum of financial services.
5. Improved competitiveness vis-a-vis nonregulated, nonbanking entities.
6. Limit on unproductive time spent on organizational and administrative functions.
7. Change attitudes of elitism among various groups, due to competitive zeal.

Source: Antoinette M. Williams, "A Strategic Planning Process: The Case of Citicorp and Its Commercial Finance Subsidiary," © 1983. Reprinted by permission of Antoinette M. Williams.

Figure 13.11 Identification of Driving Forces for General Motors Venezuela

	Current	Future
GMV	Products offered: vehicles	Products offered: vehicles
BUSINESSES		
1. Passenger cars	Products offered	Products offered
2. Light duty commercial, medium duty trucks	Products offered	Products offered
3. Parts and accessories	Products offered	Products offered
4. Vehicle financing	Market needs	Market needs
5. Engines and industrial equipment	Market needs	Market needs
6. Components manufacturing	Return on profits	Products offered

Adapted from Otto K. Soulavy, "Implementation of a Formal Strategic Planning Process," © 1983. Reprinted by permission of Otto K. Soulavy.

Figure 13.12 Statement of Strategic Thrusts and Assignment of Planning Challenges for General Motors Venezuela

	Corp.	Business unit						Functions			
		1	2	3	4	5	6	M	P	E	A
Maintain market leadership	1	1	—	—	—	—	—	—	—	—	—
Obtain market leadership	—	—	2	3	3	3	3	—	—	—	—
Increase penetration	2	2	2	1	1	1	2	—	—	—	—
Reduce costs	1	1	1	3	3	3	3	1	1	2	2
Develop new products	1	1	1	3	—	1	1	—	—	1	—
Modernize manufact.	2	—	2	—	—	—	—	2	—	—	—
Emphasis on suppliers (efficiency development)	2	—	—	2	—	—	—	—	1	2	—
Improve ratio cost and people	1	2	2	3	3	3	3	2	2	2	1

Code:

For priority assignment:	For function identification:
1 Vital	M: Manufacturing
2 Important	P: Procurement
3 Secondary	E: Engineering, R&D
— Not applicable	A: Administration

The vital issues that the corporate has to address are: maintain market leadership, develop new products, reduce costs, and improve the ratio cost and people. The important issues are: increase market penetration, modernize manufacturing and the development of local suppliers.

CORPORATE PERFORMANCE OBJECTIVES

Corporate performance objectives are quantitative indicators related to the overall performance of the firm. Typically, they are financial objectives related to total revenue, profit performance and growth rate.

By articulating broad financial expectations, the corporation adds to the challenges implicit in the strategic thrusts but, at the same time, provides a more

Figure 13.13 Statement of Strategic Thrusts and Assignment of Planning Challenges for Citicorp

Strategic Thrusts	Corporate Level	Businesses			Functions	
		Ind	Inst	Cap Mkts	Legal	Personnel
1. To identify to what degree the corporation will be able to function under regulatory constraints and competitive entities encroaching on bank services.	1	2	2	2	1	—
2. To provide concrete answers to:						
a) What are those financial services which should be offered?	3	1	1	1	—	—
b) How should the marketplace be defined?	3	1	1	3	—	—
c) How should resources be allocated?	2	2	2	2	2	2
d) What will be required in the way of human and financial resources?	2	1	1	1	2	2
3. To establish an ability to find, hire, and train highly qualified people.	2	1	1	1	3	1
4. To establish a means whereby new earnings streams can be developed through adoption of innovation.	3	1	1	1	—	—
5. To maintain position as the most profitable privately owned banking institution by becoming a low cost efficient producer of financial services.	1	1	1	1	3	3
6. Develop better ability to anticipate and manage challenges faced by emerging problem countries.	2	2	2	—	2	—

CODE: 1 Vital
2 Important
3 Secondary
— Not Applicable

KEY: Ind.—Individual Banking
Inst.—Institutional Banking
Cap. Mkts.—Capital Markets

Source: Antoinette M. Williams, "A Strategic Planning Process: The Case of Citicorp and Its Commercial Finance Subsidiary," © 1983. Reprinted by permission of Antoinette M. Williams.

realistic framework to guide the desirability of proposed action programs that will emerge from the subsequent steps in the strategic planning process.

This task require first the selection of a *few* key indicators, which are essential proxies of the successful performance of the corporation, and then the assignment of historical as well as target values for each one of them. In Figure 13.14, we suggest a menu of some important indicators. In Figures 13.15 and 13.16, the corporate performance objectives for GMV and Citicorp are indicated.

Figure 13.14   Suggested Indicators for Defining Corporate Performance Objectives

SIZE
- Sales
- Assets
- Profits
- R&D Expenses

FINANCIAL RATIOS
- Profitability
  —Profit Margin
  —Return on Assets (ROA)
  —Return on Equity (ROE)
- Turnover
  —Assets
  —Inventory
  —Accounts Receivable
- Capital Structure
  —Long Term Debt-Equity
  —Total Debt-Equity

CAPITAL MARKETS
- Common Indices
  —Price per Share
  —Earnings per Share
  —Dividends per Share
  —Price Earnings Ratio
  —Market to Book Value
- Stability Indices
  —% Change in Price per Share
  —% Change in Earnings per Share
  —% Change in Dividends per Share

HUMAN RESOURCES
- Training
- Safety

GROWTH
- Sales
- Assets
- Profits
- R&D Expenses

TECHNOLOGICAL RATIOS
- Productivity
  —Engineering Standards
  —Yield from Basic Raw Materials
- Innovation
  —Successful New Products
    Launched per Year
  —New Patents
  —Technologies that should be
    Mastered
- Quality
  —Percentage of Defective
    Products
  —Product reliability
    (Quality of Design)
  —Cost and Rate of Field Repairs
- Manufacturing Costs
  —Lowest Unit Price
  —Lowest Total Price
  —Learning Curve Slope

Figure 13.15 Corporate Performance Objectives for General Motors Venezuela

Performance Indicator	Past Years		Current Year	Objectives
	1980	1981	1982	
1. SALES size M $	479	598	648	
growth %	40	24	8	10
2. PROFITS size	12	21	5	—
growth	− 25	+ 78	− 79	—
3. ASSETS size	228	298	300	
growth	5	31	1	10
RATIOS				
4. PROFITABILITY (%)				
Margin	2.5	3.5	0.7	4.0
R.O.A.	5.2	7.0	1.4	8.0
R.O.E.	21.9	35.0	7.2	30.0
5. TURNOVER				
Assets	2.1	2.0	2.2	2.5
Inventory	3.3	2.8	3.1	3.5
Accounts				
Receivable	4.6	3.8	4.1	5.0
6. CAPITAL STRUCTURE				
Long Term Debt-				
Equity	0.1	0.7	0.9	0.5
Total Debt-Equity	2.9	3.7	2.5	2.0

Source: Otto K. Soulavy, "Implementation of a Formal Strategic Planning Process," © 1983. Reprinted by permission of Otto K. Soulavy.

Figure 13.16 Corporate Performance Objectives for Citicorp (%)

Performance Indicators	Past Years (percentages)			Current Year	Objectives
	1979	1980	1981	1982	
• Return on Equity	16.1	13.5	13.7	16.4	20
• Return on Assets	0.58	0.47	0.48	0.61	0.80
• EPS Growth	14	7	4	33	15–18

Source: Antoinette M. Williams, "A Strategic Planning Process: The Case of Citicorp and Its Commercial Finance Subsidiary," © 1983. Reprinted by permission of Antoinette M. Williams.

14

STEP 3: THE MISSION OF THE BUSINESS

The mission of the business follows exactly the same characterization as the mission of the firm, except that it is conducted at a more detailed level to get a sharper understanding of each SBU.

The mission of a business is a statement of the current and future expected product, market, and geographical scope; and a definition of the way to attain competitive leadership.

Figure 14.1 presents the mission statement for the Passenger Vehicle SBU of GMV. For the sake of brevity, we only present one of the GMV's SBUs.

Sometimes it is useful to employ the format presented in Figure 14.2, to visualize the representation of an SBU in terms of existing and new products, and existing and new markets. Increasing penetration in existing products and markets very often requires improved operational efficiency at all functional levels. The extensions of existing products in new markets demand a concentrated marketing effort. Bringing in new products in existing markets puts a heavy burden on engineering and R&D, whenever new products are internally developed. What is most challenging is the work to be done when new products are intended to serve new markets. Often, such strategies can best be implemented via acquisitions.

We will introduce now another example to illustrate some of the subsequent steps in the strategic planning process. Figure 14.3 shows the mission statement of the Aluminum Company of Martin Marietta. This company is run as an independent business, and therefore can be treated as an autonomous SBU. Since there is not much sense of change in the company, the figure is limited to presenting its existing product, market, and geographical scope.

Figure 14.1 The Mission of the SBU "Passenger Vehicle" of General Motors Venezuela

SUMMARY STATEMENT
The mission of the Passenger Vehicles SBU is the assembly and wholesale of passenger vehicles for the Venezuelan market.

	CURRENT	*FUTURE*
Product Scope	• T car Chevette sedan 2Dr Chevette sedan 4Dr	Chevette sedan 2Dr Chevette sedan 4Dr Chevette station wagon
	• G car Malibu sedan 4Dr Malibu classic sedan 4Dr • J car	
		Cavalier sedan 2Dr Cavalier sedan 4Dr Cavalier station wagon
	• A car Celebrity sedan 4Dr Century sedan 4Dr Century sedan 4Dr	Celebrity sedan 4Dr Century sedan 4Dr Century sedan 4Dr Century station wagon
Market Scope	• Lower-medium ($7,000–$12,000) • Intermediate • High (over $17,000)	• Lower-medium • Intermediate • High
Geographic Scope	• Only Venezuela	• Venezuela • Possible Latin American countries in the Andean Common Market
Ways to Achieve Competitive Leadership	• Lower cost position • Quality • Technology innovation	• Differentiated products (accelerate entry of J-car)

Adapted from Otto K. Soulavy, "Implementation of a Formal Strategic Planning Process," © 1983. Reprinted by permission of Otto K. Soulavy.

Figure 14.2 Determination of Product-Market Segments within an SBU

SBU _ _ _ _ _ _ _ _ _ _ _

		Markets	
		Existing	New
Products	Existing		
	New		

Figure 14.3 The Mission of the Aluminum Company of Martin Marietta Corporation

SUMMARY STATEMENT

To be a profitable supplier of aluminum and titanium products to selected segments of the worldwide market.

Product Scope	• Primary Products —Pure and alloy ingots —Extrusion ingot (billet) • Fabricated Products —Coiled and flat sheets —Plate products —Forgings —Extrusions (Rod, Bar, and Tubing) • Titanium Products —Extrusions —Bar —Seamless pipe • Calcined Coke (carbon)
Market Scope	• Building and Construction • Transportation • Consumer Durables • Electrical • Machinery and Equipment • Containers and Packaging
Geographical Scope	• Focus on the United States domestic market • Small percentage going to the foreign metal exchange market
Ways to Achieve Competitive Leadership	• Becoming a Low-Cost Leader by Taking the Following Actions: —Achieving full integration —Modernizing plants —Improving manufacturing process efficiencies —Locating plants where there are tax advantages of low energy costs

Source: Lily K. Lai, "Corporate Strategic Planning for a Diversified Company," © 1983. Reprinted by permission of Lily K. Lai.

15

STEP 4: FORMULATION OF BUSINESS STRATEGY AND BROAD ACTION PROGRAMS

A business strategy is a set of objectives supported by well-coordinated action programs aimed at establishing a long-term sustainable advantage over competitors.

At this stage, we are interested in addressing the global direction the business should follow, expressed in terms of broad action programs defined over a multi-year planning horizon. In subsequent steps, each of these broad action programs, in turn, will have to be defined by means of a set of specific action programs with a clear implementation purpose.

The business strategy is derived from (see Figure 15.1):

—The corporate strategic thrusts and planning challenges
—The mission of the business
—Environmental scan at the business level
—Internal scrutiny at the business level.

The first two tasks of the above list have already been accomplished; therefore we will proceed by commenting on the last two tasks prior to the development of a business strategy.

ENVIRONMENTAL SCAN AT THE BUSINESS LEVEL

The environmental scan at the business level attempts to identify the degree of attractiveness of the industry in which the business belongs. We discuss two ways of performing this task.

Figure 15.1   Formulation of Business Strategy and Broad Action Programs

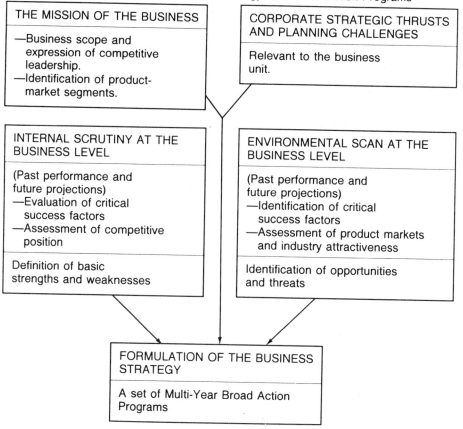

Assessment of Industry Attractiveness

The first methodology is based upon the identification of noncontrollable external factors, and it was discussed in Chapter 8 on the use of the industry attractiveness-business strength matrix in strategic planning. It can be summarized as follows:

—Identify the external factors, outside the control of business managers, which impact each SBU.
—Measure the degree of attractiveness of each of these factors in relation to the firm's "average business base," both for current state and future projections.
—Determine the opportunities and threats associated with each SBU.

Figure 15.2 shows the profile of industry attractiveness of the Passenger Cars SBU for GMV. Figure 15.3 presents a summary of the major opportunities and threats derived from this profile that impact the business.

Porter's Framework for Industry Analysis

An alternative methodology to conduct the environmental scan at the business level has been developed by Michael Porter (1980) and was explained in Chapter 3. Essentially, it identifies the following forces as determinants of the industry profitability:

—Barriers to entry
—Barriers to exit
—Rivalry among competitors
—Power of buyers
—Power of suppliers
—Availability of substitutes
—Government actions

The task to be performed is to assess how these forces are affecting the SBU in order to determine the degree of attractiveness of its industry. Figure 15.4 illustrates an application of this methodology to the Aluminum Company of Martin Marietta. Figure 15.5 summarizes the attractiveness of each one of these factors in the current and future states.

Figure 15.2 Environmental Scan for the Passenger Car SBU of General Motors Venezuela

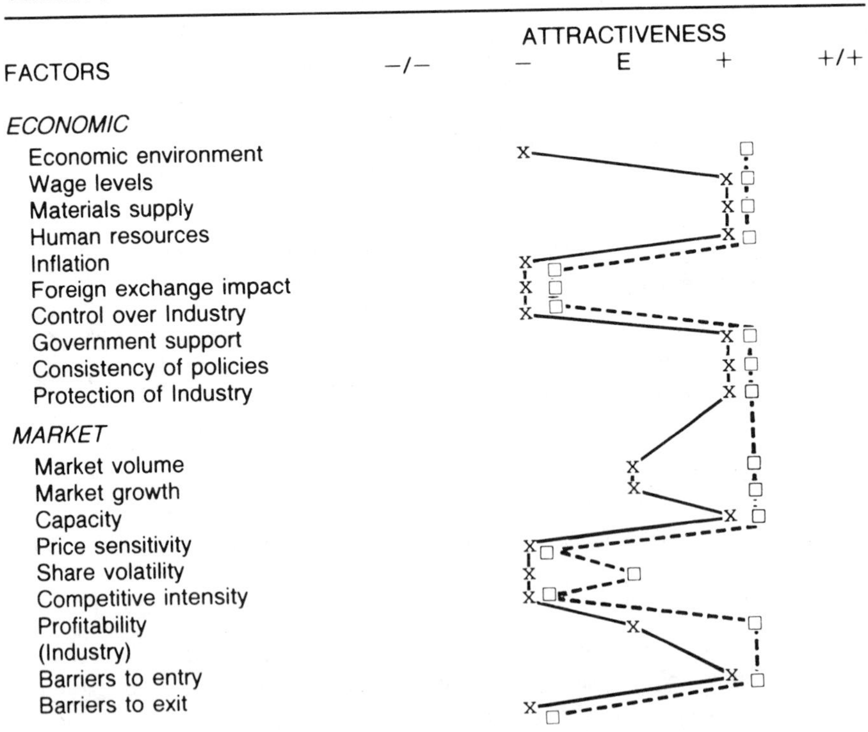

Figure 15.2 *Continued*

FACTORS	ATTRACTIVENESS				
	−/−	−	E	+	+/+

TECHNOLOGICAL
   Pace of change
   Product R&D requirements
   Process R&D
   Productivity

SOCIAL FACTORS
   Work ethic
   Degree of unionization
   Consumer protection

x———x   1983
☐- - -☐   1986

OVERALL ASSESSMENT OF INDUSTRY ATTRACTIVENESS

	LOW	MEDIUM	HIGH
CURRENT		XX	
FUTURE			X ¦ X

The current assessment is that the industry attractiveness is medium, this is mainly caused by the severe economic slow down, but it is expected that in the future, next two to three years, it will be between medium and high.

Source: Otto K. Soulavy, "Implementation of a Formal Strategic Planning Process," © 1983. Reprinted by permission of Otto K. Soulavy.

Our experience with the use of these two different frameworks to deal with environmental scan lead us to give a slight preference to the first method of analyzing the ongoing businesses of the firm. The mere process of extracting from managers the relevant factors for the analysis, forces a useful and creative probing on their part, leading towards a more pragmatic diagnostic of the industry. Certainly, Porter's framework is quite enlightening and could be used in addition to the first method to further enrich the understanding of the environment. However, we have found Porter's framework, which deals with deeper structural factors of the industry rather than with more closely related managerial

Figure 15.3　Major Forces Determining Industry Attractiveness for the Passenger Vehicle SBU of General Motors Venezuela

Major Forces Contributing to Industry Attractiveness (Opportunities)

—Barriers to entry.
—Government protection.
—Market growth potential.

Major Forces Detracting From Industry Attractiveness (Threats)

—Barrier to exit.
—Foreign exchange impact.
—Government control over industry.
—New entry, if change in regulation.
—Imports, if protection is lowered.

Adapted from Otto K. Soulavy, "Implementation of a Formal Strategic Planning Process," © 1983. Reprinted by permission of Otto K. Soulavy.

concerns, more effective in guiding the analysis of industries in which the firm does not operate, but is considering as possible entries.

Figure 15.6 provides a general list of suggested external factors which we feel could be useful in structuring the environmental scan effort.

INTERNAL SCRUTINY AT THE BUSINESS LEVEL

The internal scrutiny at the business level attempts to identify the major strengths and weaknesses of the firm against its most relevant competitors.

The performance of this scrutiny has to be supported by the following tasks:

—Identification of most relevant competitors.
—Determination of critical success factors, that is, those capabilities controllable by the firm, in which it has to excell in order to secure a long-term success over its competitors.
—Assessment of the business' strengths and weaknesses against each of the most relevant competitors.
—Identification of the overall strengths and weaknesses associated with the SBU.

Identification of the Most Relevant Competitors

A relevant competitor is one who fulfills one or more of the following conditions:

- From a market point of view

  —It has a high market share
  —It has experienced a sustained market growth
  —It earns high levels of profitability with regard to the industry average

Figure 15.4 Environmental Scan for the Aluminum Company of Martin Marietta Corporation (1983)

			Highly Unatt.	Mildly Unatt.	Neutral	Mildly Att.	Highly Att.	
BARRIERS TO ENTRY	Economies of Scale	Small					X	Large
	Product differentiation	Little	X					Big
	Brand identity	Low	X					High
	Switching cost	Low				X		High
	Access to distribution channel	Ample		X				Restricted
	Capital requirements	Low					X	High
	Access to latest technology	Ample			X			Restricted (Proprietary)
	Access to raw materials	Ample	X					Restricted
	Government protection	Nonexistent		X				High
	Experience effect	Unimportant		X				Very important
BARRIERS TO EXIT	Asset specialization	High	X					Low
	One time cost of exit	High	X					Low
	Strategic interrelationship	High			X			Low
	Emotional barriers	High	X					Low
	Government and social restrictions	High			X			Low
RIVALRY AMONG COMPETITORS	Number of equally balanced competitors	Large	X					Small
	Industry growth	Slow	X					Fast
	Fixed or Storage cost	High	X					Low
	Product features	Commodity	X					Specialty
	Capacity increases	Large increments	X					Continuously
	Diversity of competitors	High			X			Low
	Strategic stakes	High	X					Low

Figure 15.4 Continued

		Highly Unatt.	Mildly Unatt.	Neutral	Mildly Att.	Highly Att.	
POWER OF BUYERS	Number of important buyers	Few				X		Many
	Availability of substitutes of the industry products	Many				X		Few
	Buyer switching costs	Low					X	High
	Buyer's threat of backward integration	High					X	Low
	Industry threat of forward integration	Low				X		High
	Contribution to quality or service of buyer's products	Large			X			Small
	Total buyer's cost contributed by the Industry	Large fraction			X			Small fraction
	Buyer's profitability	Low			X			High
POWER OF SUPPLIERS	Number of important suppliers	Few	X					Many
	Availability of substitutes for the supplier's products	Low	X					High
	Differentiation or switching cost of supplier's products	High	X					Low
	Supplier's threat of forward integration	High			X			Low
	Industry threat of backward integration	Low	X					High

		Highly Unatt.	Mildly Unatt.	Neutral	Mildly Att.	Highly Att.	
POWER OF SUPPLIERS (CONTINUED)	Supplier's contribution to quality or service of the industry products	High			X			Small
	Total industry cost contributed by suppliers	Large fraction	X					Small fraction
	Importance of the industry to supplier group	Small				X		Large
AVAILABILITY OF SUBSTITUTES	Availability of close substitutes	Large			X			Small
	User's switching cost	Low				X		High
	Substitute producer's profitability and aggressiveness	High		X				Low
	Substitute price-value	High			X			Low
GOVERNMENT ACTIONS	Industry protection	Unfavorable			XXX			Favorable
	Industry regulation	Unfavorable						Favorable
	Consistency of policies	Low			XXXX			High
	Capital movements among countries	Restricted			X →			Unrestricted
	Custom duties	Restricted						Unrestricted
	Foreign exchange	Restricted						Unrestricted
	Foreign ownership	Limited						Unlimited
	Assistance provided to competitors	Substantial						None

Source: Lily K. Lai, "Corporate Strategic Planning for a Diversified Company," © 1983. Reprinted by permission of Lily K. Lai.

Figure 15.5 Summary of the Environmental Scan for the Aluminum Company of
Martin Marietta

	Industry Attractiveness					
	Current (1983)			Future (1988)		
	Low Attract.	Medium Attract.	High Attract.	Low Attract.	Medium Attract.	High Attract.
Barriers to Entry		X			X	
Barriers to Exit	X			X		
Rivalry among Competitors	X			X		
Power of Buyers			X		X	
Power of Suppliers	X			X		
Availability of Substitutes		X		X		
Government Actions		X			X	
OVERALL ASSESSMENT	X			X		

Source: Lily K. Lai, "Corporate Strategic Planning for a Diversified Company," © 1983.
Reprinted by permission of Lily K. Lai.

—It has demonstrated an aggressive competitive attitude against your entire
business or some important segments
—It has a highly vulnerable position against your own competitive actions.

• From a functional point of view

—It has the lowest cost structure
—It has the strongest technical base
—It has the strongest marketing
—It offers the best product quality
—It shows the highest level of vertical integration
—It exhibits the highest level of capacity utilization

Figure 15.7 portrays some basic statistics of the most relevant competitors
of General Motors Venezuela. Similarly, Figure 15.8 provides relevant information for the key competitors of the Aluminum Company of Martin Marietta,
supported by a list of financial indicators given in Figure 15.9.

Assessment of the Business' Strengths and Weaknesses

Figure 15.10 depicts a competitive profile of the Passenger Vehicle SBU of
GMV against Ford Motor Company in 1982 and 1987. A summary of the
internal scrutiny is presented in Figure 15.11, and the overall assessment of
competitive strengths is given in Figure 15.12.

Currently (1983) GMV is in disadvantage to Ford, this is a momentary
situation and caused primarily by the lack of a comparable product line, and
an excessive production capacity in the present market downturn. Ford has,
in 1983, new products for the medium segment of the market, which is the

Figure 15.6 Suggested List of External Factors

		Highly Unatt.	Mildly Unatt.	Neutral	Mildly Att.	Highly Att.
MARKET FACTORS	Market size Market growth rates Product differentiation Price sensitivity Cyclicality Seasonality Captive markets Industry profitability					
COMPETITIVE FACTORS	Competitive intensity Degree of concentration Barriers to entry Barriers to exit Share volatility Degree of integration Availability of substitutes Capacity utilization					
ECONOMIC AND GOVERNMENTAL FACTORS	Inflation Foreign exchange impact Currency transfers Wage level Raw material supply Manpower supply Legislation Regulation Taxation Government support					
TECHNOLOGICAL FACTORS	Maturity and volatility Complexity Patents Product R&D require- ments Process R&D require- ments					
SOCIAL FACTORS	Ecological impacts Work ethic Consumer protection Demographic changes Degree of unionization Personal adaptability to international markets					

segment with the greatest market growth expectancy, GMV will have a product for this segment only in mid 1984.

One should realize that there is a major difference between the future projections in the environmental scan and in the internal scrutiny process. When we are dealing with uncontrollable processes, as is the case in the environmental scan process, we are making forecasts of the future. However, in the internal

Figure 15.7 The Most Relevant Competitors of the Passenger Vehicle SBU of General Motors Venezuela

	Last year sales	3 years average growth sales	3 years average profitability	Market share
1. Ford	32.071	− 4.0	Poor	33.2
2. Fiat	10.350	+26.0	Good	10.7
3. Renault	7.788	+ 6.0	Good	8.1
GMV	46.258	+13.0	Fair	48.0
Total market	96.467	+ 0.97	Poor	100.0

Note: Financial data for the competition are not available.

Source: Otto K. Soulavy, "Implementation of a Formal Strategic Planning Process," © 1983. Reprinted by permission of Otto K. Soulavy.

scrutiny phase, the future profiles represent not a forecast, but rather a desirable position that we would like to achieve against our leading competitors. This will have to be translated into a consistent set of action programs and resource deployment that would allow us to fulfill the desirable competitive profile.

The corresponding assessment of strengths and weaknesses for the major aluminum companies in North America is presented in Figure 15.13, and a competitive profile of the Aluminum Company of Martin Marietta against Alcoa and Alcan is shown in Figure 15.14. All this and previous information is finally summarized in Figure 15.15, which provides an assessment of Martin Marietta's competitive strength in this industry. The overall information contained in those charts represents the minimum type of intelligence which is needed to grasp thoroughly the competitive position of an SBU.

Position of the SBU in the Industry Attractiveness-Business Strength Matrix

The analysis we have just completed can be summarized by positioning the SBU in the industry attractiveness-business strength matrix. This might not seem to be a very helpful representation at the SBU level, but it is extremely valuable when the information collected for all the SBUs of the firm is gathered together for purposes of representing the portfolio of businesses. We will take this issue up again in step 6 of the planning process.

Figures 15.16 and 15.17 present the current and future positions of the Passenger Vehicle SBU of GMV, and the Aluminum Company of Martin Marietta respectively.

Development of Broad Action Programs for each Business Unit

This is the key task of this step. All previous analysis should lead to an intelligence definition of broad action programs intended to exploit the inherent capabilities of the firm, and position the business toward a long-term advantage with regard to its competitors.

Figure 15.8 The Most Relevant Competitors of the Aluminum Company of Martin Marietta

Company	1981 Sales ($ million)	1981* Market Share (%)	1981 Net Incomes ($ million)	1981 Primary Capacity (000 tons)	Average Annual Growth Rate 1977–81 (%)	5 Year Average ROI (%)	5 Year Average ROE (%)	5 Year Average COE (%)	5 Year Average ROS (%)	5 Year Average Asset Turnover (times)	M/B Ratio
Alcoa	5,000	25	296	1,725	9.9	11.6	15.5	18.1	7.8	1.0	0.77
Alcan	4,978	24	264	1,059	13.2	13.6	18.1	19.2	7.9	0.9	0.86
Reynolds	3,481	17	87	1,150	10.3	7.9	12.0	18.5	4.1	1.1	0.54
Kaiser	2,275	11	57	724	10.3	10.7	15.8	18.5	8.0	1.0	0.65
MM	614	3	25	210	14.0	8.0	12.8	19.9**	7.7	0.8	N.A.

* Market shares are computed based on total sales of North American major primary producers.
** Cost of equity for Martin Marietta Corporation.
Source: Lily K. Lai, "Corporate Strategic Planning for a Diversified Company," © 1983. Reprinted by permission of Lily K. Lai.
Key: ROI = Return on investment
ROE = Return on equity
COE = Cost of equity
ROS = Return on sales
M/B = Market-to-Book value rate.

Figure 15.9 Financial Ratios for Major North American Aluminum Companies

Financial Ratios for North American Major Aluminum Companies	1977	78	79	80	81
1. Indicators of Profitability					
A. ROA (%) Alcoa	6.6	9.0	12.4	10.4	6.7
Alcan	8.2	10.0	11.8	13.0	7.1
Reynolds	5.0	6.0	7.6	7.3	4.1
Kaiser	6.3	7.1	9.3	9.0	5.1
B. ROE (%) Alcoa	11.3	16.2	22.3	17.6	9.9
Alcan	15.0	18.8	22.1	24.1	10.4
Reynolds	9.9	12.2	16.5	14.8	6.6
Kaiser	13.5	15.7	21.5	19.1	9.2
C. ROS (%) Alcoa	5.7	7.7	10.5	9.1	6.0
Alcan	6.7	7.8	9.3	10.4	5.3
Reynolds	3.7	4.2	5.4	4.9	2.5
Kaiser*	5.8	8.7	12.2	10.8	2.5
2. Indicators of Efficiency					
A. Asset Turnover (times) Alcoa	0.9	1.0	1.1	1.0	0.9
Alcan	0.9	1.0	1.0	1.0	0.8
Reynolds	1.0	1.1	1.2	1.2	1.1
Kaiser	1.0	1.0	1.0	1.0	0.9
B. Inventory Turnover (days) Alcoa	85	78	70	65	71
Alcan	142	129	119	127	150
Reynolds	117	107	92	80	92
Kaiser	92	84	75	72	90
C. Average Collection Period (days) Alcoa	45	46	48	49	47
Alcan	51	49	56	57	58
Reynolds	38	38	40	40	41
Kaiser	47	53	52	51	51

* For aluminum only

Figure 15.9 *Continued*

Financial Ratios for North American
Major Aluminum Companies

	AAGR**	1977	78	79	80	81
3. Indicators of Growth						
A. Sales Growth Rate (%)						
Alcoa	11.2	16.8	18.6	18.1	7.6	-3.3
Alcan	13.4	14.0	22.5	18.1	19.0	-4.5
Reynolds	10.8	12.9	20.3	16.8	10.5	-4.7
Kaiser	11.7	17.7	13.1	18.7	10.1	0.1
B. Net Earnings (%)						
Alcoa	15.5	35.7	60.2	64.1	-6.9	-37.0
Alcan	43.1	357.9	43.6	40.3	33.5	-51.3
Reynolds	2.9	14.9	36.6	50.3	1.8	-51.9
Kaiser	16.2	78.5	29.8	59.6	6.6	-46.3
C. Capital Expenditures (%)						
Alcoa	22.7	15.9	24.1	20.1	51.8	6.1
Alcan	47.0	72.2	39.3	48.5	51.6	27.2
Reynolds	22.3	12.6	68.6	48.9	16.6	-17.0
Kaiser	28.0	1.4	35.0	-2.8	21.3	113.2
4. Indicators of Leverage and Risks						
A. Debt Ratio (%)						
Alcoa		39.0	35.3	29.1	26.3	31.1
Alcan		36.4	31.9	28.3	30.1	40.6
Reynolds		50.0	48.8	45.7	42.4	45.0
Kaiser		46.9	44.1	38.7	34.0	46.2
B. Pretax Interest Coverage (times)						
Alcoa		4.3	6.7	10.0	9.8	4.1
Alcan		4.9	6.7	6.7	7.7	2.7
Reynolds		3.0	4.4	5.1	4.8	2.4
Kaiser		3.8	4.6	6.6	6.3	2.6
5. Indicators of Liquidity						
A. Current Ratio						
Alcoa		2.2	2.1	2.0	2.0	2.4
Alcan		2.3	2.2	2.4	2.1	2.3
Reynolds		2.6	2.4	2.1	1.9	1.7
Kaiser		1.7	1.6	1.6	1.5	1.3

** AAGR: Average annual growth rate for 1977–1981

Figure 15.9 Continued

	1977	78	79	80	81
B. Quick Ratio					
Alcoa	1.0	1.1	1.2	1.2	1.1
Alcan	0.9	1.1	1.2	0.9	0.8
Reynolds	0.9	1.2	1.0	0.9	0.6
Kaiser	0.9	0.9	0.9	0.8	0.5
6. Research and Development					
A. R&D Expense to Sales					
Alcoa	1.5	1.4	1.2	1.4	1.7
Alcan	0.9	0.9	0.8	0.9	1.0
Reynolds	1.0	0.9	0.9	0.9	0.9
Kaiser	0.7	0.6	0.5	0.6	0.6
7. Indicators of Market Valuation					
A. Market to Book Ratio					
Alcoa	0.90	0.81	0.78	0.75	0.62
Alcan	0.74	0.82	0.93	1.09	0.72
Reynolds	0.67	0.62	0.54	0.52	0.35
Kaiser	0.71	0.72	0.67	0.69	0.44
B. P/E Ratio					
Alcoa	8.4	5.4	3.8	4.6	6.5
Alcan	5.3	4.7	4.7	5.0	7.1
Reynolds	7.0	5.3	3.5	3.8	5.5
Kaiser	5.5	4.9	3.4	3.8	5.0

Source: Lily K. Lai, "Corporate Strategic Planning for a Diversified Company," © 1983. Reprinted by permission of Lily K. Lai.

Figure 15.10 Competitive Profile of the Passenger Vehicle SBU of General Motors Venezuela against Ford Motor Company

STRENGTHS

FACTORS	−/−	−	E	+	+/+

MANUFACTURING
Location and number
of plants
Size of plant

Age of plant

Human resources

Logistic management
systems
Quality

Procurement local
material
Procurement imported
material
Productivity

Capacity utilization

Unionization

MARKETING
Dealer network

Human resources

Distribution system

Service system

Market research

Fleet accounts

Breadth of product
line
Brand loyalty

Price competitiveness

Business image

R&D AND ENGINEERING
R&D facilities

Human resources

Development of
local parts
Designing of local
tailored products

x——x 1982
□- - -□ 1987

343

Figure 15.10   *Continued*

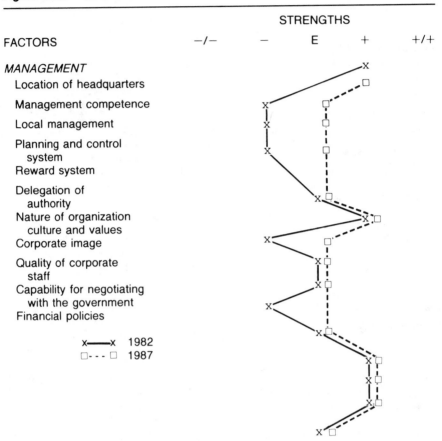

FACTORS

STRENGTHS

−/−   −   E   +   +/+

MANAGEMENT
  Location of headquarters
  Management competence
  Local management
  Planning and control
    system
  Reward system
  Delegation of
    authority
  Nature of organization
    culture and values
  Corporate image
  Quality of corporate
    staff
  Capability for negotiating
    with the government
  Financial policies

    x——x 1982
    □- - -□ 1987

Source: Otto K. Soulavy, "Implementation of a Formal Strategic Planning Process,"
© 1983. Reprinted by permission of Otto K. Soulavy.

The broad action programs should:

—Respond to the corporate strategic thrusts.
—Neutralize potentially adverse impacts from the external environment, and
  exploit opportunities detected in the environmental scan phase.
—Correct major weaknesses and reinforce the basic strengths identified during
  the internal scrutiny and competitive analysis processes.
—Suggest a priority for resource allocation in terms of the following categories
  (which we discussed in Chapter 4):
    —Build aggressively
    —Build gradually
    —Build selectively
    —Maintain selectively

Figure 15.11 Summary of the Internal Scrutiny for the Passenger Vehicle SBU of General Motors Venezuela

	BUSINESS STRENGTHS					
	Current			Future		
	Low	Medium	High	Low	Medium	High
Manufacturing		X				X
Marketing	X				X	
R&D and Engineering		X			X	
Management		X				X
OVERALL ASSESSMENT		X			X	

Source: Otto K. Soulavy, "Implementation of a Formal Strategic Planning Process," © 1983. Reprinted by permission of Otto K. Soulavy.

—Prove viability
—Divert-liquidate
—Competitive harasser

Figure 15.18 shows the broad action programs for the Passenger Car SBU of GMV.

Figure 15.12 Overall Assessment of Competitive Strength for the Passenger Vehicle SBU of General Motors Venezuela

---

Major Strengths

1. New, modern production facilities. GMV just put into service a completely rebuilt production facility in Valencia, Venezuela, to assemble the new front-wheel drive model.
2. Quality of products.
3. Dealer network.
4. Business image.

Major Weaknesses

1. Location and number of plants. GMV operates out of three different plants located in different cities. These locations make the logistics of supplying local and important materials difficult.
2. Low capacity utilization. Due to the current economic recession, most of the added capacity cannot be utilized, leaving GMV with a heavy burden of amortization against its competitors.
3. Bad service record.
4. No representation in the intermediate market segment.
5. Lack of autonomy to choose the sources of its products based on economic considerations. All decisions are made in Detroit.
6. Inflexible financial policies.

Source: Otto K. Soulavy, "Implementation of a Formal Strategic Planning Process," © 1983. Reprinted by permission of Otto K. Soulavy.

Figure 15.13 Summary Assessment of Major North American Aluminum Companies

Company	Key Strengths	Key Weaknesses
Alcoa	1. Industry technology leader	1. No participation in other industry
	2. Largest market share in 1981	2. Not low cost leader
	3. Relatively stable earnings, low leverage, and high liquidity	
	4. Broad product lines	
	5. Global sales and resource base	
	6. Emphasis on high growth markets and high technology products	
Alcan	1. Low cost leader, primarily due to low cost energy	1. No participation in other industry
	2. More profitable than other major aluminum companies	
	3. Second largest market share in 1981, but highest growth in sales, earnings, and investment. It might have been number one in market share in 1982	
	4. Lowest negative spread, highest M/B and P/E ratios	
	5. Global sales and resource base	
Reynolds	1. Domination in the packaging markets	1. Worst financial results among the big fours
	2. Product innovation	2. Old equipments
	3. Leader in aluminum recycling	3. Poor management
		4. No participation in other industries
Kaiser	1. Nonaluminum diversification	1. Poor labor relations
	2. Price leader in market segments they participate	2. Relatively high leverage and low liquidity
	3. Focus on markets where dominant position and healthy margins can be achieved	3. High fabrication costs

Source: Lily K. Lai, "Corporate Strategic Planning for a Diversified Company," © 1983. Reprinted by permission of Lily K. Lai.

With regard to the Aluminum Company of Martin Marietta, the situation is rather different. Based on the competitive structure and strengths of the aluminum industry, it seems that divestiture is the best course of action for Martin Marietta to take. Porter (1980) proposes four basic alternatives for business in a declining industry. Their objectives as well as their implications for the aluminum industry are now discussed:

• Leadership

The objective of this strategy is to gain new market share and become either the only one or the leader of few firms in the industry. Alcan seems to be following this strategy because of its comparative cost advantage.

• Niche

The firm pursuing this strategy will identify a segment (or segments) of the industry that will maintain stable demand and has structural characteristics allowing higher returns. Alcoa is pursuing this strategy by concentrating on

Figure 15.14 Competitive Profile of the Aluminum Company of Martin Marietta against Alcoa and Alcan

Areas	Factors	− −	−	E	+	+ +
MANUFACTURING	Location and number of plants					
	Sizes of plants					
	Ages of plants					
	Integration					
	Human resources					
	Logistics management systems					
	Quality					
	Procurement					
	Capacity utilization					
	Unionization					
MARKETING	Location & number of sales offices					
	Location & number of warehouses					
	Human resources					
	Distribution system					
	Market research					
	Price competitiveness					
	Breadth of product line					
	Brand loyalty					
	Sales force productivity					
	Distribution and service productivity					
	Business image					
R&D and ENGINEERING	R&D Facilities					
	Human resources					
	Development of new products					
	R&D funding					
	Patents					

Figure 15.14 *Continued*

Areas	Factors	--	-	E	+	++
MANAGEMENT	Location of corporate headquarters				o *	
	Management competence				o *	
	Planning & control systems		*	o		
	Reward system				o *	
	Delegation of authority				o *	
	Fitness of organizational culture and values		o *			
	Corporate image				o	*
	Quality of corporate staff		o	*		
	Capability for negotiating with the environment		o *			
	Financial strength			o *		
FINANCIAL RESULTS	Market share	o	*			
	Sales growth				o	*
	Return on investment		o	*		
	Return on equity	o	*			
	Asset turnover			o *		
PRODUCT LINES	Product mix			o *		
	Quality				o *	
	Price			o *		
	Image			o *		

* Current
o   Future
++ Extremely Strong
+   Strong
E   Even
-- Extremely Weak
-   Weak

Source: Lily K. Lai, "Corporate Strategic Planning for a Diversified Company," © 1983. Reprinted by permission of Lily K. Lai.

relatively high growth markets and high technology products because of its leadership position in technology.

- Harvest

In the harvest strategy, the firm seeks to optimize cash flow from the business by curtailing new investment, dropping marginal accounts, deferring maintenance, reducing R&D and advertising, closing inefficient plants, and so forth. Kaiser seems to have adopted a strategy of selective harvesting.

Figure 15.15 Summary of the Internal Scrutiny for the Aluminum Company of Martin Marietta

Areas	COMPETITIVE STRENGTHS					
	Current			Future		
	Low	Medium	High	Low	Medium	High
Manufacturing	✓			✓		
Marketing	✓			✓		
R&D and Engineering		✓		✓		
Management		✓			✓	
Financial Results	✓			✓		
Product Lines	✓				✓	
OVERALL ASSESSMENT	✓			✓		

Source: Lily K. Lai, "Corporate Strategic Planning for a Diversified Company," © 1983. Reprinted by permission of Lily K. Lai.

Figure 15.16 Position ot the Passenger Vehicle SBU of General Motors Venezuela in the Industry Attractiveness-Business Strength Matrix

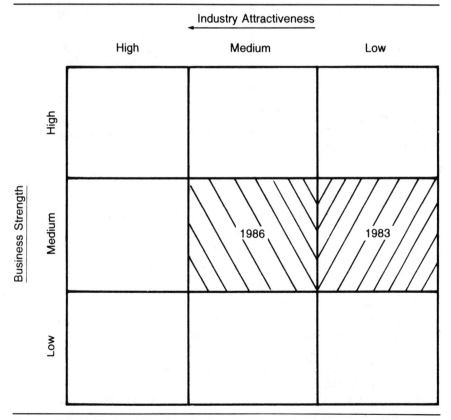

Source: Otto K. Soulavy, "Implementation of a Formal Strategic Planning Process," © 1983. Reprinted by permission of Otto K. Soulavy.

Figure 15.17   Position of the Aluminum Company of Martin Marietta in the Industry Attractiveness-Business Strength Matrix

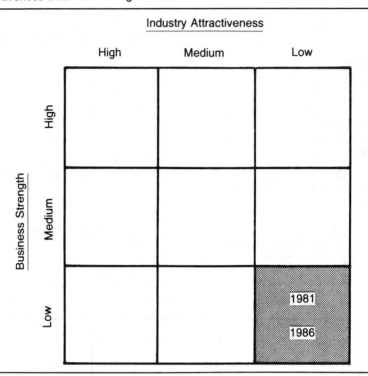

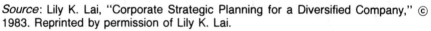

Source: Lily K. Lai, "Corporate Strategic Planning for a Diversified Company," © 1983. Reprinted by permission of Lily K. Lai.

• Quick Divestment

This strategy rests on the premise that the firm can maximize its net investment recovery by selling the business early in the decline.

Based on Porter's framework, it seems natural to recommend a divestment of the Aluminum Company of Martin Marietta Corp., for the following reasons:

—The Aluminum Company of Martin Marietta does not have a competitive strength relative to its competitors.

—Aluminum is considered a commodity product with a declining market in an unfavorable industry characterized by high fixed costs, low profit margins, rising bargaining power of suppliers, high barriers to exit, a growing number of substitutes, and increased competition from state-owned producers driven by political considerations, and so forth.

—We cannot identify any strategic need for the Corporation to remain in the aluminum business.

Figure 15.18   Broad Strategic Action Programs for the Passenger Vehicle SBU of General Motors Venezuela

SUGGESTED BUSINESS PRIORITY: MAINTAIN AGGRESSIVELY			
Broad Action Programs	Major Milestones per Year		
	1984	1985	1986
1. Replace G car (Malibu) with J car	Completed by January 1984		
2. Add Chevette and Century	Completed by January 1984		
3. Consolidate production in one plant	Close the Caracas plant by January 1984	Move the T model to the Valencia plant	Close the Chevette plant at Caracas and consolidate the personnel with the truck plant
4. Replace the rear wheel drive Chevette with the T model		Completed by 1985	
5. Gain market leadership in all segments			Consolidate leadership position in intermediate market segment
6. Improve service		Reduce to half the actual level of complaints	

Although intuitively this alternative seems to represent a logical course of action, it still needs to be probed deeper and supported by a careful financial analysis. This will be conducted in Step 6 of the planning process.

REFERENCE

Porter, Michael E., *Competitive Strategy*, The Free Press, New York, 1980.

16

STEP 5: FORMULATION OF FUNCTIONAL STRATEGY AND BROAD ACTION PROGRAMS

The business strategy assumes the long-term development of a business through the articulation of well-coordinated programs, many of them having a functional content. Therefore, the functional strategies should be an integral part of the business strategy. Whenever there is complete functional autonomy at the business level, most of the functional strategies are indeed imbedded in the business broad action programs. There is only one important exception to that, arising when there are specific strategic thrusts related exclusively to the functional management, whose resolution does not reside at the business level.

When businesses share centralized functional resources, there is still another level of concern regarding functional strategies. Although, as we do recommend, functional managers might have been strongly involved in the development of the corresponding functional strategies supporting each business, there might still be some inconsistencies in search of reconciliation. These are presented when the central functional managers analyze all the functional requirements originated by the totality of businesses. When adding up all these requirements, there could emerge legitimate reasons for disagreement between businesses and functional managers. These disagreements could generate a nonconcurrent vote on the part of the functional manager, which could either be resolved through direct discussions between the affected parties, or could escalate at the corporate level in the next step of the planning process.

Summarizing, functional strategies get formulated at three levels:

—At the business level, where functional managers actively participate in their formulation.

—At the functional level, where the functional managers have to respond to the corporate thrusts involving directly the specific function, and not contained in any proposed business plan. These functional broad action programs should be supported by an environmental scan and an internal scrutiny process, similar to those discussed at the business level, except that now the focus of attention is the actual standing and proper development of functional capabilities.

—At the intersection of business and functional levels, when functional managers cast a concurrence or a nonconcurrence vote, after the business strategies have been developed. If agreement cannot be reached among them whenever a nonconcurrence exists, the issue would escalate at the corporate level.

In the example of GMV, there are five major functions which continue to operate centrally: Procurement, Engineering, Finance, Manufacturing (small staff only), and Reliability and Quality Control. The first task conducted by these centralized functional managers was to consolidate the functional programs proposed by business managers. Figure 16.1 lists the manufacturing program presented by the two most important SBUs of GMV:

—Passenger Vehicles; and
—Light duty commercial and medium duty trucks.

The form contained in Figure 16.1 simply shows all of the broad action programs generated by the SBU manager, which have a manufacturing content,

Figure 16.1 Consolidation of the Functional Programs Proposed by Business Managers of General Motors Venezuela

FUNCTION: MANUFACTURING		
SBU	BROAD ACTION PROGRAM	CONCURRENCE AND NONCONCURRENCE
Passenger Vehicles	—New J car for January 1984	Timing too short, not possible until August 1984
	—Add station wagon to Chevette model January 1984	OK
	—Add station wagon to Century January 1984	OK
	—Consolidate manufacturing plants pass	Timing has to be determined by a study.
	—New FWD T in 1985	OK, if decision taken now
Light-Duty Commercial and Medium-Duty Trucks	—Replace C-10 January 1984	Not possible until 1985
	—Evaluate replacement of trucks	Manufacturing can cooperate in study
	—Start C-75 diesel in January 1984	OK

Source: Otto K. Soulavy, "Implementation of a Formal Strategic Planning Process," © 1983. Reprinted by permission of Otto K. Soulavy.

as well as a statement of concurrence or nonconcurrence on the part of the functional manager.

Next, Figure 16.2 shows the broad action programs recommended by the manufacturing manager. These programs should be comprehensive enough to support all manufacturing requirements proposed by the SBU managers, as well as providing appropriate responses for the strategic thrusts which imply manufacturing challenges.

Figure 16.2 Broad Strategic Action Programs for Functional Units of General Motors Venezuela

FUNCTION: MANUFACTURING			
Broad Action Programs	Major Milestones per Year		
	1984	1985	1986
1. Close the Caracas production facility smoothly and retaining the good people.		Completed by January 1985	
2. Implement the Roll-on Roll-off program* in the Valencia plant.	Start in March 1984	Completed by the end of 1985	
3. Increase productivity (output-people)	3% increase	6% increase	10% increase
4. Integrate the manufacturing operations into the SBU concept.	Completed by the end of 1984		
* New method of shipping components.			

Adapted from Otto K. Soulavy, "Implementation of a Formal Strategic Planning Process," © 1983. Reprinted by permission of Otto K. Soulavy.

17

STEP 6: CONSOLIDATION OF BUSINESS AND FUNCTIONAL STRATEGIES AT THE CORPORATE LEVEL

This step in the planning process calls for a critical review and sanctioning at the corporate level of the set of broad action programs proposed by business and functional managers. It requires the involvement of all key executives who share responsibility for shaping the strategic direction of the firm.

In this step, the following issues have to be addressed:

—Resolution of nonconcurrence conflicts
—Balancing the business portfolio of the firm with regard to:
  —Short-term profitability versus long-term development
  —Risks versus returns
  —Cash flow balance
—Defining the availability of strategic funds, the debt policy, and maximum sustainable growth
—Preliminary evaluation of proposed action programs and assignment of priorities for resource allocation to each business.

The resolution of nonconcurrence conflicts requires reaching a consensus among interested parties. We will not give any further consideration to this matter, since its treatment heavily depends on the specific circumstances surrounding each individual issue.

BALANCING THE BUSINESS PORTFOLIO OF THE FIRM

Having developed individual assessments and proposals for broad action programs at the business and functional levels, it is time to look at them from

Figure 17.1 Overall Portfolio of General Motors Venezuela

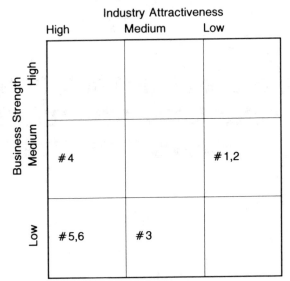

CURRENT SITUATION (Early 1983)

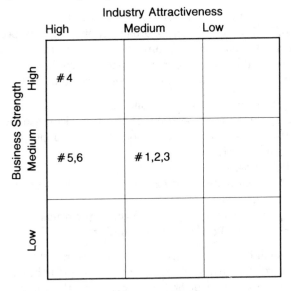

FUTURE POSITION (1986)

KEY

#1 Passenger vehicles
#2 Light duty commercial
and medium duty trucks
#3 Parts and accessories

#4 Retail and wholesale financing
#5 Engines and industrial products
#6 Components manufacturing

Adapted from Otto K. Soulavy, "Implementation of a Formal Strategic Planning Process," © 1983. Reprinted by permission of Otto K. Soulavy.

the overall perspective of the corporate level. The different portfolio matrices, discussed in Part II of this book, constitute valuable tools to accomplish this task. The popularity enjoyed by these tools resulted primarily from their effectiveness in providing a compact and graphical method portraying the strengths of the portfolio of businesses of the firm.

GMV limited the portfolio analysis to the use of the industry-attractiveness and business strength matrix. Figure 17.1 describes the current and future positions within that matrix of the SBUs defined by GMV. Figure 17.2 gives key financial information on the current portfolio of businesses, for 1982. It shows the clear dependency on passenger and commercial vehicles which account for 94 percent of sales and near 81 percent of profits, with a discouragingly low return on assets of 6 percent. The overall attractiveness of this portfolio is not very high. However, this situation is deemed to be temporary, because it

Figure 17.2   Key Financial Information on the Current Portfolio of Businesses of General Motors Venezuela

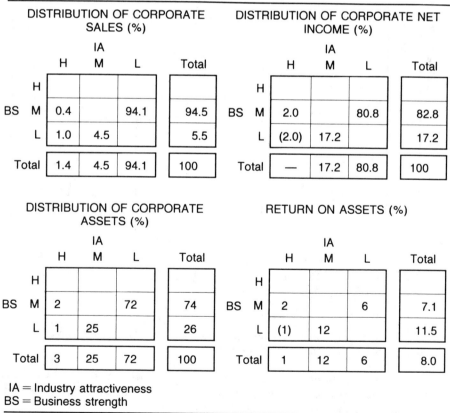

DISTRIBUTION OF CORPORATE SALES (%)

	IA H	IA M	IA L	Total
BS H				
BS M	0.4		94.1	94.5
BS L	1.0	4.5		5.5
Total	1.4	4.5	94.1	100

DISTRIBUTION OF CORPORATE NET INCOME (%)

	IA H	IA M	IA L	Total
BS H				
BS M	2.0		80.8	82.8
BS L	(2.0)	17.2		17.2
Total	—	17.2	80.8	100

DISTRIBUTION OF CORPORATE ASSETS (%)

	IA H	IA M	IA L	Total
BS H				
BS M	2		72	74
BS L	1	25		26
Total	3	25	72	100

RETURN ON ASSETS (%)

	IA H	IA M	IA L	Total
BS H				
BS M	2		6	7.1
BS L	(1)	12		11.5
Total	1	12	6	8.0

IA = Industry attractiveness
BS = Business strength

Source: Otto K. Soulavy, "Implementation of a Formal Strategic Planning Process," © 1983. Reprinted by permission of Otto K. Soulavy.

Figure 17.3 Overall Portfolio of Martin Marietta Corp., Displayed in the Industry Attractiveness-Business Strength Matrix

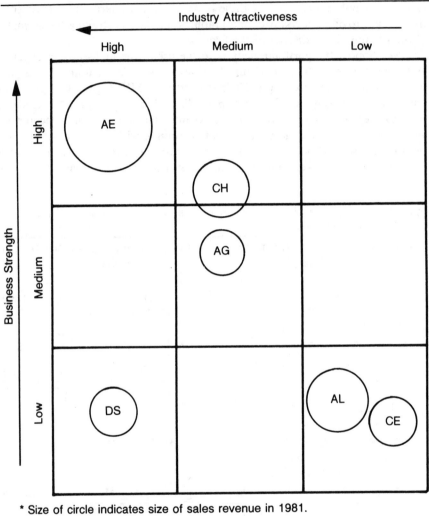

* Size of circle indicates size of sales revenue in 1981.
**AE = Aerospace,   CE = Cement,
    AG = Aggregates, CH = Chemicals,
    AL = Aluminum,   DS = Data Systems.

Source: Lily K. Lai, "Corporate Strategic Planning for a Diversified Company," ©
1983. Reprinted by permission of Lily K. Lai.

is produced mainly by the poor current economic performance in Venezuela.
Accordingly, GMV is intending to improve or maintain its competitive position,
as shown in the bottom half of Figure 17.1.

    In the case of Martin Marietta, several portfolio matrices were used to describe
the overall strength of its portfolio, constituted by six SBUs:

—Aerospace, providing full development, design, manufacturing, field support, and logistics services for sophisticated weapons systems.

—Aluminum

—Aggregates, representing construction aggregates (such as crushed stone, sand, and gravels primarily for highway and general construction), and high-grade silica sands (used mainly in the glass and foundry industry).

—Cement, primarily Portland and Masonry cement sold for use in the construction industry.

Figure 17.4 Overall Portfolio of Martin Marietta Corp., Displayed in the Growth-Share Matrix

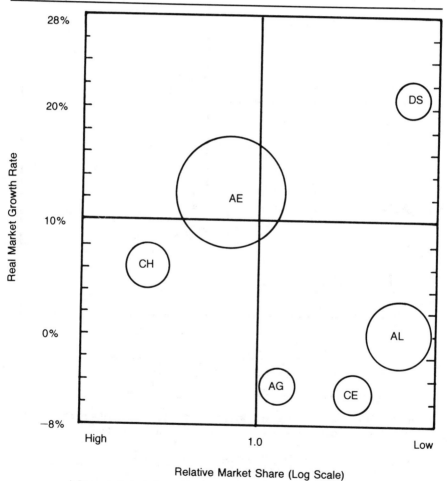

Relative Market Share (Log Scale)
* Size of circle indicates size of sales revenues in 1981.

Source: Lily K. Lai, "Corporate Strategic Planning for a Diversified Company," © 1983. Reprinted by permission of Lily K. Lai.

Figure 17.5   Overall Portfolio of Martin Marietta Corp., Displayed in the Profitability Matrix*

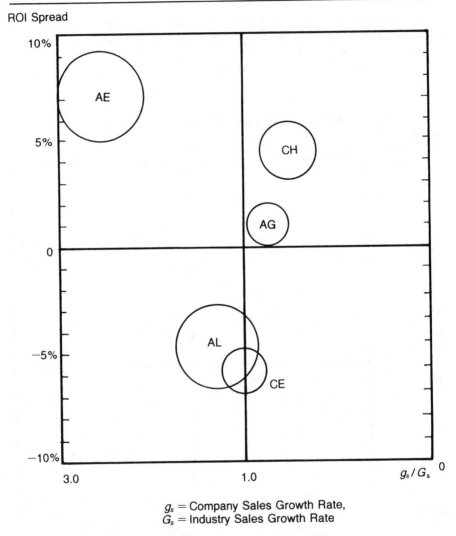

ROI Spread

g_s = Company Sales Growth Rate,
G_s = Industry Sales Growth Rate

* Size of circle indicates size of sales revenues in 1981.

The scale in the horizontal axis has been reversed with regard to the normal Marakon matrix, to facilitate comparisons with the other portfolio matrices.

Source: Lily K. Lai, "Corporate Strategic Planning for a Diversified Company," ©️ 1983. Reprinted by permission of Lily K. Lai.

Figure 17.6 Estimated βs for Proxy Companies in Relevant Markets for Martin Marietta Operating Companies

Industry/ Company	Value Line β Estimate	Debt-Equity	Estimated Marginal Tax Rate
Aerospace			
E-Systems	1.25	0.17	0.42
Fairchild	1.35	0.39	0.40
Northrop	1.30	0.03	0.29
Raytheon	1.20	0.05	0.40
Rockwell	1.05	0.15	0.48
Average	1.23	0.16	0.40
Unlevered β	1.12		
Aluminum			
Alcan	1.15	0.61	0.35
Alcoa	1.00	0.44	0.30
Kaiser	1.05	0.36	0.20
Reynolds	1.05	0.63	0.35
Average	1.06	0.51	0.30
Unlevered β	0.78		
Cement			
Lone Star	1.05	0.79	0.30
Ideal Basic	1.00	0.98	0.35
Kaiser Cement	1.15	0.78	0.35
Giant Portland	0.75	0.50	0.30
Average	0.99	0.76	0.33
Unlevered β	0.66		
Specialty Chemicals			
Betz Labs	1.00	0.01	0.46
Economics lab	1.05	0.57	0.40
Lawter International	0.80	0.02	0.35
NCH Corporation	0.80	0.03	0.48
Witco Chemical	0.95	0.51	0.44
Average	0.92	0.23	0.43
Unlevered β	0.81		

$$\beta_{\text{unlevered}} = \frac{\text{Value Line } \beta \text{ estimate}}{1 + \dfrac{\text{Debt}}{\text{Equity}} (1 - \text{marginal tax rate})}$$

Source: Lily K. Lai, "Corporate Strategic Planning for a Diversified Company," © 1983. Reprinted by permission of Lily K. Lai.

—Specialty chemicals, including concrete admixtures, refractories, and dyestuffs.
—Data systems, offering a wide range of data processing services (such as remote computer power, computer systems, and facilities management), for both private industry and government.

Figure 17.7 Estimated Parameters for the Profitability Matrix of Martin Marietta Corp.

	Cost of Capital	Return on Investment (ROI)	Investment Growth Rate (g_k)	Company Sales Growth Rate (g_s)	Industry Sales Growth Rate (G_s)
	(%)	(%)	(%)	(%)	(%)
Aerospace	19.0	26.1	18.4	39.4	19.0**
Aggregates	15.7*	16.9	18.6	2.8	3.5
Aluminum	16.5	11.8	24.6	9.2	8.5
Cement	15.7	9.9	24.8	3.4	3.4
Chemicals	16.7	21.6	16.6	10.7	14.0
Martin Marietta	18.5	18.0	23.5	23.0	—

* Assume the same risks as cement.
** This is the growth rate for the whole industry. The growth rate for the high-end technology segment of the industry is higher, but it is difficult to compute a separate growth rate.
Source: Lily K. Lai, "Corporate Strategic Planning for a Diversified Company," © 1983. Reprinted by permission of Lily K. Lai.

The portfolio of Martin Marietta's businesses is displayed in three different matrices: the industry attractiveness-business strength matrix in Figure 17.3, the growth-share matrix in Figure 17.4, and the profitability matrix in Figure 17.5. Figures 17.6 and 17.7 provide the basic parameters used in the construction of the profitability matrix.

The three matrices tend to convey consistent information about the strategic positioning of all of Martin Marietta's business. Perhaps the only discrepancy arises from the status of the Aggregates SBU, which is portrayed in a very unattractive category in the growth-share matrix, while appearing stronger in the other two matrices. Also, notice that the Aluminum SBU is squarely depicted as a loser in all three matrices.

DEFINING THE AVAILABILITY OF STRATEGIC FUNDS, THE DEBT POLICY, AND THE MAXIMUM SUSTAINABLE GROWTH

Strategic funds are expense items required for the implementation of strategic action programs whose benefits are expected to be accrued in the long term, beyond the current budget period.

There are three major components of strategic funds:

—Investments in tangible assets, such as new production capacity, new tools, new space, and new acquisitions.
—Increases or decreases in working capital resulting from strategic commitments.
—Developmental expenses that are over and above the needs of existing business,

such as R&D expenses for new products, sales promotions, development of management systems, and so forth.

A sound method of calculating strategic funds is first to forecast the sources and uses of funds by the firm. A procedure to make this computation is suggested below.

SOURCES	USES
Earnings Depreciation New debt issuing New equity issuing Divestitures Others	Dividends Debt repayment Strategic funds —New fixed assets and acquisitions —Increases in working capital —Increases in developmental expenses
TOTAL SOURCES	= TOTAL USES
STRATEGIC FUNDS	= TOTAL SOURCES Less Dividends Less Debt repayment

The estimate of strategic funds in the case of GMV is presented in Figure 17.8.

Establishing a debt policy congruent with the company's financing requirements is another issue to be addressed at this point. The amount of strategic funds that can be invested, and the maximum sustainable growth are clearly

Figure 17.8 An Estimate of General Motors Venezuela Strategic Funds for 1983 ($ million)

SOURCES		USES	
Earnings	20.8	Dividends	9.2
Depreciation	9.8	Debt repayments	20.0
New debt issues	50.0	Strategic funds*	51.4
New equity issues	—		
Divestitures	—		
Total	80.6		80.6
* Strategic funds = 80.6 − 9.2 − 20.0.			

Adapted from Otto K. Soulavy, "Implementation of a Formal Strategic Planning Process," © 1983. Reprinted by permission of Otto K. Soulavy.

determined by the capital structure selected by the firm. In the case of GMV, the debt policy calls for a total debt equal to twice the equity, that is to say:

$$\frac{D}{E} = 2.0$$

The maximum sustainable growth that can be obtained by using the internally generated resources and the recently defined debt policy for GMV, can be estimated by using the relationship:

$$g = p\left[ROA + \frac{D}{E}(ROA - i) \right]$$

The meaning of these symbols and the value they have in the case of GMV are:

g = maximum sustainable growth expressed as a yearly rate of increase of the equity base (the debt-equity ratio is assumed to remain constant, so g represents also the increase in debt).

p = percentage of retained earnings = 56%
ROA = after tax return on assets   = 8%
D/E = debt-equity ratio   = 2.0
i = after-tax interest of debt   = 6%

Therefore:

$$g = 0.56[8 + 2(8 - 6)] = 6.7\%.$$

PRELIMINARY EVALUATION OF PROPOSED ACTION PROGRAMS AND ASSIGNMENT OF PRIORITIES FOR RESOURCE ALLOCATION TO EACH BUSINESS

There are two major tasks to be conducted at this stage of the planning process. One requires the assignment of priorities to each business, in consonance with their corresponding strategic positioning. We favor the use of the following categories of strategic growth as expressions of resource allocation priorities:

—Build aggressively
—Build gradually
—Build selectively
—Maintain aggressively
—Maintain selectively
—Prove viability
—Divest-liquidate

Their specific meaning was discussed in Chapter 3.

The second task is to assign the total available resources of the firm among available SBUs. We commented in Chapter 4 on the two philosophies which have been developed around that issue: either to assign resources to the SBUs according to their strategic priorities and let the SBU managers allocate those resources among specific projects; or directly assign those resources on a project-by-project basis. As we indicated, we favor the first approach.

The actual assignment of priorities and resources can be facilitated by using the market-to-book value model for each individual business, as explained in Chapter 10.

We will now proceed to illustrate the implementation of these tasks.

In the GMV case, Figure 17.9 summarizes the essential information contained in the resource allocation task. It first provides the priorities suggested by each SBU, and the final approved priorities at the corporate level. In the case of the Aluminum Company of Martin Marietta Corp., a more comprehensive financial analysis was conducted in order to evaluate the four strategic alternatives recommended by Marakon (as discussed in Chapter 10): hold, build, harvest, and divest. In Figure 17.10 we present a summary of the basic parameters for the first three of these alternatives, as well as an estimate of the net cash flow for 1983. It can be observed, if the cash flow is a fair estimate, that none of the alternatives contributes a positive amount to the market value of the operation. All of them appear as subtracting value. Therefore, the divest strategy surges again as a most powerful alternative, which should be given careful

FIGURE 17.9 Assignment of Priorities and Resource Allocation at the Corporate Level for General Motors Venezuela

Business	Suggested Priority	Approved Priority	Targeted Resources
1. Passenger cars	Maintain aggressively	Maintain selectively	21
2. Commercials & Trucks	Build gradually	Maintain selectively	15
3. Parts & Acc. selectively	Build selectively	Build selectively	2
4. Financing viability	Prove viability	Build aggressively	5
5. Engines & Ind. Equip.	Build selectively	Build selectively	3
6. Component manufacture	Build gradually	Build gradually	5
		TOTAL	51

Source: Otto K. Soulavy, "Implementation of a Formal Strategic Planning Process," © 1983. Reprinted by permission of Otto K. Soulavy.

consideration. In fact, we can at least say that liquidating will produce a positive value, mainly when considering that the company holds current assets of $428 million which are very liquid, and has a fairly modern plant which accounts for $776 million in fixed assets. On the other hand, current liabilities and long-term debt amount to $630 million. Therefore, to break even, the firm should sell the plant for only 26 percent of its net value, because we can assume that current assets are worth the same $428 million they are valued in the books:

Net proceeds from liquidating the firm:

Current assets	$428
Fixed assets (26% of $776)	202
Total	630
− Debt outstanding	630
NET TOTAL	0

It appears most likely that the fixed assets are worth more than $202 million, because not only is it a very modern plant, but the average M/B ratio for the industry is around 0.5.

Figure 17.10 The Basic Strategies for the Aluminum Company of Martin Marietta

	Hold	Build	Harvest
Annual Sales Increase (%)	3	5	2
Return on Sales (%)	4.0	3.0	5.0
Working Capital and Sales (%)	30	30	30
Net Plant Increase (%)	3	5	2
Maintenance Investment and Net Plant (%)	11	11	11
Depreciation and Net Plant (%)	6	6	6
Deferred Tax and Net Earnings (%)	6	6	6
Cash Flow Calculation (1983)			
Net Earnings	26	20	32
+ Depreciation	39	41	38
+ Deferred Tax	2	1	4
− Capital Expenditures	92	106	83
− Working Capital	6	10	4
Net Operating Cash Flow 1983	−31	−54	−13

Source: Lily K. Lai, "Corporate Strategic Planning for a Diversified Company," © 1983. Reprinted by permission of Lily K. Lai.

18

STEPS 7 AND 8: SPECIFIC ACTION PROGRAMS AT THE BUSINESS AND FUNCTIONAL LEVELS

Specific action programs translate the broad action programs defined both at the business and functional levels into very concrete tasks which can be evaluated and monitored. They constitute a structured, coherent, and timed continuum of actions, supporting each broad action program, with a clearly identified schedule of completion, in a relatively short time span, covering from six to eighteen months.

A normalized description of specific action programs facilitates their later evaluation and comparison at the corporate level, so we recommend the inclusion of the following items in that description.

—A verbal description
—A statement of priority indicating the desirability of the program for the competitive position of the firm
  — "Absolute first priority"—postponement will hurt the competitive position significantly.
  — "Highly desirable"—postponement will affect the competitive position adversely.
  — "Desirable"—if funds were to be available, the competitive position could be enhanced.
—The estimated costs and benefits
—The schedule of completion
—The identification of a single individual responsible for its implementation

Figure 18.1 Definition and Evaluation of Specific Action Programs at the Business Level for General Motors Venezuela

BUSINESS: PASSENGER VEHICLES

BROAD ACTION PROGRAM: GAIN MARKET LEADERSHIP IN ALL SEGMENTS

Program Description	Priority*	$ Cost	Manpower Requirements	Scheduled Completion	Responsibility
1. Dealer Training	A	400,000	Dealer Coordination Department 14 persons	December 1984	Dealer Coordination
2. Advertising	A	500,000	Advertising Department 2 persons	September 1984	Marketing Manager
3. Promotion based on rebates	B	1,200,000	Marketing Organization 8 persons	June 1984	Marketing Manager
4. Improve market intelligence through marketing research efforts	C	200,000	Marketing staff and external consultants 2 persons	October 1984	Marketing Chief of Staff

* Categorize priorities in accordance with the following:
  A = *Absolute First Priority*—postponement will significantly hurt our position.
  B = *Highly Desirable*—postponement will adversely affect our position in the market.
  C = *Desirable*—if funds were to be available to enhance our position.

Adapted from Otto K. Soulavy, "Implementation of a Formal Strategic Planning Process," © 1983. Reprinted by permission of Otto K. Soulavy.

—The procedure for controlling its execution (normally of the project control kind, like Critical Path Method and Gantt-schedules).

Figure 18.1 corresponds to the set of specific action programs required to implement the broad action program "Gain Market Leadership in All Segments" for the Passenger Vehicle SBU of GMV. It conveys the minimum amount of information required to define and monitor those programs. Their collective impact will be an increase of sales of about $20 million per year for the next three years. This should represent an added contribution to profits of $300,000 in 1984, $600,000 in 1985, and $800,000 in 1986, net of strategic expenses.

A sample form to be used in requests for capital appropriations is given in Figure 18.2. Much more detailed information could be collected, if so required by the corporate level, to identify the nature of cash flows through the planning horizon, as well as the breakdown of expenses implicit in the project.

The final allocation of strategic funds at the corporate level will be based on the information provided by all SBUs in the form of specific action programs. To support the businesses of the firm, the corporation will consider the requests for capital investment, as well as the needs for an increase in working capital or in other strategic expenses.

Figure 18.2   Request for Capital Appropriation

A. Business Identification _____

B. Project Name _____

C. Responsible Manager _____

D. Type of Request
   1. Legal Requirements
   2. Cost Reduction and Productivity Improvements
   3. Maintenance of Existing Business
   4. Expansion of Existing Business
   5. New Business Development
   6. Energy Conservation
   7. Other (Explain) _____

E. Other Businesses Affected
   1. Business _____ , ____ %

   2. Business _____ , ____ %

   3. Business _____ , ____ %

F. New Project?

   ☐ Yes ☐ No

   If No, identify number ____ and year ____ of first capital appropriation.

Figure 18.2 *Continued*

G. Resources Requested

	Total Project	Current Budget	Current Year Forecast	Coming Year	Next Year
1. Property, Plant & Equipment	_____	_____	_____	_____	_____
2. Working Capital	_____	_____	_____	_____	_____
3. Total Capital	_____	_____	_____	_____	_____
4. Total Amount Requested from Corporation	_____	_____	_____	_____	_____

H. Description and Summary Justification of Project

I. Projected Cash Flows

When information is available, and for all projects over $200,000, fill in this section:

	Pre-Operational Years			Operational Years				
Estimated Sales — Cost of Goods Sold								
Operational Profits General Administrative and Marketing Expenses								
Profit before Taxes — Less Taxes								
Profit After Taxes + Depreciation — Investment — Increase in Working Capital ± Other Corrections to Determine Cash Flow								
Net Cash Flow								

Confidence in economic estimates:

☐ Solid Backing   ☐ Reasonable   ☐ Guess

Figure 18.2 *Continued*

J. Economic Indicators of the Project
   1. Cost of Capital   _____ %
   2. Time Horizon   _____ years
   3. NPV of Cash Flows $_____
   4. Internal Rate of return   _____ %
   5. Payback   _____ years

K. Key Milestone Schedule
   1. Appreciation Request Approved _____
   2. Start Engineering   _____
   3. Start Construction   _____
   4. Project Complete   _____

19

STEPS 9, 10, 11, AND 12: THE FINAL CYCLE OF STRATEGIC PLANNING. RESOURCE ALLOCATION AND THE BUDGETING PROCESS

Step 9 of the planning process involves allocation of resources and definition of performance measurements for management control. At this stage, a final commitment of strategic resources should be made. From the total funds appropriate for investments and strategic expenses, we have to deduce those which are required to fulfill legal obligations or correspond to approved commitments to ongoing projects.

The appropriation process for the remaining funds requires the completion of the following tasks:

—Collection and classification of all the information submitted by SBUs and functional units.
—Analysis of the coherence between the strategic role assigned to SBUs and functional units, and the requests for funds.
—Analysis of economic indicators, and value creation potential of the proposed programs.
—Final allocation of resources for the coming year.
—Development of performance measurements to facilitate the controlling and monitoring of the broad and specific action programs supporting business and functional strategies
  • In the short-run
  • Over an extended planning horizon.

There are three primary categories of information which we find essential to be submitted by the SBU managers in order to guide the resource allocation process. First is a brief narrative concerning the key descriptive elements of the SBU, generated from the previous steps in the planning process. Figure 19.1 provides a form containing some suggestions for structuring this task.

Second, the SBU should provide basic financial information related not only to its operating base, but also to the strategic funds necessary for its future

Figure 19.1 Summary of Business Strategy by SBU

Business ---

Mission Statement

Industry Perspective

Market Overview	Competitive Environment
Narrative and Total Available Market	*Narrative*
Trends	*Competitors Profile and Market Share*

Business Description

Markets and Distribution	Products-Technology Scope	Manufacturing
Business Sales ---------------- After-Tax Profits ------------		

Industry Attractiveness and Business Strength (Current and Future)

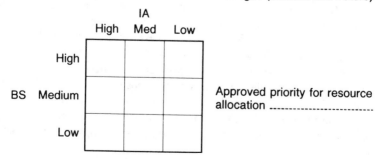

Approved priority for resource allocation -------------------------

Figure 19.1 *Continued*

Environmental Scan	Internal Scrutiny
Opportunities	*Strengths*
Threats	*Weaknesses*

Broad Action Program	Specific Action Programs	Resources Requested	Statement of Benefits	Statement of Performance and Goals	Milestones

development. Figure 19.2 presents a simplified format to communicate this information.

Third, it is required to identify the key performance indicators for each SBU, with a statement of its historical realization, as well as projected targets. An example of this type of information is given in Figure 19.3. Notice that this will constitute one of the foundations for the subsequent control of the SBU.

We have alluded already to the two different philosophies regarding the degree of centralization in the resource allocation process. When the corporate level of a firm limits itself to a gross allocation of resources among SBUs, without intervening in the assignment of those resources within the SBU, it has already performed its key decisions in Step 6 of the process. At that stage in the planning cycle, financial evaluation based on broad assessments of performance by SBU (such as the M/B model) should have provided the necessary assistance to allocate resources compatible with the strategic positioning of the SBU. What is left to be done in this case is simply a consolidation of all the information originated at the SBU level, checking for final consistency between the assigned priorities and requested funds. Figure 19.4 suggests an approach to undertake this task.

Figure 19.2 Summary of Financial Information and Strategic Funds by SBU

Business _____

Numbers in $, except when indicated)	History			Current Year		Projections			
	19__	19__	19__	19__	Actual	Budget 19__	19__	19__	19__
Total Market Market Share (%) Company Sales — Operating Cost of Goods Sold									
Gross Operating Margin — Operating SG&A									
Operating Margin — Strategic Expenses									
SBU Margin — Taxes									
SBU Net Income + Depreciation — Capital Investments — Increases in Working Capital									
Contribution-Request of funds to the Corporation									

Figure 19.3 Business Performance Objectives by SBU

		Business Performance Objectives									
		History				Current Year		Projections			
Indicators of Performance		19__	19__	19__	19__	Actual	Budget 19__	19__	19__	19__	19__
Size	Sales										
	Assets										
	Profits										
	R&D Expenses										
Growth	Sales										
	Assets										
	Profits										
	R&D Expenses										
Profit-ability	Profit Margin										
	ROA										
Turnover	Assets										
	Inventory										
	Accts. Receivable										

Technological*	Productivity	
	Innovation	
	Quality	
	Mfg. Costs	
Human Resources	Training	
	Safety	

* Indices need to be defined.

Figure 19.4　Resource Allocation Among Businesses According to the Strategic Positioning of SBUs

1. Portfolio of Businesses and Final Priorities by SBY

Industry
Attractiveness

	H	M	L
H			
M			
L			

Business Strength

Resource allocation priorities	List of SBUs
Build Aggressively	
Build Gradually	
Build Selectively	
Maintain Aggressively	
Maintain Selectively	
Prove Viability	
Divest/Liquidate	

2. Checking Consistency Between SBU Priority and Total Funds Requested-Approved

List of SBUs from higher to lower priority	Classification of Specific Action Programs			Total Requested	Total Approved
	A	B	C		
Total Requested					X
Total Approved				X	

The second philosophy for resource allocation advocates for total centralization in the assignment of resources at the corporate level, in a project by project basis. The information contained in the "Request for Capital Allocation" (Figure 18.2) will be central in guiding those decisions. There are two further issues which need to be carefully addressed in this case. First, not every request for funds can necessarily be put in terms of a project subject to precise financial evaluation, as is the case with many of the strategic expenses needed to support the development of a business. Ordinarily, these requests are subject to approval in the annual operating budget. However, we favor an explicit recognition of all strategic funds at this stage of the resource allocation process. Second, after having completed the approval of independent projects, one might detect inconsistencies between the resulting resources assigned to a business unit, and its originally intended strategic priorities.

These considerations, together with the extraordinary demands for detailed involvement from the corporate level to pass judgments on matters which might not be totally grasped by those managers, have made many firms abandon these centralized practices of resource allocation in favor of a global assignment to SBUs.

Also, as part of this step, we have to prepare a consolidation for the whole firm of the financial information and strategic funds presented by SBUs (Figure 19.2). A similar chart for GMV is presented in Figure 19.5.

Finally, one should develop a set of Performance Objectives for the corporation, similar to those given in Figure 19.3 for each SBU, but including also some measures pertaining to the capital market (such as earning per share, dividends per share, and market-to-book value), and other financial indices that can only be properly defined at the corporate level (such as return on equity, debt-equity ratio, and so forth).

Once all strategic programs have been approved, and resources allocated accordingly, business and functional managers are left with the task of translating those commitments into detailed operational budgets, and precise statements of strategic funds.

Normally, this is accomplished with the help of the three conventional financial statements: balance sheet, profit and loss statement, and sources and applications of funds. Those statements exhibit historical as well as projected information, with the current year displayed in monthly figures. Moreover, a fourth document is used to present the operating performance indicators, again with historical and projected targets, constructed similarly to the financial statements just described.

These financial statements should be prepared at every operating level in the organization, and aggregated upward for the final consolidation at the corporate level. Needless to say, most business firms look at the budget as *the* final element for planning and control, which drives, as a central thrust, the behavior of the key managers. This is why it is so important that the budget does not merely represent myopic operational commitments, but richly incorporates oper-

Figure 19.5   The Consolidation of Strategic Funds for General Motors Venezuela

STRATEGIC FUNDS STATEMENT

GENERAL MOTORS DE VENEZUELA

	HISTORY				PROJECTIONS		
	1980	1981	1982	1983	1984	1985	1986
Net income	16.5	24.2	0.3	(13.3)	6.6	16.6	26.6
Depreciation	15.6	12.2	22.9	34.4	30.0	31.7	30.7
Increase in deferred taxes	—	3.1	—	—	3.3	—	—
SOURCES OF FUNDS	32.1	36.5	23.2	21.1	40.0	48.3	57.3
Capital expenditures	10.8	30.4	101.7	55.9	28.0	10.0	8.0
Increase in working capital	2.0	74.8	(100.0)	(33.0)	16.0	10.1	10.0
USES OF FUNDS	12.8	105.2	1.7	22.9	44.0	20.1	18.0
Net cash provided (required)	19.3	(68.7)	21.5	(1.8)	(4.0)	28.2	39.3
Increase in debt	(7.6)	80.6	1.4	1.8	4.0	(21.5)	(32.6)
Year end debt	133.0	213.6	215.0	216.0	220.0	198.5	165.9
MAXIMUM AFFORDABLE DIVIDEND	11.7	11.9	22.9	—	—	6.7	6.7

Source: Otto K. Soulavy, "Implementation of a Formal Strategic Planning Process," © 1983. Reprinted by permission of Otto K. Soulavy.

tional efficiency as well as strategic developmental efforts. It is to facilitate the accountability in these two modes that we have constantly insisted in separating operational from strategic funds, and ultimately, operational from strategic expenses and results.

Since the preparation of budgets involves a well-known methodology, we will not address it here.

Part Four

THE CONGRUENCY BETWEEN ORGANIZATIONAL STRUCTURE AND STRATEGY

20

ORGANIZATIONAL DESIGN

INTRODUCTION

Organizations are formed whenever the pursuit of an objective requires the realization of a task that calls for the joint efforts of two or more individuals. We can identify the following major components in the definition of an organization (Galbraith 1977):

—Organizations are composed of individuals and groups of people,
—seeking the achievement of shared objectives,
—through division of labor,
—integrated by information-bound decision processes,
—continuously through time.

Organizations are developed around the concept that a complex task can be subdivided into simpler components by means of division of labor. The design of a structure to attain the organizational goals requires addressing two primary issues: how to perform this division of labor, and how to coordinate the resulting tasks.

The purpose of this chapter is to suggest a methodology to design the structure of formal organizations. Chapter 21 illustrates the application of this methodology to an actual situation. We will concentrate our attention on the design of formal organizations in business firms. However, the issues and methodologies presented might be extendable to other forms of organizations.

The central notion we adopt is derived from the contingency theory of organizational design, which states that there is no single set of principles to shape the structure of an organization. Rather, each organization should develop its structure in tune with its internal characteristics and the relationships with its environment. Therefore, from the outset, we are forced to recognize that the question of organizational design does not admit a simple answer. There is no mechanistic "how to do" recipe. Instead, this part outlines the basic concepts of design that can be translated into broad guidelines to support the task of structuring an organization.

The organizational structure may be defined as "the relatively enduring allocation of work roles and administrative mechanisms that creates a pattern of interrelated work activities, and allows the organization to conduct, coordinate, and control its work activities" (Jackson and Morgan 1978). Thus, this structure is not only a hierarchical allocation of authorities and responsibilities. It encompasses all the managerial processes that concur in the realization of the tasks undertaken by the organization. The nature of the interdependence between structure and processes is the central concern of Chapter 5 of this book.

The major organization archetypes (functional, divisional, and matrix), are discussed in this chapter. Although in practice we seldom encounter actual organizations structured in accordance with these pure archetypes, it is useful to reflect on their advantages and disadvantages to gain some insights into the question of organizational design.

Later in this chapter, a brief historical overview is presented. The classical theory, the human relations theory, the organizational design-making theory, and the contingency theory are discussed. The notion of contingency is central in the formulation of a unitary concept of design that calls for *segmentation* of an organization into units, *differentiation* of units to adapt to unique environmental conditions, and *integration* of units to insure a coordinated pursuit of the organizational objectives.

Finally, we present recommendations for organizational design, which addresses both the *basic* and *detailed* organizational design tasks. The basic structure is heavily dependent upon the strategic positioning of the organization, while the detailed structure is more related with operational matters. The need to *fit* structure and managerial processes to the strategic and operational demands of the organization is also discussed.

This chapter follows closely the presentation in Hax and Majluf (1981).

ORGANIZATIONAL ARCHETYPES

We turn in this section to the analysis of three archetypes that represent distinct forms of organizational structures: *functional, divisional,* and *matrix*. They are important design anchors, because these organizational structures have been extensively tested and studied, and their advantages and disadvantages are relatively well known. In fact, in practice, most organizations present combinations of these three archetypes resulting in what we designate as a *hybrid* organization.

Moreover, this section disucsses the historical evolution of the organizational structure observed in U.S. firms.

Functional and Divisional Organizations

Functional and divisional forms constitute the classical opposite archetypes for organizational design.

The functional form is structured around the *inputs* required to perform the tasks of the organization. Typically, these inputs are *functions* or *specialties* such as: finance, marketing, production, engineering, research and development, and personnel. Figure 20.1 presents the organization chart of Admiral Corporation which is structured primarily around the functions of Finance and Administration, Operations, and Sales and Marketing.

The divisional form is structured according to the *outputs* generated by the organization. The most common distinction of the outputs is in terms of the *products* delivered. However, other types of outputs could serve as a basis for divisionalization, such as programs and projects. Also, markets, clients, and geographical locations could serve as criteria for divisionalization.

Figure 20.2 presents the Organizational Chart of The Anaconda Company, which has five main product divisions: Primary Metals Division, Anaconda Aluminum Company, Anaconda Wire and Cable Company, Anaconda American Brass Company, and Forest Products Division. The functions of Administration and Finance are held at the corporate level. The detailed organization of the Primary Metals Division, presented in Figure 20.3, shows a typical functional structure with Operations, Industrial Relations, Sales, Mining Research, and Safety reporting to an Executive Vice President.

The full spectrum of attributes of the functional and divisional forms is not totally displayed in the charts above. There is a pervasive character of these organizational structures that differentiate the resulting management style: the functional form is more *centralized*, the divisional form is more *decentralized*. A functional organization tends to develop highly qualified technical skills and a climate conducive to technical excellence and high efficiency. It provides a "critical mass" for the career advancement of its professionals. But its inherent stress on specialization pushes the decision-making process upwards, because only at the top do we find the confluence of all inputs required for a final decision.

A different situation exists in divisional organizations, where some functional specialization is lost in favor of added autonomy. Many decisions can be resolved at the divisional manager's level, preventing an overburdened top hierarchy. The middle-layer of managers created in divisional organizations provides an effective training ground for general management skills. Though in charge of only one segment of the overall business, divisional managers are exposed to a full range of managerial problems. That experience gives them a decisive advantage over functional managers, who are confronted with situations involving only their narrow fields of specialty.

An excellent characterization of the distinct managerial profiles required un-

Figure 20.1 Example of a Functional Organization—Admiral Corporation (1971)

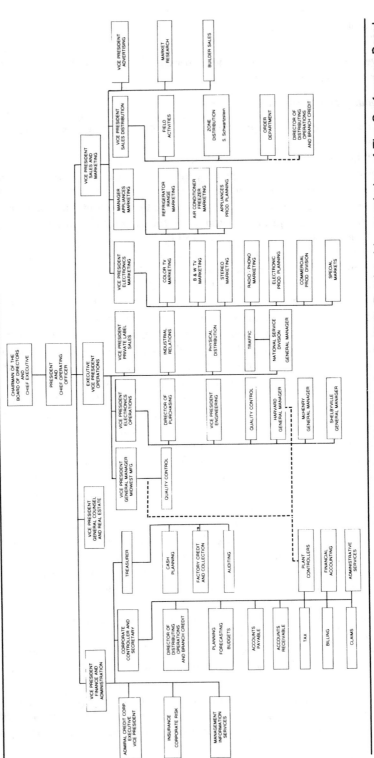

Source: A. R. Janger, *Corporate Organization Structures: Manufacturing,* © 1973. Reprinted by permission of The Conference Board, Inc., New York, NY.

Figure 20.2 Example of a Product Division Organization—The Anaconda Company (1972)

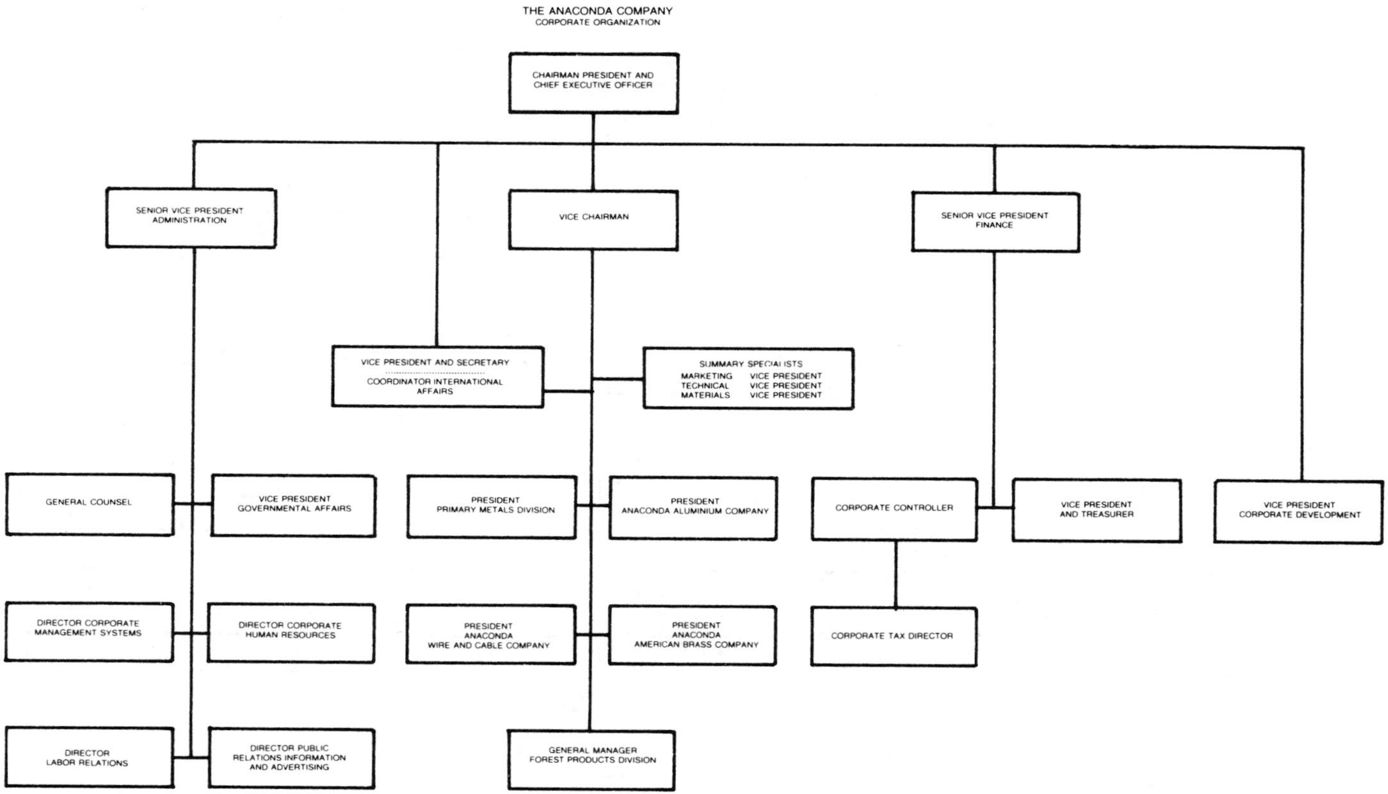

THE ANACONDA COMPANY
CORPORATE ORGANIZATION

CHAIRMAN PRESIDENT AND CHIEF EXECUTIVE OFFICER

SENIOR VICE PRESIDENT FINANCE

VICE PRESIDENT CORPORATE DEVELOPMENT

VICE PRESIDENT AND TREASURER

CORPORATE CONTROLLER

CORPORATE TAX DIRECTOR

VICE CHAIRMAN

SUMMARY SPECIALISTS
MARKETING VICE PRESIDENT
TECHNICAL VICE PRESIDENT
MATERIALS VICE PRESIDENT

PRESIDENT ANACONDA ALUMINUM COMPANY

PRESIDENT ANACONDA AMERICAN BRASS COMPANY

VICE PRESIDENT AND SECRETARY
COORDINATOR INTERNATIONAL AFFAIRS

PRESIDENT PRIMARY METALS DIVISION

PRESIDENT ANACONDA WIRE AND CABLE COMPANY

GENERAL MANAGER FOREST PRODUCTS DIVISION

SENIOR VICE PRESIDENT ADMINISTRATION

VICE PRESIDENT GOVERNMENTAL AFFAIRS

DIRECTOR CORPORATE HUMAN RESOURCES

DIRECTOR PUBLIC RELATIONS INFORMATION AND ADVERTISING

GENERAL COUNSEL

DIRECTOR CORPORATE MANAGEMENT SYSTEMS

DIRECTOR LABOR RELATIONS

Source: A. R. Janger, *Corporation Organization Structures: Manufacturing,* © 1973. Reprinted by permission of The Conference Board, Inc., New York, NY.

Figure 20.3 Example of a Product Division Organization—The Anaconda Company—Primary Metals Division (1972)

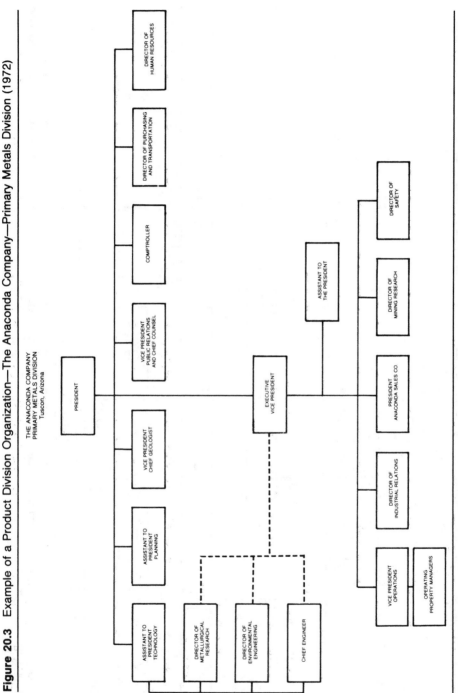

THE ANACONDA COMPANY
PRIMARY METALS DIVISION
Tuscon, Arizona

PRESIDENT

ASSISTANT TO PRESIDENT TECHNOLOGY

ASSISTANT TO PRESIDENT PLANNING

VICE PRESIDENT CHIEF GEOLOGIST

VICE PRESIDENT PUBLIC RELATIONS AND CHIEF COUNSEL

COMPTROLLER

DIRECTOR OF PURCHASING AND TRANSPORTATION

DIRECTOR OF HUMAN RESOURCES

DIRECTOR OF METALLURGICAL RESEARCH

DIRECTOR OF ENVIRONMENTAL ENGINEERING

CHIEF ENGINEER

EXECUTIVE VICE PRESIDENT

ASSISTANT TO THE PRESIDENT

VICE PRESIDENT OPERATIONS

OPERATING PROPERTY MANAGERS

DIRECTOR OF INDUSTRIAL RELATIONS

PRESIDENT ANACONDA SALES CO

DIRECTOR OF MINING RESEARCH

DIRECTOR OF SAFETY

Source: A. R. Janger, *Corporate Organization Structures: Manufacturing,* © 1973. Reprinted by permission of The Conference Board, Inc., New York, NY.

der these two structures has been proposed by Vancil (1978) and reproduced in Figure 20.4. It is not surprising, therefore, that a traumatic adaptation in managerial style takes place whenever a functional organization changes its structure to a divisional form. The previous functional managers, with their narrow concerns for professional specialization, have to develop a broad entrepreneurial spirit, which is not an easy transition.

There is a certain alignment between authority and responsibility in functional organizations that is absent in divisional forms. An illustration may be useful to clarify this point. A manufacturing manager in a functional organization is fully responsible for the operation concerning plant facilities. His responsibilities completely match his authority.

Turn now to a divisional organization with two divisional managers responsible for two different product lines. If these product lines are manufactured in a common plant, an unavoidable ambiguity results in the accountability of the plant operations. One or both divisional managers do not have total authority over the output of that plant. In this case, at least one divisional manager has more responsibility than authority.

Figure 20.4 Division Managers and Functional Managers—Dimensions of the Task

	DIVISIONAL MANAGER	FUNCTIONAL MANAGER
Strategic		
Orientation	Entrepreneurial	Professional
Relevant environment	External	Internal
Objective of Task	Adaptability	Efficiency
Operational		
Responsibility	Broad; Cross-functional	Narrow; Parochial
Authority	Less than responsibility	Equal to responsibility
Interdependence on others	May be high	Usually low
Personal		
Style	Proactive; initiator	Reactive, Implementor
Ambiguity of Task	High	Low
Performance Evaluation		
Measurements	Profit; Growth; Return on Investment	Costs, compared to standards or budgets
Quality of Feedback	Slow; Garbled	Rapid; Accurate
Risks and Rewards		
Risk of Failure	Higher	Lower
Compensation Potential	Higher	Lower

Source: Reproduced by permission of Financial Executive Research Foundation, Morristown, N.J.

The resolution of conflicts among managers is also different in functional and divisional organizations. The functional organization has a trouble-free functional line, but conflicts of interest among functional managers are usually handled at the top level. The general manager must act as the final decision-maker and arbitrate disputes among specialities, because he is the only one fully accountable for the performance of the organization. This situation could be aggravated by a tendency to develop parochial orientations in each functional group. Since in a divisional organization middle managers are accountable for the performance of their individual businesses, there is a clear incentive for them to resolve conflicts of interest by direct negotiations among themselves. Normally, ground rules are instituted to facilitate this accomodation process, such as the development of negotiated transfer prices for goods flowing among divisions.

The direct profit accountability of each segment of a divisional organization creates a genuine business climate at the divisional level that has important motivational implications. In contrast, the principal motivator in functional organizations is technical excellence more than business prominence. This attitude may be considered a drawback in a highly competitive environment.

Both functional and divisional forms are extensively used in structuring organizations. Functional forms are more predominant in organizations having single or dominant products, while divisional forms emerge as diversification increases. An empirical study conducted by Rumelt (1974), based on observations of Fortune 500 firms, reports a notorious shift from functional to divisional structure from 1950 to 1970. Figure 20.5 registers Rumelt's findings. Some arguments given to explain this shift are the increase in diversification by those firms in those elapsing years, the alleged higher efficiency of divisional forms, and their ability to deal with growth and cope with size and complexity. However, a conscious effort must be made to retain critical technical expertise when a divisional structure is adopted. In fact, most divisionalized corporations still retain a central R&D function.

An interesting example pointed out by Janger (1973) shows the change undertaken by Kendall Company from a divisionalized organization in 1970 to a functional one in 1972 (see Figures 20.6 and 20.7). This case, which is contrary to the normal evolution of most corporations, might represent an attempt to regain specialization and efficiency by adopting a functional form.

As complexity begins to grow in the context of the evolution of an organization, decentralization is a must. It becomes impossible for the top manager to retain his role as the sole coordinator of all the activities of the organization. Even more important, he is unable to understand intimately the variety of businesses in a diversified setting to provide the necessary strategic guidance. Therefore, in most complex organizations the valid question is not whether to decentralize, but what the degree of decentralization should be. Solomons (1965) suggests four thoughtful requirements for successful divisionalization:

First, the divisions should be sufficiently independent in terms of production and marketing resources to facilitate separate accountability.

Figure 20.5 Estimated Percentage of Functional and Divisional
Organizations 1949–1969

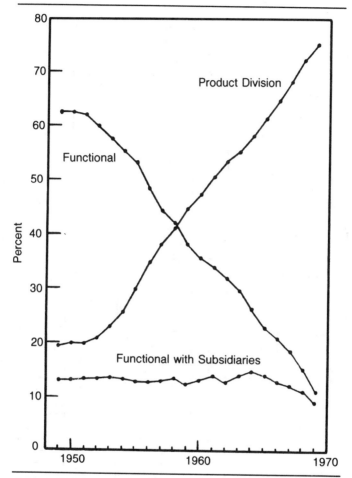

Source: Richard P. Rumelt, *Strategy, Structure, and Economic
Performance*. Boston: Division of Research, Harvard Business
School, 1974, p. 66. Reprinted by permission.

Second, though substantial independence of divisions from each other is a
necessary condition for successful divisionalization, if carried to extremes, it
would destroy the very idea that such divisions are integral parts of a single
business. This suggests some degree of interdependence among divisions.

Third, no division, by seeking its own profit, should reduce that of the corporation. This can be accomplished by developing planning, budgeting, and monitoring systems designed to stimulate divisional initiatives, while preventing actions
counterproductive to the overall corporate performance.

Figure 20.6 Evolution of an Organization Structure from Divisional to Functional—The Kendall Company 1970—Divisionalized Organization

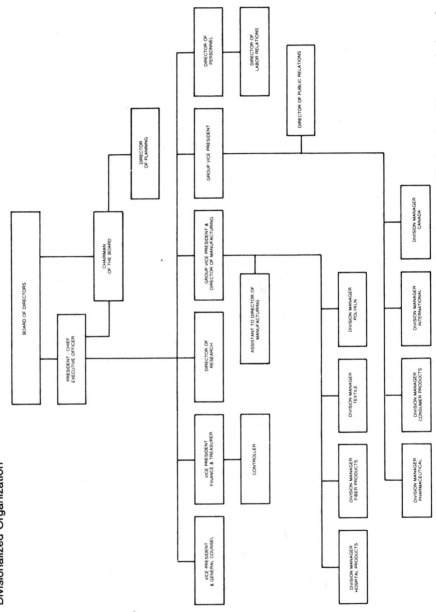

Source: A. R. Janger, *Corporate Organization Structures: Manufacturing,* © 1973. Reprinted by permission of

Figure 20.7 Evolution of an Organization Structure from Divisional to Functional—The Kendall Company 1970—Functional Organization

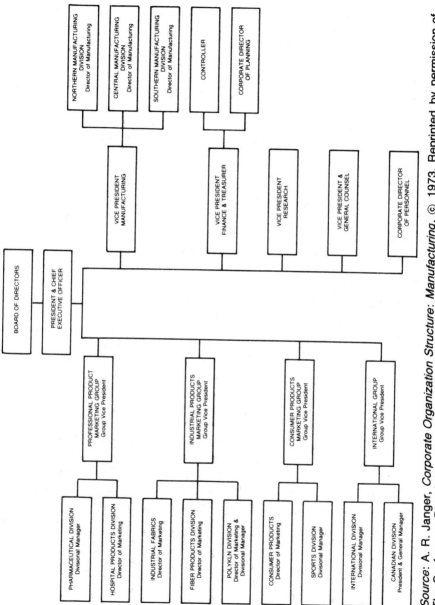

Source: A. R. Janger, *Corporate Organization Structure: Manufacturing,* © 1973. Reprinted by permission of The Conference Board, Inc., New York, NY.

Fourth, corporate managers, should exercise self constraints in issuing directives to divisional managers.

Sloan (1963), one of the foremost architects of the modern American corporation, addresses the significance of this last point by emphasizing the conscious need, on the part of the Chief Executive Officer, to restrain his personal involvement on divisional matters. This is not an easy task to do since the final accountability for corporate performance still resides on the chief executive's shoulders. However, no successful decentralization can be accomplished without relinquishing part of his authority to the divisional managers. This creates a definite imbalance of responsibility and authority at that level. Vancil (1978) labels this unresolved definition of responsibilities as a necessary "Managerial Ambiguity by Design," which is only resolved as a result of day-to-day personal interaction between the Chief Executive Officer and his divisional manager.

A final comment is worth making on the second criterion for successful decentralization stated above. By requiring some degree of interdependence among divisions, Solomons (1965) seems to cast some doubt on totally unrelated diversifications as a successful strategy to pursue. This statement encounters some support in Rumelt's findings (1974), who detects the highest level of performance in those organizations seeking related diversification strategies.

Matrix Organizations

Functional and divisional organizations are structured around *one* central design concept. Inputs (functions or specialties) are the molding principle in functional organizations, and outputs (products, programs, markets, and geographical locations) are the basic dimensions for divisional forms. This clear identification of a main guideline in the definition of a structure stems from the "unity of command" principle of classical writers, that ordinarily has been interpreted as the *one-boss* rule. Whenever a single focus is selected as the basis for organizational design, a single individual can be assigned responsibility for the management of an organizational unit in charge of performing that task. This leads to the one-boss concept. Matrix organizations are a fundamental departure from this unitary notion. They are structured around *two* or more central design concepts. A classical example of matrix organization is Dow Corning, reported by Goggins (1974), and illustrated in Figure 20.8, where the intersection of business units and functions determines the matrix responsibilities. Geographical locations and time dimensions are added components in the matrix structure of Dow Corning.

Under the matrix organizational form a person has *two (or more)* bosses. For example, an engineer belongs to both the engineering department and some well-defined project, and he must report simultaneously to the engineering manager and the corresponding project manager.

There is a large amount of inherent ambiguity in a matrix organization that may strike as counterproductive under a more traditional perspective. In fact, the implementation of a matrix structure requires properly designed managerial

Figure 20.8 Example of Matrix Organization—Dow Corning (1974)

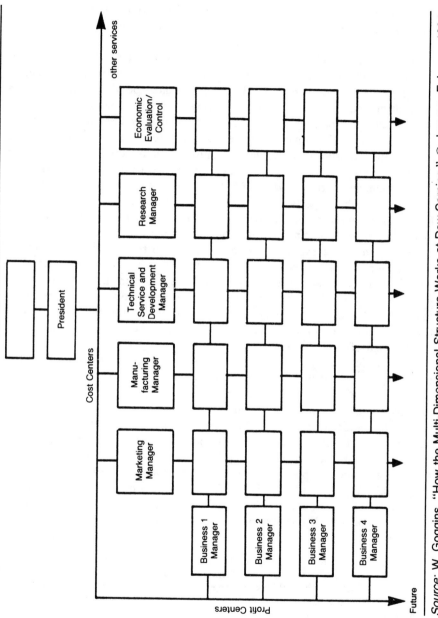

Source: W. Goggins, "How the Multi-Dimensional Structure Works at Dow-Corning," © January–February 1984, p. 56. Reprinted by permission of Harvard Business Review, Boston, Ma.

support systems, and people adequately sensitized to the matrix environment.

Galbraith and Nathanson (1978) identify some of the characteristics they judge important for successful development of a matrix climate: the adoption of a multi-dimensional profit reporting system consistent with the matrix design concepts; the establishment of a reward structure leaning toward total corporate profitability; the development of career paths based on multi-functional, multi-businesses, and multi-country experiences; and most importantly, a basic change in the role of the top executive. He must balance the views emerging from different dimensions, act in a more participative manner, develop a judgement for priorities, and be prepared to act as an arbiter in conflicting situations.

Goggins (1974), commenting about the matrix experience at Dow Corning, suggests the importance of complete communication and intelligent use of information as keys for matrix effectiveness. He also speaks of the establishment of an environment of trust and confidence to make the two-boss system work, and mentions the importance of having a set of managerial support systems, like: management by objectives, personnel reviews, planning processes, economic evaluation, profit reporting, and new business staging.

Despite the belief expressed by these authors in the possibility of a matrix organization to work effectively, serious doubts have been cast on its successful implementation. A natural tendency exists to depart from the two-boss conflict inherent in the ideal matrix. An argument can be made for the emergence of only one *real* boss, who is the one physically closer, controls the budget, assigns tasks, determines performance and rewards, and is central to the future career development of the subordinate.

An empirical study performed by Kahn, and others (1964) concludes that the ambiguity in the unit of command principle generates frustration, low productivity, and high absenteeism. Moreover, matrix organizations tend to generate multiple and conflicting loyalties, require people with high tolerance for ambiguity, create conflict of roles, confusion around the actual authority, difficulties with the reward system, and problems of power inversion (the subordinate may reject a demand from a boss, arguing instructions from "the other boss.")

A more balanced exposition about matrices is made in an Organization Planning Bulletin of General Electric (1976), that describes matrices not as a panacea but as a difficult organizational form that may be the unique solution to balance the management of a business between competing points of view: A matrix organization is not a

. . . bandwagon that we want you all to jump on, but rather that it's a complete, difficult, and sometimes frustrating form of organization to live with. It's also, however, a bellwether of things to come. But, when implemented well, it does offer much of the best of both worlds. And all of us are going to have to learn how to utilize organizations to prepare managers to increasingly deal with high levels of complexity and ambiguity in situations where they have to get results from people and components *not* under their direct control.

Davis and Lawrence (1977) define three preconditions that have to be met before the organization considers the matrix as a potential structural form.

Otherwise, there are alternative managerial systems that can reinforce more traditional organizational forms without having to resort to the full implementation of a matrix. Those preconditions are:

1. Outside pressure for dual focus.

   As already noted, the first necessary requirement for the development of a matrix organization is the coexistence of more than one fundamental focus of managerial concern.
2. Pressures for high information-processing capacity.

   A second necessary requirement for the adoption of a matrix organization is the existence of a need for processing massive amounts of information at key managerial levels. This need could result from: changing and unpredictable environmental demands, increased task complexity due to diversification of both products and markets, and strong interdependence among managers for the execution of a given task. The absorption of this voluminous information is facilitated through the intimate coordination assured by the two boss system.
3. Pressures for shared resources.

   The final necessary condition for developing a matrix organization occurs whenever great pressures for high efficiency force the sharing of critical resources; such as physical facilities, capital and human resources, and professional experience. The matrix organizations guarantee great efficiency in the utilization of these resources by sharing them among all products or projects, while maintaining a functional centralized control.

Furthermore, Davis and Lawrence suggest that a matrix does not result from the mere adoption of a matrix structure, but also requires the establishment of a *matrix system*, a *matrix culture*, and a *matrix behavior*.

The path from a traditional organization to this highly demanding matrix form is facilitated by a gradual implementation of the concept via integrating mechanisms of increased sophistication that enhance lateral relations. These mechanisms are discussed later in this chapter. Only a gradual approach to the complex and ambiguous operation of a matrix organization gives the people involved the time needed to adapt their behavior to the demands of this organizational form.

Hybrid Organization

The basic organizational forms presented previously are abstractions of a more complex reality. In general, the structure of organizations stems from more than one of these pure models, though the dominant pattern can be traced back to one of them. In fact, most divisional organizations have a number of functional specialties centralized at the corporate level.

Vancil (1978) sampled around 300 divisionalized corporations and reported the following percentages of firms having decentralized functions.

Administration	54%
R&D	64%
Manufacturing	70%
Distribution	79%
Sales	82%

He concluded from these empirical results that there is a stronger tendency to decentralization for functions closer to the final consumer.

The structure of United States Gypsum Company provided in Figure 20.9 illustrates a hybrid organization. There are three main product divisions: Construction Products, Industrial Products, and Specialty Products. There is an international division for all Mexico companies. Some functional activities are centralized under an Executive Vice President. Corporate Development, Administration, and Finance functions are at the corporate level.

Consequently, an organizational structure in a real case is usually a *hybrid* of the basic archetypes, and the challenge of organizational design is to seek a proper balance among these three alternatives to respond more effectively to the performance of the organizational tasks.

We have observed that most divisional organizations retain some centralized functions. Likewise, most large functional organizations tend to create an independent subsidiary or a divisional business operation to add autonomy to secondary segments of its businesses. Similarly, organizations often adopt partial matrix structures to link selected products with related functions.

Evolution of the Organizational Structure: The Case of the American Industrial Enterprise

The pioneer research in this area is due to Alfred Chandler, who published in 1962 his book *Strategy and Structure*. Chandler suggests that American industrial enterprises experience a developmental sequence along the following four phases:

> . . . the initial expansion and accumulation of resources; the rationalization of the use of resources; the expansion into new markets and lines to help assure the continuing full use of resources; and, finally, the development of a new structure to make possible continuing effective mobilization of resources to meet both changing short-term market demands and long-term market trends.*

In this evolutionary path there is a transition from a simple functional organization to a multidivisional form.

Galbraith and Nathanson (1978), building on the contributions of many authors, propose the evolutionary model presented in Figure 20.10. This model

---

* Alfred A. Chandler, Jr., *Strategy and Structure: Chapters in the History of the American Industrial Enterprise*, © 1962, p. 385. Reprinted by permission of The MIT Press, Cambridge, MA.

Figure 20.9 Example of a Hybrid Organization—United States Gypsum Company (1972)

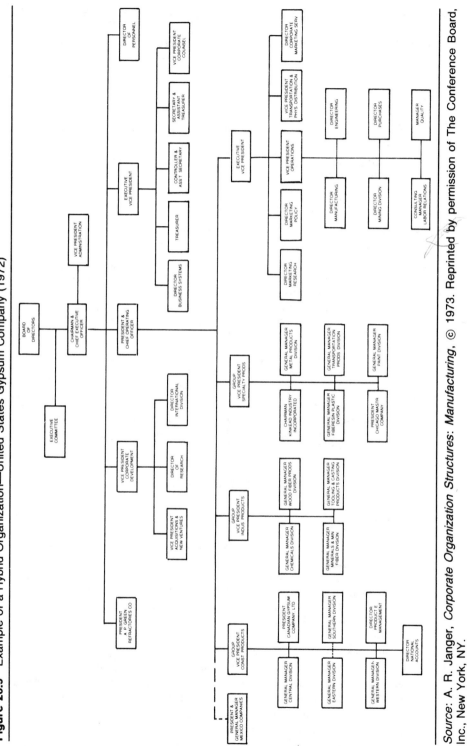

Source: A. R. Janger, *Corporate Organization Structures: Manufacturing*, © 1973. Reprinted by permission of The Conference Board, Inc., New York, NY.

Figure 20.10   An Evolutionary Model of the Organizational Structure

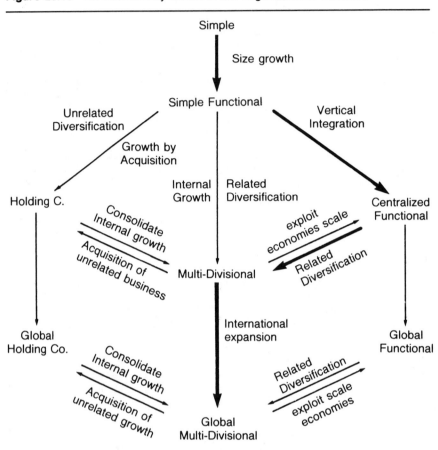

Strategies leading to a new structure

Dominant growth paths for U.S. firms: Chandler's Developmental reference

Source: Jay Galbraith and D. A. Nathanson, *Strategic Implementation*: *Role of Structure and Process*, © 1978, p. 115 or p. 69, or p. 118. Reprinted by permission of West Publishing Co., St. Paul, MN.

assumes that business firms can add any source of diversity to evolve into a new form (like new functions, new related markets, and new unrelated product lines), and that there is no set sequence through which firms must move in lock step. The route suggested by Chandler (indicated with darker lines in the figure) is the dominant but not unique path for U.S. firms.

The stages of this model are a consequence of the organizational growth. The first step moves the firm from a *simple* informal structure to a *simple functional* form, with a more extended division of labor. Then, there is a second layer of alternative stages that result from the expansion strategy chosen by the firm, once the pure growth in size reaches a plateau. The centralized functional form is achieved by a process of vertical integration that adds new functions and develops a solid functional foundation.

A second evolutionary path emerges when a simple functional firm adds new related products, or expands its geographical coverage. In this case, the firm grows into a *multidivisional organization*. If it adds unrelated product lines the firm becomes a *holding company*. These two organizational forms follow a divisional structure, but in the multidivisional firm the managerial processes stress their interdependence. As a consequence of this, the management of a multidivisional company tends to be centralized while in the holding company it is heavily decentralized.

Finally, each one of these types may be further expanded along an international dimension. This brings in a qualitative change in the operations of the organization. New fundamentally different cultural and institutional realities, that call for a special handling of international activities, need to be recognized. This is properly reflected in the definition of a *global functional*, a *global multidivisional*, and a *global holding* types, as direct extension of previously defined organization forms for an international setting.

The essential notion in this evolutionary map is Chandler's thesis that *structure follows strategy*. Briefly explained, the normal expansion of a firm's activities opens new alternatives for growth and diversification. The firm's structure has to match the strategy chosen; for example, related diversification goes with a multidivisional company, and unrelated diversification with a holding company. Chandler observes that the change in structure has followed the strategic change with some delay, due to an "overconcentration on operational activities by the executives responsible for the destiny of their enterprises, or from their inability, because of past training and education and present position, to develop an entrepreneurial outlook." The implementation of a new strategy in the framework of the old structure produces increasing inefficiencies and organizational tensions that eventually lead to the adoption of a new structure.

A BRIEF OVERVIEW OF ORGANIZATIONAL DESIGN THEORIES

Organizational design is not a field sufficiently developed to offer a mature set of theoretical principles, proved in practice, and applicable to a wide variety of situations. At least four important design theories have been proposed in the literature, and each one of them offers some valuable insights. They are: the *classical theory*, the *human relations theory*, the *decision-making theory*, and the *contingency theory*. This section presents an overview of these approaches to organizational design.

Our discussion of the various organizational theories will be brief. More detailed presentations can be found in many good texts on management and organization, such as: Dessler (1976), Galbraith (1977), Gannon (1977), Gibson, Ivancevich, and Donnelly (1976), Jackson and Morgan (1978), Mouzelis (1967), and Stoner (1978).

The Classical Theory

The central idea of the classical theory is that, regardless of the nature of the organization, there are certain universal principles that should be followed to obtain a successful performance. The most significant exponents of this theory are the *bureaucratic model* of Weber (1947), the *principles of management* of Fayol (1949), and the *scientific management* school of Taylor (1911). In Figures 20.11, 20.12, and 20.13 we summarize some of the most widely known ideas of the classical school of organization design. Without going into a detailed analysis of these ideas, it is important to stress that they have caused a long

Figure 20.11 Bureaucratic Model of Max Weber

An Ideal Organization Should Have the Following Characteristics:

1. A well defined hierarchy
2. Division of labor practiced along function specialties
3. A well defined system of rules outlining the rights and duties of subordinates and their officers
4. A set of well defined procedures and methods to perform the work
5. Impersonal relations
6. Employment and promotion decisions based on merit and competence.

Figure 20.12 Principles of Management of Henri Fayol

1. *Division of Labor*   to allow high levels of specialization
2. *Authority and Responsibility*   both should be equal for an individual manager
3. *Discipline*   resulting from good leadership, fair agreements, and judiciously enforced penalties
4. *Unity of Command*   each person has one and only one boss
5. *Unity of Direction*   activities with the same objective should be directed by only one manager
6. Subordination of the individual interest to the common good
7. *Remuneration*   based on fairness
8. *Centralization*   the proper balance between centralization and decentralization should be chosen
9. *Scalar Chain*   a clear and graded scale of authority from the top should exist
10. *Order*   materials and people should be in the right place at the right time
11. *Equity*   management should be both friendly and fair to their subordinates
12. *Stability*   high personnel turnover should be avoided
13. *Initiative*   should be stimulated
14. *Esprit de corps*   workers should have a sense of attachment to the organization

Figure 20.13 Principles of Scientific Management of Frederick Taylor

1. Develop a science for each element of an individual's work
2. Scientifically select, train, teach, and develop each worker
3. Closely cooperate with the worker to insure that the work is performed in accordance with the scientific principles
4. Assure an appropriate division of work and responsibility betweem labor and management

lasting impact, particularly among practicing managers. Many modern organizations still adhere strongly to principles such as equality of authority and responsibility, unity of command, limited span of control, and unity of direction. In fact, many managers still think that the classicist principles constitute the fundamental foundations in which a sound organizational structure should be based.

The most important critics of the classical theory are Merton (1957), Gouldner (1915), and Selznick (1953). Merton argues that the rules required for the bureaucratic organization make people ignore the actual objectives that these rules are supposed to advance. There is a loss of perspective that transforms the fulfillment of these rules in the final aims being sought. At the same time, decision making becomes routine, and no attention is paid to environmental changes and the need for strategic adaptation.

Gouldner points to a perverse behavior that induces conflict between chief and subordinate. Bureaucratic rules define minimum levels of acceptable behavior which are taken by employees as a standard which they do not need to exceed. Supervisors react against this undesirable behavior by imposing more stringent rules which increase the level of tension between them and their subordinates, and offer no guarantee that a behavior more coherent with the ends of the organization may be exacted from them. On the contrary, the process seems to convey more and more tension with increasingly complex and narrow rules being added each time.

Selznick finds that the units in a bureaucratic organization tend to develop their own goals which are not necessarily coincident with the goals of the organization.

All these critics contradict the a priori expectation of Weber that a bureaucratic organization is linked with superior performance.

The Human Relations Theory

Mainly as a reaction to the null role played by the individual in the classical design theories, the human relations school proposed that the performance of an organization depends *exclusively* on the human characteristics and behavior in an organizational setting. Important subjects are individual needs, motivation, perceptions, attitudes, values, leadership, informal group behavior, communications, and so forth. This approach is rooted in the now classical Hawthorne

Figure 20.14 A Contrast Between Classical and Participative Organization

Classical Design Organization

1. *Leadership process* includes no perceived confidence and trust. Subordinates do not feel free to discuss job problems with their superiors, who in turn do not solicit their ideas and opinions.
2. *Motivational process* taps only physical, security, and economic motives through the use of fear and sanctions. Unfavorable attitudes toward the organization prevail among the employees.
3. *Communication process* is such that information flows downward and tends to be distorted, inaccurate, and viewed with suspicion by subordinates.
4. *Interaction process* is closed and restricted; subordinates have little effect on departmental goals, methods, and activities.
5. *Decision process* occurs only at the top of the organization; it is relatively centralized.
6. *Goal-setting process* is located at the top of the organization, discourages group participation.
7. *Control process* is centralized and emphasizes fixing of blame for mistakes.
8. *Performance goals* are low and passively sought by managers who make no commitment to developing the human resources of the organization.

Participative Organization

1. *Leadership process* includes perceived confidence and trust between superiors and subordinates in all matters. Subordinates feel free to discuss job problems with their superiors, who in turn solicit their ideas and opinions.
2. *Motivational process* taps a full range of motives through participatory methods. Attitudes are favorable toward the organization and its goals.
3. *Communication process* is such that information flows freely throughout the organization—upward, downward, and laterally. The information is accurate and undistorted.
4. *Interaction process* is open and extensive; both superiors and subordinates are able to affect departmental goals, methods, and activities.
5. *Decision process* occurs at all levels through group process; it is relatively decentralized.
6. *Goal-setting process* encourages group participation in setting high, realistic objectives.
7. *Control process* is dispersed throughout the organization and emphasizes self-control and problem solving.
8. *Performance goals* are high and actively sought by superiors, who recognize the necessity for making a full commitment to developing, through training, the human resources of the organization.

Adapted from R. Likert, *The Human Organization* (New York: McGraw-Hill Book Co., 1967), pp. 197–211.

studies (Mayo 1933, Roethlisberger and Dickson 1939), but it is better expressed for organizational purposes in the work of Likert (1961, 1967). He recognizes four organizational types in the continuum from "classical" to "human" organizations, that he labels System 1, or Exploitive Authoritative; System 2, or Benevolent Authoritative; System 3, or Consultative; and System 4, or Participative. Figure 20.14 contrasts the main characteristics of Systems 1 and 4. Likert concludes from his study that the maximum performance is attained by means of a System 4 or participative structure. Also, he suggests a practical way to attain this kind of structure which rests in the notion of the *linking pin*. In Figure 20.15, each working group is represented by a triangular structure, whose working style is totally participative, and each dot (the linking pin) represents a person who acts as transmitter and coordinates between two horizontally or vertically adjacent groups.

The Organizational Design-Making Theory

The most valid commentaries on the propositions of the human relations school come from the organizational decision-making theories (Simon 1976, March and Simon 1958, Cyert and March 1963). They claim that individual behavior must be analyzed within the decision making framework provided by the organi-

Figure 20.15 A Model for a "Human Organization"

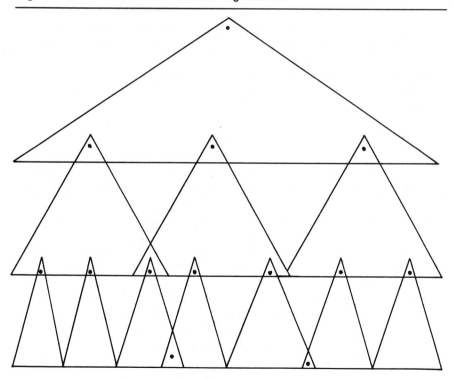

zation in the rational pursuit of its objectives. Mouzelis (1967) suggests that "division of labor; standard procedures, authority, communications, and training are important organizational features setting limits to and shaping the decisional environment of the individual." Under this perspective, the organizational structure is seen as a set of decision making units in a communication network, and the emphasis is on the actual decision making process, the resolution of conflict, the coordination among units, and the information flow. Cyert and March propose four basic principles of decision making which are: quasi resolution of conflict, uncertainty avoidance, problemistic search, and organizational learning. The *quasi resolution of conflict* suggests that the different coalitions in an organization have conflicting goals, and for the organization to operate it does not have to resolve those conflicts. "Most organizations, most of the time exist and thrive with considerable latent conflict of goals. Except at the level of nonoperational objectives, there is no internal consensus. The procedures for *resolving* such conflicts do not reduce all goals to a common dimension or even make them obviously internally consistent."

To deal with their uncertain environment, organizations use an *uncertainty avoidance* strategy. Either they develop fast reactive strategies to manage unexpected situations, or they arrange a negotiated environment to exert some control over unplanned events.

Problemistic search means that organizations direct their search effort toward the solution of a very specific problem (search is motivated). Also, this search uses preferably simple models (search is simple minded). Finally, the search is conducted from the organizational perspective of the environment (search is biased).

Organizational learning assumes that organizations exhibit an adaptive behavior through time. Figure 20.16 gives a condensed view of the organizational decision-making process as proposed by Cyert and March.

The Contingency Theory

The contingency theory approach also reacts against the extreme positions of both the classical and human relations schools, and advances a more intuitively appealing conclusion which integrates those two opposing views: the best organizational design is contingent upon the environmental conditions that the organization faces. There are situations in which a more formal organization performs better, and others in which a more participate one is more appropriate. The most important empirical works that lead towards a contingency approach are now briefly discussed.

Burns and Stalker (1961 define the *mechanistic* and *organic* forms of organization which roughly correspond to the formal organization of classical theory and to the informal-participative form of the human relations school (see Figure 20.17). They conclude, from an empirical study, that the mechanistic structure seems to perform better under a relatively stable environment, while the organic structure appears to be superior in a turbulent one. The conditioning of the

Figure 20.16   Organization Decision Process in Abstract Form Proposed by Cyert and March

Quasi-resolution of conflict	Uncertainty avoidance	Problemistic search	Organizational learning
Goals as independent constraints. Local rationality. Acceptable-level decision rules. Sequential attention to goals	Feedback-react decision procedures. Negotiated environment	Motivated search. Simple-minded search Bias in search	Adaptation of goals. Adaptation in attention rules. Adaptation in search rules

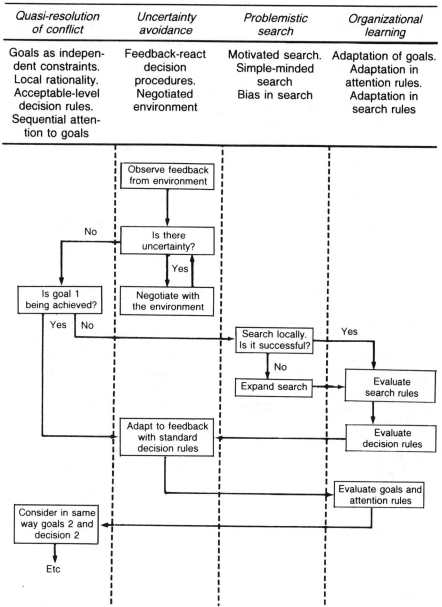

Figure 20.17   Characteristics of Organic and Mechanistic Organizations

Characteristics of Structure	Mechanistic Organizations	Organic Organizations
1. Division of labor	Functional specialization for departmentation by function	Job enlargement and job enrichment
2. Hierarchy of authority	Clearly defined and centralized	Decentralized and participative
3. Jobs and procedures	Formal and standardized	Flexible
4. Behavioral processes		
a. Motivation	Primarily economic	Both economic and non-economic
b. Leadership style	Authoritarian	Democratic
c. Group relations	Formal and impersonal	Informal and personal
d. Communication	Vertical and directive	Vertical and lateral consultative

Source: M. J. Gannon, *Management: An Organizational Perspective*, © 1977, p. 89. Reprinted by permission of Little, Brown and Company, Boston, MA.

organizational structure to the environmental situation becomes the basis for the contingency approach to organizational design.

Joan Woodward (1965) tries to determine if some specific structural characteristics could be associated with superior performance in a population of about 100 manufacturing firms. Her conclusion is that some consistent structural pattern seems to emerge only when firms of similar technology are associated together. She distinguishes three basic technologies: unit (job-order, batch, and non-repetitive processing), mass-production (assembly lines and highly labor intensive), and process or automated (continuous flow and highly capital intensive). The median structural parameters found in Woodward's study are summarized in Figure 20.18. The most successful firms in each group have parameters close to the median. Also they are more "organic" for unit and process technologies. Though some doubts have been raised on the general validity of Woodward's findings, there is certain consensus on the conclusion that, in high performing firms, the organizational structure is somewhat affected by technology.

Figure 20.18   The Relationships Between Certain Organizational Characteristics and Technology

	Job Order	Mass Production	Process Manufacturing
Median levels of management	3	4	6
Median executive span of control	4	7	10
Median supervisory span of control	23	48	15
Median direct to indirect labor ratio	9:1	4:1	1:1
Median industrial to staff worker ratio	8:1	5.5:1	2:1

Source: Rensis Likert, *The Human Organization*, © 1967, p. 50. Reprinted by permission of McGraw-Hill Book Company, New York, NY.

As we have commented earlier in this chapter, Chandler's work (1962) looks at organizations from an historical point of view. He observes that the major strategic shifts of manufacturing firms in this century may be typified as volume expansion, geographic dispersion, vertical integration, and product differentiation. The important conclusion in his work is that to be effective a firm has to adapt its structure to follow the strategy or mission of the organization. This process involves the creation of new functions, new administrative needs, new local focus, and an added requirement for coordination of the variety of units generated in the growth process.

Lawrence and Lorsch's study (1967) provides a consolidation of all emerging contingency notions in the concepts of *differentiation* and *integration*. It is one of the most important modern works in organizational design and provides the most widely accepted platform for the analysis of this problem.

As indicated before, organizations are based on the subdivision of a complex endeavor into simpler tasks. Only when a complex objective can be expressed in terms of simpler goals, the joint effort of a multitude of people can lead to the pursuit of a common aim. The division of work, effort, responsibility, and authority is translated by the *segmentation* of the organizational structure into a set of units ordered in a hierarchical tree.

Lawrence and Lorsch observe that

> . . . the act of segmenting the organization into departments would influence the behavior of organizational members in several ways. The members of each unit would become specialists in dealing with the particular tasks. Both because of their prior education and experience and because of the nature of their task, they would develop specialized working styles and mental processes.

This is the concept of *differentiation* that they formally define as "the difference in cognitive and emotional orientation among managers in different functional departments." The empirical measurement of the degree of differentiation is done in four dimensions:

—managers' orientation toward particular goals—difference in the goals among units
—managers' orientation toward time—long versus short term
—managers' interpersonal orientation—formal-hierarchical versus informal-participative
—variation in the formality of the structure—hierarchical levels, reward system, and control system.

The tendency of units in the organization to develop specialized behavior to deal with their particular subenvironment poses a strain in the final achievement of common organizational objectives. "The members of each department develop different interests and differing points of views, [and] they often find it difficult to reach agreement on integrated programs of action." Lawrence and Lorsch define *integration* as: ". . . the quality of the state of collaboration that exists among departments that are required to achieve unity of effort by the demands of the environment."

Classical integrating mechanisms are the hierarchy, standard rules and procedures, and planning and information systems. But the demands posed by the complexity of the modern environment call for enhanced possibilities of coordination and interactions. This is achieved through *lateral relations*, which may be implemented at very different levels of intensity. The lateral integrating mechanisms, in order of increasing complexity, are listed by Galbraith (1973):

—Direct informal contacts among managers in lateral positions.

—Creation of a liaison role between two independent groups: A person plays a liaison role in an organization whenever the interests of his official unit make advisable a long lasting participation in another unit of the organization. For example, the person that the marketing department assigns as its representative in the development of an information system is in a liaison role. An ambiguity emerges in this case, because he is hierarchically subordinated to the marketing manager, but he spends most of his efforts with the management information system group.

—Creation of a task force: A task force is formed by a group of people belonging to different units of the organization, having a temporary assignment, with a specific objective and time table. Again, a hierarchical ambiguity emerges, since each one of the task force members are subordinated both to their respective group heads, and to the task force head.

—Use of permanent coordinating teams: The most common form of a permanent coordinating team used by organizations is the committee. The only difference with the task force is that committees are permanent while task forces are temporary. The central problem in structuring a committee is the selection of its leader.

—Creation of a temporary coordinating manager: When activities cut across functional or divisional units of the organization, a temporary manager is often designated to fill a coordinating role. A major government order that is overrun, or a specific investment project that needs cross-functional attention, might call for the assignment of an individual whose primary role is to coordinate the tasks that are needed for a successful completion of that order or project. The temporary coordinating manager normally does not have any formal authority. He has to act either by persuasion, pressure, or by whatever authority has been informally delegated to him by the person responsible for his assignment.

—Creation of a permanent coordinating manager: When a project or product focus needs a constant coordinating attention, a permanent integrating manager role might be required. In this case, the only additional source of authority that this manager might enjoy, with regard to his temporary counterpart, is partial or total control over the project or product budget. It is clear, however, that his responsibility greatly exceeds his formal authority.

—Establishment of the matrix organization form: The most extreme form of forced coordination is the acceptance of a plurality of managerial responsibilities, characteristic of the matrix system.

The Lawrence and Lorsch study shows that the performance of a firm goes up when the level of differentiation and integration are responsive to changes in the environment. Figure 20.19 provides a comparison of the different integrative mechanisms used by successful firms in the plastics, food, and container industries. The turbulence in the environment is measured by the percent of products introduced in the last ten years. It may be observed that the integrating devices and integrating managers in these firms increases with the change in the environment.

Another significant result reported by Lorsch and Allen (1973) shows the major integrating devices used by four conglomerate firms (see Figure 20.20). It is of no surprise to find direct managerial contacts and coordinating group vice presidents high on the list of important coordinating mechanisms. Additional integrating devices used by all firms are the budgeting system (which coordinates tactical programs), approval for major capital investments (which coordinate strategic implementation actions), and incentive compensation systems (which provide a common ground for managerial motivation).

The ordered application of segmentation, differentiation, and integration provides a formal mechanism to support the strategy of a firm with a harmonious structural framework. Failing to develop the appropriate structure will have a negative impact on the development of the firm's strategy.

STEPS IN THE DESIGN OF THE ORGANIZATIONAL STRUCTURE

The basic principle for organizational design is that structure follows strategy. Under this premise, organizational design must be viewed as an integral part of the strategic positioning of the firm. The selected structure should facilitate the development and implementation of the long-term directions of the businesses of the organization. Certainly, the structure should also permit the efficient execution of short term operational tasks. Finally, the organizational structure

Figure 20.19 Comparison of Lateral Relations Used by Most Successful Firms in Three Different Industries

	Plastics	Food	Container
% New products in last 20 years	35%	15%	0%
Integrating devices	Rules Hierarchy Goal setting Direct contact Teams at 3 levels Integrating Depts.	Rules Hierarchy Goal setting Direct contact Task forces Integrators	Rules Hierarchy Goal setting Direct contact
% Integrators-managers	22%	17%	0%

Source: Jay Galbraith, *Designing Complex Organizations*, © 1973, p. 111. Reprinted by permission of Addison-Wesley Publishing Co., Reading, MA.

Figure 20.20　Major Integrative Devices in Four Conglomerate Firms

	Firm 1	Firm 2	Firm 3	Firm 4
PAPER SYSTEMS				
Five-year planning system	X*	X	X*	X
Annual budgeting system	X*	X*	X*	X*
Quarterly budget forecast			X*	
Monthly budget review	X	X*	X*	X*
Monthly operating reports	X*			
Approval system for major capital and expense items	X*	X*	X*	X*
Cash management system	X	X	X*	X
Formal goal-setting system performance evaluation and incentive compensation system	X*	X*	X*	X*
Approval system for hiring, replacement, and salary changes of key division personnel	X*			
INTEGRATIVE POSITIONS				
Group vice presidents	X*	X*	X*	X*
Divisional "specialists" in corporate controller's office				X
COMMITTEES, TASK FORCES, AND FORMAL MEETINGS				
Annual meetings between corporate and division general managers	X	X		
Group management committees	X			X*
Technical evaluation board for capital projects				X*
Permanent cross-divisional committees			X	
Line management task forces				X*
Ad hoc cross-divisional meetings for functional managers	X	X		
DIRECT MANAGERIAL CONTACT	X*	X*	X*	X*

X indicates presence of devices in each firm.
* indicates those devices that managers believed play the most significant role in corporate-divisional relations.
Source: Jay Lorsch and Stephen A. Allen, *Managing Diversity and Interdependence.* Boston: Division of Research, Harvard Business School, 1973, p. 59. Reprinted by permission.

should be regarded as the hub which facilitates the linkage between all the administrative processes seeking strategic and operational effectiveness. This subject is the central topic of Chapter 5.

The main strategic decisions are the selection of the portfolio of businesses of the firm, and the long term development of each individual business. Therefore, an organizational structure should facilitate the allocation of resources among its various businesses, support the implementation of the preferred strategy for each individual business, and permit the adaptation of existing businesses to a changing environment.

Two distinct steps should be recognized in the organizational design process. The first step is the definition of a *basic organizational structure*. This basic structure represents the major segmentation of the businesses the firm is engaged in through a hierarchical order which reveals the priorities managers assign to the firm's central activities. Only the primary echelons of the organizational chart, which are untimately linked to the strategic positioning of the firm, are recognized in this step.

A second step in the organizational design process is the definition of a *detailed organizational structure*. At this stage, the basic organizational structure is fleshed out with the numerous specific details that pertain to the operational domain of the firm.

Normally, a number of basic alternatives might emerge as competitors for a final design, each one originating different combinations at the detail level. The process of selecting a final structure implies a soul searching effort, of a fairly subjective nature, where key top executives engage in a time consuming activity of proposing, defining, testing, and selecting alternative configurations.

The design of an organizational structure is completed with the specification of a *balance* between the organizational structure chosen and the managerial processes that go with it: planning, management control, communication and information, and evaluation and reward.

The steps in the organizational design process are now more extensively discussed. The application of these steps to a real case study is presented in Chapter 21.

Design of a Basic Organizational Structure

The fundamental objective of this step is to translate the strategic positioning of the firm in terms of a set of distinctive units ordered in the highest hierarchical levels of the organizational structure. Since the focus of strategy is business development, this step requires the full recognition of the businesses the firm is engaged in, and its further segmentation into manageable units.

A simple way to begin the search for business segmentation is to prepare a list of the *critical dimensions* for the business activities. Normally, this list includes:

—Products
—Markets: Industrial, Commercial, Government, OEM, and so forth
—Functions: Production, Sales, Marketing, Finance, Administration, Personnel, R&D, Engineering, and so forth
—Technologies
—Geographic Locations: of markets and production and distribution facilities.

A business segment is composed of an orderly assignment of some or all of the above dimensions. A relatively independent business encompasses a combination of products, markets, and some autonomous capacity for product change.

Some companies decide to organize its basic structure in accordance with its primary businesses segmentation. This is normally the case in divisionalized firms, where each division has production and marketing responsibilities, as well as some decentralized functional support. Under these conditions, there is a clear alignment between the strategic and operational objectives of the organization.

However, a basic segmentation following business categories is not always desirable or possible. A company might choose a functional focus as the primary dimension for its basic structure. This selection reflects operational efficiency and technical excellence as the fundamental concern for organizational design. Similarly, market location as a primary dimension stresses the importance of a good customer service; and the choice of clients or markets attempts to emphasize the need for a special coverage of a market segment.

In any event, this step of the organizational design process calls for a hierarchical recognition of the critical dimensions identified above, with the purpose of obtaining a focus for the basic segmentation. Unfortunately, rarely the basic structure can be simply expressed in terms of a unique dimension. In the process of designing this structure, managers are confronted with a complex choice among competing focuses that must be subjected to a thoughtful tradeoff. A careful weighing of the advantages and disadvantages will most likely lead to a primary structure which is not homogeneous.

For example, in Figure 20.21, some primary units correspond to products, some to functions, some to clients, and some to geographical regions (international versus domestic focus).

The absence of a homogeneous criterion of segmentation and the lack of symmetry are not the exception but the rule in the formulation of a basic organizational structure. More than one organizational level is usually required to capture the implications of the choice made by managers. One could say that it is possible "to read" the strategy of the organization from the arrangement of its basic structure.

A good example to illustrate this point is provided by the du Pont organization in 1956 depicted in Figure 20.22. Notice that there are four major dimensions exhibited in that chart: functions (manufacturing, controller, industrial relations, sales, and research), products (nylon, orlon, dacron, and rayon), markets (home furnishing, industrial markets, mens wear, and womens wear), and geographical areas (regions I, II, III, and IV). It is clear from the organizational chart that a first priority is assigned to the functional concern, with products receiving a secondary priority, while marketing and regional coverage are assigned a third priority.

When a corporation decides not to organize in accordance with its business segments, a special effort should be made to provide a managerial focus superimposed upon the basic organization structure. A most notorious example of this kind of situation is given by the basic structure of Texas Instruments in the late 1970s shown in Figure 20.23.

Figure 20.21 Example Showing the Multiplicity of Criteria Used in the Definition of a Strategic Focus

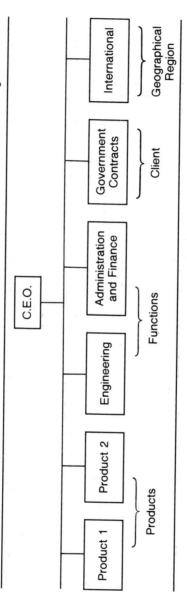

Figure 20.22 du Pont Fibers Organization (1956)

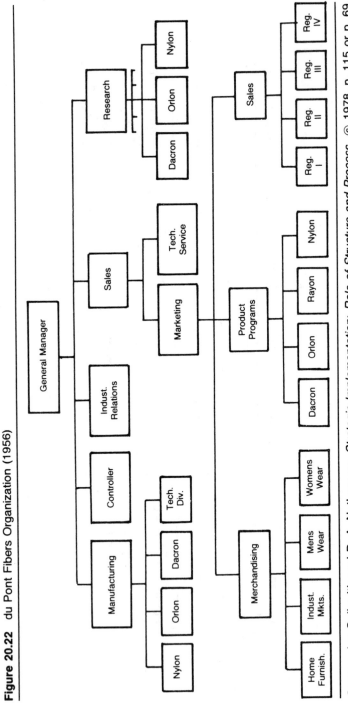

Source: Jay Galbraith and D. A. Nathanson, *Strategic Implementation: Role of Structure and Process*, © 1978, p. 115 or p. 69, or p. 118. Reprinted by permission of West Publishing Co., St. Paul, MN.

Figure 20.23 The Basic Organizational Structure at Texas Instruments

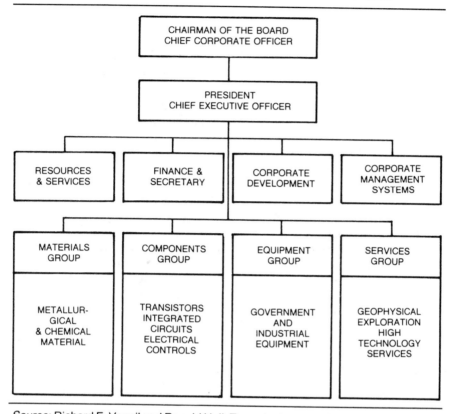

Source: Richard F. Vancil and Ronald Hall, Texas Instruments Incorporated: Management Systems, 1972. Boston: Harvard Business School, case 9–172–054, Exhibit 2, page 14. Reprinted by permission.

The four major groups were both suppliers and customers of each other. This required a high degree of operational coordination at the highest hierarchical level, which was accomplished through a great deal of committee activity. However, the resulting lack of autonomy among the groups was more than compensated for by the ability of the organization to quickly transfer any technological improvement in either materials, components, or subassemblies to all the relevant product lines. This allowed Texas Instruments to have an extraordinary capacity to compete successfully in products in which they had not been the initial innovators, such as electronic calculators. The organizational structure suggested that the primary strategic focus of TI was not restricted to a narrowly defined set of products, but its concern was rather with the effective use of a common technological base to manufacture and market products characterized by a very short life-cycle.

The TI structure was further broken down into divisions and departments, these being organized as profit centers. In order to achieve a strategic focus within that basic structure, an interesting matrix was established by crossing operational line responsibilities and strategic action programs (see Figure 20.24). Within this setting, the strategic responsibilities are formulated in terms of objectives, strategies, and tactics (OST). Each broad strategic objective is supported by a number of strategies specifically conceived to guarantee that this objective is achieved. In turn, each strategy is expressed in more concrete terms as a set of well defined tactical programs. The responsibility for the correct execution of a tactical program is given to a Department Head. In the example of Figure 20.24, tactical program 4 has been assigned to the Head of Department 2. The responsibility for a specific strategy may fall at departmental, divisional, or group level, depending on the tactics that go with that strategy. If the responsibilities for those tactics fall with a unique Department Head, he is made accountable for the strategy in question. For example, in Figure 20.24, tactics 1, 2, and 3 have been assigned to Department 1; therefore, the head of that department is responsible also for strategy 1. Similarly, we can see that the Head of Division 1 is made accountable for strategy 2, because he is the lowest level with full control over the tactics that accompany that strategy. It is important to emphasize in this example that a matrix form of organization can result not only as the traditional intersection between products and functions, but also as the crossing of strategic and operational responsibilities.

The definition of a basic structure is the central point in the organizational

Figure 20.24 A Matrix Structure Linking Operational and Strategic Responsibilities

Operational Responsibilities / Strategic Responsibilities			Group A					
			Division 1			Division 2		
			Dept. 1	Dept. 2	Dept. 3	Dept. 4	Dept. 5	Dept. 6
Objective 1	Strategy 1	Tactical Program 1	X					
		Tactical Program 2	X					
		Tactical Program 3	X					
	Strategy 2	Tactical Program 4		X				
		Tactical Program 5	X					
		Tactical Program 6			X			

design process, because it provides the frame in which the organization is going to develop its strategic and operational activities. In other words, the performance of the organization is largely determined by the choice of a basic structure.

Most likely, at the end of this step the managerial team will not be able to make a final selection. More than one basic segmentation may fit well with the needs of the firm under the premises of this broad analysis. Consequently, the result from this initial effort may be more than one basic organizational structure, whose characteristics need to be further analyzed to come out with a final decision.

In Chapter 5 we comment on the coordinating mechanisms available when the business segmentation does not coincide with the basic organizational segmentation of the firm.

Detailed Organizational Design

The objective sought in the detailed organizational design phase is two-fold: to identify all the operational tasks the organization should undertake in the pursuit of its daily activities, and to assign those tasks to the major organizational segments identified in the basic structure previously defined. The basic structure brings the selected strategy into the design process, while the detailed analysis comes to recognize the operational centralized functional activity (such as marketing or distribution), and the presence of a local demand at the divisional level might call for a functional liaison individual reporting to the centralized functional manager, but subordinated to the divisional manager.

Many questions surge naturally from people familiar with the organization to test the responsiveness of its structure against a multitude of situations that are important to consider. For example, one might ask how a request from an individual customer located in a remote area for a specific product or service would be handled under the proposed structure. If, when answering that question, one detects ambiguities, lack of efficiency, or undesirable splitting of responsibilities, some structural overhauling would have to be performed.

More specifically, some questions to be addressed are:
If the organization is mainly functional,

—How to insure that products are given their share of attention? Are integrating managers necessary in the role of product directors?
—Should the marketing function be subdivided by product? by client? by region? Should sales be centralized or regionalized?
—How should the production function be subdivided? by plants? by production stages? by products? by geographical regions?
—How R&D is going to interact with engineering, production, and marketing functions?
—How would distribution be responsible to local requests for delivery of products manufactured in several plants?
—How to provide an effective training ground for general managers? How to evaluate managerial performance in a strategic mode?

—If the firm engages in a strategy of growth via acquisition, how to integrate the newly acquired firms into the functional structure?

—If the firm expands its business to cover international markets, how to deal with the different business needs in each country?

—What integrative mechanisms should be placed to coordinate functional activities at a level other than that of the Chief Executive Officer (CEO)?

—How to prevent an overloaded CEO principally concerned with operational matters?

—How to prevent excessive "parochialism" among functional managers?

If the organization is mainly divisionalized around product lines,

—Which functions should be centralized and which decentralized?

—For centralized functions, should they report to the CEO or to a lower hierarchical level?

—If plants, distribution facilities, warehouses, and resources in general, are shared by more than one product line, who is in charge of them? How to insure that each division obtains a fair treatment?

—How to deal with regional affairs?

—Are there special clients that require preferential attention? How to handle these situations?

—For decentralized functions, how to assure the presentation of economies of scale and operational efficiency?

—Should divisionalization be conducted by major product lines, by geographical areas, by type of technology?

—How to deal with international activities?

—How much autonomy each division should have, both in operational and strategic modes? What coordination mechanisms should be enforced among divisions?

Along the more detailed analysis performed for each one of the alternative structural designs, some of the options will be discarded from further consideration, because of undesirable characteristics surfaced by this more careful inquiry. In the end, only two or three alternatives should be competing. For the final selection, the detailed analysis performed in this step provides a visceral understanding of the strategic and operational implications for each design under scrutiny.

Balance between Organizational Structure and Managerial Processes

The positioning of units and subunits of the organization in an ordered hierarchical network must be completed with the definition of all complementary managerial systems. The full fledged operations of these systems provide a background of integrative relationships that the simple organizational structure fails to represent. Moreover, these systems must be designed both to reinforce the primary focus chosen by the organization, and to support those activities relegated to a secondary level in the definition of the organizational structure. For example, a planning system in a functional organization must be specially sharp in the definition of strategic business units, because the primary structure does not give sufficient weight to the identification of businesses the firm is engaged in, and this may weaken the long term strategic positioning of the firm. On the other hand, the segments defined in divisional organizations are more long-term oriented, but the operational efficiency is enhanced by giving ample autonomy to the divisional manager and by linking his rewards with the divisional performance. In this way, some balance and some alignment is established between the long and short term concerns.

Galbraith and Nathanson (1978) provide a complete description of the characteristics that all managerial systems are supposed to have for some of the organization types they define: simple functional, centralized functional, multidivisional, holding, and global multidivisional (see Figure 20.25). The point to notice is that the need exists to adjust the characteristics given to the structure and the managerial processes.

A similar point has been made by firms like the Boston Consulting Group and Arthur D. Little. They suggest that the characteristics of a business are largely dictated by life-cycle considerations. The most natural strategies are: promotion in the introductory phase, investment in the growth phase, milking in the maturity phase, and harvest for withdrawal in the decay phase. The notion is that a different strategy is needed for each stage in the life-cycle; and, consequently, a special organizational structure, managerial style, and set of skills are required to manage a business through its economic life. Figure 20.26 presents what Arthur D. Little (1974) suggests is a balanced set of requirements in each stage of the product life.

To conclude, we can say that the design of all managerial support systems, the actual selection of a managerial leadership, and the degree of formality in each organizational unit must be *fitted* to the basic and detailed structures selected, and to the strategic and operational considerations that suggested that organizational structure in the first place.

SYMPTOMS OF AN INADEQUATE ORGANIZATIONAL STRUCTURE

As shown in this chapter, the organizational structure is a framework with two primary roles: support the full fledged implementation of strategic programs, and permit the normal conduction of the firm's operating activities.

External and internal changes call for a continuous adjustment of the organizational structure, in order to insure an optimum handling of strategic and operating activities. However, practice has shown that despite these adjustments

Figure 20.25 Managerial Characteristics of Each Type of Organization Structure

TYPE CHARACTERISTIC	(S) Simple	(F) Functional	(H) Holding	(M) Multi-Divisional	(G) Global—(M)
Strategy	Single Product	Single Product and Vertical integration	Growth by Acquisition unrelated diversity	Related diversity of product lines—internal growth some acqusition	Multiple products in multiple countries
Inter-unit and Market Relations					
Organization Structure	Simple functional	Central functional	Decentralized Profit Centers around product divisions Small Headquarters	Decentralized Product or area division profit centers	Decentralized profit centers around World wide product or area divisions
Research and Development	Not institutionalized Random search	Increasingly institutionalized around product and process improvements	Institutionalized search for new products and improvements—Decentralized to divisions	Institutionalized search for new products and improvements—Centralized guidance	Institutionalized search for new products which is centralized and decentralized in centers of expertise
Performance Measurement	By personal contact subjective	Increasingly impersonal based on cost productivity but still subjective	Impersonal based on return on investment and profitability	Impersonal based on return on investment profitability with some subjective contribution to whole	Impersonal with multiple goals like ROI, profit tailored to product and country
Rewards	Unsystematic paternal based on loyalty	Increasingly related to performance around productivity and volume	Formula based bonus on ROI or profitability Equity rewards	Bonus based on profit performance but more subjective than holding—Cash rewards	Bonus based on multiple planned goals More discretion Cash rewards
Careers	Single function specialist	Functional specialists with some generalist interfunctional moves	Cross function but intra-divisional	Cross function inter-divisional and corporate-divisional moves	Interdivisional Intersubsidiary Subsidiary/Corporate moves
Leader Style and Control	Personal Control of strategic and operating decisions by top management	Top control of Strategic decisions Some delegation of operations three plans procedures	Almost complete delegation of operations and strategy within existing businesses indirect control three results and selection of management and capital funding	Delegation of operations with indirect control three results Some decentralization of strategy within existing business	Delegation of operations with indirect control three results according to plan Some delegation of strategy within countries and existing businesses Some political delegation
Strategic Choices	Need of owner vs. needs of firm	Degree of integration Market share Breadth of Product line	Degree of diversity Types of business Acqusition targets Entry and Exit from businesses	Allocation of resources by business Exit and Entry from businesses Rate of Growth	Allocation of resources across businesses and countries Exit and entry into businesses and countries Degree of ownership and type of country involvement

Reprinted by permission of G. D. Searle & Company, Skokie, IL.

Figure 20.26 Managerial Characteristics by Stage of Product-Life Cycle

Management Activity or Function	Embryonic Industry	Growth Industry	Mature Industry	Aging Industry
Managerial Role	Entrepreneur	Sophisticated market manager	Critical administrator	"Opportunistic milker"
Planning Time Frame	Long enough to draw tentative life cycle (10)	Long-range investment payout (7)	Intermediate (3)	Short-range (1)
Planning Content	By product/customer	By product and program	By product/market/function	By plant
Planning Style	Flexible	Less flexible	Fixed	Fixed
Organization Structure	Free-form or task force	Semi-permanent task force, product or market division	Business division plus task force for renewal	Pared-down division
Managerial Compensation	High variable/low fixed, fluctuating with performance	Balanced variable and fixed, individual and group rewards	Low variable-high fixed group rewards	Fixed only
Policies	Few	More	Many	Many
Procedures	None	Few	Many	Many
Communication System	Informal/tailor-made	Formal/tailor-made	Formal/uniform	Little or none, by direction
Managerial Style	Participation	Leadership	Guidance/loyalty	Loyalty
Content of Reporting System	Qualitative, marketing, unwritten	Qualitative and quantitative, early warning system, all functions	Quantitative, written, production oriented	Numerical, oriented to written balance sheet
Measures Used	Few/fixed	Multiple/adjustable	Multiple/adjustable	Few/fixed
Frequency of Measuring	Often	Relatively often	Traditionally periodic	Less often
Detail of Measurement	Less	More	Great	Less
Corporate Departmental Emphasis	Market research; new product development	Operations research; organization development	Value analysis / Data processing / Taxes and insurance	Purchasing

Source: Arthur D. Little, Inc., *A System for Managing Diversity,* © 1974. Reprinted by permission of Arthur D. Little, Inc., Cambridge, MA.

organizations need, from time to time, a more comprehensive overhaul. As a structure grows older, it usually lacks the flexibility to accommodate new strategic and operational demands. The managerial team should maintain an eye on signs of stress that evidence an inadequate structure, because keeping it longer than necessary may impair the normal growth and development of a firm.

Some of the most common symptoms that can be traced back to an inadequate organizational structure are:

1. Lack of opportunities for general manager development: That is usually the case of functionally oriented organizations.
2. Insufficient time devoted to strategic thinking due to: Too much concentration on operational issues; excessive decision making at the top; or overworked key personnel.
3. Intensive antagonistic working climate: The motivational and reward system should be in tune with the given structure. An antagonistic climate may be signaling a problem of balance between structure and processes.
4. Lack of definition in portfolio business planning, neglect of special markets, and inappropriate setting for maximizing growth and profit. These are among the clearest evidence of an organizational structure which cannot accommodate the new strategic positioning of the firm.
5. Lack of coordination among divisions: This points to a failure of integrating mechanisms.
6. Excessive duplication of functions in different units of the firm: The differentiation among units is not well established. Some redefinition of tasks or the fusion of some units might be advantageous.
7. Excessive dispersion of functions in one unit of the firm: Determine if the differentiation of tasks warrants the segmentation of this unit.
8. Poor profit performance and low return expectations: The organizational structure cannot escape a major revision in a situation like this. The firm should examine its strategy and adopt an organizational structure suitable for the implementation of the agreed strategy.

REFERENCES

Arthur D. Little, Inc., *A System for Managing Diversity*, Cambridge, MA, December 1974.

Burns, T., and G. Stalker, *The Management of Innovation*, Tavistock Publishing Co., London, 1961.

Chandler, Alfred A., Jr., *Strategy and Structure: Chapters in the History of the American Industrial Enterprise*, The MIT Press, Cambridge, MA, 1962.

Cyert, R. M., and J. C. March, *A Behavioral Theory of the Firm*, Prentice-Hall, Inc., Englewood Cliffs, NJ, 1963.

Davis, S. M., and P. R. Lawrence, *Matrix*, Addison Wesley Publishing Co., Inc., Reading, MA, 1977.

Dessler, G., *Organization and Management: A Contingency Approach*, Prentice-Hall, Englewood Cliffs, NJ, 1976.

Fayol, Henry, *General Industrial Management*, translated by Constance Storrs, Pittman and Sons, Ondon, 1949.

Galbraith, Jay, *Designing Complex Organizations*, Addison-Wesley, Reading, MA, 1973.

Galbraith, Jay, *Organization Design*, Addison-Wesley, Reading, MA, 1977.

Galbraith, Jay, and D. A. Nathanson, *Strategy Implementation: The Role of Structure and Process*, West Publishing Co., St. Paul, MN, 1978.

Gannon, M. J., *Management: An Organizational Perspective*, Little, Brown, Boston, MA, 1977.

General Electric, *Organization Planning Bulletin*, September 1976.

Gibson, J. L., J. M. Ivancevich, and J. H. Donnelly, Jr., *Organizations: Behavior, Structure, Processes*, Business Publications, Inc., Dallas, TX, 1976 (2nd edition).

Goggins, W., "How the Multi-Dimensional Structure Works at Dow-Corning," *Harvard Business Review*, Vol. 52, No. 1, January–February 1974, pp. 54–65.

Gouldner, A. W., *Patterns of Industrial Bureaucracy*, Free Press, Glencoe, IL, 1953.

Hax, Arnoldo C., and Nicolas S. Majluf, "Organizational Design: A Survey and an Approach," *Operations Research*, Vol. 29, No. 3, May–June 1981, pp. 417–447.

Jackson, J. H., and C. P. Morgan, *Organization Theory: A Macro Perspective for Management*, Prentice-Hall, Englewood Cliffs, NJ, 1978.

Janger, A. R., *Corporate Organization Structures: Manufacturing*, The Conference Board, Inc., New York, 1973.

Kahn, R., D. Wolfe, R. Quinn, and J. Snoek, *Organizational Stress: Studies in Role Conflict and Ambiguity*, John Wiley, New York, 1964.

Lawrence, Paul, R., and Jay W. Lorsch, *Organization and Environment: Managing Differentiation and Integration*, Richard D. Irwin, Inc., Homewood, IL, 1967.

Likert, Rensis, *New Patterns of Management*, McGraw-Hill, New York, 1961.

Likert, Rensis, *The Human Organization*, McGraw-Hill, New York, 1967.

Lorsch, Jay, and S. Allen, *Managing Diversity and Interdependence*, Division of Research, Harvard Business School, Boston, MA, 1973.

March, J., and Herbert Simon, *Organizations*, John Wiley, New York, 1958.

Mayo, E., *The Human Problems of an Industrial Civilization*, Macmillan, New York, 1933.

Merton, Robert K., *Social Theory and Social Structure*, Free Press, Glencoe, IL, 1957 (2nd edition).

Mouzelis, N. P., *Organization and Bureaucracy: An Analysis of Modern Theories*, Aldine Publishing Co., Chicago, IL, 1967.

Roethlisberger, F. J., and W. J. Dickson, *Management and the Worker*, Harvard University Press, Cambridge, MA, 1939.

Rumelt, Richard, *Strategy, Structure, and Economic Performance*, Division of Research, Harvard Business School, Boston, MA, 1974.

Selznick, P., *TVA and the Grass Roots*, The University of California Press, Berkeley, CA, 1949.

Simon, Herbert A., *Administrative Behavior: A Study of Decision-Making Processes in Administrative Organization*, Free Press, New York, 1976 (3rd edition expanded with new introduction).

Sloan, Alfred P., Jr., *My Years with General Motors*, edited by John McDonald with Catharine Stevens, Anchor Books, Doubleday, Garden City, NY, 1963.

Solomons, David, *Divisional Performance: Measurement and Control*, Richard D. Irwin, Inc., Homewood, IL, 1965.

Stoner, J. A. F., *Management*, Prentice-Hall, Englewood Cliffs, NJ, 1978.

Taylor, Frederick W., *The Principles of Scientific Management*, Harper and Row, New York, 1911.

Vancil, Richard, *Decentralization: Managerial Ambiguity by Design*, Dow Jones-Irwin, Homewood, IL, 1978.

Weber, M., *The Theory of Social and Economic Organization*, translated by A. M. Henderson and T. Parsons, Free Press, New York, 1947.

Woodward, Joan, *Industrial Organization: Theory and Practice*, Oxford University Press, Oxford, England, 1965.

21

A CASE STUDY ON MATCHING STRATEGY AND STRUCTURE

INTRODUCTION

The structure of an organization is no longer viewed as a rigid definition of hierarchical levels and interrelationships among different groups. Managers use the organizational design process as a fundamental tool for implementing and communicating the strategic direction selected for the firm.

This chapter discusses a case study concerned with the identification of alternative structures for a business firm and the recommendation of one of those alternatives to be adopted. Throughout the chapter, the central scheme relies on matching strategy and structure. However, in the actual process of evaluating the various organizational designs, proper weight was given to the behavioral dimensions of the problem. Personalities, individual competences, cultural traditions, and managerial styles dominated our discussions. The utmost concern in the minds of those involved in the study was the question regarding their personal positions and spheres of influence that would have resulted under each alternative. Many concessions and departures from an "optimal alternative" had to be made to accommodate for these personal trade-offs. We have purposely omitted all comments to this regard for the sake of brevity as well as for the preservation of the legitimate confidentiality of those issues.

Since Chandler's historical analysis of a selected group of American firms (1962), it has been strongly advocated that "structure follows strategy"; that is to say, that the organizational structure should be designed so as to facilitate the strategic pursuit of a firm. Our work is strongly influenced by this axiom. However, it should be recognized that strategy and structure is a two-way street, in which strategy is certainly influencing the resulting organizational design, but also the existing structure somehow constrains the strategic alternatives of the firm.

The basic methodology that we adopted in our study is presented in the previous chapter. Our discussion closely follows Hax and Majluf (1983).

The objective of this chapter is to illustrate the application of this methodology to the design of an organizational structure for a company wholly-owned by a U.S. Corporation. The Company has been engaged primarily in the sales, service, and distribution of large and small equipment, which in turn were manufactured and developed by another Company belonging to the same Corporation. That equipment is sold to a variety of commercial, industrial, and government markets. The equipment needs special types of chemical products as primary inputs for its operation and specialized computer systems support.

To maintain the confidentiality of the information pertaining to this case, all the specific characteristics of the Company businesses have been altered.

BRIEF DISCUSSION OF THE EXISTING ORGANIZATION

The primary organizational structure of the Company is presented in Figure 21.1. Initially the Company was organized according to a pure functional form, where the managerial functions represented were Distribution, Sales, Services (all of them included under the Regional Centers), Marketing, and Financial Control. Manufacturing, Research, and Development were not part of the Company's activities. Those functions were represented within other sister Companies of the Corporation.

However, as time passed, new responsibilities were added to the Company. Primarily, the acquisition of Computer Systems, Inc., involved in data management. This new unit constituted an autonomous business, managed in a completely decentralized way, with self-sufficient functional support which included Research, Development, and Manufacturing.

Moreover, the Company acquired a small firm, Chemicals, Inc., with Manufacturing, Research, and Development capabilities for the chemical products needed to operate the major equipment.

These two acquisitions provided an integrated capability of the Company's businesses. Now, the Company was not only able to distribute, sell, and service major equipment, but also manufacture, develop, and market the chemicals and computer systems to support the equipment's operation.

Finally the Company began to expand its international operations into Canada and Mexico. This introduced an international concern that did not exist previously.

These new responsibilities seriously affected the organizational structure of the Company, changing it from a functional organization into a hybrid organization with functions, products, and international dimensions.

Even more important, new developments were expected for the immediate

Figure 21.1 Existing organization

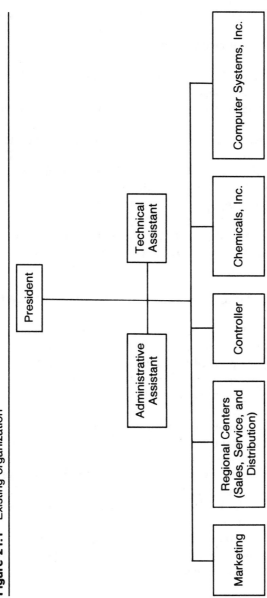

future. Among them we can cite the possible expansion of activities in Central and South America, the absorption of two new business concerns, and a significant projected growth in almost all product lines. Furthermore, potential new acquisitions were under consideration. All of these events triggered a serious concern on the part of the top management of the Company to critically review the present organizational structure and to propose more effective organizational alternatives.

Figures 21.2 and 21.3 provide the organizational charts describing the existing structure of the Regional Centers and Computer Systems, Inc., respectively. It is worth noting that the Regional Centers are the fundamental operational core of the Company, including a regionalized Sales, Service, and Distribution coverage. Moreover, the Regional Center Vice President had a centralized responsibility for Sales Training and Implementation, National Distribution, Materials Control, Government Accounts, and the overall management of customers' orders. This is clearly evident in the organigram of the Regional Centers of Figure 21.2. Also important to reemphasize is the self-standing nature of the Computer Systems, Inc. organization given in Figure 21.3. Computer Systems, Inc. operated as an independent business unit with all the necessary managerial functions reporting to the Computer Systems Vice President.

CRITIQUE OF THE EXISTING ORGANIZATION

The first task undertaken in our attempt to provide organizational alternatives for the Company was to reflect upon the most pressing problems of a general nature that could be traced back to the current structure. A consensus emerged in identifying the following issues as the most important to be addressed in a new proposal for the organizational structure:

1. lack of opportunities for general management development;
2. too much concentration on operational issues;
3. lack of a portfolio-management vision;
4. lack of coordination with other Companies within the Corporation;
5. intensive antagonistic environment;
6. neglect of special markets (such as government accounts and international business accounts);
7. excessive concentration of decision making at the top;
8. organization not appropriate for maximizing growth and profit;
9. overworked key personnel.

All of the issues listed above not only reveal problems that result from an inappropriate organizational structure, but also eloquently point out to the need for an organizational structure that better permits the development of a formal strategic and operational planning system. Such a system should balance the

Figure 21.2 Existing Organization of Regional Centers

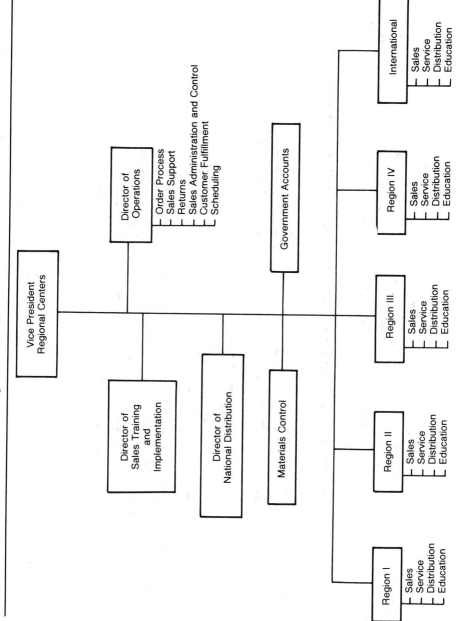

Figure 21.3 Existing Organization—Computer Systems, Inc.

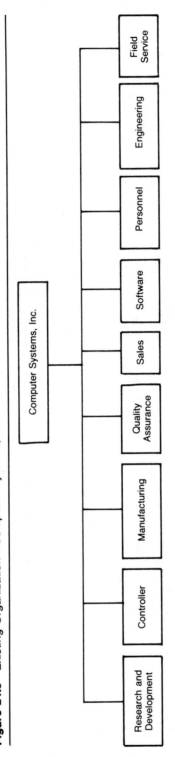

long term concerns of the Company with the proper pressures for short term performance.

PRIMARY CRITERIA FOR THE DESIGN OF A NEW ORGANIZATION

In order to determine the basic segmentation of responsibilities in an organization, one is forced to select one dimension which is perceived to be the dominant force of the organizational activities. In this case, there are three primary dimensions that could be candidates for this focus of attention. They are:

1. functions;
2. business segments;
3. geographical areas.

Functions

The functional form of organization is structured around the inputs required to perform the organizational task. Typically, these inputs are centered around professional specialties or disciplines such as finance, marketing, production, sales, engineering, research and development, and personnel. The functional form leads to a centralization of the management activities, since it is only at the highest level where the responsibility of coordinating all functional tasks resides. A functional organization tends to develop highly qualified technical skills and a climate conducive to technical excellence and high efficiency. It provides a "critical mass" for the career advancement of its professionals. But its inherent strength on specialization pushes the decision-making process upward, because only at the top we find the confluence of all inputs required for the final decision.

Business Segments

The selection of business segments as the dominant dimension for organizational design allows for an effective exploitation of the opportunities which might be available in each individual business segment. A business-focused organization leads to a divisionalized segmentation, in which every division is relatively autonomous in an operational sense. The division then becomes a self-sustaining business in its own right, having a legitimate business climate which allows for the identification of genuine profit centers. Each individual business unit cannot only operate efficiently in the day-to-day operations, but can carry on effectively long term strategic actions pertaining to their development. Thus, each business division provides an excellent training ground for the development of general managers. The top manager of the organization is significantly relieved from the routine operational tasks and can therefore exercise a much more meaningful role in planning the business portfolio and overall divisional growth.

This form of organization allows for the strategic development of each major business of the firm, either by internal growth or by the consolidation of new acquisitions into the appropriate business segments.

Geographical Areas

For organizations covering wide geographical territories with a strong need for maintaining a high level of services responsive to the individual idiosyncrasies of each area, a geographical divisionalized organization could be appropriate. Thus, the basic segmentation results in regional managers who, when taken to an extreme, can be in total control of all the functions and businesses in their own region.

As is apparent from this very brief discussion, an organizational structure in a complex situation normally does not have a single dominant dimension, but rather becomes a hybrid structure. In such a structure, some centralized functions can report directly to the president, some regionalization focus can emerge either at the first or second organizational level, and some business divisions can also report to the president.

IDENTIFICATION OF THE CRITICAL DIMENSIONS FOR THE COMPANY'S ORGANIZATION

As a first attempt to single out the organizational dimensions relevant to the Company, we constructed a list of the major products, markets, locations, and functions represented in the current Company's activities. That list is given in Figure 21.4.

Figure 21.4 Identification of Major Products, Markets, Locations, and Functions

Products	Markets	Locations	Functions
Major Equipment —Large & Small 　Equipment A —Large & Small 　Equipment B —Large & Small 　Equipment C Computer Systems Chemicals	Commercial Clients —Large & Small Industrial Clients —Large & Small Government Clients	Markets —USA —Canada —Mexico —Central America —South America Plants —Detroit —Los Angeles —Boston —New Orleans	Marketing Sales Distribution Manufacturing Research & 　Development Finance Service Education & 　Training Project 　Engineering

Furthermore, in order to define the major business segments of the Company, we constructed a matrix of products and markets, which is shown in Figure 21.5. From that Product-Market segmentation it became clear that the primary businesses could be characterized as follows:

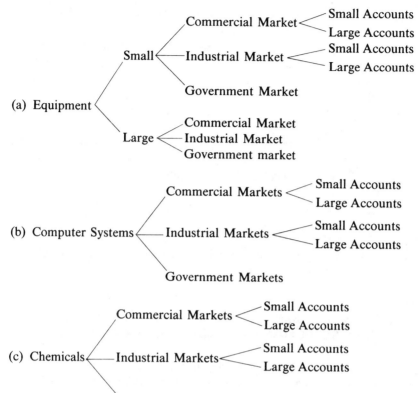

Figure 21.5 Identification of Product-Market Segments

Products / Market	Commercial Clients		Industrial Clients		Government Clients
	Large	Small	Large	Small	
Large Equipment A	X		X		X
Large Equipment B	X		X		X
Large Equipment C	X		X		X
Small Equipment A	X	X	X	X	X
Small Equipment B	X	X	X	X	X
Small Equipment C	X	X	X	X	X
Computer Systems	X	X	X	X	X
Chemicals	X	X	X	X	X

Notice that a business is not necessarily a product line. In the case of Equipment, it is important to distinguish both Large and Small Equipment, as well as Commercial, Industrial, and Government Markets, each of them split into Small and Large Accounts. This segmentation allows managers to detect the different opportunities that each business offers.

Finally, the Company's President provided his own personal objectives for the design of an alternative organizational form. His instructions were as follows:

1. permit a shift of the President's time from routine day-to-day decisions to actions pertaining to business development and strategic management;
2. organize to facilitate absorption of new acquisitions;
3. do not break new businesses;
4. allow for the development of general managers.

Statements 1 and 4 clearly eliminate the pure functional form as an organizational alternative. Moreover, statements 2 and 3 can be interpreted as favoring a business divisionalized form.

DESIGN OF A BASIC ORGANIZATIONAL STRUCTURE: THE SELECTION OF LEADING ALTERNATIVES

As we had indicated before, the first step in the organizational design process is the recognition of competing forms for the basic organizational structure. This basic structure identifies the primary echelons of the organizational chart which are linked to the strategic positioning of the firm.

We recognized four major alternatives for the basic organizational structure of the Company. These alternatives are:

1. Alternative Organization Based on Primary Businesses
2. Alternative Organization Based on a Centralized Sales, Service, and Distribution Function
3. Alternative Organization with Geographical Regions and Business Segments
4. Alternative Organization with Geographical Regions and Centralized Manufacturing

These basic organizational alternatives are presented in Figures 21.6, 21.7, 21.8, and 21.9, respectively.

Obviously many other alternatives were discussed in the first stage of our study. However, they were discarded after a more in-depth analysis because they were clearly dominated by either one or more of the four basic alternatives indicated above.

We will now proceed to comment briefly on the salient characteristics of each of the leading basic structure alternatives.

Figure 21.6 Alternative Organization Based on Primary Businesses

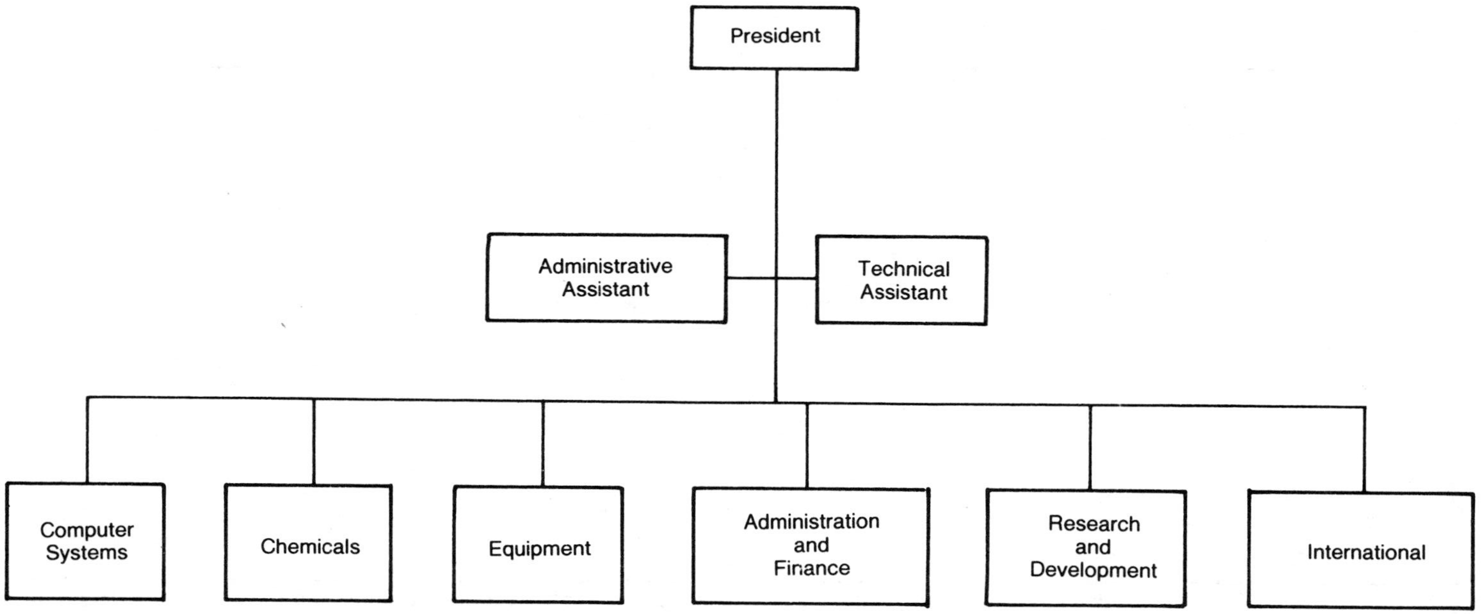

Figure 21.7 Alternative Organization Based on a Centralized Sales, Service, and Distribution Function

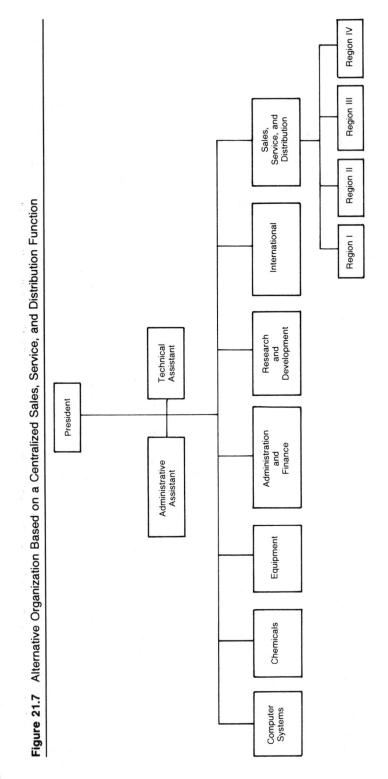

Figure 21.8 Alternative Organization with Geographical Regions and Business Segments

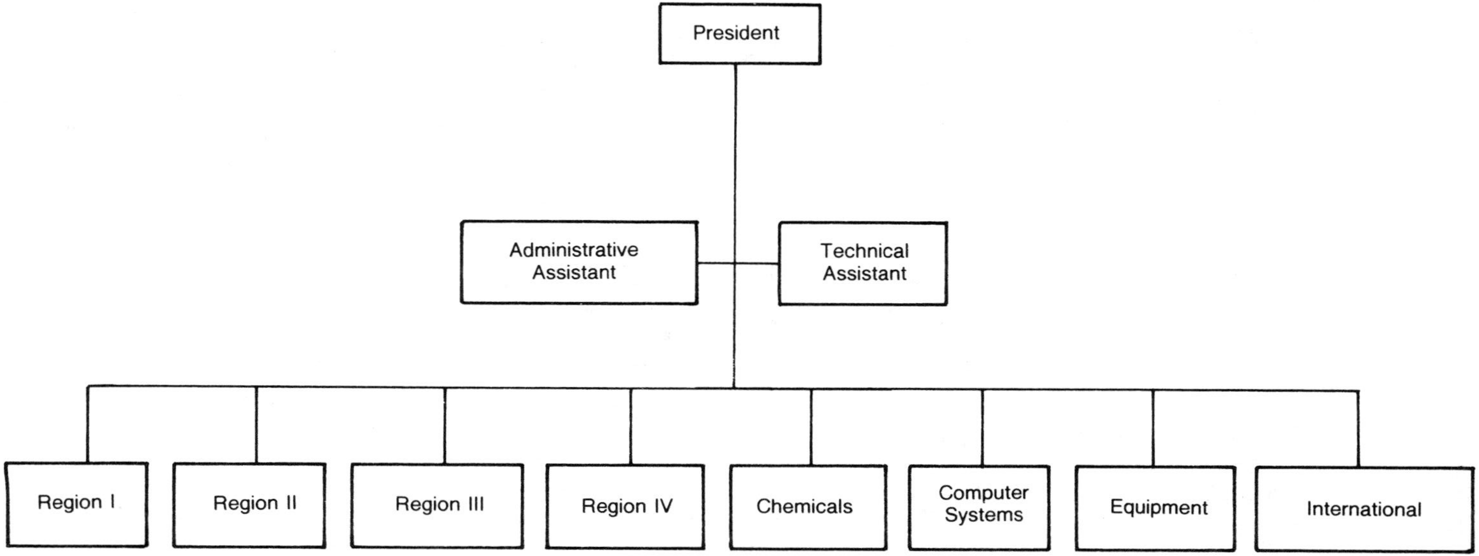

Figure 21.9 Alternative Organization with Geographical Regions and Centralized Manufacturing

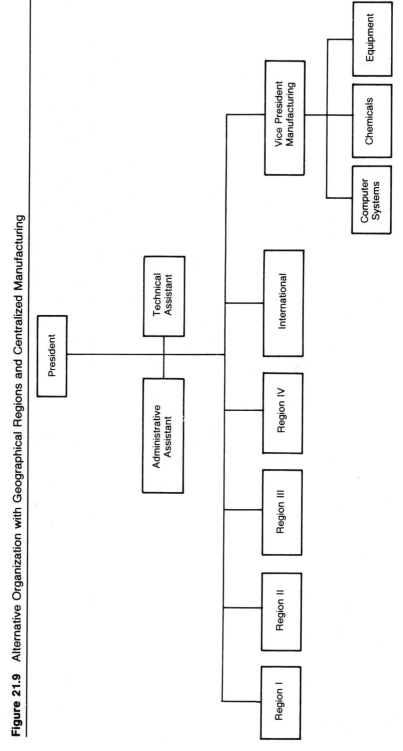

Alternative Organization Based on Primary Businesses

The heart of this alternative (see Figure 21.6) is the identification of three primary autonomous businesses: Computer Systems, Chemicals, and Equipment. Although these businesses are closely related to one another, the adoption of this organizational form might contribute to the realization of opportunities unique to each individual segment. That is to say, that Chemicals and Computer Systems not only will be developed to satisfy the important role they should play in supporting the Equipment operation, but they can also seek penetration in other markets, not necessarily tied to the Equipment business environment. The strategic implications of adopting this organizational form are enormous. It means that the Company will no longer view itself as being solely in the business of Equipment, but as being in three autonomous, although related, business segments.

Other characteristics worth noting in this basic structure are:

—There is a centralized Administration and Finance function to provide the normal Controller's duties for the whole Company, as well as handling centralized personnel, and business development and planning functions. The Controller's responsibilities include the development of a financial system that allows for the effective monitoring of the long and short term performance of each business unit. It is important to recognize that this organizational structure permits a new business-oriented management control system to be implemented.

—There is a centralized Research and Development function for the whole Company to facilitate a coordinated Research and Development activity for all its business segments.

—The staff offices of Technical Affairs and Administrative Assistant are kept unmodified from their current status.

—This organization permits appropriate emphasis on the emerging international responsibilities by ultimately identifying and appointing a manager for an International segment.

Alternative Organization Based on a Centralized Sales, Service, and Distribution Function

Given the predominant role played by the Regional Centers in the existing organization of the Company, a primary contender for an alternative basic organization should be one having a regional geographical segmentation as its dominant dimension.

However, such an alternative is not easy to develop if one wants to respect the four objectives for the design of an organization form given by the Company's President outlined earlier in this chapter. His concern to facilitate absorption of new acquisitions without breaking new businesses, and his determination to adopt a structure that would facilitate the strategic development of the major businesses of the Company makes it desirable for us to maintain a segmentation focus having Computer Systems, Chemicals, and Equipment as primary units. A geographical focus can be brought in by establishing a centralized Sales, Service, and Distribution function which is further segmented by geographical regions. That function would serve a purpose quite similar to the existing Regional Centers, but under a business-oriented organizational structure.

Figure 21.7 describes the first two hierarchical levels of such an organization. The comparisons of Figure 21.7 with the organizational alternative based on primary businesses, depicted in Figure 21.6, simply shows the addition of a new centralized function, while preserving all the other organizational units. However, there are fundamental differences in the way in which the Company will operate, both in the short and the long run, under these two organizational forms.

The organizational alternative that has a centralized Sales, Service, and Distribution function (Figure 21.7) allows for a comprehensive geographical regionalization, which generates the following major advantages:

—It provides a single Company's image to all customers.
—It permits better coordination among the various businesses of the Company in the interface with customers.
—It assures efficiency at the operational level.
—It is consistent with the current Regional Center concept, and, therefore, would encounter less resistance in its implementation.

However, the major disadvantages of the geographical regionalization alternative relative to the business-oriented organization (Figure 21.6) are:

—It divides managerial accountability between Sales, Service, and Distribution on the one hand, and the business segments on the other. This makes sound management control principles very hard to apply.
—There is a loss of strategic focus for specific business development, since the business units do not possess complete autonomy in Sales, Service, and Distribution.
—It forces newly acquired, self-standing businesses to be broken.
—The Company President would have to play a very strong integrating role to coordinate the operational activities of the business units with the centralized function of Sales, Service, and Distribution. This will prevent a major concentration of the President's time to the strategic directions of the Company.

It should be clear from the above remarks that the business-oriented segment organization alternative responds more effectively to the criteria that were proposed as the basis for a new organization, particularly with respect to allowing for a strong strategic focus for business development.

Alternative Organization with Geographical Regions and Business Segments

Figure 21.8 shows a segmentation based on four major geographical regions and the three basic business units: Computer Systems, Chemicals, and Equipment. This alternative is dominated by the alternative just discussed—the Centralized Sales, Service, and Distribution function—which reduces the span of control of the Company President and separates him from the operational routines of running the day-to-day activities of the Regional Centers.

Since our previous analysis suggested a strong preference for the alternative based on a business-oriented segmentation over the alternative based on Centralized Sales, Service and Distribution function, we can abandon from further consideration the organization with Geographical Regions and Business Segments.

Alternative Organization with Geographical Regions and Centralized Manufacturing

Figure 21.9 shows an organizational alternative that preserves the four Regional Center managers, but has the three basic business units reporting to a Vice President of Manufacturing. This alternative would make the Computer Systems, Chemicals, and Equipment businesses simply cost centers in charge of providing the goods to be required by the Regional Center managers. We discarded this alternative since it would have unduly emphasized the operational concerns of the Company, sacrificing its strategic business focus.

We have provided only a synoptic description of the arguments that were given to support our final recommendation to adopt the business-oriented organization for the Company. In the actual study we examined in detail all the four basic alternatives discussed above.

DETAILED DESIGN: DESCRIPTION OF EACH ORGANIZATIONAL UNIT OF THE BUSINESS-ORIENTED ALTERNATIVE

Having selected a preferred basic alternative, the second step in the design process is the definition of the associated detailed organizational structure.

We will limit ourselves to provide some brief comments to characterize the nature of each of the units reporting to the President of the Company under the alternative organization based on primary businesses (see Figure 21.6).

Computer Systems

Figure 21.10 shows the proposed organizational chart for the Computer Systems business. Since Computer Systems has been operating already as a self-sustaining unit, its organization does not change significantly. It is proposed that in the future, Sales and Marketing would be combined in a single subunit, which would both improve the necessary coordination of these functions, as well as reduce the span of control of the Computer Systems Vice President.

Chemicals

Figure 21.11 presents the organizational chart for the Chemicals segment. The most important element to bear in mind is that the Advertising and Distribution Management functions reporting to the Vice President of Chemicals not only

Figure 21.10 Proposed Organization for Computer Systems

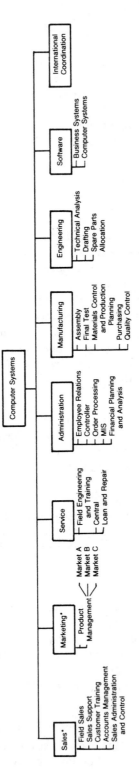

* Sales and Marketing could be combined, which will reduce the span of control of the Computer Systems Vice President.

Figure 21.11 Proposed Organization for Chemicals

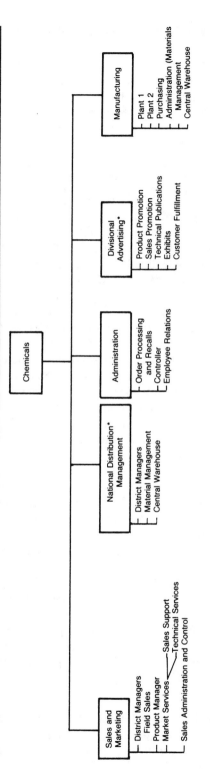

* Denotes centralized divisional functions.

443

serve those functional needs for the Chemicals business, but also are centralized functions for Computer Systems and Equipment. We could have opted for a centralized functional structure reporting directly to the President. We rejected that alternative because it would have loaded the President with operational responsibilities. Since Chemicals is the business that most heavily needs Distribution and Advertising support, it was an obvious choice to assign those centralized functions to Chemicals.

Equipment

The Equipment organizational chart (see Figure 21.12) singles out a unit responsible primarily for manufacturing Small Equipment. The remaining functions (Sales and Services, Marketing, Management Development and Training, and Administration) are common for both Small and Large Equipment. At least for the time being, Large Equipment will still be produced and developed by a sister company. This explains the absence of Manufacturing and Research and Development for Large Equipment.

An important issue to be recognized in the Equipment organization is the presence of regional managers reporting to the Sales and Services unit. Naturally, given the broad geographical area coverage of the Company's activities, it is essential to have Sales and Services regional managers' offices. The question is to whom those regional managers should report and how Sales and Services forces from different businesses should be coordinated. The answer to those questions is to maintain regional managers subordinated to the Equipment business, given the very strong importance of Sales and Services functions for that group. However, the Sales forces from Chemicals and Computer Systems would also be using those regional physical facilities, as is currently done between Equipment and Computer Systems Sales forces. The coordination of the Sales activities between different businesses will be assured by continuing the current practice of giving commissions to sales people for all types of sales. This allows for the payment of double commissions for a single sales as necessary, and so preserves a strong supporting effort of the Sales force. In addition, monthly meetings will be conducted among all sales people in a given regional office to coordinate sales efforts across the board in that region.

It should also be recognized that the Marketing function of Equipment has centralized Company responsibilities for activities concerning: governmental accounts, legislative affairs, and divisional market research. This means that in those activities the Marketing group is not only overseeing the interests of the Equipment business, but also the interests of Computer Systems and Chemicals. Similarly, the Management Development and Training group has equally centralized Company responsibilities for that particular function.

Administration and Finance

Figure 21.13 describes the proposed organizational chart for Administration and Finance. It is important to recognize that this function has been expanded beyond the traditional Controller's responsibility, by adding an Office of Business

Figure 21.12 Proposed Organization for Equipment

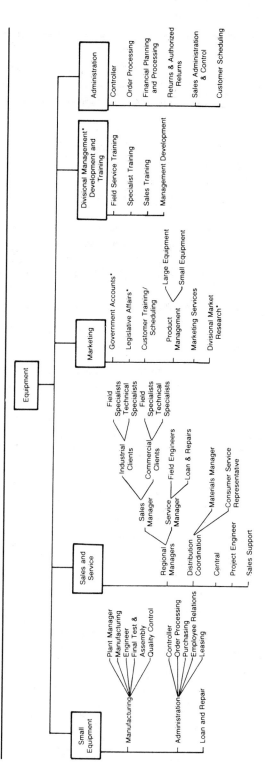

* Denotes centralized divisional functions.

Development and Planning for the whole Company. This Office will play an essential role in establishing the processes, practice, and tools to facilitate the implementation of the strategic and operational planning system of the Company.

Research and Development

The proposed organizational chart for the Research and Development function is presented in Figure 21.14. Notice that we have opted for a centralized Research and Development function. We decided on this alternative because we consider it essential to allow for a strong Research and Development group with a significant critical mass. Decentralizing that function would have resulted in the proliferation of small Research and Development efforts under each business, preventing cross-fertilization and allowing for separate and uncoordinated programs to take place. Although a centralized Research and Development function creates some problems for the coordination of Research and Development with a specific Manufacturing and Marketing function of each business, we believe this is a bearable price to pay to implement coordinated Research and Development programs among the businesses.

International

The Company had recently accepted new business responsibilities in Mexico. It is contemplating in the future to expand those responsibilities to Central America, and eventually to South America and the Caribbean. Those commitments create a need for a concentrated focus of activities with an international concern. It is mandatory to achieve a deep understanding of the business, social, and political climates in those international areas. Furthermore, special instru-

Figure 21.13   Proposed Organization for Administration and Finance

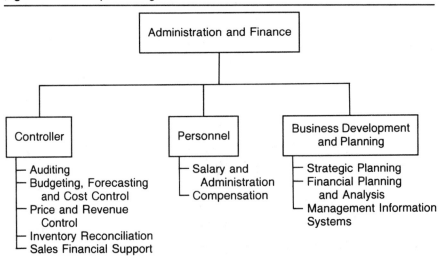

Figure 21.14 Proposed Organization for Research and Development

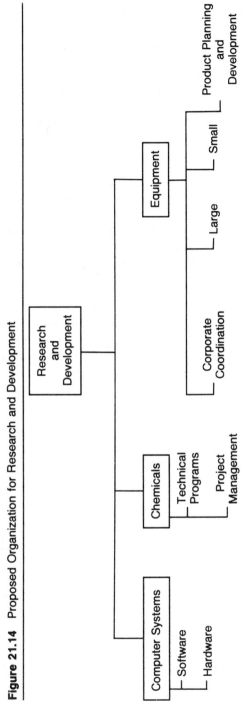

ments might have to be developed to serve those special markets and tailor-made prices and marketing policies would have to be adopted.

At this time, where the Company has a very embryonic presence in the international market, the international unit is merely composed of a single manager. The fact that he reports directly to the President of the Company is a clear indication of the high priority that the development of an international scope has for the Company. As these activities grow, we envision a further segmentation of the international unit into three potential territories: Mexico and Central America, Canada, and South America. At the time this study was conducted, these were the targets for international penetration.

TESTING THE PROPOSED ORGANIZATIONAL
STRUCTURE AGAINST THE CURRENT ORGANIZATION

Numerous questions were raised to test the effectiveness of the proposed structure. To achieve this goal we conducted several tests aimed at contrasting the performance of the proposed organization against the existing one, under a variety of critical decisions. As an illustration on how this methodology was applied, we will comment on a particularly challenging project requiring important inputs from several businesses and managerial functions. The project identified for these purposes was the development of a Small Equipment that would use a specific type of chemical material (Equipment—Alpha). This project required the performance of the following major planning tasks:

1. business plan
2. product marketing
3. advertising program
4. sales
5. service
6. distribution
7. training
8. servicing
9. acquisition plans
10. budgeting and finance
11. interfacing with other divisions of the Company
12. Chemicals and Equipment delivery schedule
13. manufacturing, quality control, and shipment
14. check-up
15. profit and loss statements
16. manufacturing of Chemicals
17. methods approval
18. regulations and quality assurance
19. financial approval and final approval.

Figure 21.15 illustrates the participation of each of the major line and functional managers in the development of the Equipment—Alpha project. This

Figure 21.15 Involvement of Various Managerial Levels in the Execution of Tasks for the Development of Equipment—Alpha and Current Organization

Mgt. Level \ Tasks	1	2	3	4	5	6	7	8	9	10	11	12	13	14	15	16	17	18	19
President	X	X	X	X	X	X	X	X	X	X		X	X	X	X	X	X		X
Marketing	X	X	X	X		X	X		X	X	X	X	X	X	X	X	X	X	
Regional Centers	X	X		X	X	X	X	X		X		X	X	X		X		X	
Service	X	X			X		X	X		X	X			X					
Controller	X	X		X					X	X	X	X	X	X	X	X			X
Corporate Officer 1											X								
Chemicals, Inc.	X		X	X			X	X	X	X		X	X	X	X	X		X	
Corporate Officer 2				X		X						X	X			X			
Corporate Officer 3																X	X		
Corporate Officer 4					X								X		X	X	X	X	
Corporate Officer 5									X	X					X				X

Figure 21.16 Involvement of Various Managerial Levels in the Execution of Tasks for the Development of Equipment—Alpha and Proposed Organization

Mgt. Level \ Tasks	1	2	3	4	5	6	7	8	9	10	11	12	13	14	15	16	17	18	19
President	X								X	X									X
Chemicals, Inc.		X	X	X		X			X	X		X	X			X	X	X	
Small Equipment		X	X	X	X	X	X	X	X	X	X	X	X	X	X			X	
Large Equipment							X												
R&D																	X		
Administration and Finance	X	X		X					X	X					X				X
Data Management											X								
Corporate Officer 4															X		X	X	
Corporate Officer 5									X	X									X

figure should be contrasted with Figure 21.16, which shows similar involvement under the proposed organization.

The following conclusions emerge from that comparison. The number of executive involvements have been reduced from 95 in the current organization to 48 in the proposed organization. The depth of involvement has been reduced from 11 to 9. The President's participation has been greatly reduced. His involvement is mostly in critical decisions that have long term impact, while he has been removed from the more operational issues. The proposed organization shows a much clearer assignment of responsibilities concentrated in the Small Equipment and Chemicals businesses. This is a highly desirable outcome, given the nature of the project. To summarize, the proposed organization shows a better concentration of responsibilities at the important managerial levels. This prevents a dispersion of responsibilities throughout the organization that would necessarily call for the direct President's coordination in a multitude of issues.

CONCLUSION

The case study just described represents an illustration on how to implement the two-stage approach for organizational design that we outline in Chapter 20. Although any case study has the inherent limitation of being restricted to a particular situation, we believe our experience can be useful to guide a manager confronted with the task of redesigning his or her organization. We found the available literature to be lacking on specific examples of this sort.

A disciplined approach for organizational design can facilitate the task of developing a new organizational structure by bringing in all important information related to the strategic posture of the firm—which is the essence of the first step in identifying basic organizational alternatives—as well as the definition of operational tasks—which are handled at the detailed segmentation stage.

REFERENCES

Chandler, A. D., Jr., *Strategy and Structure: Chapters in the History of the American Industrial Enterprise*, M.I.T. Press, Cambridge, MA, 1962.

Hax, Arnoldo C., and Nicolas S. Majluf, "Organizational Design: A Case Study on Matching Strategy and Structure," *Journal of Business Strategy*, Vol. 4, No. 2, pp. 72–86, Fall 1983.

Lawrence, P. R., and J. W. Lorsch, *Organization and Environment: Managing Differentiation and Integration*, Richard D. Irwin, Homewood, IL, 1967.

Pascale, R. T., and A. G. Athos, *The Art of Japanese Management: Applications for American Executives*, Simon and Schuster, New York, 1981.

Waterman, R. H., Jr., "The Seven Elements of Strategic Fit," *The Journal of Business Strategy*, Vol. 2, No. 3, Winter 1982, pp. 69–73.

INDEX